FROI

COMPREHEN~~S~~ ~~~~ ~~GUIDE~~

VANCOUVER & VICTORIA '94-'95

by John Gottberg
Assisted by Bill Nikolai
and Richard Payment

PRENTICE HALL TRAVEL

NEW YORK • LONDON • TORONTO • SYDNEY • TOKYO • SINGAPORE

FROMMER BOOKS

Published by Prentice Hall General Reference
15 Columbus Circle
New York, NY 10023

ISBN 0-671-84697-3
ISSN 1045-9316

Design by Robert Bull Design
Maps by Geografix Inc.

Frommer's Editorial Staff
Editorial Director: Marilyn Wood
Editorial Manager/Senior Editor: Alice Fellows
Senior Editors: Sara Hinsey Raveret, Lisa Renaud
Editors: Charlotte Allstrom, Thomas F. Hirsch, Peter Katucki, Theodore
Stavrou
Assistant Editors: Margaret Bowen, Christopher Hollander, Alice Thompson, Ian Wilker
Editorial Assistants: Gretchen Henderson, Douglas Stallings
Managing Editor: Leanne Coupe

Special Sales
Bulk purchases (10+ copies) of Frommer's Travel Guides are available to
corporations at special discounts. The Special Sales Department can produce
custom editions to be used as premiums and/or for sales promotion to suit
individual needs. Existing editions can be produced with custom cover
imprints such as a corporate logo. For more information write to: Special
Sales, Prentice Hall Travel, 15 Columbus Circle, New York, New York 10023.

CONTENTS

FOREWORD by Arthur Frommer

LIST OF MAPS

by Arthur Frommer

When professional groups from northern California and the Pacific northwest hold their yearly meetings and conventions, they often do so in Vancouver; I once spoke in that city before an association of lawyers from Seattle and Spokane who were meeting for both recreation and education in Vancouver. Imagine—people from some of the most compelling and attractive cities of America were going for their own fun and games to this unofficial capital of Canada's West Coast!

You have only to see it once to understand the reasons for that choice: A setting of raw wilderness dominated by water and fjords, deep green forests and high mountains; a city of sophisticated nightlife and shops; graceful skyscrapers lining clean and well-ordered streets; ships filling its giant harbor; a successful, prosperous city of quiet manners and cultured people. In some respects it resembles San Francisco, but has a distinct foreign flavor that residents of the city work hard to maintain. This is no offshoot of the United States, but a proud national treasure of Canada.

It has a giant Chinatown and a fast-growing Asian population. It has nearly a dozen intensely foreign ethnic neighborhoods possessing their own publications, organizations, culture, and cuisine. Scattered about town is a lively theater scene that boasts original productions dealing with themes of Canadian interest, with only an occasional Broadway import. And only 60 miles away, it has one of the continent's trendiest ski areas—the immensely popular Whistler, with its state-of-the-art lifts and lodges.

Most tourists combine a visit to Vancouver with one to the charming, turn-of-the-century Victoria, and so does this book. From Vancouver, you simply take a $9.00, 95-minute "car boat" of the BC Ferries to that touch of Britain in the New World whose architecture is largely of the period described by its name. You can later return to the U.S. mainland by a ferry sailing from Victoria to Seattle. Or you can start in Seattle and proceed via Victoria to Vancouver in the other direction. Because the Seattle-Victoria-Vancouver route is so very popular, we've devoted a great many pages to Victoria in this guidebook and feel sure you'll enjoy the old-English-style pleasures of Victoria (with its lawn bowling, yachting, high teas, and year-round garden exhibits) and the ecological treasures of the immense Vancouver Island on which it is found.

On one memorable, cost-conscious trip some years ago, I traveled north from Vancouver along the famous "Inside Passage" to key cities in southeast Alaska. I crossed by ferry from Vancouver to Vancouver Island, drove a rental car to Port Hardy on the northernmost tip of that island, took an inexpensive 15-hour cruise to Prince Rupert on another BC Ferry, and then switched from there to one of the ships of the Alaska Marine Highway System going to Juneau and Skagway, Alaska. The very same do-it-yourself trip can still be taken today at a fraction of the price charged by those monumental cruise ships stuffed with 1,200 to 2,000 passengers that ply the waters of Alaska in summer.

Independent travel, with a single companion or with family members, is one of the key themes of the Frommer travel books, and it is the main point of this guide to Vancouver and Victoria. We write primarily for the many individuals, couples, and families who prefer to select their own lodgings, travel on dates of their own choosing, and go wherever they themselves wish—people who savor the profound rewards and emotions of independent travel.

Reading the initial manuscript of this guidebook to Vancouver and Victoria, I was again reminded of those joys of independent travel and earnestly recommend the same approach to you. Have a good trip!

INVITATION TO THE READERS

In researching this book, I have come across many wonderful establishments, the best of which I have included here. I am sure that many of you will also come across appealing hotels, inns, restaurants, guesthouses, shops, and attractions. Please don't keep them to yourself. Share your experiences, especially if you want to comment on places that have been included in this edition that have changed for the worse. You can address your letters to:

John Gottberg
Frommer's Vancouver & Victoria '94–'95
c/o Prentice Hall Travel
15 Columbus Circle
New York, NY 10023

A DISCLAIMER

Readers are advised that prices fluctuate in the course of time and travel information changes under the impact of the varied and volatile factors that affect the travel industry. Neither the author nor the publisher can be held responsible for the experiences of readers while traveling. Readers are invited to write to the publisher with ideas, comments, and suggestions for future editions.

SAFETY ADVISORY

Whenever you're traveling in an unfamiliar city or country, stay alert. Be aware of your immediate surroundings. Wear a moneybelt and keep a close eye on your possessions. Be particularly careful with cameras, purses, and wallets, all favorite targets of thieves and pickpockets.

CHAPTER 1

INTRODUCING CANADA'S PACIFIC COAST

1. HISTORY, GEOGRAPHY & PEOPLE

2. ART & ARCHITECTURE

3. RECOMMENDED BOOKS

Few places on Earth are as tailor-made for vacationers as Canada's spectacularly beautiful southwestern corner.

Focused around one of the world's great metropolises, Vancouver, and one of its most charmingly quaint and walkable cities, Victoria, this is a region where worldly sophistication goes hand-in-hand with a zest for the out-of-doors. Here is the marriage of city and wilderness, of forward-looking progress and primordial protectiveness, of suave urbanity and rugged rusticity.

A typical British Columbian will fight fiercely for wilderness conservation while struggling to keep up with the Joneses (or Wongs, as the case may be). For residents of this province, a day spent in the mountains is as likely as an evening at the opera; often both are enjoyed on the same day. And speaking about cosmopolitanism: It wouldn't be unusual for a Greek Canadian who is employed by a Hong Kong multinational firm to take a German colleague out after work for ale at a British pub, followed by dinner at an East Indian restaurant and then on to a Japanese nightclub.

Vancouver, a city of half a million people in a metropolitan area of 1.6 million, is surrounded and deeply indented by water on three sides with a backdrop of evergreen-cloaked mountains. Some call it the most beautiful city in the world, ranking it ahead of San Francisco, Hong Kong, and Rio de Janeiro. Few Americans paid it much attention before Expo '86, the resoundingly successful world's fair that initiated a tourism boom. But the business world, especially that of the Pacific Rim, had discovered Vancouver long before—because of large foreign investments here, Asian businesspeople often refer to the city as "Hongkouver." Indeed, Canada's window to the west has become increasingly important as the 21st century approaches.

Some people claim that Victoria is "more English than the English." A former trading post built on a superb natural harbor, it has evolved over a century and a half into a peaceful garden city. The two principal businesses of its 300,000 inhabitants are government (British Columbia's provincial functions are based here) and tourism. Visitors who stroll up and down the streets will find numerous shops that specialize in Waterford crystal, Victorian antiques, and woolen tartans, not to mention fish and chips. And no one should leave town without enjoying high tea at the venerable Empress Hotel.

Outside the cities, British Columbia lives up to its publicity as "Super, Natural." Most of Vancouver Island, 280 miles long and

50–75 miles wide, is a spectacular wilderness. Eagles and elk wander its 7,000-foot mountains, and sea lions and whales frolic in its seaward fjords. Victoria is on Vancouver Island, whereas Vancouver is on the mainland. Despite streamlined ferry and air connections, Victoria's relative isolation has contributed significantly to its small-city character.

The Whistler/Blackcomb resort area, 75 road miles north of Vancouver, has been acclaimed by *Ski* magazine readers as North America's second-most-popular ski resort (after Vail, Colorado). Along the Sunshine Coast, north of Vancouver, and throughout the islands of the Strait of Georgia, life revolves around small fishing villages and tiny farm communities. Even the heavily populated Lower Mainland region, which extends east from Vancouver nearly 100 miles along the Fraser River lowlands and south to the U.S. border, is speckled by wetland sanctuaries and hot springs, all beneath the gaze of towering mountain sentinels on its northern edge.

1. HISTORY, GEOGRAPHY & PEOPLE

HISTORY

For centuries before the arrival of white settlers, Canada's Pacific coastline was dominated by various native tribes, including Coast Salish (in the Fraser Delta), Nootkas, Kwakiutls, Bella Coolas, Tsimshians, and Haidas. It is believed that these tribes were descendants of a Fraser River culture that thrived around the time of Christ. Archeologists have found stone carvings, utensils, and fishing tackle that exemplify supreme artistry and skill.

The British Columbian coastal tribes were blessed with an abundance of food and natural resources. Excellent hunters and trappers, they hunted deer, bear, ducks, and geese with bow and arrow. They snared salmon, black cod, and herring; harpooned seals and sea lions; and stalked the sea otter for its warm fur. Children gathered berries from the forest undergrowth, dug clams, and plucked crabs from tidal flats. The seemingly endless forests, especially the easily split cedar, provided the raw material for houses, clothing, and utensils. The abundant resources enjoyed by these tribes enabled them to conduct a steady trade with the peoples of the interior, especially up the Fraser River.

The society of these coastal groups was complex and sophisticated. They saw their lives as an integral part of the natural world, and their religion was based on kinship and communication among all living things—differences between animate beings were considered to be superficial. Clans were named for legendary creatures—for example, the Raven, Eagle, and Whale—which, it was believed, could appear in such human form as teachers or heroes.

Totemic symbols identified these real or imaginary animals. They appeared most often on totem poles, which were carved to honor the dead, to document social events, and to record history and oral tradition. Masks and houseposts also enabled woodcarvers to demonstrate their art.

Wealth and lines of descent, both patrilineal and matrilineal, led to a hierarchy within the clans. Within each clan it was important to maintain one's social position and to improve it by acquiring greater wealth or performing heroic deeds. One of the primary means for accomplishing this was the *potlatch:* The chief or clan leader would invite neighboring leaders of equal or greater wealth to visit him; he would then feed, house, and entertain them for weeks on end. Thus, by giving away much of his wealth, he could elevate his own social rank. Protocol then demanded that his humbled guests reciprocate by inviting him to future potlatches, where he would be honored with even more riches than he had doled out.

It is estimated that 80,000 Native Canadians lived along British Columbia's Pacific coast when the first white explorers arrived. Spanish ships skirted the coast in 1774, and the ubiquitous English navigator Capt. James Cook charted parts of Vancouver Island's coastline in 1778. Their glowing reports of the area's wealth of sea otter, beaver, and other furs whetted the interest of British and American traders. Capt. George Vancouver—who had been a 21-year-old lieutenant on Cook's earlier voyage of discovery—took possession of the area for Great Britain in 1792. (It is said that young Lt. Peter Puget exclaimed to Captain Vancouver, "This is the most beautiful place I've ever seen!" The captain's alleged reply: "Yes, but you should have seen it 14 years ago.")

By this time, European settlers were moving west. In July 1793, Alexander Mackenzie completed a cross-Canada journey by water and on foot. In 1808, Simon Fraser reached the Pacific near modern Vancouver after traveling down the river later named in his honor. His expedition opened the way for the Hudson's Bay Company to establish a series of fur-trading posts on the Fraser River, including Fort Langley in 1827, which was the first settlement in the Lower Mainland. Located about 28 miles upstream from the mouth of the Fraser River, today it is a national historic park.

Ongoing conflict between Great Britain and the United States ended in 1846 when the Oregon Treaty established the boundary between the United States and Canada at the 49th parallel "to the middle of the channel which separates the continent from Vancouver's Island; and thence southerly through the middle of the said channel, and of Fuca's Straits to the Pacific Ocean."

Fort Victoria, founded as Fort Camosun in 1843, became the western headquarters of the Hudson's Bay Company. When Vancouver Island was designated a Crown Colony in 1849, Victoria became its administrative center. The island colony was united with British Columbia in 1866, and when, in 1871, British Columbia became the fifth province of the Dominion of Canada, Victoria was declared the provincial capital.

The fur industry waned in the early part of the 19th century, and gold (rather than sea otters) became the base upon which British Columbia grew and prospered. Alluvial gold was discovered in the lower Fraser River valley in 1858, and four years later in that part of the upper Fraser known as Cariboo country. By 1865—some $25 million in gold dust later—the rush was over. But during those few years thousands of new settlers had discovered a home here. Victoria mushroomed on the strength of gold income, as steamships plied the lower Fraser and a coach road connected the navigable portion of the river with the Cariboo.

The first settlement on Burrard Inlet was established in the early

1860s after coal was discovered. Soon thereafter, timber emerged as a commercially more important product, and the Hastings Sawmill became the focus of the young community. Since liquor was not permitted on company land, an opportunist named John Deighton (nicknamed "Gassy Jack" after his gift for gab) opened a saloon in nearby Maple Tree Square in 1867. Business was so successful that a community called Gastown grew up around Deighton's saloon. The Gastown settlement was approved as a town site by the provincial government in 1870 and was officially named Granville.

The town's future was more or less assured in 1884 when the Canadian Pacific Railroad chose it as the western terminus for Canada's first transcontinental railway. On April 6, 1886, when the track was completed, Granville became incorporated as the city of Vancouver. But barely two months later, on June 13, the city of 1,000 was obliterated by fire, a forest slash burn that ran out of control. Very few buildings survived (the only one standing today is St. James Anglican Church, at the corner of Cordova and Gore Streets).

The city founders wasted no time in rebuilding their city. In fact, by Christmas 1886, there were about 800 buildings—a construction rate of more than four a day. The Hotel Vancouver opened in 1887, the 1,000-acre Stanley Park in 1888, the Granville Street Bridge in 1889, the Orpheum Theatre in 1890, and the Hudson's Bay Company department store in 1893. A steamship line between Vancouver and Asia initiated service in 1891, and a century of transpacific trade began.

When the Panama Canal opened in 1915, making it feasible to export grain and lumber to Europe, British Columbia experienced a boom the likes of which hadn't been seen since the gold rush of the mid-19th century. Investors laid out thousands of dollars for timberland and mining territory. When settlement of Canada's barren inland prairies began, the call for lumber and other supplies went out to British Columbia. In the first decade of the 20th century, B.C.'s population more than doubled to 400,000 and Vancouver's population climbed to well over 100,000.

Victoria, meanwhile, was also flourishing. Money earned in manufacturing and timber helped the city gain a reputation for its beautiful homes (notably the spectacular Craigdarroch Castle, built in 1889) and magnificent gardens (like the remarkable Butchart Gardens, created in 1904 from a worked-out limestone quarry). The governmental city didn't suffer a disastrous fire like Vancouver's, but it endured something potentially worse—a smallpox epidemic in 1892, attributable to a ship that had arrived from Asia. Had it not been for the availability of the cowpox vaccine, the city of 16,000 people might have been decimated.

As Vancouver expanded around the railroad, Victoria resigned itself to its role as British Columbia's "second city." With a sunnier, milder climate than either Vancouver or Seattle, Victoria was becoming a tourist draw for refugees from both cities, who traveled to Victoria by steamer. Most visitors stayed in the posh new Empress Hotel, built in 1908. It was adjoined by an extensive rose garden and by the Crystal Gardens, a glass-roofed, indoor, saltwater swimming pool that became the social center of Victoria.

Hard times plagued both cities during the years of World War I and the subsequent Great Depression. The onset of World War II, however, created new opportunities in timber, mining, and shipbuilding.

Today, wood processing remains a major industry in both cities. Sufficient power for sawmills, plywood, and paper production comes from hydroelectric plants farther inland. Vancouver and Victoria support thriving fishing fleets, and their ice-free harbors greet vessels from all over the world. The Port of Vancouver, with its extensive docks as well as its mineral and grain-elevator facilities, is the third most active port in North America in terms of foreign tonnage.

In 1986 Vancouver celebrated its 100th birthday with the most publicized event in its history, the five-month-long Expo '86. The main theme of the world's fair was transportation. It was no coincidence that the most ambitious public transport project in the city's history—the SkyTrain light-rail rapid-transit system—had opened earlier that same year. Victoria hopes to make a similar splash when the British Commonwealth Games, a mini-Olympics, are held in the garden city in 1994.

GEOGRAPHY

British Columbia's mountains were formed millions of years ago— about the same time as the U.S. Rocky Mountains—by a great geologic uplift and folding. Glaciers followed, carving the troughs for the Strait of Georgia and for inland waterways that were fed by melting ice waters and torrential rains.

It's easiest to think of southwestern British Columbia as a mountainous land punctuated by waterways. The largest of those bodies of water is the Strait of Georgia, which separates Vancouver Island from the Canadian mainland. Averaging about 20 miles across, it's the dominating physical feature between the Vancouver Island Ranges and the Fraser Plateau.

The Fraser River, which cuts an 850-mile-long swath through the British Columbian mountains from its source in Jasper National Park, broadens over its last 100 miles into a gentle valley before reaching the Strait of Georgia. The Fraser Valley supports most of the population of British Columbia, including Vancouver, which lies on the northern edge of its delta. Another deep indentation, the Burrard Inlet, marks the boundary between Vancouver and the ruggedly mountainous North Shore.

Victoria lies 60 miles from Vancouver, almost due south, at the southeastern edge of Vancouver Island. The Juan de Fuca Strait separates the island from Washington State's Olympic Peninsula, 20 miles distant. The Haro Strait, which cuts an 8-mile-wide path between Vancouver Island and Washington's San Juan Islands, acts as a capillary linking the Strait of Georgia with the Juan de Fuca Strait, Canada's artery to the Pacific Ocean.

The region's geography is responsible not only for its beauty but for its mild and often rainy climate.

Most weather systems move into southwestern British Columbia off the jet streams that follow the moderate Japan Current, which curls past the west coast of Vancouver Island after leaving the Gulf of Alaska. That coastline is often bathed by rain clouds that stall on the island's mountainous 7,000-foot-high spine. Fronts that find their way around Vancouver Island, often passing by sheltered Victoria, can't get beyond the wall of peaks behind Vancouver and the Lower Mainland. Downtown Vancouver receives about 57 inches of rain a year, most of it between October and March; the average high temperature ranges from 74°F (23°C) in July to 41°F (5°C) in January.

Victoria receives about half the annual rainfall of Vancouver—26 inches—to go with temperatures that range from 72°F (22°C) in July to 43°F (6°C) in January. The average length of winter snow cover is 11 days in Vancouver, but a mere 3 days in Victoria.

PEOPLE

Three-quarters of British Columbia's citizens live in the province's southwestern corner. Individuals of British descent (English, Scots, Irish, and Welsh) comprise the largest percentage (about 40%) of Vancouverites and Victorians, but they are by no means the only significant group.

In fact, it's now estimated that 25% of all Vancouverites, and perhaps 225,000 British Columbians, are Chinese or of Chinese descent. Tens of thousands of them have recently immigrated from Hong Kong, moving their families and considerable financial assets out of Asia because of the impending return of Hong Kong to mainland China. Previous waves of Chinese migrants came to Canada's west coast in 1858 because of the Fraser Valley gold rush and in the 1880s to help build the trans-Canada railway.

Life for the Chinese in British Columbia has not always been easy: From their earliest arrival and through much of the 20th century they were treated as second-class citizens; they did not achieve the right to vote until the late 1940s. Today, however, they are perhaps the wealthiest ethnic group in the province. Vancouver's Chinatown, several square blocks around the intersection of Main and Pender Streets (east of downtown) is the second largest in North America (after San Francisco's). Victoria's Chinatown is not so large, but it is no less significant.

Indians and Pakistanis comprise another highly visible ethnic group; more than 65,000 of them live in greater Vancouver. Most Indian nationals who emigrate to Canada belong to the monotheistic Sikh religion, which is a minority faith in India. Baptized Sikh men wear colorful turbans to cover the tightly coiled hair they must never cut. As influential merchants, their principal ethnic center is the Punjabi Market on Main Street between 49th and 51st Avenues.

Although French-speaking Canadians have equal status with their English-speaking countrymen, French Canadians comprise a scattered minority of about 80,000 in British Columbia. They have their own newspaper, radio and television station, and a sizable community—Maillardville, in Coquitlam—east of Vancouver in the Fraser Valley. In fact, Coquitlam has the only bilingual school system in the province.

Southern European immigrants—Italians (about 48,000) and Greeks (9,000)—have established distinct communities in both Vancouver and Victoria, as well as a number of popular restaurants. In Vancouver, the principal Italian district is along Commercial Drive north and south of Broadway; the Greek community is centered near the University of British Columbia, along Broadway between McDonald and Alma Streets.

An estimated 150,000 Germans, 65,000 Dutch, and 50,000 Ukrainians also live in British Columbia. Many emigrated from their native lands following World War II and took up farming in the Fraser Valley or the lowlands of Vancouver Island. Other European immigrants, especially Scandinavians, found work in lumbering or fishing,

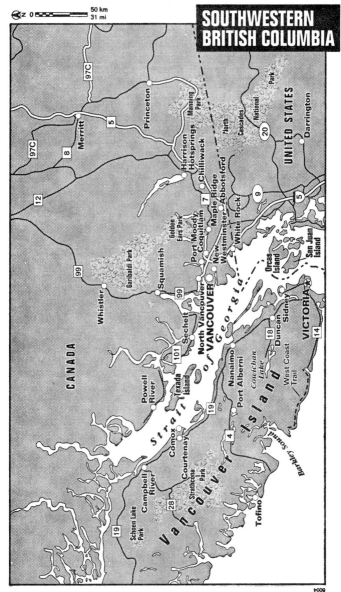

much as they had done in their homelands. There are also sizable ethnic communities of Japanese, Vietnamese, and Filipinos in southwestern British Columbia.

The Native Canadian population of 60,000—about one-third of whom live in southwestern B.C.—have a far lower average income and higher mortality rate than the white population. Three bands of Coast Salish live on two large reserves in Greater Vancouver—one located beneath the north end of the Lion's Gate Bridge in North Vancouver and the other on the Burrard Inlet near the foot of Mount

Seymour. A half dozen more reserves are located in metropolitan Victoria and the adjacent Saanich Peninsula.

2. ART & ARCHITECTURE

True British Columbian art is that of the indigenous coastal tribes. Today, contemporary Native and non-Native artists have adapted their totemic designs to silver jewelry, wood and jade carving, paintings and drawings, ceramics, and more traditional basketry. Galleries specializing in Native art are found throughout the province, including Water Street in Vancouver's Gastown and Government Street in downtown Victoria. Don't miss Haida artist Bill Reid's classic cedar sculpture *Raven and the First Men* in the University of British Columbia's Museum of Anthropology.

Emily Carr, a native of Victoria, is B.C.'s single most famous artist. Especially well known for her sketches and almost mystical paintings of coastal rain forests and Native culture, Carr turned to writing later in life. By the time of her death in 1945 at the age of 74, she had produced six incisive autobiographical books. The Emily Carr Room in the Vancouver Art Gallery houses 157 paintings and drawings she bequeathed to the people of British Columbia. The Emily Carr College of Art and Design on Vancouver's Granville Island carries on the work she began as a teacher. More of her art is on display at her longtime home in Victoria and at the Emily Carr Gallery.

Today's B.C. artists are as likely to be working in fabrics or ceramics as on canvas. A large number of artists have studios on Granville Island; many more are scattered widely through both communities.

Two names stand out in British Columbian architecture, one from the past and one from the present. Between 1893 and 1930 Francis Mawson Rattenbury designed Victoria's landmark Empress Hotel and Parliament Buildings, as well as the famous hotels in Banff and Lake Louise and a number of courthouses and banks throughout British Columbia. Arthur Erickson is Canada's greatest living architect, a genius who seems able to make buildings blend with their surroundings. Among his creations are the Museum of Anthropology at the University of British Columbia and, in downtown Vancouver, the law courts at Robson and Howe Streets and the MacMillan Bloedel tower on West Georgia Street. Although they never met, the two men collaborated on one project: Erickson converted the courtrooms and corridors of Rattenbury's Robson Square Courthouse into the Vancouver Art Gallery.

3. RECOMMENDED BOOKS

A large writers' community is thriving in southwestern British Columbia, though few of its members have achieved the fame of Canadian writers Margaret Atwood and Mordecai Richler. Events such as the annual Vancouver Writers Festival, which takes place in late October, help the community to prosper.

British Columbia's most successful commercial writer in recent years has been W. P. Kinsella, a resident of White Rock on the U.S. border. Author of 18 books, Kinsella gained recognition so slowly that at first he had to support himself by managing a pizza parlor and driving a taxi in Victoria. But in 1988 his baseball novel, *Shoeless Joe* (Ballantine) was turned into the successful movie *Field of Dreams* starring Kevin Costner. Perhaps now the world will discover his fine collections of Native Canadian stories, such as *The Miss Hobbema Pageant* (HarperCollins) and *Box Social* (Ballantine).

Southwestern British Columbia is home to an active group of poets, some of whom are Native sons and daughters. Works by Robin Skelton, P. K. Page, Susan Musgrave, Robert Bringhurst, Joe Rosenblatt, Dorothy Livesay, and Marilyn Bowering are among the best.

A good source of information on British Columbia's Native population is *A Guide to B.C. Indian Myth and Legend* by Ralph Maud (Talonbooks). Contemporary Native artist Bill Reid is profiled in *The Black Canoe: Bill Reid and the Spirit of Haida Gwaii* by Robert Bringhurst and Ulli Steizer (University of Washington Press).

Although there are many fine books on British Columbia's history, Terry Reksten's *Rattenbury* (Sono Nis) stands alone as a fascinating profile of B.C.'s most famous architect and his times. A detailed history of British Columbia is presented in *The West Beyond the West* by Jean Barman (University of Toronto Press). Rural life can be experienced through Rosemary Neering's book *Down the Road: Journeys Through Small-Town British Columbia* (Whitecap Books).

Among the excellent guidebooks on southwestern British Columbia, I think Jurgen Gothe's *First Rate* (Brighouse) may be the most entertaining volume of restaurant critiques I've ever read. Shoppers can rely on Anne Garber's *The Vancouver Shopper* (Elloitt Fairweather), now in its third edition.

Visitors with children should look for *Kids! Kids! Kids! in Vancouver* by Daniel Wood (Douglas & McIntyre) or *Kids! Kids! Kids! and Vancouver Island* by Daniel Wood and Betty Campbell (Douglas & McIntyre), which tell everything families need to know. A good book *for* children is *Siwitl: A Whale's Story* by Alexander Morton (Orca Books). Hikers can probably make good use of the trail guides published by Gordon Soules of North Vancouver or by the Mountaineers of Seattle. As for coffee-table volumes, it would be hard to beat the Bob Herger–Rosemary Neering project, *The Coast of British Columbia* (Whitecap).

CHAPTER 2

PLANNING A TRIP TO VANCOUVER & VICTORIA

Don't wait until you're on your way to read this chapter. It contains information that will help you plan your trip. And it is designed to save you time, money, luggage space, and perhaps aggravation.

In the following pages, you'll get a crash course on traveling in British Columbia. I've tried to answer the following questions: (1) Where can I get basic tourist information on Vancouver and Victoria? (2) What travel documents must I carry? (3) What is the Canadian currency system like? Is my American money good? What about my credit cards? (4) What are the best times to go? (5) What should I pack? (6) What health precautions should I take? (7) What about insurance? (8) Where can I get medical or legal aid if I should need it?

1. INFORMATION, ENTRY REQUIREMENTS & MONEY

SOURCES OF INFORMATION

Your first contact should be **Tourism British Columbia** (tel. toll free 800/663-6000 in North America). The provincial government tourist agency has detailed information on all areas of British Columbia. This book deals with only two of them.

Tourism B.C. has two offices in the United States—both on the West Coast: 2600 Michelson St., Suite 1050, Irvine, CA 92715 (tel. 714/852-1054; fax 714/852-0168); and 720 Olive Way, Suite 930, Seattle, WA 98101 (tel. 206/623-5937; fax 206/447-9004).

The agency's head office is in the Parliament Buildings, Victoria, BC V8V 1X4 (tel. 604/387-1683; fax 604/387-1420). Most tourist requests are handled at 865 Hornby St., 8th Floor, Vancouver, BC V6Z 2G3 (tel. 604/685-0032; fax 604/660-3383).

Your next sources are the visitors' bureaus for the respective cities. For **Tourism Vancouver,** write or call the Vancouver Travel InfoCentre, P.O. Box 49296, Vancouver, BC V7X 1L3 (tel. 604/683-

2000, or toll free 800/888-8835; fax 604/683-2601). For **Tourism Victoria,** write or call 1175 Douglas St., Suite 710, Victoria, BC V8W 2E1 (tel. 604/382-2160, or toll free 800/663-3883; fax 604/361-9733).

If you're planning to spend time outside the cities, get in touch with the following groups as well: For mainland B.C., the **Tourism Association of Southwestern British Columbia,** 1755 W. Broadway, Suite 204, Vancouver, BC V6J 4S5 (tel. 604/739-9011; fax 604/739-0153); and for Vancouver Island, the **Tourism Association of Vancouver Island,** 45 Bastion Sq., Suite 302, Victoria, BC V8W 1J1 (tel. 604/382-3551; fax 604/382-3523).

Canadian government tourism offices are often located together with consulates in major American cities. Since these offices provide information on Canada as a whole, they may not have too much detailed information on Vancouver and Victoria.

ENTRY REQUIREMENTS

DOCUMENTS Citizens and legal, permanent residents of the United States do not need passports or visas to cross the U.S. border into Canada. It's a good idea, however, to carry identification papers (a birth certificate will do) in case any questions arise. Naturalized citizens should be able to produce a naturalization certificate; permanent residents are advised to carry their alien registration (green) cards. Visitors 18 years of age and under, if traveling without a parent or guardian, should carry a letter of authorization stating their name and the length of their trip.

Citizens of countries other than the United States need a valid passport to enter Canada, whether directly or via the United States. Many also require visas. Inquiries should be directed to the Canadian embassy, high commission, or consulate in their home countries before departure for North America.

American citizens wishing to study or work in Canada must receive authorization to do so prior to arrival. Work permits are granted only if no Canadian citizen or permanent resident is deemed qualified for the job—the government is quite strict about this. Interested persons should check with a Canadian embassy or consulate for details.

CUSTOMS In most instances, clearing Customs at Vancouver Airport is a breeze for U.S. citizens and residents. **Canada Customs, Pacific Region,** which is responsible for British Columbia and the Yukon Territory to the north, is headquartered at 333 Dunsmuir St., Vancouver, BC V6B 5R4 (tel. 604/666-0545, or 604/666-1802 at the airport). Canadian Immigration officials can be reached by calling 604/666-2171.

The nearest **U.S. Customs and Immigration Services** checkpoint to Vancouver, and one of the busiest in North America, is the Peace Arch station north of Seattle (tel. 206/332-5771), where a full staff is on duty 24 hours a day. There are also U.S. Customs officers located on the second level of the Vancouver International Airport terminal in Room 2223 (tel. 604/278-1825 for Customs, 604/278-3360 for Immigration).

Clearing Customs either entering or leaving Canada is normally a fast, painless procedure. The typical northbound (entering Canada) questions are: "Where do you live? Where are you going? How long do you plan to be gone? What's the purpose of your trip? Are you carrying any fruit, vegetables, or firearms?" Then the Customs official usually says, "Okay, fine, go ahead." Southbound, you'll hear similar questions: "What is your citizenship? Where do you live? How long have you been gone? Did you buy anything in Canada that you are returning home with? (What?) Are you carrying any fresh produce?" Unless you give a "wrong" answer, act suspicious, or are overly reluctant to answer, you're home free.

Customs Regulations   Each American resident entering Canada for a visit of at least 24 hours may import duty free for consumption in Canada: 40 ounces (1.1 liter) of liquor or 24 cans or bottles of beer; one carton of cigarettes (200); 50 cigars; 2.2 pounds (1kg) of pipe tobacco; and perfume. (You must be 16 years old to purchase tobacco. Remember, too, that although the drinking age in British Columbia is 19, you can't buy alcoholic beverages in Washington state if you're under 21.) Gifts to be left in Canada valued at more than $40 (Canadian) are subject to duty on the excess amount. Canadian residents returning to Canada after a 48-hour absence have the same limits on liquor and perfume, but their purchases cannot exceed a total value of $100. They are limited to 400 grams of loose tobacco, in addition to cigars and cigarettes. Once a year, they may also import $300 of merchandise after a seven-day absence.

You can bring in almost anything you want, but there are strict regulations on importing plants, meats, and firearms. Hunters with valid licenses can bring in some gear, but handguns and fully automatic firearms are prohibited. In any case, *all* firearms must be declared at the border. If you want to fish, you must obtain a license. Pet animals may be admitted with proper vaccination records, but you should inquire in advance about necessary procedures. (Don't forget to talk to U.S. Customs about bringing your pet back home!)

Americans returning to the United States after a minimum 48-hour stay in Canada, but not more than once a month, may bring back duty free one liter of liquor, 100 cigars, one carton of cigarettes, and other items whose value does not exceed $400 (U.S.). Canadians traveling to the States may bring in 150 milliliters (less than six ounces) of alcoholic beverages or perfume, one carton of cigarettes, 50 cigars or two kilograms of tobacco, and other merchandise. Inquiries may be directed to the **U.S. Customs Service,** 1301 Constitution Ave. NW, Washington, DC 20229-0001.

MONEY

CURRENCY   There's little difference between the United States and Canada in terms of currency systems. Both are decimal based, and both call their monetary units **dollars and cents.** Canadian dollars come in the same denominations as U.S. dollars, but they're easier to tell apart—they come in different colors. What's more, a $1 coin (called a "Loonie") has replaced the $1 bill.

At press time, the American dollar is worth about 20% more. What this means is that every Canadian dollar you spend actually costs you only about 82¢ in U.S. money. To put it another way, if you budget $1,000 U.S. for your trip, you can spend almost $1,220 Canadian.

Greenbacks are widely accepted in Canada. Banks and other financial institutions offer a standard rate of exchange that may vary

THE CANADIAN DOLLAR & THE U.S. DOLLAR

At this writing $1 U.S. = approximately $1.22 Canadian (or $1 Canadian = 82¢ U.S.). This rate fluctuates from time to time and may not be the same when you travel to Canada. Therefore, this table should be used only as a guide:

Can.$	U.S.$	Can.$	U.S.$
0.25	0.21	11.00	9.02
0.50	0.41	12.00	9.84
0.75	0.62	13.00	10.66
1.00	0.82	14.00	11.48
2.00	1.64	15.00	12.30
3.00	2.46	20.00	16.40
4.00	3.28	25.00	20.50
5.00	4.10	50.00	41.00
6.00	4.92	75.00	61.50
7.00	5.74	100.00	82.00
8.00	6.56	150.00	123.00
9.00	7.38	200.00	164.00
10.00	8.20	250.00	205.00

slightly day by day. Commercial establishments, most of which welcome U.S. dollars, may offer a lower rate of exchange—or a higher one. The Canadian government urges visitors to use Canadian money to avoid exchange problems when traveling there, but I've never encountered any exchange problems with U.S. dollars beyond an occasional unfavorable rate.

You can bring into or take out of Canada any amount of money, but if you are importing or exporting sums of $10,000 or more, you must file a report of the transaction with U.S. Customs.

TRAVELER'S CHECKS Traveler's checks, in U.S. or Canadian funds, are the safest way to carry money, and they are universally accepted by banks (which may charge a small fee to cash them) and by larger commercial establishments.

CREDIT & CHARGE CARDS Major credit and charge cards are widely accepted in British Columbia, especially American Express, MasterCard, and VISA, and, to a lesser extent, Diners Club, Carte Blanche, and EnRoute. The amounts spent in Canadian dollars will automatically be converted by your company to U.S. dollars when you are billed.

IMPORTANT NOTE

Unless noted otherwise, all prices quoted in this book are in Canadian dollars.

BANKING HOURS Normal banking hours in Canada are 10am to 3pm Monday through Friday, although many banks stay open later, particularly on Friday.

TAXES Taxes are of special interest to visitors. *Everyone,* Canadian or not, must pay a 10% tax on hotel rooms and a 6% provincial tax on almost everything else except food and restaurant meals. Most goods and services *also* carry a 7% federal tax, better known as the "GST." Foreign tourists may be able to get most of this GST refunded if they spend at least $100 (Canadian) on their visit. For details, call toll free 800/66-VISIT and/or see "Taxes" in "Fast Facts: Vancouver" in Chapter 3.

2. WHEN TO GO —
CLIMATE, HOLIDAYS & EVENTS

Any time of year is a good time to visit, depending on your interests. The Vancouver-Victoria climate is Canada's balmiest, with warm summers and mild, rainy winters.

The six-month tourist season runs from April through September. Hotels often raise their prices 20%–30% during this period, but they are still fully booked. On the other hand, the weather is nicer (with rainfall sporadic, not continual), special events are far more numerous, and many seasonal attractions are open only during the tourist season. The days are long in these northern climes (16 hours of daylight in mid-June), encouraging one to participate in a variety of outdoor sports and activities.

The off-season is less expensive, less crowded, easier to get reservations in, and more conducive to indoor activities. Remember to bring an umbrella! Winter sports-lovers don't have far to travel to reach some of the continent's best-loved and most challenging ski resorts.

CLIMATE The month-by-month temperature range in Vancouver and Victoria is almost identical. The difference is in precipitation: Victoria, protected from southerly chinook breezes by Washington's Olympic Range, gets far less rain/snow than Vancouver, which lies against the mountains that attract rain clouds. The average annual rainfall in Vancouver is 57 inches; in Victoria, it's just 26 inches.

Vancouver's Average Temperatures and Days of Rain

	Jan	Feb	Mar	Apr	May	Jun	July	Aug	Sept	Oct	Nov	Dec
Temp. (°F)	36	39	43	49	55	60	64	63	57	50	43	39
Temp. (°C)	3	4	7	9	13	16	18	18	14	11	7	4
Days Rain	20	17	17	14	12	11	7	8	9	16	19	22

Victoria's Average Temperatures and Days of Rain

	Jan	Feb	Mar	Apr	May	Jun	July	Aug	Sept	Oct	Nov	Dec
Temp. (°F)	38	40	43	47	54	57	62	61	57	50	43	40
Temp. (°C)	3	5	6	9	12	14	17	16	14	10	6	4
Days Rain	16	14	13	10	8	7	5	6	8	13	16	18

HOLIDAYS   The official public holidays in the province of British Columbia are: New Year's Day (Jan 1); Good Friday, Easter, Easter Monday (Apr 1–4, 1994); Victoria Day (May 23, 1994); Canada Day (July 1); B.C. Day (Aug 1, 1994); Labour Day (Sept 5, 1994); Thanksgiving (Oct 10, 1994); Remembrance Day (Nov 11); Christmas (Dec 25); and Boxing Day (Dec 26).

VANCOUVER & VICTORIA CALENDAR OF EVENTS

The following are some of the area's events.

JANUARY

- ☐ **Polar Bear Swim,** English Bay, Vancouver. January 1.
- ☐ **Pacific Cup Oldtimers Hockey Tournament,** Victoria. Late January.

FEBRUARY

- ☐ **Chinese New Year celebration,** Chinatown, Vancouver. Includes a parade. Date varies.
- ☐ **Flower Count,** Victoria. Late February.

MARCH

- ☐ **Pacific Rim Whale Festival,** Tofino and Ucluelet, Vancouver Island. Late March.

APRIL

- ☐ **International Wine Festival,** Vancouver. Early April.
- ☐ **Victoria Society Orchid Show,** Victoria. Early April.
- ☐ **Antique Car Easter Parade,** New Westminster, Lower Mainland. Easter Sunday.
- ☐ **TerrifVic Dixieland Jazz Party,** Victoria. Late April.

MAY

- ☐ **Greater Victoria Music Festival,** Victoria. Early May.
- ☐ **Victoria Home Tour,** Victoria. Early May.
- ☐ **Cloverdale Rodeo,** Cloverdale, Lower Mainland. Mid-May.
- ☐ **Vancouver International Children's Festival,** Vancouver. Mid-May.
- ☐ **Country Music Fair and Jamboree,** Coombs, Vancouver Island. Mid-May.

☐ **Queen Victoria Day Celebration,** Burnaby Village Museum, Vancouver. May 23.
☐ **Victoria Day Parade,** Victoria. May 23.
☐ **Empire Days,** Nanaimo, Vancouver Island. Mid-May.
☐ **Tea Cup Boat Races,** Victoria. Mid-May.
☐ **Port Day,** North Vancouver. Mid-May.
☐ **Country Music Festival,** Mill Bay, Vancouver Island. Late May.

JUNE

☐ **Fishing Derby,** Port Alberni, Vancouver Island. Early June.
☐ **Fraser River Festival,** Delta, Lower Mainland. Early June.
☐ **Kite Festival,** Harrison Hot Springs, Lower Mainland. Early June.
☐ **Children's Art Festival,** Whistler, Sunshine Coast. Mid-June.
☐ **International Dragon Boat Festival,** Vancouver. Mid-June.
☐ **North Vancouver Folkfest,** North Vancouver. Mid-June.
☐ **DuMaurier International Jazz Festival,** Vancouver. Mid-June.
☐ **Jazz Fest International,** Victoria. Mid-June.
☐ **Victoria International Boat Race,** Victoria. Mid-June.
☐ **Gastown Grand Prix Bicycle Race,** Gastown, Vancouver. Late June.
☐ **Folkfest,** Victoria. Late June.

JULY

☐ **Canada Day,** Vancouver, Victoria, and all over British Columbia. July 1.
☐ **Steveston Salmon Festival,** Vancouver. Early July.
☐ **Busker International Festival of Street Performers,** Victoria. Early July.
☐ **Abbotsford Berry Festival,** Lower Mainland. Early July.
☐ **Harrison Festival of the Arts,** Harrison Hot Springs, Lower Mainland. Arts festival in the Fraser River valley east of Vancouver; attracts fine performing artists from around the world. Early July.
☐ **Summer Music Festival,** Comax, Vancouver Island. July.
☐ **International Festival,** Victoria. Spotlights classical performances almost nightly. July to mid-August.
☐ **Agricultural Fair,** Mission, Lower Mainland. Mid-July.
☐ **Old Time Fiddlers' Jamboree,** Coombs, Vancouver Island. Mid-July.
☐ **Pacific Rim Summer Festival,** Ucluelet and Tofino, Vancouver Island. Late July.

✪ ***VANCOUVER SEA FESTIVAL*** *This is one of the city's biggest events, featuring four days of concerts, parades, and fireworks over English Bay, and concluding with a bathtub race across the Strait of Georgia from Nanaimo.*
   Where: *Vancouver.* ***When:*** *Mid-July.* ***How:*** *For information on the festival, contact Tourism Vancouver (tel. 604/631-2831 or toll free 800/888-8835).*

☐ **Vancouver Folk Music Festival,** Vancouver. Mid-July.

☐ **Bathtub Race Week,** Nanaimo, Vancouver Island. Mid-July.
☐ **Early Music Festival,** University of British Columbia, Vancouver. Mid-July to mid-August.
☐ **Vancouver Chamber Music Festival,** Vancouver. Late July.
☐ **Country Blues Festival,** Whistler, Sunshine Coast. Late July.
☐ **Coombs Rodeo,** Coombs, Vancouver Island. Late July.
☐ **Fort Festival of the Performing Arts,** Fort Langley, Lower Mainland. Late July.

AUGUST

☐ **British Columbia Day,** Vancouver. August 1.
☐ **Powell Street Festival,** Vancouver. Japanese festival. Early August.
☐ **Salmon Derby,** Nanaimo, Vancouver Island. Early August.
☐ **Vancouver International Comedy Festival,** Vancouver. Early August.
☐ **Abbotsford International Airshow,** Abbotsford, Lower Mainland. Early August.
☐ **Festival of the Written Arts,** Sechelt, Sunshine Coast. Mid-August.
☐ **Vancouver International Triathlon,** Vancouver. Mid-August.
☐ **International Festival of Dance,** Victoria. Mid-August.
☐ **Whistler Classical Music Festival,** Whistler, Sunshine Coast. Mid-August.
☐ **Summer Music Festival,** Squamish, Sunshine Coast. Mid-August.

✪ *XV COMMONWEALTH GAMES* *Victoria will command the attention of citizens of the British Commonwealth the world over as host of the 15th Commonwealth Games. Athletes from 66 nations will converge on the B.C. capital to match skills in 10 sports in this mini-Olympics: track and field, swimming and diving, badminton, bowling, boxing, cycling, gymnastics, shooting, weight lifting, and wrestling. A complementary cultural program of fine and performing arts—the Commonwealth Celebration '94—will be staged from January through October in Victoria and southern Vancouver Island, highlighted by a series of August events.*
*   **Where:** Victoria. **When:** August 18–28, 1994. **How:** For information on the games, contact the Victoria Commonwealth Games Society, P.O. Box 1994, Victoria, BC V8W 3M8 (tel. 604/380-1994).*

☐ **SunFest,** Victoria. Mid-August.
☐ **Pacific National Exhibition,** Vancouver. The 10th largest fair in North America. Late August.
☐ **Molson Indy Vancouver,** Vancouver. Late August.

SEPTEMBER

☐ **Classic Boat Festival,** Victoria. Early September.
☐ **Bluegrass Festival,** Chilliwack, Lower Mainland. Early September.

- [ ] **Vancouver Fringe Festival,** Vancouver. Art festival emphasizing counterculture (or at least out-of-the-mainstream) art forms. Mid-September.
- [ ] **Terry Fox Run,** Vancouver. Mid-September.
- [ ] **Victoria Fringe Festival,** Victoria. Art festival emphasizing counterculture (or at least out-of-the-mainstream) art forms. Late September.

OCTOBER

- [ ] **Vancouver International Film Festival,** Vancouver. Early October.
- [ ] **Thanksgiving,** Burnaby Village Museum, Vancouver. Mid-October.
- [ ] **Vancouver Writers Festival,** Vancouver. Mid-October.
- [ ] **Halloween,** Vancouver. October 31.
- [ ] **Oktoberfest,** Vancouver. Various weekends.

NOVEMBER

- [ ] **Remembrance Day Parade,** Vancouver and Victoria. November 11.

DECEMBER

- [ ] **Christmas Lights Display,** Burchart Gardens, Victoria. Entire month.
- [ ] **Christmas Craft Market,** Granville Island, Vancouver. Until Christmas Eve.
- [ ] **Hyack Christmas Carol Cruises on the Fraser River,** Vancouver. Mid-December.
- [ ] **Christmas Carol ships,** English Bay and Burrard Inlet. Mid to late December.
- [ ] **Christmas Lighted Boat Parade,** Inner Harbour, Victoria. Around Christmas.
- [ ] **First Night,** Vancouver and Victoria. A merchant-sponsored, alcohol-free party in the downtown streets that has proven to be immensely popular. December 31.

3. HEALTH & INSURANCE

HEALTH Canadian hospital and medical services are comparable to those in the United States, except that medical care has become nationalized in Canada. Daily hospitalization rates vary; in-patient care can start at $900. Be sure you have insurance coverage.

Major hotels have doctors and dentists on call. If you need a referral, call the **College of Physicians and Surgeons of British Columbia** in Vancouver (tel. 773-7758) or the **College of Dental Surgeons of British Columbia,** also in Vancouver (tel. 736-3621), weekdays between 8am and 4pm. In case of an emergency, dial 911 or 0 (zero) for an operator anywhere in the province.

INSURANCE American travelers should review their health-insurance plans to see if adequate coverage is provided for travel outside the United States. For those who are not adequately covered, traveler's health insurance is recommended and widely available. Check with any travel agent or insurance company.

Auto insurance is compulsory in B.C. through the Insurance Corporation of British Columbia (ICBC). Basic coverage consists of "no-fault" accident benefits and third-party legal liability coverage of a minimum of $200,000. If you plan to drive in Canada, before you leave the States, check with your insurance company to make sure that your policy meets this requirement. Your company should issue a financial responsibility card, which you must present along with your vehicle registration and driver's license in case you have an accident. To report accidents to ICBC, call 520-8222 in Vancouver, 383-1111 in Victoria, or toll free 800/663-3051 anywhere in the province.

4. WHAT TO PACK

My first rule of thumb is: Travel as light as possible. Never carry more than you can handle yourself without assistance. Ideally, you shouldn't have more than one suitcase, and a carry-on bag that fits neatly under your seat on the airplane or in the overhead rack on a bus or train. If you're driving, you can allow yourself to carry a little more.

The clothing you bring will depend on the time of year you come and whether you plan to ski or to swim. In summer, casual lightweight clothing will suffice most of the time, but always carry a sweater for cool nights. Men should have a jacket and tie, and women an evening dress, if formal dining is on the agenda. In winter, you'll want a heavy jacket or coat, preferably waterproof. Gloves and a rain hat are a good idea, too.

Any time of year, a pair of sturdy and comfortable walking shoes is imperative. An umbrella is always a wise accessory, but it is essential from mid-September to mid-April.

There are a few items that could prove to be extremely useful during your stay: (1) a travel alarm clock, so that you don't have to depend on your hotel for wake-up calls; (2) a Swiss army knife, which has a multitude of uses from bottle opener to screwdriver; (3) a small flashlight, especially in winter when it gets dark early; (4) a washcloth in a plastic bag, in case your budget hotel doesn't provide one; (5) a pair of light wooden (not plastic) shoe trees to air out your footwear after you've spent a long day on your feet; and (6) a magnifying glass for reading the small print on maps.

There's one more thing you must never, ever travel anywhere without—your sense of humor.

Medicine If you're taking a prescription medication, it's wise to bring a copy of the prescription in case it needs to be renewed in Canada. It's advisable, also, to bring your eyeglasses/lens prescription in case your glasses get broken or lost and must be replaced. And for minor emergencies, I always carry a small first-aid kit containing an antibiotic ointment, bandages, aspirin, soap, a thermometer, and motion-sickness pills.

Electrical Appliances   Canada's electricity is 110 volts alternating current, just as in the United States, and it uses the same kind of outlets. You can bring and use any appliance without requiring an adapter. Just remember what I said about traveling light.

5. TIPS FOR THE DISABLED, SENIORS, SINGLES & FAMILIES

FOR THE DISABLED   Virtually every higher-priced accommodation, and most of those in the moderate range, have special rooms for the handicapped. Some budget hotels may also have suitable facilities. In all cases, it's important to book well ahead of time to reserve space.

Wheelchair travelers can obtain specific information about traveling in British Columbia by contacting the **Canadian Paraplegic Association,** 780 SW Marine Dr., Vancouver, BC V6P 5Y7 (tel. 604/324-3611).

Services for the hearing-impaired are available at the **Western Institute for the Deaf and Hard of Hearing,** 2125 W. Seventh Ave., Vancouver, BC V6K 1X9 (tel. 604/736-7391; TDD phone 604/736-2527). On Vancouver Island, services for the hearing-impaired are supplied by **Island Deaf and Hard of Hearing** at 835 Humboldt St., Suite 302, Victoria, BC V8V 4W8 (tel. 604/384-8088; TDD phone 604/384-3105). There's also a 24-hour Message Relay Centre: voice phone 604/681-2913 in Vancouver, or toll free 800/972-6503 outside Vancouver; TDD phone 604/681-1932 in Vancouver, or toll free 800/972-6509 outside the city.

Vancouver has a **Handicapped Resource Centre** (tel. 604/873-3371) and also assists disabled persons with transportation needs (tel. 264-5000).

FOR SENIORS   Travelers over the age of 65—in many cases 60, sometimes even 55—may qualify for discounts not available to the younger adult traveler. Some hotels offer rates 10%–20% less than the officially quoted rate; inquire at the time you make reservations. Public transportation systems and many privately owned attractions give seniors discounts of up to half the regular adult fare or admission price. Get in the habit of asking for your discount.

Vancouver has a program that assists senior citizens with transportation needs (tel. 264-5000).

If you are retired and are not already a member of the American Association of Retired Persons, consider joining. The AARP card is valuable throughout North America in your search for travel bargains.

FOR SINGLES   Traveling alone in Vancouver or Victoria won't present any more difficulties than in any U.S. city. In many cases, there will be fewer problems. Both cities are safe and clean, with low crime rates and modern transportation systems.

Young budget travelers know that the best places to meet others of similar values are youth hostels and universities. If you're a bit older and more sophisticated, you'll find it easy to start a conversation in the cafés of Vancouver's Robsonstrasse and the tearooms near Victoria's Inner Harbour.

Organized tours are a wonderful place to meet other singles looking for no-strings-attached companionship while sightseeing and dining.

FOR FAMILIES   Children often get special discounts that are not available to adults or even seniors. For instance, many hotels allow children to stay free with their parents in the same room. The upper age limit for a "child" may vary from 12 to 18, so be sure to check in advance.

Youngsters are almost always entitled to discounts on public transportation and admission to attractions. Though every entrance requirement is different, you'll often find that kids of 5 and under are free, those of elementary-school age are entitled to half price, and older students (through high school) get significant discounts.

You should also keep your eyes open for family rates at various attractions. These allow the whole clan admission for little more than the tab for just mom and dad.

If you happen to be in the area in mid-May, don't miss the Vancouver International Children's Festival at Vanier Park; it's the foremost event of its kind in North America. Another not-to-be-missed Vancouver event is the Pacific National Exhibition in late August. French-speaking children enjoy La Fête Colombienne des Enfants at Crescent Beach, near White Rock—just north of the U.S. border, in late May and early June.

Parents know all too well that whereas it's hard to take children into a classy restaurant, it may be unpleasant to take them into a "greasy spoon." Have no fear: Both Vancouver and Victoria offer a wide range of family-oriented restaurants. I've included several in Chapter 5, "Vancouver Dining."

Every family planning a vacation in southwestern British Columbia should obtain a copy of *Kids! Kids! Kids! in Vancouver.* First published in 1978, and frequently revised and expanded since, this book by teacher-broadcaster Daniel Wood includes more than 1,000 ideas for places to go and things to do in Vancouver and the Lower Mainland. A companion volume, *Kids! Kids! Kids! and Vancouver Island,* includes Victoria.

6. GETTING THERE

Getting to Canada's southwestern corner is no longer the arduous journey it was in the days of George Vancouver, Alexander Mackenzie, and Simon Fraser. For many West Coast Americans, it's certainly easier than traveling to New York; and for Easterners it can take less time than to cross the Atlantic to Europe. Air, rail, bus, private car, and even ship are all viable means of transportation to Vancouver.

BY PLANE   Vancouver International Airport is Canada's second busiest (after Toronto's), with flights continually arriving from and departing for airports throughout North and South America, Europe, Asia, and the Pacific. Victoria has a small international airport for regional flights from Vancouver and Seattle, as well as a number of smaller cities and towns. Visitors flying to southwestern British

Columbia from outside the area, therefore, always arrive in Vancouver first.

Special excursion fares may offer savings of up to 40% over regular economy fares. They may have certain requirements, however; for example, you may have to travel both ways on a Monday through Thursday, stay over a weekend, and purchase your ticket a minimum number of days (usually 30) before your trip. Ask a travel agent or call individual airlines to inquire about taking advantage of these special discount opportunities.

BY TRAIN The national **VIA Rail Canada** (tel. toll free 800/ 561-8630 for fares and reservations) service, sadly, has announced cutbacks, which will inevitably put as-yet-undetermined glitches in long-distance rail travel to Vancouver and Victoria from the east. The trans-Canada journey is one of the world's most spectacular train trips—especially the portion between Calgary and Vancouver, where the track winds through the Canadian Rockies. Travelers from the American Midwest can take Amtrak and connect with VIA Rail in Winnipeg; from the East, connections can be made in Montréal or Toronto. There is a ferry link for extending rail travel from Vancouver on to Victoria.

From the south, Amtrak has a direct San Diego–Los Angeles–San Francisco–Portland–Seattle–Vancouver route; connections to Victoria are made by boat in Seattle.

BY BUS This is the most economical method of traveling virtually anywhere in North America. Bus travel is usually cheaper and often faster than train, and bus routes are more flexible in case you want to stop off along the way. On the other hand, buses are more cramped, meals are available only at rest stops, and inner-city stops are frequent. What's more, trying to sleep on an overnight bus trip can be exhausting.

Greyhound Bus Lines, the only company that crosses the border into Canada from the United States, has such an extensive network that you can probably reach British Columbia's west coast with only a couple of transfers. Greyhound offers a variety of discount fares and unlimited-travel passes in addition to its regular fares. For information on fares and schedules, call any Greyhound station in North America.

Greyhound doesn't continue on to Victoria, but you can transfer to **Pacific Coach Lines** at the Vancouver bus depot, 150 Dunsmuir St. (tel. 662-8074).

West Coast budget travelers might want to consider **The Green Tortoise,** P.O. Box 24459, San Francisco, CA 94124 (tel. toll free 800/227-4766), a "youth hostel on wheels" with sleeping space on the bus. Twice-weekly trips are scheduled year-round between Los Angeles, San Francisco, Portland, and Seattle, where transfers can be made to Greyhound (for Vancouver) or ferry (for Victoria). Fares (less than $100 from L.A. to Seattle) are paid in cash to the driver.

BY CAR There are two principal routes to Vancouver. One—from the south—is U.S. Interstate 5 through Seattle; it becomes Route 99 at the British Columbia border. The second, from the east, is Trans-Canada Highway 1.

To reach Victoria by car is somewhat more complicated, simply because you must put your car on a ferry. Direct sea runs to Victoria originate in Seattle (via I-5) and Port Angeles, Washington (via U.S.

101); and car-ferry connections to Vancouver Island (and thus by road to Victoria) begin in Anacortes, Washington (via I-5), and Tsawwassen and Horseshoe Bay, British Columbia (both via Route 99).

BY SHIP It's possible to take a cruise ship from California to Vancouver or Victoria, but only during the summer. The Cunard, Princess, Royal Viking, and Sitmar lines sail from San Francisco to Alaska with stopovers in either or both cities to load new passengers. Several other cruise lines begin the Alaska run at Canada Place in Vancouver. Consult *Frommer's Alaska '94–'95,* by this same author, for details.

Several daily year-round services connect certain Washington cities with Victoria and Vancouver Island. **Washington State Ferries** (tel. 206/464-6400 or 604/381-1551, or toll free 800/843-3779 in Washington) makes two runs daily in summer (once a day during the rest of the year) between Anacortes, Wash., and Sidney, north of Victoria, via the San Juan Islands. **Black Ball Transport** (tel. 206/457-4491) runs a car-ferry between Port Angeles, Wash., and Victoria. And the privately owned **Victoria Clipper** (tel. toll free 800/888-2535) operates nonstop service between Seattle and Victoria's Inner Harbour.

Two additional daily passenger-only ships serve the Inner Harbour during the peak tourist season: Victoria Rapid Transit's **Victoria Express** from Port Angeles, May through October (tel. 206/452-8088 or 604/361-9144); and Gray Line Cruises' **MV Victoria Star** from Bellingham, Wash., via the San Juan Islands, June through October (tel. 206/371-5222, or toll free 800/443-4552).

Within British Columbia, **B.C. Ferries** (tel. 604/386-3431 or 604/669-1211) has several routes from the mainland to towns on Vancouver Island. **Royal Sealink Express** has a passenger-only ship connecting downtown Vancouver (tel. 604/687-6925) with downtown Victoria (tel. 604/382-5465). Details on all routes are provided in Chapter 10, "Getting to Know Victoria."

CHAPTER 3

GETTING TO KNOW VANCOUVER

1. ORIENTATION
2. GETTING AROUND
• FAST FACTS:
  VANCOUVER

Welcome to Vancouver! The journey is over and now you're ready to explore. But you feel a little lost and wouldn't mind a helping hand to show you the ins and outs of the city.

That's what this chapter is designed to do. First I'll tell you how to get into town and find things once you're there. Then I'll give you the scoop on getting around the city by public or private transportation. Finally, I'll present what is called the "Fast Facts" of the place—a miscellany of essential facts that you might have been hesitant to ask about but that could make a big difference in how much you enjoy your stay.

1. ORIENTATION

ARRIVING

Located just 19 miles north of the U.S. border, Vancouver is readily accessible by plane, train, and road.

BY PLANE

VANCOUVER INTERNATIONAL AIRPORT More than 10 million air passengers pass through Vancouver International Airport each year, arriving from (or departing for) more than 250 destinations in 40 countries aboard some 19 major carriers, including Air Canada, Air New Zealand, British Airways, Canadian Airlines, Cathay Pacific, Continental, Japan Air Lines, KLM Royal Dutch, Lufthansa, Qantas, and Singapore Airlines.

The airport is located eight miles south of downtown Vancouver on Sea Island, in the Fraser River delta adjacent to suburban Richmond.

An $18-million program is under way to improve the airport's facilities at its two terminals. The Main Terminal building serves incoming and outgoing foreign and domestic flights. The South Terminal is the base for smaller scheduled or charter airlines serving British Columbia, including Air B.C., Bute Air, Harbour Air, Shuswap Air, Waglisla Air, and Wilderness Airlines.

The international arrivals lounge is on Level 1 of the Main Terminal; the domestic arrivals lounge is on Level 2. The ticket and check-in area is on Level 3; Transport Canada administrative offices are on Level 4. Within the terminal building, travelers will find restaurants and cocktail bars, bookstores and newsstands, florists and chocolate shops, duty-free shops, and a seafood specialty shop. Services include banks and currency exchange, a post office, a barbershop, hotel reservation telephones, and public phones. **Tourist Information Centres** located on Levels 1 and 3 (tel. 276-6101) are staffed daily from 6:30am to 11:30pm.

Parking is available at the airport for more than 3,600 vehicles, one-third of them in a long-term lot. Call 276-6106 for parking information and charges.

Courtesy buses serve hotels in the immediate airport vicinity, and a shuttle bus links the Main and South Terminals.

GETTING INTO TOWN   The airport is easily accessible by three bridges. Travelers heading into Vancouver will take the Arthur Laing Bridge, which leads directly into Granville Street (Hwy. 99)—the most direct route to downtown.

Airport Express bus service to downtown Vancouver is provided by Perimeter Transportation (tel. 273-9023). A bus leaves from Level 2 every 15 minutes daily from 6:30am to 10:30pm, then every 30 minutes until 12:15am. It leaves various downtown sites every half hour between 5:35am and 10:55pm—check at your hotel for the nearest pickup point. The fare is $8.25 one way, $14 round-trip. The trip takes 30 minutes.

Public buses also stop at both terminals. Visitors who prefer the $1.35 ($2 during rush hours) trip downtown should board the no. 100 New Westminster bus at the terminal and request a transfer to the no. 20 or no. 17 bus at Marine Drive.

Nearly 400 **taxis** serve the airport; the typical fare to downtown Vancouver is $20.

AirLimo (tel. 273-1331), the city's only flat-rate limousine service, operates between the airport and downtown Vancouver with one-way fares of $26 per limo, not per person. It operates 24 hours a day and accepts major credit cards.

Numerous **car-rental firms** have desks at the airport with vehicles ready for drivers. They include Avis (tel. 273-4577), Budget (tel. 278-3994), Dominion (tel. 278-7196), Hertz (tel. 278-4001), and Tilden (tel. 273-3121). It's best to make reservations well ahead of time, however, especially during busy periods.

BY TRAIN

The main **Vancouver railway station** is at 1150 Station St. (tel. 669-3050), just south of Chinatown and adjacent to the old Expo '86 site near Main Street and Terminal Avenue. It's an ideal location for getting downtown—from the train platform, just walk a short block to SkyTrain's Main Station; it's only two stops to the Granville Station (or four stops to the Waterfront Station).

BY BUS

The bus terminal for both **Greyhound Bus Lines** (tel. 662-3222) and **Pacific Coach Lines** (tel. 662-8074) is at 150 Dunsmuir St., near B.C. Place Stadium. The downtown hotels are within easy walking distance from here, and SkyTrain's Stadium Station is just next door.

Bus transfer to Vancouver from Seattle-Tacoma International Airport is available through **Quick Coach Lines** (tel. 604/526-

2836). The bus stops at the Delta Pacific Inn in Richmond and the Sandman Inn, 180 W. Georgia St., in downtown Vancouver. The three-hour trip costs $32 one way, $60 round-trip.

BY CAR

If you're driving, you'll probably be entering the city by one of two routes:

Highway 99 from the Washington border passes under the

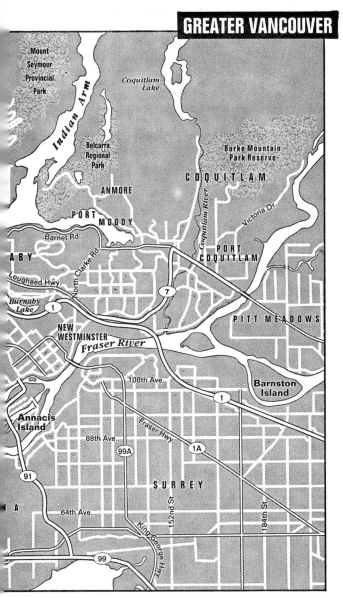

South Arm of the Fraser River through the George Massey Tunnel, then goes over the North Arm on the Oak Street Bridge, at which point it's no longer a freeway, but a busy city street. To find a bridge across False Street heading downtown, you'll have to get off Oak Street. Either turn west to Granville Street (preferred) or east to Cambie Street, then turn north again. Both routes head directly downtown.

Trans-Canada Highway 1 is a limited-access freeway all the way to Vancouver's eastern boundary. Exit at Cassiar Street, take a left at Hastings Street (the first light), adjacent to the Pacific National Exhibition grounds, and follow Hastings (Hwy. 7A) about four miles to the heart of downtown. (If you stay on Hwy. 1 and cross the Second Narrows Bridge into North Vancouver, you'll be on the most direct route to Whistler.)

Canada accepts all valid U.S. driver's licenses, and vice versa. Proof of insurance is required in the event of an accident (see "Health and Insurance" in Chapter 2). Make sure you have your vehicle registration with you. Wearing seat belts is mandatory in British Columbia.

BY SHIP

Vancouver's **cruise-ship terminal** (tel. 666-4452) is at Canada Place, the multisailed architectural wonder jutting into Burrard Inlet. About 200 sailings (up to four at once) arrive and depart from here annually between May and October. Although buses and taxis greet arriving ships, it's just a short walk from Canada Place to the central business district.

B.C. Ferries (tel. 669-1211) arriving from Vancouver Island dock either at Tsawwassen (from Sidney) or Horseshoe Bay (from Nanaimo). Highway 17 from Tsawwassen joins Hwy. 99 just before the Massey Tunnel; then follow the driving instructions given above for cars. From Horseshoe Bay, Hwys. 1 and 99 head back toward North Vancouver, with connections to downtown Vancouver on Hwy. 99 across the Lion's Gate Bridge.

TOURIST INFORMATION

The **Vancouver Travel InfoCentre,** Pavilion Plaza, 4 Bentall Centre, 1055 Dunsmuir St. (near Burrard Street; P.O. Box 49296), Vancouver, BC V7X 1L3 (tel. 604/683-2000, or 604/683-2772 for hotel reservations, or toll free 800/888-8835), is your single best source of tourist information. Established in the heart of the business and shopping districts by Tourism Vancouver, it has a large staff to answer any and all tourist inquiries. It also sells bus passes and tickets to sports and entertainment events. Open May to Labor Day, daily from 8am to 6pm, the rest of the year, Monday through Saturday from 8:30am to 5:30pm.

Another InfoCentre operates during the summer season only outside Eaton's department store at Georgia and Granville Streets, open daily from 9am to 5pm. A third InfoCentre in Stanley Park is open daily May 1 to Labor Day, from 9am to 5pm.

Tourism B.C. has three information centers outside Vancouver's city limits: in Richmond on Hwy. 99 just north of the Massey Tunnel, open daily year-round; in White Rock at 1224 King George Hwy., open daily in summer, weekdays in winter; and in North Vancouver at 131 E. 2nd St., near Lonsdale Quay, open daily May to September only.

CITY LAYOUT

Central Vancouver extends like a tongue into Burrard Inlet. Surrounded on three sides by water, the peninsula is crowned by stunning Stanley Park, which encompasses its seaward half. Its southern portion, in direct contrast to the park's green serenity, is the most intensively developed area in North America north of San Francisco and west of Chicago. Beyond this downtown core, the city sprawls for many miles east to the city of Burnaby, south to the Fraser River, and west to the Strait of Georgia.

To get your bearings, it may be helpful to start at Robson Square, the focal point of downtown. This three-block complex of terraces, gardens, waterfalls, restaurants, exhibition halls, skating rink, theaters, and government buildings is an ideal place to orient yourself.

If you stand on the square's top terrace and look toward the Vancouver Art Gallery (built in the early 20th century as a courthouse), you're facing north. (It's actually northeast, but everyone thinks of it as north, because of the diagonal grid layout of the downtown streets.) Beyond the gallery, north across the Burrard Inlet, are suburban West and North Vancouver, reached by the Lion's Gate and Second Narrows Bridges. Behind them, farther north, is the North Shore Range, whose peaks include Grouse Mountain and two other developed ski areas.

To the west is the Strait of Georgia and Vancouver Island, Stanley Park, English Bay, and the West End. East are B.C. Place Stadium, Chinatown, and Exhibition Park; farther east is the Trans-Canada Highway, which traverses the country from coast to coast.

South of Vancouver lies False Creek, which is spanned by three bridges. Within the narrow inlet, beneath the Granville Bridge, is Granville Island. Vanier Park, site of the Vancouver Museum and other attractions, is at the inlet's mouth. The spacious campus of the University of British Columbia is about four miles west. The North Arm of the Fraser River, which marks Vancouver's southern boundary, is five miles south; farther south is Vancouver International Airport (and, even farther, the U.S. border). In between lies most of residential Vancouver.

MAIN ARTERIES & STREETS   Downtown Vancouver is laid out on a grid: The streets generally run north-south (actually northeast-southwest) from Burrard Inlet to False Creek and east-west (actually northwest-southeast) from Chinatown to Stanley Park. Your perch in Robson Square is on **Robson Street,** the city's primary shopping and dining strip. (In fact, the area extending west of you for five or six blocks is called Robsonstrasse, a label no doubt bestowed for its European appeal.) Robson Street extends all the way from B.C. Place Stadium to Stanley Park; it also marks the approximate southern border of the central business district, which extends north about four blocks to West Hastings Street, west about two blocks to Burrard Street, and east about two blocks to Seymour Street.

Georgia Street, which parallels Robson one long block to the north, leads directly to Stanley Park and the Lion's Gate Bridge on the west and across a viaduct to Main Street on the east. Many upscale hotels and stores, as well as the post office and bus station, are on or adjacent to this street. Two and three blocks farther north, Pender and Hastings Streets extend east through Chinatown; Hastings skirts the southern edge of the historic Gastown district and continues all the way east to the Trans-Canada Hwy. and well into Burnaby.

The most important **north-south streets** are Burrard, which connects at its south end with the Burrard Bridge; Howe, a one-way street southbound onto the Granville Bridge; and Seymour, a one-way street northbound off that same bridge. **Granville Street,** which runs between them, is a pedestrian mall (with bus and taxi access only) for several blocks. The SkyTrain Terminal, SeaBus Terminal, and Canada Place are at its north end.

Across the Granville Bridge, Granville Street becomes Hwy. 99 to the airport; at 70th Avenue, Hwy. 99 turns east to Oak Street as it heads to the border. **Broadway,** which intersects both Granville and Oak Streets about six blocks south of the Granville Bridge, is a major east-west thoroughfare (Hwy. 7) which becomes the Lougheed Hwy. as it enters Burnaby. **Main Street,** the north-south artery through Chinatown, turns southeast as it crosses Broadway and becomes Kingsway (Vancouver's major cheap-motel strip), which leads to New Westminster.

NEIGHBORHOODS The **West End**——that section of downtown west of Thurlow Street, as far as Stanley Park—is reputed to have the highest population density of any urban area in North America except Manhattan. It tends to be upscale and sophisticated. **Old Gastown,** at the northeast fringe of downtown, was Vancouver's first urban-renewal project in the '60s and '70s; today it retains a bohemian ambience. Vancouver's **Chinatown** is the second largest in North America; focused around the intersection of Main and East Pender Streets, it even has its own cultural center. The Punjabi Market, built along Main Street between 49th and 51st Avenues, is the primary shopping area for the **East Indian** community. **Little Italy** runs along Commercial Street near Broadway; the largest concentration of **Greek** Canadians is also on Broadway, but near UBC around McDonald Street. **Kerrisdale,** around 41st Avenue and West Boulevard (west of Granville), is a quaint and charming community without any particular ethnic identification. **Shaughnessy,** between Arbutus and Cambie Streets, and 16th and 33rd Avenues, is an elegant older neighborhood of posh mansions on tree-lined streets.

FINDING AN ADDRESS Downtown, numbering on north-south streets starts at Powell Street (or, for all practical purposes, Burrard Inlet); on east-west streets at Carrall Street. In fact, **Carrall Street** (and, south of False Creek, Ontario Street) is the geographic line from which streets are designated "east" or "west." **Powell and Dundas Streets** form the boundary between "north" and "south." South of False Creek, it's easy to find an address because all the east-west streets are numbered—except Broadway (9th Avenue) and King Edward Avenue (25th Avenue).

MAPS Tourist InfoCentres provide free maps that show downtown in detail and the main routes through the rest of the city. If you need a more comprehensive map—which may be helpful if you plan to stay more than a few days—check bookstores or service stations.

2. GETTING AROUND

BY PUBLIC TRANSPORTATION

The **Vancouver Regional Transit System (BC Transit)** operates virtually around the clock, with regular service on the busiest routes from 5am to 2am, and late-night "Owl" service on several downtown-suburban routes until 4:20am. The system covers more than 1,500 square miles of the Lower Mainland. Information is available by calling 261-5100 between 6:30am and 11:30pm. Schedules are available at many places around the city, including InfoCentres.

The system includes SkyTrain, SeaBus, and the well-established fleet of buses and trolleys.

SKYTRAIN The pride of the system is SkyTrain, a fully computerized, magnetically propelled train that runs 16 miles (26km) from downtown to Surrey via Burnaby and New Westminster. It takes 35 minutes to cover the 17 stations, 13 of which are elevated; the four downtown stations are underground. A new line is being built to Coquitlam; another line to Richmond is in the planning stages.

SEABUS SeaBus crosses the Burrard Inlet from Waterfront Station (SkyTrain's terminus) to Lonsdale Quay in North Vancouver. The SS *Beaver* and SS *Otter* carry more than 400,000 passengers a year; neither has ever had to curtail service because of the weather. Boats leave Monday through Friday every 15 minutes from 6:15am to 6:30pm, then every 30 minutes until 1am; on Saturday, every half hour from 6:30am until 12:30pm, then every 15 minutes until 7:15pm, then every half hour until 1am; on Sunday and holidays they run every half hour from 8:30am until 11pm.

BUS Among the most popular bus routes is the hourly "Around the Park" service (no. 52) through Stanley Park from late April to late October. Other buses to keep in mind: no. 1 (Gastown–English Bay loop), no. 3 and 8 (English Bay/downtown–Marine Drive), no. 4 and 10 (UBC–Exhibition Park via downtown), no. 50 (Gastown–Broadway/False Creek), no. 51 (Granville Island), no. 100 (Port Coquitlam–Vancouver Airport via Marine Drive; from downtown, transfer from no. 20 or 17), no. 120 (Burnaby–New Westminster), no. 246 (North Vancouver), no. 250 (West Vancouver–Horseshoe Bay), no. 406 (Richmond–Steveston), no. 601 (Tsawwassen–Vancouver Island ferry). Many routes to Surrey, Langley, and other communities begin at the New Westminster SkyTrain station.

FARES Fares are the same for train, boat, or bus. You can travel within the City of Vancouver day or night for the same $1.35 fare (70¢ for children 5–13 and seniors 65 and over). Books of 20 "FareSaver" tickets cost $25.65 ($14 concession price).

Visitors can buy a **DayPass,** good for one day's unlimited travel on buses, SeaBus, and SkyTrain, after 9:30am Monday through Friday or all day on Saturday, Sunday, and holidays. Priced at $4 for adults, $2 for children 5–13 and seniors 65 and over, it may be purchased in advance or on the day of use. Tickets and passes are sold at InfoCentres, convenience stores, drugstores, credit unions, and other outlets with a "FareDealer" symbol in the window.

During rush hours (Monday through Friday before 9:30am and from 3 to 6:30pm), fares climb to $1.75 (90¢ for children 5–13 and seniors 65 and over) for travel from Vancouver to North Vancouver, West Vancouver, Richmond, Burnaby, or New Westminster, and $2.50 ($1.25 for children 5–13 and seniors 65 and over) to Delta, Surrey, Coquitlam, and points beyond.

Bus fares must be paid in exact change (no bills accepted).

Single-fare tickets are sold at machines in SeaBus terminals and SkyTrain stations. Transfers, issued on request when you board a bus, are valid for 90 minutes for travel in any direction.

BY TAXI

Taxi fares are reasonable unless you're traveling in the wee hours, when you'll have to pay double. In the downtown area, you can expect to travel for less than $4, except during the rush-hour traffic. The typical fare to the airport, eight miles distant, is $20. It's appropriate to tip the driver.

It may be hard to hail a taxi except downtown; your best bet is to call for a pickup. Taxi companies include **Black Top** (tel. 681-2181), **Checker Taxi** (tel. 731-1111), and **MacLure's** (tel. 731-9211).

BY CAR

The convenience of having a car at your disposal is a luxury you should not dismiss lightly. Although rush-hour traffic can be heavy in Vancouver and gas expensive, and although the city has its share of inattentive drivers, it's easy to find your way around and you may feel it's worth a little aggravation not to be dependent on the routes and schedules of public transportation.

CAR RENTALS   A great many visitors drive to Vancouver. Those who don't can rent a vehicle from one of the following firms: **ABC,** 255 W. Broadway (tel. 873-6622); **Avis,** 757 Hornby St. (tel. 682-1621, or toll free 800/331-1212); **Budget,** 450 W. Georgia St. and 1030 Denman St. (tel. 263-5555, or toll free 800/527-0700 for both); **Hertz,** 1128 Seymour St. (tel. 688-2411, or toll free 800/654-3131); **Rent-a-Wreck,** 1085 Kingsway (tel. 876-7155); **Thrifty,** 1400 Robson St. (tel. 688-2207, or toll free 800/367-2277); or **Tilden,** 1140 Alberni St. (tel. 685-6111). For long-term travelers, there's also **Canada Camper R.V. Rentals,** 1080 Millcarch St., Mitchell Island, Richmond (tel. 327-3003).

PARKING   All major downtown hotels have parking lots for guests, with varying daily charges. There's parking at **Robson Square** (enter at Smythe and Howe Streets), the **Pacific Centre** (Howe and Dunsmuir Streets), and **The Bay** (Richards near Dunsmuir). You'll find **parking lots** at Thurlow and Georgia Streets, Thurlow and Alberni, and Robson and Seymour.

Metered **street parking** is in high demand downtown and rules are strictly enforced (for this reason you should carry a pocketful of Canadian coins). Unmetered parking on side streets may be a long trek from where you're going. Read the signs carefully: If you park in a designated rush-hour lane, expect to have your car towed away.

DRIVING RULES   Driving rules in British Columbia are similar to those in the United States. (Canadians gave up driving on the left side of the street early in the 20th century.) The biggest difference is that you'll have to deal with the metric system: Speeds and distances are in kilometers and gas is sold by the liter. It's legal to turn right on a red light after you've come to a full stop. Wearing seat belts is mandatory; children under 5 must be in kids' car seats; helmets are compulsory for motorcyclists.

AUTO CLUB   Members of the American Automobile Association

(AAA) can get assistance from the **B.C. Automobile Association** at 999 W. Broadway, Vancouver (tel. 732-3911). The association's special road-service number is 293-2222.

BY BICYCLE

Even though bike paths are limited in number, cycling is extremely popular in Vancouver. The 5½-mile paved seawall path around Stanley Park and the circuit around the University of British Columbia are two favorites, but even the busiest city streets can easily be negotiated by cautious riders. Riding on sidewalks is illegal.

Many places rent bicycles, including **Bayshore/West Point Cycles,** 1876 W. Georgia St. (tel. 688-2453); **Robson Cycles,** 1463 Robson St. (tel. 687-2777); **Spokes Bicycle Rentals,** 1798 W. Georgia St. (tel. 688-5141); and **Stanley Park Rentals,** 676 Chilco St. (tel. 681-5581). Ask for a copy of "The Vancouver Bicycle Map," which points out potential trouble spots like busy streets, dangerous intersections, and steep hills to help riders select their routes.

Bicycles are allowed on the SeaBus at any time except rush hours; there's no extra charge. Bicycles are not allowed in Hwy. 99's George Massey Tunnel beneath the South Arm of the Fraser River, but a tunnel shuttle service operates from mid-May to September, four times daily—at 8am, 11am, 3pm, and 7pm southbound and 30 minutes later northbound. From May 1 to Victoria Day (the third weekend of May), the service operates on weekends only.

For other information, call the hotline of the **Bicycling Association of B.C.** (tel. 731-7433).

ON FOOT

I'm a strong advocate of walking whenever possible. Not only do you get exercise, but you see a lot more, experience the ambience of a place, and orient yourself much more quickly. In dry weather, Vancouver is a good walking city, with much scenic beauty and many points of interest. And one of the most pleasant excursions is a brisk early-morning stroll around Stanley Park. Don't worry: It's completely safe—no muggers.

FAST FACTS *VANCOUVER*

Airport   See "Arriving" in "Orientation," above in this chapter.

Area Code   Vancouver's telephone area code is 604.

Babysitters   Major hotels usually can arrange babysitting service on short notice, although they would prefer to be notified a day ahead. Moppet Minders Child and Home Services (tel. 325-3150) will send a babysitter to you with 24 hours' notice.

Banks   Most banks are open Monday through Friday from 10am to 3pm. Some are also open on Saturday.

Business Hours   Typical business hours are 8am to 5pm Monday through Friday, with a lunch break from noon to 1pm.

Business Services   Most major hotels offer secretarial, fax, and other services for a fee.

Climate   Vancouver's climate is mild and rainy much of the year, with average highs of 64°F (17.5°C) in July and average lows of 36°F (2.5°C) in January. Most of the abundant rainfall occurs during the winter months. See "When to Go" in Chapter 2 for details.

Consulates   The U.S. Consulate is at 1075 W. Georgia St. (tel. 685-4311). About 40 countries, mainly Pacific Rim and European, have consulates in Vancouver as well. Check the *Yellow Pages* for listings.

Currency   As this was being written, $1 U.S. was equal to $1.22 Canadian; inversely, 82¢ U.S. equaled $1 Canadian.

American dollars are widely accepted as payment at most hotels, restaurants, and shops throughout the Vancouver area. But not every outlet gives the same exchange rate as banks—some offer better, others worse. It has been my experience that banks at the border charge a higher commission than banks in Vancouver itself for changing American dollars into Canadian dollars. I've also found exchange rates to be a few cents better per dollar at small banks than at major banks.

Typically, a Canadian bank sells notes for a couple of percentage points less than the declared exchange value (e.g., $1.21 Canadian to $1 U.S. at this writing) and buys at a couple of percentage points higher (e.g., $1.23). This, of course, is where the bank makes its money. Merchants may offer an exchange rate of anywhere from 10% to 20%.

The **International Securities Exchange** has three downtown currency-exchange offices: at 1036 Robson St. near Burrard (tel. 683-4686), 1169 Robson St. near Bute (tel. 683-9666), and 734 Granville St. near Georgia (tel. 683-4879).

See "Information, Entry Requirements, and Money" in Chapter 2 for more information.

Dentists   Some major hotels have a dentist on call. Otherwise, you can get referrals from the College of Dental Surgeons of B.C. (tel. 736-3621) Monday through Friday between 8am and 4pm.

Doctors   Hotels typically have a doctor on call. The College of Physicians and Surgeons of B.C. (tel. 733-7758) will provide the names of three doctors if you call Monday through Friday between 8am and 4pm.

Drugstores   The Shopper's Drug Mart, 1125 Davie St. (tel. 685-6445), is open Monday through Saturday from 9am to midnight and on Sunday from 9am to 9pm. It has the longest hours of any downtown pharmacy. In the suburbs, several Safeway stores have late-night pharmacies.

Electricity   As in the States, 110 volts, alternating current.

Emergencies   Dial **911** for fire, police, ambulance, and poison control.

Eyeglasses   Try London Drugs, 1187 Robson St. (tel. 669-7374), or Tru-Valu Optical, 833 W. Broadway (tel. 873-3941). If you wear contact lenses, get in touch with the Image Contact Lens Centre at 815 W. Hastings St. (tel. 681-9488) or 1189 Robson St. (tel. 685-3937).

Hairdressers   This style-conscious city is teeming with hairdressers. Many major hotels have their own salons, and others are located along Robsonstrasse and in shopping arcades.

Holidays   See "When to Go" in Chapter 2.

Hospitals   St. Paul's Hospital is right downtown at 1081 Burrard St. (tel. 682-2344). Vancouver General Hospital is just south of Broadway at 855 W. 12th Ave. (tel. 875-4411). Other major hospitals include Shaughnessy Hospital, 4500 Oak St. at 29th Avenue (tel. 875-2222), and its neighbors, Children's Hospital, 4480 Oak St. (tel. 875-2345), and Grace Hospital (obstetrics), 4490 Oak St. (tel. 875-2424). In North Vancouver, there is Lions Gate Hospital, 231 E. 13th St. (tel. 988-3131).

Information See "Tourist Information" in "Orientation," above in this chapter.

Language English and French are the official languages of Canada. In British Columbia, English is the predominant language.

Laundry/Dry Cleaning One modestly priced dry cleaner is Scotty's One Hour Cleaners, 834 Thurlow St. (tel. 685-7732). There are also numerous self-service laundries around the city.

Liquor Laws You must be 19 years old to buy or drink alcoholic beverages in British Columbia. Spirits are sold only in government liquor stores, but beer and wine can be purchased from some specially licensed private stores and pubs.

Lost Property Try the Vancouver Police property room (tel. 665-2232) or, if you think you may have lost something on public transportation, B.C. Transit (tel. 682-7887).

Mail Everything you mail from Canada must bear a Canadian stamp. Postal rates vary; as I write this, it costs 48¢ to send a letter or postcard from Canada to the United States. Canadian postal codes, you may have noticed, alternate letters and numerals; it's important to put them on all your correspondence. See also "Post Office," below.

Maps You can get good city and regional maps from tourist information centers, bookshops, automobile clubs, service stations, and even hotel desks.

Metric Measurements Canada uses the metric system of measurement. For a conversion chart, see the Appendix.

Newspapers The *Vancouver Sun,* a broadsheet, is published mornings, Monday through Saturday. *The Province,* a tabloid, appears Sunday through Friday mornings. Both are sold on newsstands and in many hotel lobbies. *The Georgia Straight,* a weekly entertainment paper, comes out on Thursday.

Photographic Needs Your best bet may be London Drugs, located on the mall at 540 Granville St. (tel. 685-0105), as well as in other locations in the Greater Vancouver area. Also, try Lens & Shutter Cameras, 2912 W. Broadway (tel. 736-3461).

Police In an emergency, dial **911.** Property crime can be reported at 665-3321.

Post Office The main post office takes up a full city block at West Georgia and Homer Streets. It's open Monday through Friday from 8am to 5:30pm and it has an excellent philatelic center for collectors. There are smaller post office counters in Eaton's and The Bay, Vancouver's two big downtown department stores; some drugstores—those with the Canada Post symbol in their windows—also offer basic services Monday through Saturday. Letters and postcards to the States cost 48¢; within Canada, 42¢.

Radio and Television AM radio stations include 600 CHRX (classic rock), 690 CBU (classical, no commercials), 730 CKLG (top 40), 980 CKNW (talk and sports), 1040 CKST (alternate rock), 1130 CKWX (country), and 1320 CHQM (easy listening). FM stations include 99.3 CFOX (progressive rock), 102.0 CITR (alternative music), 102.7 CFRO (community radio), and 105.7 CBC (classical, no commercials).

Among television stations, CBUT (Channel 2, cable 3) and BCTV (Channel 8, cable 11) are Canadian network affiliates, and U-TV (Channel 10, cable 13) is independent. All three major American networks as well as the Public Broadcasting System are received from Seattle.

Religious Services Downtown churches include Central Presbyterian Church, 1155 Thurlow St. (tel. 683-1913); Christ Church Cathedral (Anglican), 690 Burrard St. (tel. 682-3848); First Baptist Church, 969 Burrard St. (tel. 683-8441); First Church of Christ Scientist, 1160 W. Georgia St. (tel. 685-7544); Holy Rosary Cathedral (Roman Catholic), 646 Richards St. (tel. 682-6774); and St. Andrew's Wesley United Church, 1012 Nelson St. (tel. 683-4574).

Major non-Christian places of worship near downtown include the Akali Singh Sikh Temple, 1890 Skeena St. (tel. 254-2117); the Beth Israel Synagogue, 4350 Oak St. (tel. 731-4161); the Universal Buddhist Temple, 525 E. 49th Ave. (tel. 325-6912); and many others, including Hindu and Muslim.

Restrooms Look in the same places you would in the States, including hotels, restaurants, shopping malls, and other public places.

Safety Whenever you're traveling in an unfamiliar city or country, stay alert. Be aware of your immediate surroundings. Wear a moneybelt and don't sling your camera or purse over your shoulder—wear the strap diagonally across your body. These precautions will minimize the possibility of your becoming a victim of crime. Every society has its criminals; it's your responsibility to be aware and alert even in the most heavily touristed areas.

Shoe Repairs Try Robson Shoe Renew, 1108 Robson St., or a major department store.

Taxes Hotel rooms are subject to a 10% tax. The provincial sales tax is 6% (excluding food, restaurant meals, and children's clothing). For specific questions, call the B.C. Consumer Taxation Branch (tel. 660-4500).

Most goods and services are subject to a 7% Canadian federal goods and services tax (GST). Americans and other foreign tourists can usually have this tax refunded if they spend at least $100 Canadian during their visit. (The refund does not apply to car rentals, parking, restaurant meals, room service, tobacco, or alcohol.) Hotels and tourist information offices can provide application forms. Save your receipts. For details on the GST, call toll free 800/66-VISIT.

Taxis See "Getting Around," above in this chapter.

Telephones They work just like those south of the border, with local calls normally costing 25¢. And, yes, your telephone credit card is good here. The area code for all of British Columbia is 604.

Time Vancouver is in the Pacific time zone—the same as Seattle, San Francisco, and Los Angeles. Daylight saving time is in effect from April to October.

Tipping It's appropriate to tip 15% for restaurant meals, 50¢ per bag for porters, and $1 a day for the housekeeper if you're staying more than a couple nights in your hotel. You may tell taxi drivers to "keep the change."

Transit Information See "Getting Around," above in this chapter.

Useful Telephone Numbers Royal Canadian Mounted Police Tourist Alert, for urgent messages only (tel. 264-2466 May–August); Distress Line Crisis Centre (tel. 733-4111); Rape Crisis Centre (tel. 872-8212); Victims of Violence (tel. 665-2187); Poison

Control Centre (tel. 682-5050); SPCA animal emergency (tel. 879-7343); B.C. Highway Report (tel. 660-9775).

   Water   Tap water is safe to drink everywhere.

   Weather   See "Climate," above, and "When to Go" in Chapter 2. For current forecasts, call 664-9010; for a marine forecast, dial 270-7411.

VANCOUVER ACCOMMODATIONS

Vancouver has a wide choice of fine accommodations in all price ranges. The average tourist will find the same high standards as in any Western city.

In this listing, I have organized accommodations first by geographic area and then by price.

GEOGRAPHIC AREAS Accommodations are listed in the following areas of the city: "Downtown," "The West End" (the area between downtown and Stanley Park, west of Thurlow Street), "East of Downtown" (east of Main Street, a heavily residential area with several major thoroughfares), "South of Downtown" (the area extending from Main Street west of the University of British Columbia and south from False Creek to the Fraser River), "Near the Airport" (the area within easy shuttle distance of Vancouver International Airport, especially the suburb of Richmond), "The North Shore" (the twin suburbs of North Vancouver and West Vancouver on the north shore of the Burrard Inlet), "Gastown/Chinatown" (which are roughly bounded by the waterfront to Pender Street on the north, Richard Street on the west, Keefer Street on the south, and Gore Avenue on the east), and "West of Downtown" (the area near the University of British Columbia).

PRICE CATEGORIES In general I have used four price categories, according to summer rates for two persons: "Very Expensive" ($175 and up a night), "Expensive" ($125–$175), "Moderate" ($75–$125), and "Budget" (under $75). *Prices are quoted in Canadian dollars* and do not include the 10% provincial sales tax; you will also be charged the 7% goods and services tax.

The listed rates are the officially quoted, or "rack rates," and don't take into account any individual or group discounts. Even in the upper price brackets there are many ways to pay much less. One hotel sales director told me that wise travelers should always try to secure reduced rates. He suggested asking for corporate rates. If you don't work for a corporation, identify a big firm (a bank, for instance) and you'll save 20%–35% off listed rack rates. Family emergencies warrant a medical rate. There are union rates and university rates. Travel-industry rates are 25% off in summer, 50% off in winter. Weekend rates are often 50% lower than midweek business travelers' rates, especially in the off-season. Speak up to save—if you don't ask, they won't tell you!

RESERVATIONS Reservations are always important, but are absolutely essential from June to September and during other holiday periods. If you arrive without a reservation and have trouble finding a room, call **Tourism Vancouver** (tel. 682-2772). They will try to help, but you may have to settle for something several miles from downtown.

BED-AND-BREAKFASTS If you find it difficult to get a hotel room, or if you prefer to stay in a bed-and-breakfast, the following agencies try to match visitors and hosts with similar interests:

A Home Away From Home Bed & Breakfast Agency, 1441 Howard Ave., Burnaby, BC V5B 3S2 (tel. 604/873-4888).

Born Free Bed & Breakfast of B.C., 4390 Frances St., Burnaby, BC V5C 2R3 (tel. 604/298-8815).

Canada-West Accommodations Bed & Breakfast Registry, P.O. Box 86607, North Vancouver, BC V7L 4L2 (tel. 604/929-1424).

Copes' Choice Bed & Breakfast Accommodations, 864 E. 14th St., North Vancouver, BC V7L 2P6 (tel. 604/987-8988 or 988-7264).

Old English Bed & Breakfast Registry, P.O. Box 86818, North Vancouver, BC V7L 4L3 (tel. 604/986-5069; fax 604/298-5917).

Town & Country Bed & Breakfast in B.C., P.O. Box 74542, 2803 W. Fourth Ave., Vancouver, BC V6K 1K2 (tel. 604/731-5942).

Westway Accommodation Registry, P.O. Box 48950, Bentall Centre, Vancouver, BC V7X 1A8 (tel. 604/273-8293).

All of the above are members of the **British Columbia Bed & Breakfast Association,** P.O. Box 593, 810 W. Broadway, Vancouver, BC V5Z 4E2 (tel. 604/276-8616), an umbrella group formed at the request of Tourism British Columbia to promote tourism and quality control. Each member home is inspected for cleanliness, comfort, courtesy, and service to ensure high standards.

The rates vary widely, but may be as low as $45 single, $60 double, and range to about $120 for special suites. Indicate your preferred price range when making reservations. Fireplaces, Jacuzzis, and heated swimming pools are sometimes available in the higher price categories. Credit cards are usually accepted.

1. DOWNTOWN

VERY EXPENSIVE

DELTA PLACE HOTEL, 645 Howe St., Vancouver, BC V6C 2Y9. Tel. 604/687-1122, or toll free 800/268-1133. Fax 604/689-7044. 179 rms, 18 suites. A/C MINIBAR TV TEL **SkyTrain:** Granville.

$ Rates: May–Sept, $205 single; $225 double; $152 weekends. Oct–Apr, $190 single; $210 double; $105 weekends. Suites to $950. Children stay free in parents' room. AE, DC, ER, JCB, MC, V.

Parking: $12, underground.

This luxurious modern hotel is small enough to ensure individual service but large enough to be able to provide every possible amenity.

Formerly called the Mandarin Hotel, it's right in the downtown business and shopping district. Businesspeople love it because *every* room has executive service with upscale amenities.

The first hint that your room is special is its doorbell. Within, you'll find solid oak cabinets and furnishings, including a custom-built leather-top desk and a TV hidden in an armoire. There are three telephones, including one in the Italian marble bathroom, which has a separate shower and oversize bathtub. Most rooms open onto private balconies. Other touches include terry-cloth bathrobes, umbrellas, shoeshine service, and a free morning newspaper.

Dining/Entertainment: Le Café, on the second floor, is the fine dining room, with entrées priced at $11.50–$16.50. The West Coast cuisine features local seafood and produce. Open for breakfast and lunch as well, it provides a children's menu. The Clipper Lounge has a daily Asian buffet and lunch entrées.

Services: 24-hour room service, concierge, valet cleaning.

Facilities: Indoor swimming pool, squash and racquetball courts, weight/exercise room, whirlpool, sauna (with TV), massage room, steam room, business center, meeting/banquet space for 100, no-smoking rooms and facilities for the handicapped.

FOUR SEASONS HOTEL, 791 W. Georgia St., Vancouver, BC V6C 2T4. Tel. 604/689-9333, or toll free 800/332-3442 in the U.S., 800/268-6282 in Canada. Fax 604/684-4555. 330 rms, 55 suites. A/C MINIBAR TV TEL **SkyTrain:** Burrard.
$ Rates: Year-round, $185–$235 single; $210–$260 double; $260–$705 suite. AE, CB, DC, JCB, MC, V. **Parking:** $13.

From the Rolling Stones to former Prime Minister Brian Mulroney, a wide range of visitors has chosen this 28-story hotel. It's easy to miss the Howe Street entrance but not the stunning greenhouselike rotunda that connects it to the 200-store Pacific Centre shopping mall. Built in 1976, the hotel has a subtle Asian decor, starting with the lotus-seated Buddha that greets guests.

The rooms continue the Asian motif in their art and bonsai plants. Rich wood furnishings include a glass-top desk and an armoire containing the remote-control television. The rooms have a minimum of two phones (sometimes four), clock radios, VCRs, hairdryers, terry-cloth bathrobes, and marble-top vanities. The deluxe rooms have French doors which separate the king-size bedroom from the living area, and two baths. Nearly two-thirds of the rooms are reserved for nonsmokers.

Dining/Entertainment: Chartwell, which has hosted such celebrities as Queen Elizabeth II, the late Malcolm Forbes, and Mick Jagger, is considered one of Canada's elite restaurants. The moderately priced Seasons Café, open early to late, extends to the rotunda overlooking Pacific Centre. A $27.50 brunch is served on Sunday around the fountain in the Garden Lounge; on Friday and Saturday nights, a dessert buffet is offered to patrons of the lounge's piano bar.

Services: 24-hour room service, concierge, laundry and valet service, complimentary shoeshine, twice-daily housekeeping; children get cookies and milk in the evening, room-service menus, and their own robes.

Facilities: Indoor/outdoor pool, fitness center, weight/exercise room, aerobics classes, whirlpool, saunas, banquet/meeting space for 800; tennis courts in new adjoining office tower.

HOTEL VANCOUVER, 900 W. Georgia St., Vancouver, BC V6C 2W6. Tel. 604/684-3131, or toll free 800/828-7447 in U.S., 800/268-9411 in most of Canada, 800/268-9420 in Ontario and Québec. Fax 604/662-1929. 508 rms, 42 suites. A/C MINIBAR TV TEL **SkyTrain:** Burrard.

$ Rates: Late Apr to Nov, $200–$260 single; $225–$285 double; packages from $95 single. Nov to late Apr, $115–$175 single; $140–$200 double; packages from $83 single. Suites to $1,520. AE, CB, DC, ER, MC, V. **Parking:** $9.

The grande dame of the city's hospitality industry, the Hotel Vancouver has hosted royalty and celebrities since King George VI stayed here four days after the hotel opened in May 1939. The hotel's steeply pitched green copper roof is characteristic of a 16th-century French château; artisans from 10 countries spent 12 months carving its classical facades. The lobby, reminiscent of the Edwardian era with its antique armchairs and sofas, is equally remarkable for its huge crystal chandeliers and marble pillars. No less than 166 tons of marble—25 different types—was used for the interior design.

The spacious, soundproof rooms have pastel color schemes and standard furnishings. Business-class rooms are equipped with colonial antique furnishings, working desks, and conference phones. The rosewood-paneled Entree Gold executive floor offers direct check-in with a concierge on the floor, a private lounge and boardroom, and free local phone calls. Both categories include breakfast.

Dining/Entertainment: There's 15th-floor dining and dancing with a spectacular city view at the Roof Restaurant and Lounge. The highbrow Timber Club specializes in West Coast cuisine. Griffin's Bistro serves breakfast, lunch, tea, and dinner in a garden atmosphere. The Lobby Lounge offers a luncheon menu as well as piano music each evening.

Services: 24-hour room service, complimentary morning coffee and newspaper, twice-daily housekeeping, overnight pressing and shoeshine, valet laundry, babysitting, secretarial service; small pets are allowed.

Facilities: Indoor pool, wading pool, Jacuzzi, health club with kinesiologist and masseuse, weight room, saunas, tanning bed, banquet/meeting space for 1,500, car rental, bank, beauty salon, barbershop, shoeshine stand, shopping arcade, no-smoking rooms and facilities for the handicapped.

HYATT REGENCY VANCOUVER, 655 Burrard St., Vancouver, BC V6C 2R7. Tel. 604/683-1234, or toll free 800/233-1234. Fax 604/689-3707. 612 rms, 34 suites. A/C MINIBAR TV TEL **SkyTrain:** Burrard.

$ Rates: Apr 16–Oct, $190–$210 single; $210–$230 double; $330–$650 suite; weekend discounts from $130 single. Nov–Apr 15, $140–$170 single; $160–$190 double; $280–$650 suite; weekend discounts from $85 single. AE, CB, DC, ER, MC, V. **Parking:** $12.50.

From the spacious street-level lobby to the panoramic windows of the 34th-floor meeting and banquet rooms, Vancouver's largest hotel is also one of its finest. And it's situated adjacent to the Royal Centre mall and movie complex.

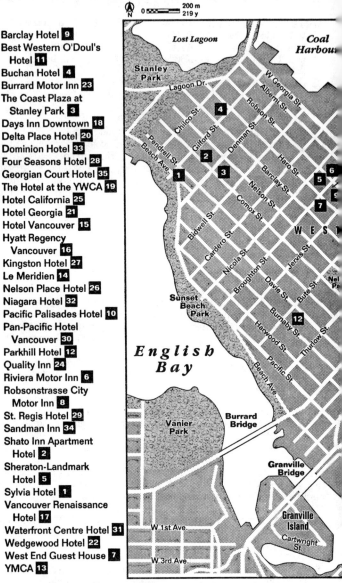

The hotel recently completed an $11-million refurbishing: The guest rooms have been decorated in subtle shades of purple with a hint of Oriental-style furnishings—lacquered tables, brass lamps, oversize closets, and baths. Many rooms have security vaults, and the corner rooms come with balconies. Several floors of executive rooms and walnut-furnished suites offer a concierge and private lounge, complimentary breakfast, and special amenities.

Dining/Entertainment: Fish & Co., needless to say, specializes in seafood. It's one of Vancouver's best seafood restaurants for lunch,

CENTRAL VANCOUVER ACCOMMODATIONS

Burrard Inlet

Canada Place

W. Pender St.
Melville St.
W. Cordova St.
W. Hastings St.
Water St.
Dunsmuir St.
Victory Sq.
Abbott St.
Carrall St.

N D

Robson Sq.

Burrard St.
Hornby St.
Howe St.
Granville St.
Seymour St.
Richards St.
Homer St.
Hamilton St.
Cambie St.
Beatty St.

W. Georgia St.
Robson St.
Post Office
Bus Depot
Stadium

Nelson St.
Helmcken St.
Drake St.
Davie St.
Pacific Blvd.

Cambie St. Bridge

Creek

False

W. 1st Ave.
MOUNT PLEASANT
W. 3rd Ave.

Post Office ⊠

Information ⊖

6006

dinner, and Sunday-brunch buffet. The Café, open daily for all meals, offers a salad and pasta bar. Weekday lunch buffets are also available in the intimate Peacocks Club Lounge and the lively Gallery Bar. Both feature nightly piano music, but this may be preempted in the Gallery by big-screen sports.

Services: 24-hour room service, concierge, laundry and valet service, doctor and dentist on call, summer program for children; staff members collectively speak 32 languages.

Facilities: Outdoor pool, health club, weight and exercise machines, saunas, access to racquetball and squash courts, business center, banquet/meeting space for 2,000, no-smoking rooms.

LE MERIDIEN, 845 Burrard St., Vancouver, BC V6Z 2K6. Tel. 604/682-5511, or toll free 800/543-4300. Fax 604/682-5513. 397 rms, 47 suites. A/C MINIBAR TV TEL **SkyTrain:** Burrard.

$ Rates: May–Sept, $150–$180 single; $150–$200 double; $250–$325 suite. Oct–Apr, $140–$150 single; $140–$170 double; $200–$240 suite. Children under 18 stay free in parents' room. AE, CB, DC, DISC, ER, JCB, MC, V. **Parking:** $12, underground; valet parking available.

Classical elegance in the European style is the hallmark of this hotel managed by Air France. You'll feel as if you're walking into an 18th-century mansion. Rather than entering a vast lobby, you'll encounter a series of serene rooms with marble floors, Oriental carpets, antique furnishings, and chandelier-bedecked hallways hung with oil paintings. Soothing classical music provides the final touch.

The guestrooms are equally elegant, with silk bedspreads, TVs hidden in armoires, impressively large desks, and botanical prints on the beige walls. Each bathroom has a telephone, marble-top vanity, scale, hairdryer, and bathrobe. Each room is also stocked with an umbrella for Vancouver's rain.

Next door is La Grande Résidence, with 162 suites for those who plan to stay in Vancouver at least 30 days. Hollywood production companies often make their home base here.

Dining/Entertainment: Le Club is among the city's finest restaurants. Café Fleuri serves breakfast and lunch daily in an informal French provincial setting; the café also offers a popular Sunday brunch, and on Friday and Saturday evenings there's a seafood buffet and Chocoholic Bar for dessert lovers. La Promenade lounge and Gerard Lounge offer light snacks and piano bars.

Services: 24-hour room service and concierge, twice-daily housekeeping, laundry/valet service with 24-hour pressing, shoeshine, babysitting.

Facilities: Glass-covered indoor pool, outdoor deck, weight/exercise room, whirlpool, women's sauna, men's steam room, tanning, massage, hairstylist, business center, meeting/banquet space for 350, gift shop, florist, car rental, nine no-smoking floors and 12 rooms for the handicapped.

PAN-PACIFIC HOTEL VANCOUVER, 300-999 Canada Place, Vancouver, BC V6C 3B5. Tel. 604/662-8111, or toll free 800/937-1515 in the U.S., 800/663-1515 in Canada. Fax 604/662-3815. 467 rms, 39 suites. A/C MINIBAR TV TEL **SkyTrain:** Waterfront.

$ Rates: Mid-Apr to Nov, $250–$270 single or double. Dec to mid-Apr, $180–$205 single; $210–$235 double; $200–$900 suite. Children under 18 stay free in parents' room. AE, DC, ER, MC, V. **Parking:** $17, valet.

Apart from Vancouver's natural surroundings, the city's most distinctive landmark is Canada Place with its five soaring white Teflon sails, reminiscent of a giant vessel leaving port. It houses the Vancouver Trade and Convention Centre and the Alaska cruise-ship terminal. Adjoining it is this $100-million hotel, the most expensive ever built in Canada. Guests ride an escalator to the fifth-floor lobby, which has an open eight-story atrium with its own fountain and 20-foot waterfall. Fine art displayed on the maple walls, together with rose granite floors, create a look of opulence.

All rooms are superior or deluxe, and give a feeling of simple luxury. More than 70% have king-size beds. The decor has an Asian influence. Look for beige tones, textured walls, and large marble bathrooms with telephones. Some suites have Jacuzzis, steam rooms, even baby grand pianos!

Dining/Entertainment: The Five Sails offers seafood dinners to be enjoyed with a terrific view across the Burrard Inlet to the mountains. The Suntory Restaurant is justly famous for its Japanese cuisine. Café Pacifica offers Canadian specialties; it also has a Chinese dim sum bar and a Friday-night Italian buffet featuring the creations of chef Enrico Balestra, a former opera tenor. The Cascades Lounge offers luncheon buffets and a seasonal outdoor patio bar. The hotel has its own bakery and butcher.

Services: 24-hour room service, concierge, valet laundry.

Facilities: Outdoor pool, squash and racquetball courts, indoor track, whirlpool, sauna, tanning, massage, business center, hair salon, barber, shopping arcade, art galleries, florist, gift shop, exchange bank, car rental, meeting/banquet space for 500, three no-smoking floors and 13 rooms for the handicapped.

VANCOUVER RENAISSANCE HOTEL, 1133 W. Hastings St., Vancouver, BC V6E 3T3. Tel. 604/689-9211, or toll free 800/228-9898 in the U.S., 800/268-8998 in Canada. Fax 604/689-4358. 434 rms, 19 suites. A/C MINIBAR TV TEL **SkyTrain:** Burrard. **Bus:** 19.

$ Rates: May–Sept, $160–$180 single; $180–$200 double; $350–$750 suite. Oct–Apr, $125–$145 single; $145–$165 double; $275–$750 suite. Higher rates for views. Children under 18 stay free in parents' room. AE, CB, DC, DISC, ER, JCB, MC, V. **Parking:** $8, underground.

Formerly known as the New World Harbourside, this Ramada hotel has an enviable location: It's in the heart of the financial district but overlooks the waterfront. Guests enter a lower lobby lined with 18-foot ficus trees. A black granite staircase leads to the reception area and pillared upper lobby, where a multicolored carpet sets off an area of abstract works of art.

Two color schemes are used in the guestrooms—warm rose in the north-facing harborfront rooms, cooler sage on the south-facing cityside rooms. All rooms are nicely furnished, with the added luxury of heated tile bathroom floors and hairdryers. The Dynasty Floor rooms feature more elegant furniture, in-room check-in and checkout, and other amenities. The harborfront rooms overlook a railroad yard that's scheduled to be transformed into a residential and business park.

Dining/Entertainment: The Dynasty is widely regarded as one of Vancouver's best Chinese restaurants. It's hard to top the view from Vistas on the Bay, a 20th-floor revolving restaurant open for three meals daily. The Lobby Lounge serves breakfast and a buffet lunch daily, with piano music in the evening. The Channel Bar is packed at night with karaoke enthusiasts rocking to the pulse of its high-tech laser-disk sound system.

Services: Room service 6:30am–2am daily, valet laundry, dry cleaning, concierge, airport shuttle, babysitting, business and secretarial services, multilingual personnel; Dynasty Floor guests receive a continental breakfast, tea service, newspaper, shoeshine, and turn-down service.

Facilities: Indoor pool, weight/exercise room, sauna, meeting/banquet for 800, gift shop, no-smoking rooms and facilities for the handicapped.

WATERFRONT CENTRE HOTEL, 900 Canada Place Way, Vancouver, BC V6C 3L5. Tel. 604/691-1991, or toll free 800/828-7447 in the U.S., 800/268-9411 in Canada. Fax 604/691-1999. 489 rms, 29 suites. A/C MINIBAR TV TEL **SkyTrain:** Waterfront.

$ Rates: Nov to late Apr, $200–$240 single; $220–$260 double. Late Apr to Oct, $200–$250 single; $225–$275 double. Weekend packages from $115 single or double. Suites $350–$1,700. AE, CB, DC, ER, MC, V. **Parking:** $12.

An enclosed walkway links the new Waterfront Centre, located on the shores of Burrard Inlet, with Canada Place, the Vancouver Trade and Convention Centre, and the cruise-ship terminal. The downtown business district, historic Gastown, Chinatown, and the new Coal Harbour waterfront are all within walking distance. Opened in July 1991, this hotel makes the most of its harbor and mountain views, inside and out. An eclectic 45-piece art collection, including the paintings and sculpture of young, emerging Canadian artists, enhances the hotel's ambience in the lobby and other public areas.

All guestrooms include remote-control color TV with in-house movie channels, clock radio, telephones with data-transmission capability (many with two lines), individual climate control, full bath amenities, and complimentary morning coffee and newspapers. There are two superior room categories: Business Class offers business travelers express check-in, complimentary continental breakfast, superior amenities and twice-daily maid service; Entree Gold guests, lodged on a private floor with its own concierge, also enjoy the use of a private lounge and boardroom with complimentary cocktail-hour canapés.

Dining/Entertainment: Diners in the glass-enclosed Heron's Restaurant are treated to vistas of forested Stanley Park, an outdoor terrace, and the Mediterranean-inspired cuisine of chef Thomas Dietzel. The open kitchen, with its showcase rôtisserie, serves up "nouvelle classique" dinner menus as well as breakfast and lunch buffets. Sunday-brunch diners may couple their meal with a guided tour of the hotel's art collection. Heron's Lounge offers cocktails and light meals.

Services: Laundry/valet, business center, babysitting, luggage storage, safety-deposit boxes.

Facilities: Heated outdoor swimming pool, fitness club, whirl-pool, steam rooms, massage, full meeting and convention facilities, bank and car-rental desks, no-smoking rooms, and rooms for the handicapped.

WEDGEWOOD HOTEL, 845 Hornby St., Vancouver, BC V6Z 1V1. Tel. 604/689-7777, or toll free 800/663-0666. Fax 604/688-3074. 60 rms, 33 suites. A/C MINIBAR TV TEL **SkyTrain:** Burrard.

$ Rates (including continental breakfast): $150–$200 single; $170–$220 double; $270 suite; $370 penthouse. AE, CB, DC, ER, JCB, MC, V. **Parking:** $10, underground, valet.

In 1983, Greek immigrant Eleni Skalbania bought a dilapidated apartment building for $4.5 million, spent another $3 million on renovations, and transformed an ugly duckling into an elegant and sophisticated swan. That swan is the Wedgewood, where European and Middle English styles mingle in a delightfully arty atmosphere. Skalbania's personal touch—she may greet you herself in the warm, cozy lobby, or drop by your table in the dining room—is everywhere, from the antique furnishings to the one-of-a-kind oil paintings.

The rooms are as tastefully decorated as the rest of the hotel, with light-wood furnishings, fine-art prints, potted plants, and private flower beds on the balconies. All except 18 rooms are upgraded executive-class rooms with appropriate extras. Some suites even have fireplaces.

Dining/Entertainment: Bacchus Ristorante offers breakfast and Italian cuisine daily, a sumptuous brunch buffet on Sunday, and live entertainment and dancing. The piano lounge has live entertainment nightly except Sunday beneath an imposing oil painting of Bacchus himself, the Roman god of wine. Afternoon tea is served between 2 and 4pm.

Services: 24-hour room service, twice-daily housekeeping, limousine service, morning newspaper, box of chocolates for every new guest, secretarial services, babysitting; small pets permitted.

Facilities: Squash courts, weight room, aerobics, sauna, whirlpool, massage, hair salon, no-smoking rooms.

EXPENSIVE

GEORGIAN COURT HOTEL, 773 Beatty St., Vancouver, BC V6B 2M4. Tel. 604/682-5555, or toll free 800/663-1155. Fax 604/682-8830. 160 rms, 20 suites. A/C MINIBAR TV TEL **SkyTrain:** Stadium.

$ Rates: May–Sept, $130–$150 single; $150–$170 double. Oct–Apr, $99–$119 single; $115–$135 double. AE, DC, ER, MC, V. **Parking:** $6.

Many of the standing ovations delivered across the street at B.C. Place Stadium, or a block away at the Queen Elizabeth Theatre, should go to the Georgian Court. This hotel is a class act, an intimate European-style hostelry with faultless service. The lobby is a veritable work of art with its mahogany, brass, and beveled glass. Rich handcrafted furnishings grace the restaurant and guestrooms.

Each room offers both quiet air conditioning *and* windows that open. The vanity and dressing table are topped with marble, and the closet is larger than most travelers need. Each room is equipped with three phones—bedside, desktop, and bathroom. Executive-floor guests receive complimentary breakfasts and other special touches.

Dining/Entertainment: The William Tell Restaurant is among Canada's finest. Rigney's Bar & Grill, named for a former B.C. Lions football player, has a sports-bar atmosphere. The posh Club Lounge, which features a baby grand piano and a mahogany-paneled bar, offers a continental breakfast and evening entertainment.

Services: Room service, concierge, turndown service, complimentary morning newspaper.

Facilities: Health club with Universal gym, whirlpool, and sauna; gift and sundry shop (open mornings and evenings); no-smoking rooms, facilities for the handicapped, and special rooms for women travelers; small meetings and banquets accommodated.

HOTEL GEORGIA, 801 W. Georgia St. (at Howe St.), Vancouver, BC V6C 1P7. Tel. 604/682-5566, or toll free 800/663-1111. Fax 604/682-8192. 310 rms, 3 suites. A/C TV TEL **SkyTrain:** Granville.

$ Rates: May to mid-Oct, $130–$140 single; $140–$150 double. Mid-Oct to Apr, $120–$130 single; $130–$140 double. Suites $225–$450. Children under 16 stay free in parents' room. AE, CB, DC, ER, MC, V. **Parking:** $9.

This huge brick building from the Georgian era has an impressive lobby with gold-touched woodwork, beautiful brass chandeliers, a big fireplace, and heavy carpeting. Wide, low-lit corridors lead to comfortable gray-carpeted rooms with standard furnishings and basic amenities.

Dining/Entertainment: The Cavalier Grill, off the main lobby, evokes a feeling of British royalty with its red upholstery and wood decor. It serves continental cuisine. The George V Pub, in the dungeonlike lower level, offers traditional English-pub fare and evening sing-alongs. The Night Court Lounge offers light meals, dancing, and a sports-and-trivia hookup, while the Patio Lounge serves business lunches.

Services: Room service, valet laundry.

Facilities: Meeting/banquet space for 400, jeweler, gift shops, hair salon, barber, shoeshine.

MODERATE

BURRARD MOTOR INN, 1100 Burrard St. (at Helmcken St.), Vancouver, BC V6Z 1Y7. Tel. 604/681-2331. 70 rms. A/C TV TEL **Bus:** 22.

$ Rates: May–Oct, $63 single; $75 double; $83 twin. Nov–Apr, $52 single; $62 double; $69 twin. Kitchenette $6 extra. AE, DC, ER, MC, V. **Parking:** Free.

This in-city motel succeeds in creating a garden image. All rooms face an inner garden courtyard that hides a parking garage; behind closed doors, even the carpets are garden green. You'll find the basic amenities and standard furnishings, including a working desk. Kitchenettes and no-smoking rooms are available. Small pets are permitted.

The Greenhouse restaurant serves three meals daily, and there's an adjoining lounge.

DAYS INN DOWNTOWN, 921 W. Pender St., Vancouver, BC V6C 1M2. Tel. 604/681-4335, or toll free 800/325-2525. Fax 604/681-7808. 80 rms, 5 suites. TV TEL **SkyTrain:** Burrard.

$ Rates: May–Sept, $95 single; $105 double; $125 twin; $135 suite. Oct–Apr, $74 single; $84 double; $104 twin; $114 suite. Children under 12 stay free in parents' room. AE, DC, DISC, ER, JCB, MC, V. **Parking:** Free 6pm–9am.

A Vancouver classic located discreetly in the heart of the financial district, this seven-story stone building—formerly the Abbotsford Hotel—has twice undergone major renovations to enhance its beauty. Its elegant lobby makes liberal use of art deco–style brass.

The individually decorated rooms are also bright, with striped coverlets and red upholstery.

The Bombay Bicycle Pub is popular for lunch and after-work drinks. There's also the Chelsea Restaurant, open daily, and the Bull & Bear Lounge, with a big-screen TV. All are snug and cozy, with "gaslight" illumination, dark-wood paneling, and evocative old prints.

Room service, valet laundry, VCR and movie rental, business and secretarial service (minimal charge), and no-smoking rooms are available. There's also a health club and squash court (one block away) and a travel agent.

QUALITY INN, 1335 Howe St. (at Davie St.), Vancouver, BC V6Z 1R7. Tel. 604/682-0229, or toll free 800/228-5151. Fax 604/662-7566. 157 rms and junior suites, 14 one-bedroom suites. A/C TV TEL **Bus:** 4, 7, 8, 10, or 20.

$ Rates: May–Sept, $99 single; $109 double; $99–$125 suite. Oct–Mar, $69–$74 single or double; $78–$85 suite. Apr, $69–$74 single or double; $86–$93 suite. Children under 18 stay free in parents' room. AE, CB, DC, ER, MC, V. **Parking:** Free.

The red facade of this clean, modern hostelry is hard to miss beside the Granville Street Bridge on-ramp. The rooms have a country charm with knotty-pine furnishings, an imitation quilt bedspread, and a brick wall behind the bed. The rooms are ideal for families, especially the one-bedroom suites with fully equipped kitchens. They're not well suited for business travelers, however, since there are no desk phones or other business-related services.

The bright, arty Creekside Café is open daily for breakfast and dinner. Lunch is served in the Creekside Lounge. A valet laundry is available, plus an outdoor swimming pool and a meeting room. There's complimentary use of the facilities at a nearby fitness club.

SANDMAN INN, 180 W. Georgia St. (at Homer St.), Vancouver, BC V6B 4P4. Tel. 604/681-2211, or toll free 800/SANDMAN. 216 rms. A/C TV TEL **SkyTrain:** Stadium.

$ Rates: May–Sept, $99.75 single; $103.75 double; $107.75 twin. Oct–Apr, $79.75 single; $83.75 double; $87.75 twin. AE, CB, DC, ER, MC, V. **Parking:** Free.

The flagship of this popular western Canada motel chain has an outstanding location opposite the Queen Elizabeth Theatre and the Airporter bus terminal. The rooms are adequate, with standard furnishings. The decor varies from beige to dusty rose, with floral or paisley bedspreads and drapes. Local phone calls are free; some rooms feature minibars.

The Heartland Restaurant serves three meals daily, and has take-out service. The JR Country Club is downtown Vancouver's number-one country-and-western bar. The Sportsline Lounge has a big-screen TV, pool table, and darts. There's a valet laundry, indoor pool, whirlpool, saunas, meeting/banquet space for 250, gift shop, and a car-rental desk.

BUDGET

THE HOTEL AT THE YWCA, 580 Burrard St., Vancouver, BC V6C 2K9. Tel. 604/662-8188, or toll free 800/663-

1424 in the U.S. Northwest and western Canada. Fax 604/681-2550. 169 rms. TEL **SkyTrain:** Burrard.

$ **Rates:** $46–$52 single; $58–$65 twin; $63–$68 double; $66–$72 triple; $72–$77 family room. Seventh night free for weekly stays. Group rates and senior discounts. MC, V.

A modern 13-story residence, this Y welcomes women, men, couples, families, and groups. The rooms are larger than those at the YMCA; some even have private bathrooms, though usually the facilities are shared. There are five TV lounges and five communal kitchens; only women may use the swimming pool, sauna, and weight room. The neon-lit cafeteria offers meals for about $4.50.

HOTEL CALIFORNIA, 1176 Granville St., Vancouver, BC V6Z 1L8. Tel. 604/688-8701. Fax 604/688-8335. 130 rms (100 with bath). TV TEL **Bus:** 4, 7, 8, 10, or 20.

$ **Rates:** May–Oct, $35 single; $40 double. Nov–Apr $30 single; $35 double. MC, V.

Completely renovated to soundproof the guestrooms from the live rhythm and blues in the downstairs lounge, this hotel is nicer than its exterior might suggest. All except 30 of the spacious bedrooms have full bathrooms (with a tub or shower); the others share facilities. The furnishings are basic but satisfactory. In addition to the lounge, the hotel has a pub where food is available.

KINGSTON HOTEL, 757 Richards St., Vancouver, BC V6B 3A6. Tel. 604/684-9024. Fax 604/684-9917. 60 rms (30 with bath). TEL **Bus:** 15.

$ **Rates** (including continental breakfast): May–Oct, $35 single without bath, $50 single with bath; $40 double without bath, $65 double with bath; $60 twin without bath, $75 twin with bath. Nov–Apr, $30 single without bath, $45 single with bath; $35 double without bath, $60 double with bath; $55 twin without bath, $70 twin with bath. Student and senior discounts. AE, MC, V. **Parking:** Free.

Although not luxurious, this clean, modern bed-and-breakfast inn maximizes what it has to offer. The exterior has been refurbished in the European style with a small outdoor patio. The rooms are small but nicely furnished; half are equipped with private baths and color TVs. The rest have handbasins and shared facilities. A continental breakfast is served in a small lounge; desserts are available from room service in the evening. Intrepid travelers are glad to find a sauna and guest laundry. But be warned: This three-story hotel has no elevator.

NELSON PLACE HOTEL, 1006 Granville St., Vancouver, BC V6Z 1L5. Tel. 604/681-6341. Fax 604/685-5414. 100 rms. TV TEL **Bus:** 4, 7, 8, 10, or 20.

$ **Rates:** May–Oct, $50 single; $60 double or twin. Off-season discounts available. Children under 12 stay free in parents' room. AE, DC, MC, V. **Parking:** Free.

An older but adequately maintained building, the Nelson Place has a small but homey lobby and cozy bedrooms hung with historic map prints. The restaurant serves breakfast and lunch daily. The lounge has live music Wednesday through Saturday nights, and the adjoining Champagne Charlie's basement pub features exotic dancers (i.e., strippers).

ST. REGIS HOTEL, 602 Dunsmuir St. (at Seymour St.),

Vancouver, BC V6B 1Y3. Tel. 604/681-1135. Fax 604/683-1126. 84 rms. TV TEL **SkyTrain:** Granville.

$ Rates: May–Oct, $50 single; $55 double; $60 twin. Nov–Apr, $45 single; $50 double; $55 twin. Children under 12 stay free in parents' room. AE, DC, DISC, ER, MC, V.

An older hotel located right downtown, the St. Regis has a large (if spare) lobby and spacious guestrooms that sleep four. All rooms provide full modern baths, comfortable furnishings, and lots of closet space. The Cottage Gardens coffee shop serves three meals on weekdays, breakfast and lunch on weekends. There's a lounge with big-screen TV and a pub featuring exotic dancers. The desk will handle laundry. Small pets are permitted.

YMCA, 955 Burrard St. (at Barclay St.), Vancouver, BC V6Z 1Y2. Tel. 604/681-0221. 111 rms (none with bath), 120 beds. **Bus:** 22.

$ Rates: May–Sept, $28 single, $139 per week; $47 double. Oct–Apr, $24 single, $126 per week; $37 double. Additional cot in room $7.50. MC, V. **Parking:** $3.75 per day.

Both the men's and women's rooms are small and undistinctive, but they're spotlessly clean. There's a single bed, a table, a desk with a lamp, a walk-in closet—and that's it. The washrooms and showers are shared, along with pay phones and a coin-op laundry. Some rooms provide TVs for an additional nightly charge of $2. Guests may use the Y's athletic facilities, including an indoor pool, gymnasium, weight room, and racquetball courts. Jonathan T's, a small café, is open Monday through Saturday for low-cost breakfasts and lunches. No liquor is allowed.

2. THE WEST END

VERY EXPENSIVE

THE COAST PLAZA AT STANLEY PARK, 1733 Comox St. (at Denman St.), Vancouver, BC V6G 1P6. Tel. 604/688-7711, or toll free 800/663-1144. Fax 604/685-7210. 85 rms, 182 suites. MINIBAR TV TEL **Bus:** 8.

$ Rates: $180–$250 single; $200–$270 double; $210–$290 suite. Children under 18 stay free in parents' room. AE, CB, DC, ER, JCB, MC, V. **Parking:** $5, underground.

If this 35-story luxury hotel were renamed "Squirrel Plaza," some folks might chuckle, but few could object. After all, Lucy, Cindy, Boom Boom, and the other tree-climbing rodents that venture into the pink marble lobby are treated royally—so much so, in fact, that doormen and bellhops carry hazelnuts in their pockets.

The guestrooms are off-limits to the little guys, however. Every one of the spacious rooms has a balcony, clock radio, coffee-maker, and the sort of furnishings one expects in a fine hotel. Limited Edition floors have special touches. Most suites—which comprise two-thirds of the units—have full kitchen facilities.

Dining/Entertainment: Windows on the Bay, a rooftop restaurant, serves fine West Coast cuisine dinners high above English Bay and Stanley Park. The modern Brasserie has an open kitchen that offers three meals daily. Shampers is a popular lobby-level pasta bar and night club with a piano bar Monday through Thursday and disco on Friday and Saturday.

Services: 24-hour room service, concierge, valet laundry, downtown and airport limousine service. Limited Edition guests receive a complimentary breakfast, morning paper, and other services.

Facilities: Indoor pool, health club, squash courts, saunas, games, piano, gift shop, full meeting and convention facilities, no-smoking floors, rooms for the handicapped; the 30-store Denman Mall is right next door.

WESTIN BAYSHORE, 1601 W. Georgia St., Vancouver, BC V6G 2V4. Tel. 604/682-3377, or toll free 800/228-3000. Fax 604/687-3102. 517 rms, 33 suites. A/C MINIBAR TV TEL **Bus:** 19 or 242.

$ Rates: Mid-Apr to Oct, $165–$190 single; $215–$230 double; $310 junior suite; $450–$1,375 full suite Nov to mid-Apr, $95–$119 single; $139–$169 double; $255–$750 suite. Children 18 or under stay free in parents' room. AE, CB, DC, ER, MC, V. **Parking:** $7.

Beautifully landscaped grounds surround the Westin, which sits on the shore of Coal Harbour as if it were an extension of Stanley Park. The gardens and private marina are the trademark of the hotel, which pioneered in modern hospitality when it was built in 1961, and it's still going strong.

The rooms are classified by their location and view: The Tower rooms, which are the largest and provide the best views, are the most expensive. While the standard units have two phones, the Tower rooms are equipped with a bathroom extension and a modem. Corner rooms also have balconies. The junior suites enjoy deluxe amenities, which are equivalent to executive-level rooms elsewhere.

Dining/Entertainment: Trader Vic's, with its South Seas decor, offers Chinese and continental cuisine with seafood specialties. The Harbour Bar provides nightly entertainment. The Garden Restaurant offers three meals daily and a Sunday-brunch buffet, while the Garden Lounge serves lunch by day and entertains with light jazz by night.

Services: 24-hour room service, concierge, valet laundry, electronic voice mail, courtesy bus, doctor and dentist on call, secretarial services, babysitting; fishing trips and sightseeing cruises chartered through Westin Marina; small pets permitted.

Facilities: Indoor and outdoor pools, weight room, fitness trail, bicycle rentals, whirlpool, saunas, massage, meeting/banquet space for 1,000, clothing stores, jeweler, hair salon, barber, florist, gift shop, newsstand, marina with seaplane dock, no-smoking rooms and facilities for the handicapped.

EXPENSIVE

BEST WESTERN O'DOUL'S HOTEL, 1300 Robson St., Vancouver, BC V6E 1C5. Tel. 604/684-8461, or toll free 800/663-5491. Fax 604/684-8326. 119 rms, 11 suites. A/C MINIBAR TV TEL **Bus:** 8.

$ Rates: May–Sept, $140–$165 single; $150–$180 double; $250–$350 suite. Oct–Apr, $99–$109 single; $114–$124 double; $150–$250 suite. AE, DC, DISC, ER, JCB, MC, V. **Parking:** Free.

This Best Western hotel is located at the west end of the Robsonstrasse shopping strip. When it was rebuilt from scratch in 1986, the owners commissioned numerous paintings, sculptures, stained- and beveled-glass works, tapestries, and murals. As a result, the hotel displays museum-quality contemporary works of art. Its interior color scheme ranges from soft pink to burgundy, from mint to rain-forest green, accented with brass and other art deco touches.

Every room in the six-story hotel is of deluxe quality, with three phones, working desks, clock radios, and hairdryers. Each guest is assured of special attention, right down to the individually programmed electronic door locks.

Dining/Entertainment: O'Doul's Restaurant is open for three meals daily, and it emphasizes West Coast specialties. The art deco theme reaches its climax here by a tongue-in-cheek jungle theme (complete with ceramic animals). The adjoining lounge has a big-screen TV featuring sports.

Services: 24-hour room service, concierge, valet laundry, secretarial services.

Facilities: Indoor pool, exercise room, whirlpool, meeting/banquet space for 130, no-smoking rooms and facilities for the handicapped.

PACIFIC PALISADES HOTEL, 1277 Robson St., Vancouver, BC V6E 1C4. Tel. 604/688-0461, or toll free 800/663-1815. Fax 604/688-4374. 233 suites. A/C TV TEL **Bus:** 8.

$ Rates: Mid-Apr to Oct, $115–$210 suite for one or two. Nov to mid-Apr, $92–$170 suite for one or two. Penthouses from $375. AE, CB, DC, ER, MC, V. **Parking:** $8, underground secured.

These former residential apartments were renovated into a hotel in 1991 at a cost of $8 million. The two towers are separated by a lovely outdoor courtyard. A plaque in the lobby, just off Jervis Street, lists hundreds of celebrities who have stayed here. The hotel is a member of the Shangri-La International Hotel group.

The accommodations are mainly spacious one-bedroom suites, with a handful of studios and several larger units. Most have private balconies and good views. All suites are equipped either with kitchenettes (including microwave, coffee-maker, sink, and fridge/minibar) or more expensive full kitchens (with full-size appliances). Suite amenities include bathroom telephone, hairdryer, shaving/makeup mirror, terry-cloth bathrobes, and an umbrella.

Dining/Entertainment: The Monterey Lounge and Grill is open for breakfast, lunch, dinner, and Sunday brunch, as well as evening cocktail piano and jazz entertainment. The lush colors and use of marble create a cozy, informal atmosphere. In summer, the popular sidewalk patio with barbecue enables one to dine outdoors and people-watch on Robson Street.

Services: 24-hour room service, limousine service, valet laundry, tea/coffee service, daily newspaper, complimentary shoeshine, secretarial services, voice message service, doctor on call.

Facilities: Indoor swimming pool, weight/exercise room, whirlpool, sauna, massage, tanning, bicycle rentals, shopping arcade, gift shop, meeting/banquet space for 200, no-smoking floors. Access to nearby racquetball courts for a small fee.

PARKHILL HOTEL, 1160 Davie St., Vancouver, BC V6E 1N1. Tel. 604/685-1311, or toll free 800/663-1525. Fax 604/681-0208. 190 rms, 2 suites. A/C MINIBAR TV TEL **Bus:** 8.

$ Rates: $145–$165 single; $165–$185 double; $275 suite. AE, DC, DISC, ER, JCB, MC, V. **Parking:** $3.25.

Formerly called the Ming Court Hotel, this hostelry is recognized for its dedication to artistry, both in the tastefulness of its interior design (including Ming porcelains) and in the skill of its staff. The handsome rooms are all quite large (450 square feet) and provide balconies facing the downtown skyline or English Bay. The superior and deluxe rooms on the upper floors are equipped with hairdryers; the deluxe rooms also feature two phones (with PC capability), clock radios, in-room safes, and coffee-makers.

Dining/Entertainment: Byron's Grill offers continental cuisine, Byron's Lounge provides nightly entertainment Tuesday through Saturday, and Taiko Japanese Restaurant specializes in sushi, sashimi, and tempura.

Services: Room service, concierge, valet laundry, shuttle service, complimentary newspaper, babysitting, on-call doctor and dentist.

Facilities: Outdoor pool, sauna, health club, meeting/banquet space for 280.

SHERATON-LANDMARK HOTEL, 1400 Robson St., Vancouver, BC V6G 1B9. Tel. 604/687-0511, or toll free 800/325-3535. Fax 604/687-2801. 353 rms, 7 suites. A/C TV TEL **Bus:** 8.

$ Rates: May–Sept 1, $115–$175 single; $135–$195 double; $275–$425 suite. Winter discounts from $85 single or double. AE, DC, ER, MC, V. **Parking:** $4.50.

If you're looking for scenic views, look no further than Vancouver's tallest hotel—the West End's most prominent building. Rising like a sentinel over Robson Street, this 42-story structure has a simple, unpretentious lobby but fine facilities within. Every room offers a private balcony with an unobstructed view. Although not posh, the furnishings are comfortable; the deluxe rooms feature minibars.

Dining/Entertainment: Cloud 9, a 42nd-floor revolving restaurant and lounge, provides gourmet dining. The Prime Time Bar offers big-screen satellite TV sports and karaoke sing-alongs.

Services: Room service, valet laundry, seasonal tour desk.

Facilities: Exercise room, saunas, whirlpool, gift shop, car rental, meeting/banquet space for 600, corporate lounge with secretarial service for frequent business travelers, eight no-smoking floors, rooms with facilities for the handicapped.

MODERATE

BARCLAY HOTEL, 1348 Robson St., Vancouver, BC V6E 1C5. Tel. 604/688-8850. Fax 604/688-2534. 79 rms, 10 suites. A/C MINIBAR TV TEL **Bus:** 8.

$ Rates: June–Sept, $59–$75 single; $85–$95 double; $119 suite. Oct–May, $45–$59 single; $69–$79 double; $99 suite. AE, DC, MC, V. **Parking:** Free.

There is a French provincial ambience in this cozy, recently renovated hotel, which is one of Vancouver's best bargains. Snowy white inside and out, it has brass chandeliers, polished wood, and a certain old-world charm extending from the antiques in its marble foyer to the tastefully decorated guest-rooms. No-smoking rooms are available.

The Barclay Restaurant, with French specialties, serves three meals daily. The Bistro Lounge features live music nightly and outdoor seating in summer. Room service and valet laundry are offered.

RIVIERA MOTOR INN, 1431 Robson St., Vancouver, BC V6G 1C1. Tel. 604/685-1301. 40 suites. TV TEL **Bus:** 8.

$ Rates: May–Sept, $88 suite for one, $98 suite for two. Oct–Apr, $78 suite for one, $88 suite for two. AE, DC, DISC, ER, JCB, MC, V. **Parking:** Free.

One of several converted apartment blocks at the west end of Robsonstrasse, the 10-story Riviera has a tiny lobby but rather large studio and one-bedroom suites. Each one is provided with a fully equipped kitchen (fridge, four-burner stove, and all cooking utensils). The furnishings are down-to-earth—a Formica table, vinyl-covered chairs—but the views from the upper floors are spectacular. A penthouse suite is equipped with an Astroturf deck and lawn furniture, not to mention the view across Stanley Park.

SHATO INN APARTMENT HOTEL, 1825 Comox St., Vancouver, BC V6G 1P9. Tel. 604/681-8920. 22 rms. TV TEL **Bus:** 8.

$ Rates: May–Sept, $75 single; $85 double; $95 twin. Oct–Apr, $55 single; $65 double; $75 twin. Kitchen units $10 extra. MC, V. **Parking:** Free.

A modern three-story cedar structure within three blocks of Stanley Park, the inn has spacious, attractive rooms, some with kitchens and/or balconies. This friendly, family-run establishment is in a quiet neighborhood off Denman Street.

WEST END GUEST HOUSE, 1362 Haro St., Vancouver, BC V6E 1G2. Tel. 604/681-2889. Fax 604/688-8812. 7 rms. TV TEL **Bus:** 8.

$ Rates (including full breakfast): $60–$130 single; $85–$175 double. AE, DC, MC, V. **Parking:** Free.

You'll have to book well in advance to get a room in this quaint bed-and-breakfast inn, barely a block from frenetic Robson Street. This turn-of-the-century Victorian house is in the pink, the same color as its exterior walls. Each room has a private bath. There's a guest lounge with a fireplace, and a breakfast room for starting the day in gourmet style. Smoking is not permitted in the bedrooms or dining area.

BUDGET

BUCHAN HOTEL, 1906 Haro St., Vancouver, BC V6G 1H7. Tel. 604/685-5354. Fax 604/685-5367. 60 rms. TV **Bus:** 8.

$ Rates: May–Sept, $65 single; $70 double. Oct–Apr, $70 single; $75 double. Children under 12 stay free in parents' room. AE, DC, MC, V. **Parking:** $3.

This unique older building is located in a quiet residential neighborhood one block from huge Stanley Park. The rooms are small but clean, with standard furnishings; ask for a room on the brighter east side of the hotel, which overlooks a park block. The friendly staff helps to compensate for the lack of big-hotel amenities. Laundry and maid service are available. In the basement is Delilah's, a popular local hangout which serves fixed-price dinners and lots of martinis (see Chapter 5, "Vancouver Dining").

ROBSONSTRASSE CITY MOTOR INN, 1394 Robson St., Vancouver, BC V6E 1C5. Tel. 604/687-1674. 41 suites. TV TEL **Bus:** 8.

$ Rates: May–Sept, $50–$60 suite for one or two. Oct–Apr, $50 suite for one or two. AE, MC, V. **Parking:** Free.

This hostelry prides itself on its huge, comfortable rooms. Each unit is composed of a kitchen (utensils are available on request, for a deposit) with attached dining nook, a large, nicely furnished living room (with a hideaway sofa for additional guests), and a big bedroom with a walk-in closet and nine-drawer dresser.

SYLVIA HOTEL, 1154 Gilford St., Vancouver, BC V6G 2P6. Tel. 604/681-9321. 120 rms, 15 suites. TV TEL **Bus:** 1 or 8.

$ Rates: $55–$77 single or double; $82–$125 suite. AE, DC, MC, V. **Parking:** $3.

A longtime favorite among families and regular Vancouver visitors, the Sylvia is a heritage building erected as a state-of-the-art apartment house on English Bay in 1912. The imposing stone edifice, now covered with ivy, stays cool in summer, warm in winter; the staff is always exceptionally friendly. There's room service and valet laundry. Every room in the original hotel differs in size, shape, and decor; try to get a corner unit for the view. Some of the rooms have fully equipped kitchens with gas stoves; 16 rooms in a 1986 annex offer individual heating, but they're less interesting.

Sylvia's Restaurant, which serves three meals daily, specializes in meat and seafood with a continental touch. Its big windows face either the bay or a courtyard lily pond. The adjacent casual bistro is open all day, every day, for light snacks. Guests can enjoy drinks in a cozy lounge, served from a glass-enclosed bar.

3. EAST OF DOWNTOWN

MODERATE

BEST WESTERN EXHIBITION PARK, 3475 E. Hastings St. (at Hwy. 401, Cassiar St.), Vancouver, BC V5K 2A5. Tel. 604/294-4751, or toll free 800/528-1234. Fax 604/294-1269. 46 rms, 12 suites. A/C TV TEL **Bus:** 14.

$ Rates (including continental breakfast): July–Sept, $85–$95 single; $90–$105 double; $105–$115 twin. Oct–June, $65–$82 single, double, or twin. Year round $125–$170 suite. Additional persons $10. AE, MC, V. **Parking:** Free.

This is what travelers expect from Best Western establishments: clean and comfortable rooms without frills. The rooms here are newly renovated and are equipped with full baths. One- and two-bedroom suites are available, as are no-smoking rooms and rooms for the handicapped. There's a 24-hour restaurant adjacent to the motel. A sauna, whirlpool, and coin-op laundry are available to guests.

BUDGET

BURNABY CARIBOO R.V. PARK, 8765 Cariboo Place, Burnaby, BC V3N 4T2. Tel. 604/420-1722. 217 full-hookup sites, 24 tent sites. **Bus:** 101.
$ Rates: $17–$30 full-hookup site; $13 tent site. MC, V.
Surrounded by 400-acre Burnaby Lake Regional Park, this lovely spot is reached by Gagliardi Way, just north of Hwy. 1 near Port Moody. All sites have 30-amp electrical, cable TV, and telephone hookups. Heated washrooms provide free hot showers and are disabled-accessible. Facilities include an indoor pool, whirlpool, sun deck, adult lounge, games arcade, coin-op laundry, and market. There's also a sanitary dump station, a playground, shuttle-bus service, and park tours.

CARIBOO MOTEL AND TRAILER PARK, 2555 Kingsway, Vancouver, BC V5R 5H3. Tel. 604/435-2251. 33 rms, 34 trailer/RV sites. TV TEL **Bus:** 19.
$ Rates: $42–$58 single; $58–$84 double (additional person $5); $25 RV site with full hookup, including shower. Pets $4 on acceptance. MC, V. **Parking:** Free.
More like a residential community than a motel, the Cariboo has individual cabins with kitchens and private garages surrounded by lawns, trees, and shrubbery. It's great for families since there's a playground nearby. The trailer park is at the rear of the motel units.

2400 MOTEL, 2400 Kingsway, Vancouver, BC V5R 5G9. Tel. 604/434-2464. 65 rms. TV TEL **Bus:** 19.
$ Rates: $58–$125 single or double. Pets $4. MC, V. **Parking:** Free.
An everyday two-story motel and a not-so-ordinary cluster of 12 white bungalows comprise this hostelry. The cabins are special; situated on lovely landscaped grounds, they are equipped with kitchens and separate front and back doors.

4. SOUTH OF DOWNTOWN

VERY EXPENSIVE

GRANVILLE ISLAND HOTEL, 1253 Johnston St., Vancouver, BC V6H 3R9. Tel. 604/683-7373, or toll free 800/663-1840. Fax 604/683-3061. 49 rms, 5 suites. A/C TV TEL **Bus:** 51. **Aquabus** or Granville Island ferry.
$ Rates: June–Sept, $175 single; $190 double; $205–$225 suite. Oct–May, $155 single; $170 double; $185–$205 suite. Winter specials often available. AE, DC, ER, MC, V. **Parking:** $7.
Situated at the east end of Granville Island, on False Creek, this hotel enjoys a unique water location in Vancouver. Constructed like a warehouse, one side is corrugated metal, the other Mediterranean-pink concrete. A green-and-white-striped canopy connects the wings. The lobby boasts a beautiful antique sideboard with a collection of

fine porcelain. It takes just six minutes to go downtown by taking the ferry across False Creek (fare: $1.25).

The rooms are oriented to vacationers rather than businesspeople. Careful attention has been given to installing stereo cassette systems with AM/FM clock radios in the rooms, yet the desks are sized only for personal correspondence. Wooden louvers cover the windows, and framed serigraphs hang on the walls. The highlight of each room is the huge bathroom with an oversize tub, hairdryer, and bidet. If you enjoy quiet, ask for a room away from the galleria so you won't be disturbed by the music from the nightclub.

Dining/Entertainment: Beneath a three-story galleria, complete with a kinetic calliope machine that actually flies kites by pumping air from a bellows, is the Pelican Bay Restaurant and Night Club. The restaurant serves three meals daily at moderate prices, including a classic oyster stew. Late at night it becomes a Top-40 disco with a marble dance floor overlooking the marina. In the summer Balboa's Pub and Bistro serves food and drinks on the patio.

Services: Room service, valet laundry.

Facilities: Tennis courts, whirlpool, sauna, fishing and diving charters, meeting/banquet space for 200.

EXPENSIVE

HOLIDAY INN VANCOUVER CENTRE, 711 W. Broadway, Vancouver, BC V5Z 3Y2. Tel. 604/879-0511. Fax 604/872-7520. 196 rms, 2 suites. A/C TV TEL **Bus:** 9.

$ Rates: May–Sept, $130 single; $140 double. Oct–Apr, $110 single; $120 double. Year round $325 suite. AE, DC, ER, MC, V. **Parking:** Covered, free.

If "Holiday Inn" means something less than elegant to you, you may change your mind as you enter the marble-floored lobby of this handsome 16-story hotel. The rooms aren't flashy, but they're tastefully furnished and decorated with Gretchen Dow Simpson lithographs. The corner rooms have balconies; those on the west side provide great views over the False Creek Marina and Granville Island. Executive-floor rooms are equipped with minibars, hairdryers, pants presses, terry-cloth robes, and coffee machines. Small pets are permitted.

Dining/Entertainment: Stages on Broadway, open for three meals daily, specializes in light California-continental cuisine. Life-size mannequins keep an eye on diners. Stages Lounge is a favorite hangout for lounge potatoes because of its big-screen satellite system, sports, and trivia games. The Great Canadian Casino (tel. 872-5543), Vancouver's largest casino, is also located on the premises; bets from 50¢ to $25 may be placed on roulette, blackjack, and sic bo.

Services: Room service, valet laundry.

Facilities: Indoor swimming pool, weight/exercise room, sauna, tanning, video games, banquet facilities, meeting rooms; public tennis courts are within a five-minute walk.

SHERATON INN PLAZA 500, 500 W. 12th Ave. (at Cambie St.), Vancouver, BC V5Z 1M2. Tel. 604/873-1811, or toll free 800/325-3535. Fax 604/873-5103. 150 rms, 3 suites. A/C MINIBAR TV TEL **Bus:** 15.

$ Rates: $99–$140 single; $130–$155 double; $170 suite. Frequent seasonal specials. AE, CB, DC, ER, MC, V. **Parking:** $3.50.

Perhaps the most centrally located Vancouver hotel, the 17-story Plaza 500 is diagonally across from City Hall, directly opposite the new $3-million City Square shopping center, and right in the medical district. Built in 1963 and completely renovated in 1988, it features a small but tasteful lobby with an extended sun roof, marble floors and pillars, and a philodendron-laden staircase leading to the second-floor ballroom.

All rooms are spacious, well lit, and brightly decorated. Most are equipped with private balconies which on the upper floors provide views of the mountains, water, and/or downtown skyline. Standard fixtures include walk-in closets, full-length mirrors, six-drawer dressers, easy chairs, and clock radios.

Dining/Entertainment: Remington's is a California-style café serving three moderately priced meals daily in an indoor/outdoor vineyard setting. Adjacent is the Lobby Lounge, which features a piano bar and complimentary hors d'oeuvres from 5 to 7pm daily. In the hotel basement is the Jolly Alderman English pub, a local favorite for lunch and light meals.

Services: Room service, valet laundry, complimentary breakfast for corporate clients.

Facilities: Hair salon, jeweler, skin-care center, meeting/banquet space for 500; guests can use the Fitness World health club in the City Square (no pool).

MODERATE

KENYA COURT GUEST HOUSE, 2230 Cornwall Ave., Vancouver, BC V6K 1B5. Tel. 604/738-7085. 4 suites. TV TEL **Bus:** 22.

$ Rates (including breakfast): $85–$105 single or double. Additional charge for up to six guests. No credit cards. **Parking:** Free, on street (limited).

Situated on English Bay at Kitsilano Beach, this three-story heritage apartment building features a handful of large self-contained suites with private entrances. The largest sleeps six. All are clean and attractively decorated, right down to the window boxes. Some two-bedroom suites have ocean views. No smoking is permitted in the building.

A full breakfast, including coffee, juice, fruits, croissants, and bacon and eggs, is served daily in a rooftop solarium facing the mountains across English Bay. The Kenya Court also features a music room with a piano available to guests. The park across the street offers a large heated outdoor saltwater pool, tennis courts, and jogging trails.

BUDGET

CITY CENTRE MOTOR INN, 2111 Main St. (at Sixth Ave.), Vancouver, BC V5T 3C6. Tel. 604/876-7166. Fax 604/876-6727. 80 rms. **Bus:** 3 or 8.

$ Rates: May 15–Sept, $55 single or double. Oct–May 14, $45 single or double. Additional person $5 extra; children under 12 stay free in parents' room. AE, MC, V. **Parking:** Free.

A cozy modern motel near Science World on the old Expo '86 site, the City Centre provides complimentary coffee and morning pastries for guests in its lobby. The rooms are standard motel fare; kitchenettes and rooms for the disabled are available.

5. NEAR THE AIRPORT

VERY EXPENSIVE

DELTA VANCOUVER AIRPORT HOTEL, 3500 Cessna Dr., Richmond, BC V7B 1C7. Tel. 604/278-1241, or toll free 800/877-1133 in the U.S., 800/268-1133 in Canada. Fax 604/267-1975. 410 rms, 5 suites. A/C MINIBAR TV TEL **Bus:** 404 or 405.

$ Rates: Jan–May and Sept 7–Oct, $198 single or double. June–Sept 6, $220 single or double. Nov–Dec, $184 single or double. Year round $175–$375 suite. Children under 18 stay free in parents' room. AE, CB, DC, DISC, ER, JCB, MC, V. **Parking:** Free; valet available.

Fishing charters and river cruises begin from this hotel's marina on the Fraser River, just east of the airport. The 11-story Y-shaped structure caters to corporate business clients with a major business center, cellular-phone rental, and rooms designed for the working traveler. Many rooms feature private balconies.

Dining/Entertainment: The Pier, located right on the river, offers fine dining, especially fresh Northwest cuisine. The renovated Deckhouse Café, located off the main lobby, hosts casual dining. The Jetty Garden Lounge, in the main lobby, provides views of the courtyard and a limited menu.

Services: Late-hour room service, morning coffee in the lobby, valet laundry, airport shuttle; courtesy bus to the Lansdowne Shopping Centre and the Delta Pacific Resort and Conference Centre.

Facilities: Outdoor swimming pool with barbecue area, saunas, exercise bike, bicycle rentals, jogging route, gift shop, car rental, meeting/banquet space for 600, five no-smoking floors, rooms with facilities for the handicapped. At the associated Delta Pacific Resort and Conference Center, indoor tennis, squash, two swimming pools, weight room, recreational facilities, and children's center.

EXPENSIVE

DELTA PACIFIC RESORT AND CONFERENCE CENTRE, 10251 St. Edwards Dr., Richmond, BC V6X 2M9. Tel. 604/278-9611, or toll free 800/268-1133. Fax 604/276-1121. 456 rms, 4 suites. A/C MINIBAR TV TEL **Bus:** 401, 403, or 406.

$ Rates: May–Sept, $125–$150 single; $140–$160 double. Oct–Apr, $105–$130 single; $120–$140 double. Year round $150–$300 suite. Children 18 and under stay free in parents' room. AE, CB, DC, ER, MC, V. **Parking:** Free.

✪ Set amid 14 acres of landscaped gardens, this impressive property is virtually a destination resort. It takes pride in its recreation center, which comprises three swimming pools (one indoor and two outdoor), four indoor tennis courts, two squash courts, a volleyball court, weight/exercise room, quarter-mile jogging track, golf driving range, pro shop, and mountain-bike rental.

The rooms are located in two towers and a renovated Terrace wing. Those in the new South Tower are especially large and feature private balconies. The decor emphasizes a fishing or game-bird theme. The North Tower and Terrace rooms are smaller but equally nice, with wildlife prints and other attractive touches. Signature

Service offers corporate travelers complimentary breakfasts and superior amenities.

Dining/Entertainment: The exquisite Suehiro Steakhouse, located on a tranquil island, is surrounded by a Japanese garden filled with medieval Asian sculptures. It offers teppan-style lunches and dinners of beef, chicken, and seafood, as well as sushi, sashimi, and sake consommé. The Coffee Garden features breakfast buffets, light lunches, and moderately priced dinner entrées; Gilligan's Patio Bar and Grill offers patio service from May to September. Off the lobby is The Landing piano lounge.

Services: Room service, valet laundry, luggage storage; shuttle service to the airport, the Delta River Inn, and the Lansdowne Shopping Centre; small pets permitted.

Facilities: Recreation center (including Jacuzzi and sauna), children's creative center for 3- to 8-year-olds (including swimming lessons and outdoor playground), business center, gift shop, hair salon, outdoor barbecue area with cabañas, car-rental desk, cash machine, full convention facilities.

MODERATE

BEST WESTERN ABERCORN INN, 9260 Bridgeport Rd., Richmond, BC V6X 1S1. Tel. 604/270-7576, or toll free 800/663-0085. Fax 604/270-0001. 80 rms. A/C TV TEL **Bus:** 401, 403, or 406.

$ Rates: June–July, $89 single; $99 double. Aug–Sept, $95 single; $105 double. Oct–May, $85 single; $95 double. AE, DC, ER, MC, V. **Parking:** Free for first week.

Within its Tudor-style exterior, the Abercorn provides comfortable rooms and a friendly staff. Some rooms are equipped with double Jacuzzi baths or oversize tubs. There's a licensed restaurant and lounge, meeting and banquet facilities for 110, and complimentary airport shuttle service.

STAY 'N SAVE MOTOR INN, 10551 St. Edwards Dr., Richmond, BC V6X 3L8. Tel. 604/273-3311, or toll free 800/663-0298. Fax 604/273-9522. 153 units. A/C TV TEL **Bus:** 401, 403, or 406.

$ Rates: May 15–Oct 1, $87–$110 single or double. Oct 2–May 14, $64–$75 single or double. Additional person $10 extra; unit with kitchen $10 extra. Weekly rates available off-season. AE, DC, MC, V. **Parking:** Free.

It's hard to miss the distinctive blue roof, just off Hwy. 99 North at Cambie Road. The rooms are comfortable and equipped with standard furnishings. Kitchen units and rooms for the disabled are available. O'Donal's Family Restaurant is next door. The motel offers free local calls and complimentary airport shuttle service. There's a spa and exercise room, and a guest laundry.

6. ON THE NORTH SHORE

EXPENSIVE

PARK ROYAL HOTEL, 540 Clyde Ave., West Vancouver, BC V7T 2JT. Tel. 604/926-5511. Fax 604/926-6082. 30 rms. TV TEL **Bus:** 250, 251, 252, or 253.

$ **Rates:** May–Sept, $95–$155 single; $105–$165 double. Oct–Apr, $65–$85 single; $75–$95 double. AE, DC, ER, MC, V. **Parking:** Free.

A lovely ivy-covered Tudor-style mansion set in beautifully manicured English country gardens beside the Capilano River, the Park Royal is near the north end of the Lion's Gate Bridge. The Park Royal Shopping Centre is a short stroll away, and a riverside path just outside the front door leads to Ambleside Beach.

The rooms are elegant, with king-size brass-frame beds, bay windows, plush carpets, and rich wood furnishings (including love seats). You may have to book months in advance to get a room here.

Dining/Entertainment: There's an English country inn ambience in the fine dining room and intimate pub because of the large stone fireplaces and wooden beams. Their large windows face out on the beautiful gardens, and both are open seven days.

MODERATE

CAPILANO MOTOR INN, 1634 Capilano Rd., North Vancouver, BC V7P 3B4. Tel. 604/987-8185. 52 rms, 19 suites. TV TEL **Bus:** 246.

$ **Rates:** May 15–Sept, $75 single; $85 double; $100 suite. Oct–May 14, $65 single; $75 double; $100 suite. AE, DC, ER, MC, V. **Parking:** Free.

Located on the "motel strip" heading toward Capilano Canyon Regional Park, this Best Western lodging features a variety of spacious rooms, including standard units, kitchen-equipped family units, and one- and two-bedroom executive suites. There's a heated outdoor swimming pool, sauna, and guest launderette. The Dutch Pannekoek House serves breakfast and lunch daily.

LONSDALE QUAY HOTEL, 123 Carrie Cates Court, North Vancouver, BC V6M 3K7. Tel. 604/986-6111. Fax 604/986-8782. 57 rms, 13 suites. A/C MINIBAR TV TEL **SeaBus:** Lonsdale Quay.

$ **Rates:** $97.50–$117.50 single; $117–$125 double; $145 suite. AE, DC, ER, MC, V. **Parking:** $6.

Located on the upper floors of the colorful Lonsdale Quay Market adjacent to the SeaBus Terminal, this delightful small hotel is 12 minutes and an entire world away from downtown Vancouver. Extending into the inlet, the hotel offers a nonpareil view of the city skyline, as well as the flavor of a fishing port, thanks to blasts from the Cates Tugboat terminal next door.

There are twin rooms on the third floor of this two-tier inn and spacious rooms with two queen-size beds on the fourth floor. The decor is extremely pleasant and the furnishings standard, with such added niceties as a coffee-maker in every room. The westside rooms offer the best view.

Loops Restaurant serves three meals daily from a truly international menu, including Japanese, Indonesian, continental, and West Coast dishes; seafood; and pastas all for moderate prices. The open kitchen creates a welcoming ambience, a piano player performs in the evenings, and there's patio dining in summer. The Waterfront Bistro is popular among singles in their 30s and 40s for meeting and dancing; it also offers light lunches and snacks. Tugs Pub has a big-screen TV, rock 'n' roll for guests aged 19–25, and a burger menu.

The hotel offers room service, valet laundry, complimentary morning newspaper, no-smoking rooms, and facilities for the handicapped. There's also a fitness center with weights, an exercise room, whirlpool, and sauna, plus meeting and banquet space for 120.

BUDGET

CANYON COURT MOTEL, 1748 Capilano Rd., North Vancouver, BC V7P 3B4. Tel. 604/988-3181, or toll free 800/663-4059 in western Canada. Fax 604/988-3181. 77 rms, 12 suites. A/C TV TEL **Bus:** 246.

$ Rates: May–Sept, $65 single; $75 double; $110–$140 suite. Oct–Apr, $50 single; $55 double; $80–$90 suite. AE, DC, ER, MC, V. **Parking:** Free.

A clean, friendly, family-run hostelry, the Canyon Court provides spacious units with standard furnishings and satellite TV, as well as family rooms with kitchenettes, and one- and two-bedroom suites. There's a guest laundry, a heated outdoor swimming pool, courtesy coffee, and a restaurant next door.

CAPILANO R.V. PARK, 295 Tomahawk Ave., North Vancouver, BC V7P 1C5. Tel. 604/987-4722. 208 sites. **Bus:** 250, 251, 252, 253, or 254.

$ Rates: June–Sept, $18–$28 RV site. Oct–May, $16–$26 RV site. MC, V.

These year-round sites at the north end of Lion's Gate Bridge are the nearest to downtown Vancouver. They have 30-amp electrical hookups with lines for cable TV, telephone, water, and sewer, plus picnic tables. The park offers washrooms with free showers, a swimming pool, 10-person whirlpool, coin-op laundry, children's play area, video games, and a lounge. Reservations, with a deposit, are required from June to August.

GLOBETROTTER'S INN, 170 W. Esplanade, North Vancouver, BC V7N 1A3. Tel. 604/988-5141. 7 rms, 8 dorms with 55 beds. **Bus:** 236 or 246. **SeaBus:** Lonsdale Quay.

$ Rates: $13 dorm bed; $27 single; $33 double without bath, $38 double with bath. Seventh night free in winter. Key deposit $5. No credit cards. **Parking:** Free, on street.

The former Montrose Hotel is now a backpackers' hostel. Travelers will find it less rigid than a regular youth hostel: There's no curfew and everyone has a front-door key. There are men's and women's dorms, toilets and shower rooms, and a handful of shabbily furnished private rooms for couples traveling together. Guests share a kitchen (with utensils provided), a laundry, and a living room—the only room in which smoking is permitted.

GROUSE INN, 1633 Capilano Rd. (at Marine Dr.), North Vancouver, BC V7P 3B3. Tel. 604/988-7101. Fax 604/988-7102. 68 rms, 6 suites. A/C TV TEL **Bus:** 246.

$ Rates: Apr 16–May and Oct, $58–$65 single; $65–$70 double; $70–$80 twin; $80–$120 suite. June–Sept, $68–$75 single; $75–$80 double; $80–$85 twin; $80–$138 suite. Nov–Apr 15, $48–$55 single; $52–$58 double; $65–$68 twin; $80–$120 suite. AE, DC, ER, MC, V. **Parking:** Free.

Located at the foot of the road to Grouse Mountain, this motel has numerous family suites with kitchenettes. There's a restaurant and lots of activities for the children—an outdoor heated pool with a water slide and recreational facilities including a children's play area. Facilities include a coffee shop, meeting room, and laundry.

---

7. GASTOWN/CHINATOWN

BUDGET

BACKPACKERS YOUTH HOSTEL, 927 Main St., Vancouver, BC V6A 2V8. Tel. 604/682-2441. 33 rms (none with bath). **SkyTrain:** Main.

$ Rates: $10 dorm bed, $50 per week; $20 single, $100 per week; $25 double, $130 per week. No credit cards. **Parking:** Free, but limited.

Bearing a greater resemblance to a boardinghouse than to a traditional hostel, this former guest house on the edge of Chinatown has 18 three-bed dormitory rooms and 15 private rooms with single or double beds. All bathroom and shower facilities are shared, as well as the community kitchen, dining room, library, TV room, pay phone, coin-op laundry, and sauna. Bicycle rentals are popular in summer. There's no day or evening curfew; everybody receives a front-door key. There is free morning coffee; complimentary pickup from the bus depot is sometimes provided.

BUDGET INN PATRICIA HOTEL, 403 E. Hastings St., Vancouver, BC V6A 1P6. Tel. 604/255-4301. 195 rms. TV TEL **Bus:** 14 or 21.

$ Rates: $32–$42 single; $39–$55 double. MC, V. **Parking:** Free.

Most rooms in this six-story hotel east of Chinatown offer fine views of the downtown skyline. They're simply furnished but well kept. All rooms have ceiling fans and private bathrooms with showers or tubs. A pub on the premises serves food daily from 11am to 7:30pm.

DOMINION HOTEL, 210 Abbott St. (at Water St.), Vancouver, BC V6B 2K8. Tel. 604/681-6666. Fax 604/681-5855. 74 rms (37 with bath). TV **Bus:** 14 or 21.

$ Rates: Apr 15–Oct 15, $39.95 single without bath, $44.95 single with bath; $49.95 double without bath, $54.95 double with bath. Oct 16–Apr 14, $29.95 single without bath, $39.95 single with bath; $34.95 double without bath, $44.95 double with bath. AE, MC, V.

A restored 1899 heritage property in the heart of Gastown, this red-and-white brick palace is a museum of Vancouver nostalgia with a lobby full of fascinating antiques. There are no elevators; an impressive staircase leads to the neatly furnished rooms. In summer, a complimentary breakfast is served until 11am. Orlando's Fresh Pasta Bar is open until 11:30pm, and there's live music in the Lamplighter Pub, which early in this century was the first public bar in Vancouver to serve women.

NIAGARA HOTEL, 435 W. Pender St., Vancouver, BC V6B 1V2. Tel. 604/688-7574. Fax 604/687-5180. 99 rms (40 with bath). TV **Bus:** 19.

$ Rates: $30 single without bath, $45 single with bath; $35 double without bath, $50 double with bath. Children under 12 stay free in parents' room. AE, MC, V.

A handsome hewn-stone facade welcomes guests to this old hotel at the edge of Gastown. The rooms are small and sparsely furnished, but they're clean and adequate for the budget-watcher. The hotel pub serves cafeteria lunches Monday through Saturday.

8. WEST OF DOWNTOWN

BUDGET

UNIVERSITY OF BRITISH COLUMBIA CONFERENCE CENTRE, 5961 Student Union Blvd. (at Westbrook Mall), Vancouver, BC V6T 2C9. Tel. 604/822-1010. Fax 604/822-1001. 3,600 rms. A/C TV TEL **Bus:** 4, 10, 41, or 42.

$ Rates: $29–$47 single; $63 double; $80 suite. Family rates available. MC, V. **Parking:** Free May 4–Aug 26, $7 per day the rest of year.

This is an attractive option in summer (May 4 to August 26), when few students are on campus; a limited number of rooms may be available (by reservation) at other times. Three separate towers have self-contained clusters of six single bedrooms around a central kitchen, bathroom, and living room. There are also a number of studios and one-bedroom suites for couples in the nearby Walter Gage residence. The UBC Student Union across the street has a cafeteria for meals; guests may use UBC's indoor pool, sauna, whirlpool, tennis courts, and fitness center.

VANCOUVER INTERNATIONAL YOUTH HOSTEL, 1515 Discovery St., Vancouver, BC V6R 4K5. Tel. 604/224-3208. Fax 604/224-4852. 285 beds. **Bus:** 4 or 42.

$ Rates: $12.50 for IYHA members, $17.50 for Canadian nonmembers, $10 for foreign nonmembers, plus linen/blanket rental. Annual adult Canadian membership is $26.75. Family and group memberships available. Maximum stay three nights during busy periods. Family rooms by advance booking. No credit cards. **Parking:** Free, but limited.

Canada's largest youth hostel is a former air force barracks, a big white building on English Bay's beautiful Jericho Beach at Point Grey. A member of the International Youth Hostel Federation, it provides separate dormitories and washroom facilities for men and women, common activity and meeting rooms, and personal lockers. Like most youth hostels, it has fully equipped kitchens for guest use; unlike most, it also has a full-service cafeteria offering breakfast and dinner. The lounge has a large-screen satellite TV; laundry facilities are available. The building is open all day but the doors are locked at 2am. No smoking or drinking is allowed, and no pets are accepted. Bike rentals are available, and tennis courts and a sailing club are nearby. Downtown Vancouver is 30 minutes away by bus.

CHAPTER 5

VANCOUVER DINING

1. **DOWNTOWN**
2. **THE WEST END**
3. **EAST OF DOWNTOWN**
4. **SOUTH OF DOWNTOWN**
5. **NEAR THE AIRPORT**
6. **ON THE NORTH SHORE**
7. **GASTOWN/ CHINATOWN**

There are as many varieties of fine food in Vancouver as there are ethnic groups represented—and that's a lot. From hamburgers to poached salmon, Chinese to Italian, Greek to Indian, Hungarian to Ethiopian, you can get whatever your taste buds desire in this city.

The cuisine comes in all price ranges and in all settings—from seafood eateries overlooking marinas to revolving restaurants atop high-rises, from intimately styled French restaurants in quaint residential neighborhoods to overcrowded holes-in-the-wall in Chinatown.

It's hard to keep track of the exact number, but there are probably close to 2,000 restaurants in Vancouver alone, putting it in serious competition with San Francisco for the most dining establishments per capita of any city in North America. The listings in this book, while substantial, can only scratch the surface.

As with the accommodations in Chapter 4, I have listed my restaurant recommendations first by **geographical area** and then by price category. You need to decide the area where you'd like to eat. If you're staying in a downtown hotel, you can also walk to the West End (west of Thurlow Street), Gastown, or Chinatown. If you're willing to travel farther, you'll find marvelous restaurants in East Vancouver (east of Main Street, all the way to Burnaby); South Vancouver (west of Main Street and south of False Creek, all the way to the Fraser River); the airport area (Richmond and Delta); and North and West Vancouver (north of the Burrard Inlet).

The restaurants are grouped into four **price categories:** "Very Expensive" (with entrées averaging more than $20), "Expensive" (entrées $15–$20), "Moderate" (entrées $10–$15), and "Budget" (entrées less than $10). Remember that *the prices quoted here are in Canadian dollars.*

While many types of cuisine are represented here, **West Coast cuisine** may be the most intriguing. Essentially it is nouvelle cuisine modified to include ingredients readily found in British Columbia and the Pacific Northwest, focusing on seafood, game, and wild herbs. Your entrée may be fresh Dungeness crab or orange mussels from the Queen Charlotte Islands, served with kelp fettuccine, steamed fern shoots, wild chanterelle mushrooms, and acorn squash, in a sauce of peppercress cream, hazelnut butter, or loganberry liqueur. Every chef has his or her own style of preparation, so sit back and enjoy.

British Columbia also has its own **wines,** grown mainly in the

Okanagan Valley, 170 miles (as the crow flies) east of Vancouver in southern B.C.'s dry plateau country. In the hills surrounding the serpentine, 75-mile-long Lake Okanagan and the Okanagan River are more than 12 estate wineries, including Cedar Creek, Grey Monk, Divino, Gehringer Brothers, Le Compte, Quail's Gate, Hanle, and Sumac Ridge. British Columbians are very proud of their wines; while most of them lack the character and finish of California wines or a good Washington state label, they are considerably less expensive (thanks to stiff Canadian import duties). Your best bet for a good B.C. vintage is a medium-dry white, such as a chenin blanc, semillon, or riesling.

Restaurant hours vary. Lunch is typically noon to 1pm; in the evening, British Columbians rarely dine before 7pm or later in summer. **Reservations** are recommended at most restaurants and are essential at the most popular ones. Reservations may not be accepted at some of the budget and moderately priced restaurants, however; in a worst-case scenario, you'll have to join the crowd in line.

One positive word: There's no provincial tax on restaurant meals in British Columbia—just the 7% federal goods and services tax.

1. DOWNTOWN

VERY EXPENSIVE

CHARTWELL, in the Four Seasons Hotel, 791 W. Georgia St. Tel. 689-9333, ext. 6373.
   Cuisine: WEST COAST/CONTINENTAL. **Reservations:** Recommended. **SkyTrain:** Burrard.
$ Prices: Appetizers $5.50–$12; main courses $13.50–$19.50 at lunch, $19–$35 at dinner. AE, DC, ER, MC, V.
   Open: Lunch Mon–Fri noon–2pm; dinner Mon–Sat 5–10:30pm.
Chartwell was the name of Winston Churchill's family home in the English countryside, and he would have been proud to call this exquisite restaurant his own. Chartwell re-creates some of the atmosphere with rich walnut paneling, parquet floors, a roaring fireplace, piped-in classical music that seems to come from the drawing room, and even bucolic oil paintings in wall niches that look like scenes of turn-of-the-century Oxfordshire.

The food is no less inspiring. The cuisine is West Coast, yes, but with continental touches: Chef Wolfgang von Wieser offers such starters as warm smoked salmon on a bagel with wintergreens and rosemary pâté with a frozen berry sauce, followed by such lunch dishes as shrimp and monkfish pie with grilled squid or a West Coast pot-au-feu of veal, duck, chicken, and prawns. The dinner menu may include entrées like Nova Scotia lobster poached in chardonnay, local seafood, Chartwell's famous rack of lamb, and game (in winter). The celebrated dessert menu includes apple Tatin, a fresh-cut apple on a bed of pastry, caramelized, with vanilla ice cream and fresh cream. Service is what you'd expect—impeccable. Valet parking is $6.

JEAN PIERRE'S RESTAURANT, Plaza Level, 4 Bentall Centre, 1055 Dunsmuir St. Tel. 669-0360.

Cuisine: TRADITIONAL FRENCH. **Reservations:** Recommended, especially at lunch. **SkyTrain:** Burrard.

$ Prices: Appetizers $4.50–$9.95; main courses $10.50–$15.25 at lunch, $18–$23 at dinner. AE, DC, ER, MC, V.

Open: Breakfast Mon–Sat 7:30–11am; lunch Mon–Sat 11am–4pm; dinner Mon–Fri 4–10pm, Sat 5–10pm.

Under the summer sun, you might see the colorful umbrellas of a sidewalk café amid the fountains and greenery beneath the Bentall Centre's towers. At other times, you may have to search to find this

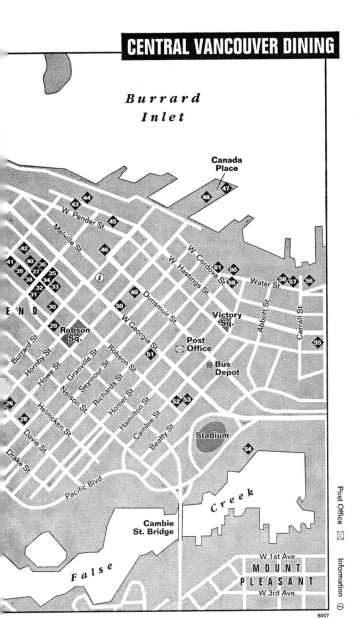

Burrard Inlet

Canada Place

W. Pender St.

Melville St.

W. Cordova St.

W. Hastings St.

Water St.

Abbott St.

Carrall St.

Dunsmuir St.

Victory Sq.

W. Georgia St.

Robson Sq.

Post Office

Burrard St.

Hornby St.

Howe St.

Granville St.

Seymour St.

Robson St.

Richards St.

Bus Depot

Nelson St.

Homer St.

Hamilton St.

Cambie St.

Beatty St.

Helmcken St.

Davie St.

Drake St.

Pacific Blvd.

Stadium

Creek

Cambie St. Bridge

False

W. 1st Ave.

MOUNT PLEASANT

W. 3rd Ave.

Post Office ☒

Information ⊙

6007

elegant little restaurant—but it's worth it! Owner Jean-Pierre Bachellerie has employed all the tricks he once learned as food and beverage manager at the Four Seasons Hotel to bring good cuisine and hospitality to a larger Vancouver public.

The menus are handwritten and change often. Spit-roasted rack of lamb, chateaubriand (straight from the rôtisserie), suprême of chicken with crab à l'armoricaine, and poached fillet of salmon aux salsifis et concombre are among the popular dishes. Jean-Pierre also offers table d'hôte for $25. There's validated parking in Bentall Centre.

LE CLUB, in Le Méridien Hotel, 845 Burrard St. Tel. 682-5511, ext. 5222.
Cuisine: WEST COAST/CONTINENTAL. **Reservations:** Recommended. **SkyTrain:** Burrard.
$ Prices: Appetizers $5.75–$11.50; main courses $17–$24. AE, CB, DC, ER, MC, V.
Open: Dinner only Mon–Sat 5:30–10pm.

Just as the Le Méridien hotel chain is consummately continental, so, too, is Le Club, the restaurant. Original oils hang on padded silk walls; fresh flowers are perfectly centered on rich wood sideboards. Everywhere there's an air of refinement. The light-green-and-salmon color scheme lends itself to conversation rather than to stifled whispers—and the food is worthy of conversation.

Diners may order à la carte or leave the meal in the hands of chef Olivier Chaleil, who offers a nightly table d'hôte, all-inclusive, for $32. Entrées might include pan-fried Oregon tilapia on a lentil-and-rosemary cream, broiled fillet of coho salmon with sun-dried tomato coulis, sautéed Black Angus tenderloin with red-pepper coulis and braised romaine, or roasted duckling marinated in honey and star anise. It's an adventure in dining with no risk attached. Valet parking is $5 plus hourly charges.

RESTAURANT SUNTORY, in the Pan-Pacific Hotel, 999 Canada Place. Tel. 683-8201.
Cuisine JAPANESE. **Reservations:** Recommended.
SkyTrain: Waterfront.
$ Prices: Appetizers $2.50–$6 at lunch, $3–$7 at dinner; à la carte dinner $4–$40; complete dinner $13.50–$110; lunch main courses $6.95–$35. AE, DC, ER, JCB, MC, V.
Open: Lunch Mon–Sat noon–2pm; dinner daily 6–10pm.

Some Japanese restaurants offer the casual ambience of a sushi bar. Some please with teppanyaki—the staccato slicing and frying of meat and vegetables on a tabletop grill. Not as common in North America are restaurants that specialize in sukiyaki and shabu-shabu—beef and vegetable dishes cooked in a broth at your table. The Suntory is unique: It's all three restaurants in one, and it also has private tatami rooms on request.

Business travelers from Tokyo and Osaka, and Canadian executives trying to win them over, find that they just can't go wrong at the Suntory. (What's more, prices are much lower than in the Land of the Rising Yen.) Sukiyaki and teppanyaki are suggested for first-time diners, but more adventurous palates would probably prefer one of the special delicacies, such as broiled eel or squid cooked in sake and mixed with marinated sea urchin. For special occasions, the 10-course *kaiseki* dinner ($65) will fulfill every dream. Valet parking is $5 (free after 6pm).

WILLIAM TELL RESTAURANT, in the Georgian Court Hotel, 765 Beatty St. Tel. 688-3504.
Cuisine: SWISS/CONTINENTAL. **Reservations:** Recommended at dinner. **SkyTrain:** Stadium.
$ Prices: Appetizers $5–$8; main courses $8–$12 at lunch, $22–$28 at dinner. AE, DC, ER, JCB, MC, V.
Open: Breakfast daily 7–10:30am; lunch Mon–Fri 11:30am–2pm; dinner Mon–Sat 6–9:30pm.

Nearly three decades have passed since Swiss-born Erwin Doebeli first opened the William Tell. He started by specializing in the French/German cuisine of Switzerland—appropriately so, for a restaurant named after his country's national hero—and almost immediately received the highest accolades of Vancouver food critics. The praise has continued to grow under its internationally acclaimed executive chef, Pierre Dubrulle. The menu emphasizes continental dishes with a West Coast influence.

The ambience is of classical elegance and perfection. Doebeli chose the highest-quality linen, china, and crystal for his table settings, and the framed historical prints on the walls are from his personal collection. The food, most of it locally grown on a 15-acre organic farm, is likewise superb. Diners can begin with blueberry champagne soup or Bündnerfleisch (rump roast), then savor a Campbell's pheasant or éminé of veal Zürichois. The wine list is astounding, but no more so than Doebeli himself, who may stop by your table to chat for a while. Parking costs $3.

EXPENSIVE

BANDI'S, 1427 Howe St., near Pacific St. Tel. 685-3391.
Cuisine: HUNGARIAN. **Reservations:** Recommended. **Bus:** 401, 403, or 406.
$ Prices: Appetizers $5–$8; main courses $13–$22. AE, MC, V.
Open: Lunch Mon–Fri 11:30am–2pm; dinner Mon–Thurs 6–11pm, Fri–Sat 5:30–11pm, Sun 5:30–10pm. **Parking:** On street.

Chef-owner Bandi Rinkhy's establishment may be the nicest thing to greet eastern European eyes this side of Budapest. Enter the warm, folksy restaurant and you'll be treated to piquant palate-pleasers that you've probably never associated with Hungary. Start, for instance, with chilled cherry soup, then move on to paraszt sonka (smoked ham with fresh horseradish and scallions). For a main course, try the duck braised in Tokaj, or borjuszelet bankar modra (slices of veal in a ragoût of sweetbreads, truffles, olives, and foie gras). Accompany your meal with longos (unleavened bread served with fresh chopped garlic), and leave room for a sweet crêpe dessert. Wow! There's on-street parking.

DYNASTY RESTAURANT, in the Vancouver Renaissance Hotel, 1133 W. Hastings St. Tel. 689-9211.
Cuisine: CANTONESE. **Reservations:** Recommended. **Bus:** 19.
$ Prices: Appetizers $8–$18; three dishes with rice (for two people) $30–$60. AE, DC, ER, JCB, MC, V.
Open: Lunch Tues–Fri 11:30am–2pm, Sat–Sun 11:30am–2:30pm; dinner Tues–Sun 6–10pm.

Vancouver's most exotic Chinese dining can be experienced behind the sign of the flying *devi,* etched in glass at the entrance to the Dynasty. An ancient Buddhist symbol that represents the highest ideals, the colorful goddess has her likeness reproduced on the specially commissioned Narumi bone china, the menu cover, and elsewhere in the restaurant. Everything here is heavenly, from the imported rosewood furniture to the fine ceramics mounted in niches in the walls.

The menu is 15 pages long and packed with such offerings as

sautéed octopus with bamboo pith, boneless pig knuckle with vinegar, deep-fried whole crispy pigeon, and goose webs and vermicelli casserole. Don't let it scare you off: Western diners will also find sliced chicken with enoke mushrooms and red dates, barbecued duck with plum sauce, and grilled Szechuan prawns. Whatever you choose, you'll find it to be *devi*-lishly good. There's validated parking at dinner and also for lunch on weekends.

IL GIARDINO DI UMBERTO, 1382 Hornby St. Tel. 669-2422.
   Cuisine: TUSCAN. **Reservations:** Required. **Bus:** 22 or 401.
$ Prices: Appetizers $6–$10; main courses $10–$15 at lunch, $15–$25 at dinner. AE, DC, ER, MC, V.
   Open: Lunch Mon–Fri noon–2:30pm; dinner Mon–Sat 6–11pm.
Of five local restaurants (and five more out of town) owned and operated by Vancouver's famed Italian chef, Umberto Menghi, this is the one that attracts the "in" crowd. Local celebrities hand the keys to their Ferraris and BMWs to natty valets ($4), then rush into "Umberto's Garden" to gawk at visiting screen stars. The ambience is of a romantic seaside villa, with leather chairs on tile floors beneath high ceilings. When the weather cooperates, there's outdoor patio dining beside a vine-draped terrace.

The menu emphasizes pasta and game. In the former category, capelletti stuffed with squash, and tortellini mascarpone are an interesting change from linguine and fettuccine. Game dishes include pheasant with polenta, quail in grappa, and reindeer prepared in a variety of fashions. Most popular of all, perhaps, are the veal dishes.

KAMEI SUSHI RESTAURANT, 811 Thurlow St., at Robson St. Tel. 684-4823.
   Cuisine: CASUAL JAPANESE. **Reservations:** Recommended, especially at lunch. **Bus:** 8.
$ Prices: A la carte $6.50–$14.45; complete meal $5.75–$12.85 at lunch, $18.25–$24 at dinner. AE, DC, MC, V.
   Open: Lunch Mon–Fri 11:30am–2pm, Sat noon–2:30pm; dinner Mon–Thurs 5–10:30pm, Fri–Sat 5–11:30pm, Sun 5–9:30pm.
Frenetic Robsonstrasse is the perfect location for this modern restaurant, which could be a transplant from Tokyo's Roppongi or Akasaka district. Chic diners of all ages and ethnic backgrounds flock to the counter to watch the sushi makers hand-roll the vinegared rice-and-raw-fish delicacies that Kamei Sushi first made popular in western Canada.

Sushi isn't the only thing on the menu, of course. Tempura and teriyaki combinations, nabemonos (noodle soups and casseroles), and special shabu-shabu and sukiyaki dinners are also available. Reserve ahead to dine in a tatami room, complete with matted floor and shoji screens. If you're not staying downtown, you can find other Kamei Sushis at 601 and 1414 W. Broadway in Vancouver, as well as in Burnaby and Richmond. Parking is on-street.

A KETTLE OF FISH, 900 Pacific St., at Hornby St. Tel. 682-6853.
   Cuisine: SEAFOOD. **Reservations:** Recommended. **Bus:** 22, 401, 403, or 406.
$ Prices: Appetizers $2.95–$25; main courses $6.95–$7.95 at lunch, $10.95–$24.95 at dinner. AE, DC, MC, V.
   Open: Lunch Mon–Fri 11:30am–2:30pm; dinner Sun–Thurs 5:30–9:30pm, Fri–Sat 5:30–10pm.

This elegant courtyard restaurant is housed near the foot of the Granville Street Bridge in a turn-of-the-century building that once served heavy industry. It has been transformed into a lush greenhouse with such warm-weather plants as rubber trees, Norfolk pines, and pandanus. In the window is a big sign: EAT LOTSA FISH. And that's what everyone does.

A laminated, fish-shaped menu lists the appetizers, but the fresh offerings are scrawled on blackboards where they are changed daily according to availability. The seafood can be grilled, barbecued, blackened, or cooked in natural butter and squeezed lemon—it's your choice. The fish chowder, a tomato-based bouillabaisse, is superb with a squeeze of lime; an ample portion of fresh wok-cooked vegetables is served with entrées. There's on-street parking or nearby pay parking lots.

NANIWA-YA SEAFOOD RESTAURANT, 745 Thurlow St., at Alberni St. Tel. 681-7307.

Cuisine: JAPANESE SEAFOOD. **Reservations:** Recommended. **Bus:** 8.

$ Prices: A la carte $2.35–$18.50; complete meals $5.75–$13.95 at lunch, $17.50–$27.95 at dinner. AE, DC, JCB, MC, V.

Open: Lunch Mon–Fri 11:30am–2:30pm; dinner Mon–Sat 5:30–11pm, Sun 5–10pm.

This delightful country-style restaurant, specially designed by a Japanese architect, was the first of its kind in Canada to allow diners to choose their own live seafood from seawater tanks on the premises. Named for owner Akio Higashio's native city, "the Osaka place" serves all food on fine Arita-yaki pottery and provides a traditional Japanese atmosphere.

Crab, lobster, shrimp, scallops, oysters, geoduck ("gooey-duck") and butter clams, and abalone can be prepared at the diner's request in a variety of ways, such as with ginger or ponzu sauce. A special 10-course dinner includes sashimi, tempura, and green-tea ice cream. On-street parking.

PICCOLO MONDO, 850 Thurlow St. Tel. 688-1633.

Cuisine: TRADITIONAL ITALIAN. **Reservations:** Required. **Bus:** 8; then walk one block north from Robson.

$ Prices: Appetizers $5–$12; main courses $10–$21. AE, DC, ER, MC, V.

Open: Lunch Mon–Fri 11:30am–2pm; dinner Mon–Sat 5:30–10pm.

In a too-small beige-and-brown room at the corner of Smythe Street is an establishment many consider to be the best Italian restaurant in Vancouver. Noted food critic Jurgen Gothe, in fact, has declared it the best restaurant in the city. Why? Because Piccolo Mondo has succeeded in being many things to many people—trendy and traditional, generous and refined, with Canada's best Italian wine list and a pared-down menu of innovative specials.

Diners are asked to choose from among 30 or more pastas; a half portion makes a dandy starter. Consider the nido di Lumache—angel-hair pasta with escargots, garlic, walnuts, and Pernod. Fish and meat main dishes vary greatly, from mahi mahi alla livornese to quail alla borghese to tripe and beef tongue. The insalata Piccolo Mondo is indeed special: It includes ham, mushrooms, and papaya. On-street parking.

THE PROW RESTAURANT, 100-999 Canada Place. Tel. 684-1339.

Cuisine: CONTINENTAL/SEAFOOD. **Reservations:** Recommended at dinner. **SkyTrain:** Waterfront.

$ Prices: Appetizers $3.25–$6.95; main courses $10.95–$19.50. AE, ER, MC, V.

Open: Lunch daily 11:30am–2:30pm; dinner daily 5:30–10:30pm.

The white sails of Canada Place are open to the breezes, as if to propel the nose of a ship into the waters of Burrard Inlet. Right at the tip of the quay, tucked into what might be (you guessed it) the prow of the ship, is the Prow Restaurant. Huge picture windows open onto the inlet and cruise-ship terminal—truly a spectacular setting.

Equally impressive is the cuisine—continental with a Pacific emphasis. You can start with mushrooms stuffed with crabmeat and sun-dried tomatoes, smothered in Brie, or grilled oysters and lettuce with a hot bacon vinaigrette; then move on to grilled mahi mahi with pineapple chutney and a light curry butter, or grilled B.C. salmon with hazelnut-roasted garlic butter. The menu also includes chicken, veal, beef and lamb dishes. Be sure to leave room for dessert. Parking is free with validation.

TAI CHI HIN, 888 Burrard St., at Smythe St. Tel. 682-1888.

Cuisine: MANDARIN/SHANGHAI. **Reservations:** Recommended. **Bus:** 22.

$ Prices: Appetizers $2–$7.50; three dishes with rice (for two people) $23–$57. AE, DC, ER, JCB, V.

Open: Lunch daily 11am–2:30pm; dinner daily 5:30–10:30pm.

The decor of this restaurant feels more like Los Angeles than Beijing. It's open and airy, with chrome, brass, and glass blocks, and pastel shades used quite liberally; indeed, it's very much a reflection of the New Age or new wave music that wafts from the sound system.

But the food is distinctly northern Chinese gourmet. The fried smoked duck with coriander and dumplings is on everyone's list of favorites. The crab-and-asparagus soup is a delicious, hearty starter; the garlic eel is an unusual entrée. Squeamish diners are sometimes put off by the rock cod: Before being prepared with ginger and scallions, it's presented to the table—live, in a plastic case, for inspection. Free valet parking.

VISTAS ON THE BAY, in the Vancouver Renaissance Hotel, 1133 W. Hastings St. Tel. 689-9211.

Cuisine: WEST COAST. **Reservations:** Recommended at dinner. **Bus:** 19.

$ Prices: Appetizers $4.75–$7.50; main courses $9–$16 at lunch, $12–$27.50 at dinner. AE, DC, ER, MC, V.

Open: Lunch daily 11:30am–2:30pm; light menu daily 2:30–5:30pm; dinner Sun–Thurs 5:30–9pm, Fri–Sat 5:30–10pm.

Chef Peter Buche, who headed up the Canadian team at the 1988 World Culinary Olympics, has a wonderful place to work: a revolving restaurant, 20 stories high overlooking Burrard Inlet, with a 360° view that includes the high peaks of the North Shore Mountains. His cuisine raises eyebrows as well.

There are so many good things on the menu that I hardly know where to begin. I might be tempted to start with the Sable Island roe scallops in roasted-pepper-and-parsley butter, followed by a wild herb salad with glazed St. Maure goat cheese. Then I'd opt for the papillote of Pacific sole with leeks, shiitake mushrooms, white wine, and cream, or perhaps the pork tenderloin dressed with Dungeness crab and macadamia nuts. There's validated parking.

MODERATE

CAFE IL NIDO, 780 Thurlow St., at Robson St. Tel. 685-6436.
   Cuisine: ITALIAN. **Reservations:** Recommended. **Bus:** 8.
$ Prices: Appetizers $4.75–$7.75; main courses $7.75–$12.75 at lunch, $11.50–$16.75 at dinner. AE, ER, MC, V.
   Open: Lunch Mon–Fri 11:30am–2:30pm; dinner Mon–Sat 5:30–10:30pm.

Tucked away in the courtyard of Manhattan Square, "The Nest" offers a charming respite from the bustle of downtown Vancouver. Surrounded by shops, offices, and apartments, you could easily imagine it in any city—Florence or Milan, for example.

The food certainly underscores the Romanesque flavor: prosciutto and melanzana appetizers, fusilli and capelletti ginger pastas, and main dishes like gamberoni e canastrelle (prawns and scallops in a vol-au-vent) and pollo diable (chicken breast in a sauce of Dijon mustard, shallots, and peppercorns). The chef's specialty is carello d'agnello (rack of lamb). The menu changes seasonally. On-street parking.

CHATEAU MADRID, 1277 Howe St., near Drake St. Tel. 684-8814.
   Cuisine: SPANISH. **Reservations:** Required. **Bus:** 401, 403, or 406.
$ Prices: Appetizers $2.95–$6.95; main courses $12.75–$16.95. AE, DC, ER, MC, V.
   Open: Dinner only, Tues–Sat 6–11pm.

Entering this original Spanish restaurant is like walking into an Iberian hacienda. Seating is intimate, handsome waiters attend your every request, and taped flamenco guitar music completes the ambience. It's almost like a more refined chapter out of the tale of Don Quixote, whose likeness graces the restaurant's logo.

You'll get such well-known Spanish dishes here as paella and pollo Asturias (chicken finished with cider), as well as lesser-known delights such as pato a la Sevillana (duckling in orange-brandy sauce) and pincho marinero (skewered seafood in a sherry-and-cream sauce). Starters include alcachofas Don Carlos (sautéed artichoke hearts with dry cured chorizo sausage). On-street parking.

JOE FORTES SEAFOOD HOUSE, 777 Thurlow St., near Robson St. Tel. 669-1940.
   Cuisine: SEAFOOD. **Reservations:** Recommended. **Bus:** 8.
$ Prices: Appetizers $3.95–$6.95; main courses $5.95–$9.95 at lunch, $9.95–$15.95 at dinner. AE, DC, DISC, ER, MC, V.
   Open: Lunch daily 11:30am–4pm; light meals daily 4–5:30pm; dinner Sun–Thurs 5:30–11pm, Fri–Sat 5:30pm–midnight.

Few cities perpetuate hero-worship for a man like Seraphim "Joe" Fortes. A Barbados-born seaman of African-Spanish extraction, he arrived in Vancouver in 1885 and quickly became a fixture in the city. For three decades, he lived in a squatter's shack on English Bay, where he was a combination lifeguard, constable, chaperone, counselor, teacher, and friend to thousands of children. His funeral cortege in 1923 was the longest in the city's history.

Today, the bar and grill that bears Joe's name is a gathering place for many of Vancouver's upwardly mobile young adults. An oyster bar shucks a dozen varieties to order. Menu selections include cultured mussels steamed in tarragon-cream sauce, seared mahi mahi with macadamia nuts and lobster sauce, and West Coast cioppino with garlic-fennel toast. There's an extensive daily fresh-fish list, and meat-lovers can choose from steaks and mixed grills. Valet parking is $4; the lot next door charges $2.

1066 HASTINGS, 1066 W. Hastings St. Tel. 689-1066.

Cuisine: WEST COAST/CONTINENTAL. **Reservations:** Recommended. **SkyTrain:** Burrard. **Bus:** 19.

$ Prices: Appetizers $3.25–$5.95; main courses $5.95–$7.75 at lunch, $9.95–$16.95 at dinner. AE, DC, ER, MC, V.

Open: Breakfast Mon–Fri 7–10:30am; lunch Mon–Fri 11:30am–3pm; light meals Mon–Fri 3–5pm; dinner Mon–Sat 5–10pm.

Hard by the financial district, less than a block from the Vancouver Renaissance Hotel, is this friendly family-owned spot. Look behind the shrubs and ivy and you'll see the umbrellas on the patio, well patronized on sunny days. Inside is a restaurant that combines a casual daytime atmosphere with an intimate evening mood, sufficiently romantic to inspire Saturday-night dinner dancing.

All ingredients used in cooking are local; they're prepared with continental and occasional Asian culinary touches. Dishes include a Northwest bouillabaisse featuring prawns, scallops, and whitefish; prawn-and-black-bean stir-fry; fresh B.C. salmon fillet topped with a delicate tomato-basil hollandaise sauce (the house special); and prime rib of beef. Leave room for dessert, such as freshly baked lemon bread pudding. Free parking in the evening.

TSUI HANG VILLAGE, 1193 Granville St., at Davie St. Tel. 683-6868.

Cuisine: CHINESE SEAFOOD. **Reservations:** Recommended in the early evening. **Bus:** 8, 10, 20, 14, or 21.

$ Prices: Appetizers $1.50–$7; three dishes with rice (for two people) $19–$46. MC, V.

Open: Daily 5pm–3:30am.

The best way to choose an Asian restaurant is to peek inside and see how many Asians are dining there. If there aren't many, you might wonder what's wrong with the food. At the Tsui Hang, there's no such worry. You'll see whole families of Chinese feasting together by the live seafood tanks. Established by immigrants from Hong Kong during the electric days preceding Expo '86, Tsui Hang moved to new, larger premises in 1992. It's rated by some as Vancouver's finest Chinese seafood restaurant.

Crab is the house specialty, prepared in the shell in your choice of sauce such as garlic-black-bean or ginger-butter-cream. The scallop dishes and whole rock cod are equally wonderful. Hot-and-sour soup is a great starter, and the almond gelatin (a sweet beancurd dish) is a perfect dessert. Late-night/early-morning diners rave about the rice porridge. Parking is free.

BUDGET

THE ELEPHANT & CASTLE, 700 Dunsmuir St., Pacific Centre. Tel. 685-4545.

Cuisine: ENGLISH PUB. **SkyTrain:** Granville.

$ Prices: $4.95–$13.95 per dish. AE, DC, ER, MC, V.

Open: Mon–Wed and Sat 11am–9pm, Thurs–Fri 11am–11pm, Sun noon–6pm.

This is the flagship of the Canadian chain of British pubs, with franchises from Victoria to Ottawa, and one in Bellingham, Washington. Its temporary Expo '86 site received international coverage when it hosted Prince Charles, Diana, and Prime Minister Margaret Thatcher. Here's where you can get a ploughman's lunch and a pint of John Smith's Yorkshire Bitter on tap in a modern, folksy atmosphere. There's parking in the Pacific Centre.

LA BODEGA, 1277 Howe St., near Drake St. Tel. 684-8815.

Cuisine: SPANISH TAPAS. **Bus:** 401, 403, or 406.

$ Prices: $1.95–$6.95 per dish. AE, DC, ER, MC, V.

Open: Mon–Sat 11:30am–1am.

This popular bar-restaurant on the ground floor of the Chateau Madrid restaurant (recommended above) is like a dark, cozy cavern with its brick walls and mounted bull's head. Choose from hot and cold tapas such as mejillones (mussels in vinaigrette or a pepper-wine sauce), albondigas (Spanish meatballs), besugo en salsa (red snapper), or empanadilla (Spanish pie). Accompany it with a fruity sangría.

LAS TAPAS, 760 Cambie St., between Georgia and Robson Sts. Tel. 669-1624.

Cuisine: SPANISH TAPAS. **Bus:** 15 or 242.

$ Prices: $1.75–$10.95 per dish. MC, V.

Open: Mon–Thurs 11:30am–10pm, Fri 11:30am–11pm, Sat 5–11pm, Sun 5–9:30pm (later if concert schedules warrant).

Conveniently located just around the corner from the Queen Elizabeth Theatre, this restaurant offers pre- and postconcert nibbles. Tapas, the appetizer-sized Spanish answer to fast food, are served in a big tiled room with a foreign decor. Such dishes as eggplant, calamares (squid), garlic shrimp, spicy chorizo sausage, and marinated lamb are available in small, medium, or large portions.

LESWICK'S ON GEORGIA, 418 W. Georgia St. Tel. 688-0939.

Cuisine: FAMILY STYLE. **Bus:** 242.

$ Prices: $3–$7.25 per dish. No credit cards.

Open: Mon–Sat 7am–8pm.

Another family restaurant, Leswick's offers clean, simple decor and cafeteria-style service with a posted menu. Breakfasts are inexpensive, burgers with the works cost just $4.25, and baked ham dinners are at the top of the line.

PRESTO PANINI CAFE, 822 Thurlow St., near Robson St. Tel. 684-4445.

Cuisine: ITALIAN FAST FOOD. **Bus:** 8.

$ Prices: $3.75–$6.75 per dish. AE, MC, V.

Open: Mon–Thurs 11am–10pm, Fri–Sat 11am–midnight.

S This small storefront offers some of the tastiest and most unusual quick meals you're likely to find anywhere: varieties of panini (a flat bread, served as a hot sandwich) and penne (a quill-shaped pasta). First-timers are drawn to the classical panini (salami, cappicolla, mozzarella, and provolone cheese, served with mustard chutney) and the penne with eggplant or artichoke hearts. The café also offers a vegetable calabeze (ginger-coconut) soup, a green salad, and antipasti. It has an espresso bar, wine, and beer.

STEAMERS AND STEWS, 900 Pacific St., at Hornby St. Tel. 682-6853.
Cuisine: SEAFOOD. **Bus:** 22, 401, 403 or 406 (two blocks from stops).
$ Prices: $3.75–$8.95 per dish. AE, DC, MC, V.
Open: Mon–Fri 11am–9:30pm, Sat–Sun 5:30–10pm.

S A casual bistro on the lower floor of A Kettle of Fish (see my recommendation, above), this little eatery is ideal for those who want a meal of angels on horseback or cold, cracked Dungeness crab without the trappings of a big dinner. And the bouillabaisse is just as good as it is upstairs.

A TASTE OF JAMAICA, 941 Davie St., at Burrard St. Tel. 683-3464.
Cuisine: JAMAICAN. **Bus:** 8.
$ Prices: $2.50–$6 per dish. No credit cards.
Open: Mon–Sat 11am–11pm, Sun 4–11pm.

S This tiny diner with just six tables and a solid diet of reggae music is where Jimmy Buffett might come searching for changes in latitude; in fact, Ziggy Marley himself has eaten here. You'll find ackee and codfish with a fried-plantain dumpling on the menu, as well as a variety of vegetable, fish, and meat curries— goat, for instance. The highlight of this meal might be an ice-cold guava or mango juice, or homemade ginger beer. There's parking behind the building for $1.75.

THE UNICORN, in the Plaza of Nations, 770 Pacific Blvd. S. Tel. 683-4436.
Cuisine: ENGLISH PUB. **SkyTrain:** Stadium. **Bus:** 15.
$ Prices: $4.95–$11.95 per dish. AE, MC, V.
Open: Mon–Thurs 11:30am–midnight, Fri–Sat 11:30am–1am, Sun noon–7pm.

"The loveliest of them all was the unicorn." When the Irish Rovers first recorded their big hit in the mid-1960s, they weren't planning to become publicans as well as musicians. They've done well, though, with this establishment on the old Expo '86 site adjacent to B.C. Place Stadium. Shepherd's pie, fish and chips, and clam chowder highlight the menu, and there's appropriate folk-oriented entertainment nightly. Parking costs $6 in nearby lots.

2. THE WEST END

VERY EXPENSIVE

CLOUD 9, in the Sheraton-Landmark Hotel, 1400 Robson St. Tel. 687-0511, ext. 7235.

Cuisine: CONTINENTAL. **Reservations:** Recommended. **Bus:** 8.

$ Prices: Appetizers $3.95–$8.95; main courses $3.75–$14.25 at lunch, $23–$30 at dinner. AE, DC, ER, MC, V.

Open: Breakfast daily 6:30–11:30am; lunch daily 11:30am–2:30pm; dinner daily 5–11pm (lounge open to 1am Mon–Sat).

Vancouver's highest restaurant, revolving at the 42nd floor of the Sheraton, provides diners with a spectacular view. Rotating once every 85 minutes, Cloud 9 affords a bird's-eye perspective on the Burrard Inlet and North Shore Mountains, on South Vancouver across English Bay and False Creek, and on Vancouver Island across the Strait of Georgia. The seating is structured to allow maximum visibility through the spacious windows.

Too often, restaurants with a spectacular view don't offer high-quality meals. Such is not the case at Cloud 9, where the food is equal to the setting. Diners might start with oysters Rockefeller ultima (with Pernod-flavored spinach and fresh crabmeat) or almond-crusted Camembert accompanied by apple and fresh mint-chutney sauce. Popular main courses include fresh salmon en papillote, wrapped and baked with prawns and scallops; and Alberta roast prime rib of beef. Parking is $1.50.

EXPENSIVE

DELILAH'S, in the Buchan Hotel, 1906 Haro St., at Gilford St. Tel. 687-3424.

Cuisine: CONTINENTAL. **Reservations:** Accepted only for parties of six or more. **Bus:** 8 to Denman Street.

$ Prices: Fixed-price dinner $15.50–$24. MC, V.

Open: Dinner only, daily 5–11pm.

★ A toast to the martini, please. This campy and crowded spot can be found one block west of Denman Street, in the basement of an aging hotel on a quiet residential street. You won't find many out-of-town visitors here; it seems that only locals are willing to arrive early and still wait hours for a table. Their first order of business is to sidle up to the bar and order a martini. There are 26 kinds—all of them too big, all of them exceptional. As you wait for your table, you can study the North Beach decor and hand-painted Florentine ceiling, or you can order another martini. Wait: Isn't that tall, flamboyant figure Delilah herself, I mean, himself? Barkeep, another martini!

Finally, you'll be seated and offered a checklist instead of a menu. You can choose either a two-course or a five-course meal; the latter includes soup, salad, appetizer, entrée, and dessert. Gourmet selections change every few months, but you can count on fine seafood and steaks, original adaptations of traditional favorites, or vegetarian meals. And after dessert? Well, you can always have another martini. Valet parking costs $4; street parking is exceedingly limited.

ENGLISH BAY CAFE, 1795 Beach Ave., at Denman St. Tel. 669-2225.

Cuisine: WEST COAST/CONTINENTAL. **Reservations:** Recommended. **Bus:** 8.

$ Prices: Appetizers $4.25–$7.65; main courses $8.25–$10.50 at lunch, $12.95–$23.45 at dinner. AE, ER, JCB, MC, V.

Open: Lunch Mon–Fri 11:30am–2pm, Sat–Sun 10:30am–2:00pm; dinner Mon–Fri 5:30–10pm, Sat–Sun 5–10pm.

This "café" is really three restaurants in one: an elegant dining room upstairs, the Sea Level Bistro downstairs (see my recommendation, below), and an outside deck with a barbecue menu (summers only). The view from all three is magnificent, especially at sunset, when all types of seaworthy craft, from sailboats to freighters, are outlined against the sun setting on the bay. But the skylit fine-dining establishment sets a high standard all day long with its rosewood furniture, exotic flower arrangements, and abstract watercolors.

A meal in the second-floor café is guaranteed to be an adventure. The daily menu offers starters such as salmon carpaccio or goat cheese and prosciutto tart, and entrées like seafood Wellington and the English Bay fillet steak, smothered with Dungeness crab and béarnaise. Daily specials may include alligator steaks. Passion-fruit flan and white-chocolate/amaretto cheesecake are among the more sinful desserts. Valet parking is $4.

HY'S MANSION, 1523 Davie St., near Nicola St. Tel. 689-1111.

Cuisine: CONTINENTAL/STEAKS. **Reservations:** Recommended. **Bus:** 8.

$ Prices: Appetizers $4–$7; main courses $15–$25. AE, DC, JCB, ER, MC, V.

Open: Dinner only, Mon–Thurs 5:30–10pm, Fri–Sat 5:30–11pm, Sun 5–9pm.

Sugar baron B. T. Rogers had this magnificent graystone built for himself in 1900. Surrounded by deftly tended grounds, it's now a heritage property with hand-carved terra-cotta fireplaces, oak-paneled halls and staircase, elaborate stained-glass windows, and an impressive downstairs bar. Vancouver's best steaks are prepared in its kitchen and served in its dining rooms with a flair that would have made old B. T. proud.

Folks with a preference for seafood and poultry will find them on the menu as well, but those in the know opt for the beef. All steaks are of the highest quality and come in generous portions. "The Only," served only at Hy's, consists of 12 prime ounces marinated in the mansion's unique steak sauce. The standard classics are also here: steak Diane, steak au poivre, filet mignon, French Canadian rib steak, and so forth. Don't forget to ask the maître d' for a tour of the mansion when you've finished. There's valet parking.

KIRIN MANDARIN RESTAURANT, 1166 Alberni St., near Bute St. Tel. 682-8833.

Cuisine: MANDARIN. **Reservations:** Recommended. **Bus:** 8; then walk one block south at Robson Street.

$ Prices: Appetizers $1.50–$28; three main dishes (for two people) $21–$115. AE, ER, MC, V.

Open: Lunch daily 11am–2:30pm; dinner daily 5–10:30pm.

As modern and showy as the downtown office tower whose ground floor it occupies, this is one upscale Chinese eatery that might be out of place in Hong Kong. It has high skylit ceilings, live-seafood tanks set into its sage-green walls, pink tablecloths, and lots of black lacquer trim. So successful has this restaurant been that a second Kirin opened at City Square, opposite City Hall and the Sheraton Plaza 500 at 12th and Cambie.

This is a restaurant for connoisseurs who can enjoy shark's-fin and bird's-nest soups at premium prices. Everyone, unless allergic, should have a live lobster or crab: They're prepared in 11 different ways, notably Shanghai style with ginger, onion, and egg. Other favorites on the 185-item menu include Szechuan hot-and-spicy fresh scallops, Peking duck, and various hot pots and chow meins. If you insist, you can get braised fish maw with sea cucumber or shrimp eggs or fish snouts. If you're here at lunchtime, there's a tasty dim sum selection. Free valet parking.

LE GAVROCHE, 1616 Alberni St., at Cardero St. Tel. 685-3924.
   Cuisine: FRENCH. **Reservations:** Recommended. **Bus:** 242.
$ **Prices:** Appetizers $6–$9; main courses $9.50–$14.50 at lunch, $16.50–$20 at dinner.
   Open: Lunch Mon–Fri noon–2pm; dinner Mon–Sat 5:30–10:30pm.

There are many who believe that this is Vancouver's finest French restaurant, and I wouldn't disagree. After all, wasn't London's Le Gavroche the first three-star Michelin restaurant outside France? This establishment, owned and operated by Jean-Luc Bertrand since the mid-1970s, is not related—but the quality is such that it could easily be a cousin. Located in an elegant old house a few steps from the Westin Bayshore, it offers a perfect cozy setting for a candlelit dinner.

Diners can start with a smoked-quail salad in a ginger-and-hazelnut dressing, rabbit pâté with quince purée, or a lobster velouté with Armagnac. Entrées include monkfish in pistachio-cream sauce, Dover sole in lemon butter, poached oysters in a seaweed-and-apple-cider sauce, and breast of duck with figs and white porto sauce. Get the idea? It's a house policy, incidentally, to use cream and butter sparingly in the preparations. The wines, especially the bordeaux, are superb in all (and I mean *all*) price ranges, and the service is attentive but unobtrusive. There's valet parking.

THE RAINTREE, 1630 Alberni St., near Cardero St. Tel. 688-5570.
   Cuisine: WEST COAST. **Reservations:** Recommended. **Bus:** 242.
$ **Prices:** Appetizers $4–$8; main courses $7–$11 at lunch, $13–$25 at dinner. AE, DC, JCB, MC, V.
   Open: Lunch Mon–Fri 11:30am–2:30pm, Sun 11am–3pm; dinner Sun–Thurs 5:30–9:30pm, Fri–Sat 5:30–10:30pm.

In this wet climate, it makes sense for the foremost purveyor of West Coast cuisine to call itself the Raintree. This is culinary theater at its best. The decor is simple and elegant, with touches of flamboyance, like the huge papier-mâché irises and tulips framed against the etched-glass dividers and pastel walls. Oversize windows face out across Burrard Inlet at Grouse Mountain. The service is personal and attentive. According to the owner Janice Lotzkar: "A restaurant to me is like a magic show, with a stage and props. People come in with an expectation—and we overwhelm them!"

The food is presented with equal artistry. Chef Anthony Hodda buys only fresh local seafood, hormone-free meats, and organic farm produce. And does he produce! Starters include sourdough clam fritters and cold smoked salmon with peppercress cream. The house salad is an unusual collection of local edible greens, including arugula, anise, and radish greens, with a dandelion/honey-mustard dressing. Dinner entrées include rockfish steamed in nori, grilled lamb in a loganberry-liqueur/pepper sauce, and kelp fettuccine with sweet peppers and mushrooms. Eat all you want (free refills) of half a dozen colorful vegetables and three homemade breads. Desserts, baked daily, include a chocolate-hazelnut-mousse torte and Okanagan apple pie. There's free parking in the lot in the evening.

THE TEAHOUSE RESTAURANT, Ferguson Point, Stanley Park. Tel. 669-3281.
   Cuisine: CONTINENTAL. **Reservations:** Required. **Bus:** 19.
$ Prices: Appetizers $3.50–$7.25; main courses $11.95–$19.95. AE, MC, V.
   Open: Lunch Mon–Sat 11:30am–2:30pm; dinner daily 5:30–10pm; brunch Sun 10:30am–2:30pm.

Like a Victorian country home, this garden mansion is located in the middle of Stanley Park, surrounded by shrubbery against a backdrop of large fir trees. Once a wartime officer's home, it was later an actual teahouse before evolving into this fine-dining establishment. Both the drawing room, with its soft pastel decor, and the conservatory, a newer glassed-in wing, present panoramic views of mountainous Howe Sound and toward Vancouver Island across the Strait of Georgia.

   The cuisine is as *haute* as the view. A diner might start with teahouse mushrooms, salad of smoked chicken breast, or duck-and-veal pâté. Among the outstanding seafood entrées are gratinée de St-Jacques au vermouth, symphony de fruit de mer, and canneloni stuffed with creamy spinach and crabmeat. Heartier eaters might opt for the rack of lamb or grilled fillet steak Café de Paris with herb butter. Free parking.

MODERATE

CAFE DE PARIS, 751 Denman St., near Robson St. Tel. 687-1418.
   Cuisine: FRENCH BISTRO. **Reservations:** Recommended. **Bus:** 8.
$ Prices: Appetizers $5–$8; main courses $14–$17. AE, MC, V.
   Open: Lunch Tues–Fri 11:30am–2pm; dinner Mon–Sat 5:30–10:30pm.

Ask almost anyone: This is the closest thing in western Canada to a Left Bank bistro. Crowded and smoky, its walls lined with etchings and the menu scrawled on a blackboard, this place will make you feel welcome, even if the service is sometimes a little icy—but then, that's Paris. Locals come back again and again. Why? For the bohemian ambience? To read *Le Monde* and listen to Piaf and Aznavour? If truth be known, it's for the pommes frites.

   Chef Patrice Suhner's steak au poivre is superb. That could also be said about his onion soup, calf brains, kidneys in cream and mustard, coq au vin, mussels baked with garlic, and other traditional preparations. Every entrée is accompanied by a generous serving of vegetables, and the wine cellar is excellent. But still they flock back for the finger food—the french fries. Even the highbrow food critics rave. Street parking.

THE CHEF AND THE CARPENTER, 1745 Robson St., between Bidwell and Denman Sts. Tel. 687-2700.
   Cuisine: FRENCH. **Reservations:** Required Sat–Sun. **Bus:** 8.

$ Prices: Appetizers $3.50–$5.95; main courses $12.95–$17.95. AE, DC, ER, MC, V.

Open: Lunch daily 11:30am–2pm; dinner daily 5:30–10pm.

There hasn't been a carpenter in the business for several years, but the chef is still attracting a regular crowd. Folks keep coming back to this cozy establishment as they might to a close friend's living room. Oil paintings and family portraits adorn the old-fashioned blue wallpaper, and lace curtains hang in the windows.

Diners might start with clams Bourgogne or a cognac pâté with veal and chicken livers, then devour a Caesar salad prepared tableside. Popular entrées include sweetbreads Lisbonne in a madeira sauce, rack of lamb in shallots, and scallops Bombay with a curry-and-pear sauce. Every plate is piled high with five vegetables, and there's always a tempting dessert selection, including homemade ice creams, parfaits, and the famous chocolate-hazelnut cake. The predominantly French wine list starts at around $15 and climbs to around $90. On-street parking available.

CHEZ THIERRY, 1674 Robson St., near Bidwell St. Tel. 688-0919.

Cuisine: COUNTRY-STYLE FRENCH. **Reservations:** Recommended; required Sat–Sun. **Bus:** 8.

$ Prices: Appetizers $5–$10; main courses $10–$16.95. AE, DC, ER, MC, V.

Open: Dinner only, daily 5:30–10:30pm.

One thing you can say about Thierry Damilano: He's a good sport. Whether he's coaching the Canadian national windsurfing team (a daytime pursuit) or practicing fencing, the friendly Frenchman always finds time to greet and entertain his guests. Many diners, in fact, order champagne (the real stuff) just to watch Damilano open it for them—with his saber—in a single lightning slash. That's the sort of trick that keeps this little (16 tables) neighborhood restaurant packed, especially on weekends.

Chef François Launay prefers traditional country recipes to nouvelle cuisine, but he prepares them with a modern touch. The duck terrine and the watercress-and-smoked-salmon salad are fine starters. Outstanding entrées include red snapper poached with sweet red peppers in a saffron sauce, and pork roast with walnuts and honey. The grillades are superb, the desserts delectable. There's on-street parking available.

THE FISH HOUSE IN STANLEY PARK, 2099 Beach Ave., Stanley Park. Tel. 681-7275.

Cuisine: SEAFOOD. **Reservations:** Recommended Sun and in summer. **Bus:** 19.

$ Prices: Appetizers $3.25–$6.95; main courses $7.95–$11.95 at lunch, $11.95–$14.95 at brunch, $9.95–$15.95 at dinner. Two-for-one "early bird" dinners before 6pm. AE, DC, ER, JCB, MC, V.

Open: Lunch Mon–Sat 11:30am–2:30pm; dinner daily 5–10pm; brunch Sun 11am–2:30pm. **Closed:** Mon Oct–Apr 1.

Long known as the Beach House, this heritage building, set amid the trees, lawns, and tennis courts of Stanley Park, was renovated and renamed by its new owner Bud Kanke in 1990. As with the two other establishments run by this successful and respected restaurateur (Joe Fortes Seafood House and The Cannery), the emphasis is on denizens of the deep, as reflected in the tastefully done maritime decor. Subdued green and burgundy are the colors of choice; together with large, bright windows, they provide the setting for the fish prints and West Coast fishing memorabilia that hang on the walls.

The dishes coming from the kitchen taste even more delectable than they look. The daily fresh sheet offers marlin, shark, skate, swordfish, and other fish, served with lemon butter. Start with a fish sampler or shrimp and corn fritters with lemon thyme yogurt sauce. Menu entrées include a tangy ginger hot pot with salmon, snapper, clams, mussels and prawns, or blackened mahi mahi with fresh-fruit salsa. Lamb, beef, and vegetarian platters are also available. Lord Stanley's Oyster Bar serves those who prefer morsels of mollusk. There's free validated parking in the evening, $1 at lunch.

ICHIBANKAN, 770 Thurlow St., near Robson St. Tel. 682-6262.
   Cuisine: JAPANESE SUSHI. **Reservations:** Not required.
   Bus: 8.
$ **Prices:** $9–$15 per dish. AE, ER, DC, JCB, MC, V.
   Open: Mon–Thurs 11:30am–10:30pm, Fri–Sat 11:30am–11pm.
In Tokyo, the name would mean "Number One Place." There's no doubt that this was the first place in Vancouver to introduce conveyor-belt sushi. That's right: In the basement of an antique-looking brick building, you can belly up to a big sushi bar, watch the *maki*-makers, and choose your own California roll from the varieties making the circuit in front of your eyes.

You'll notice four colors of plates—red, white, black, and green. Each designates a different price. When you've had enough, you'll be charged for each plate in front of you. For those who don't like sushi, there's a small selection of tempura and teriyaki dishes. On-street parking.

NAKORNTHAI RESTAURANT, 1157 Davie St. Tel. 683-6621.
   Cuisine: THAI. **Bus:** 8.
$ **Prices:** Appetizers $4.30–$5.80; dinner main courses $8.80–$13.80; lunches $4.95–$7.50. AE, DC, MC, V.
   Open: Lunch Mon–Fri 11:30am–2:30pm; dinner daily 5–11pm.
   Closed: Holidays.
If you find Szechuan cooking too hot, you'd be well advised to steer clear of Thai cuisine as well. If, however, your palate craves chiles, lemon grass, and coconut milk, the Nakornthai is for you. In an atmosphere of Thai temple art, you can sup on tom yum goong (hot-and-sour prawn soup), gang kiew-wah gai (chicken and eggplant in a green curry), nuea ob (beef strips in honey, soy sauce, and garlic), and pahd Thai (stir-fried rice noodles with tofu, shrimp, eggs, and peanuts). There's an $8.45 luncheon buffet on Thursday and Friday.

PEPITA'S, 1170 Robson St., near Bute St. Tel. 669-4736.
   Cuisine: MEXICAN/SPANISH. **Reservations:** Not accepted.
   Bus: 8.
$ **Prices:** Appetizers $2.95–$8.95; main courses $5.95–$7.95 at lunch, $6.95–$15.95 at dinner. AE, DC, MC, V.
   Open: Daily 11:30am–11pm (in summer, Fri–Sat 11:30am–midnight).

Across one wall of this lively establishment are written the words: "Viva la Luna! Viva el Sol!" In English, we'd say, "Long Live the Moon! Long Live the Sun!" And indeed, Pepita's is hopping both night and day. This is a little piece of Mexico in the middle of Robsonstrasse—red-tile floor, piñatas hanging from the ceiling around the bar, *muchos* terra-cotta flowerpots and other south-of-the-border ceramics, and mariachi or Latin salsa music on tape. Weekend evenings, a line forms outside to graze on tapas and listen to the live Spanish guitar.

All meals start with a free basket of chips and salsa. You can choose standard Cal-Mex fare like tacos, burritos, and enchiladas, or dive into a house special such as carnero al horno (roast lamb in tequila sauce) or huachinango à la Veracruzana (red snapper in tomato-and-caper sauce). Every plate comes with black beans and a healthy helping of guacamole. Street parking.

It's equally busy at Pepita's in the Kitsilano district at 2041 W. Fourth Ave. (tel. 732-8884) and in North Vancouver at 180 W. Esplanade (tel. 980-2405).

QUILICUM NATIVE INDIAN RESTAURANT, 1724 Davie St., near Denman St. Tel. 681-7044.
Cuisine: NORTHWEST COAST NATIVE. **Reservations:** Recommended. **Bus:** 8.
$ **Prices:** Appetizers $4.95–$7.95; main courses $10.95–$19.95. AE, MC, V.
Open: Lunch Wed–Fri 11:30am–2:30pm; dinner daily 5–9:30pm.

Imagine it's the mid-19th century, and the white explorers have yet to establish a settlement at the site of modern Vancouver. You descend a flight of stairs to what could be a Northwest native longhouse. It's a simple room, furnished with wooden benches and tables, and a blazing fire keeps you warm. The pillars are family totems, the masks are carved masterpieces, and the rhythm of chants can be heard in the background. This is the Quilicum—the only restaurant where diners can still feast in the manner of the original B.C. coastal residents.

The only major adjustments have been the modernization of cooking technology and the addition of seasonings to make the foods more appealing to modern palates. Smoked oolichans (small fish), herring roe on kelp, alder-barbecued oysters, and bannock bread serve as appetizers for what follows: barbecued caribou, rabbit, or goat ribs; baked juniper duck with cabbage and wild rice; or smoked salmon with fiddleheads, sweet potato, and hazelnuts. For dessert, try whipped sopalallie berries or cold raspberry soup. The artworks around you are also for sale. There's a small lot for free parking.

ROBSON GRILL, 1675 Robson St., near Bidwell St. Tel. 681-8030.
Cuisine: STEAKS/SEAFOOD. **Reservations:** Recommended. **Bus:** 8.
$ **Prices:** Appetizers $2.50–$6.95; main courses $6.95–$16.95. AE, MC, V.
Open: Mon–Wed 11:30am–12:30am, Thurs–Sat, 11:30am–1:30am, Sun 11:30am–midnight.

"RG's," as it's called, wants to be known as a restaurant that combines creative cuisine with an entertaining atmosphere. Like the turn-of-the-century railroad station it resembles, it's on the right track. Around the huge beams that support black wooden arches and wrought-iron lighting fixtures, there's seating for 290 guests. In the center of the room, near the entrance, is a large bar island; behind it is a dance floor and bandstand where local groups perform '60s and '70s rock on Friday and Saturday from 8:30pm.

Homemade soups and sandwiches are a hit at lunchtime, while eggs Haida (with smoked salmon) highlight weekend brunches. Everyday dinner entrées include salmon Wellington and chicken stuffed with pistachio and Brie. New York cheesecake is the No. 1 dessert. RG's even has a kids' menu (burgers, pasta, fish and chips) that comes with crayons. There's free parking.

BUDGET

THE FRESGO INN, 1138 Davie St., near Thurlow St. Tel. 689-1332.
   Cuisine: CAFETERIA. **Bus:** 8.
$ **Prices:** $3.50–$8 per dish. No credit cards.
   Open: Mon–Sat 8am–3am, Sun 8am–midnight.

As a late-night hangout for all types of men and women, the Fresgo is an institution for Vancouver people-watchers. A garden-style buffet/cafeteria, it serves enormous breakfasts, a classy array of hamburgers, and a variety of other tasty dishes. Davie Street night owls enjoy the taped rock music, which seems to play nonstop.

GREENHUT VIETNAMESE CUISINE, 1429 Robson St., near Broughton St. Tel. 688-3688.
   Cuisine: VIETNAMESE. **Bus:** 8.
$ **Prices:** Appetizers $2.75–$7.50; main courses $5.50–$7.25 at lunch, $6.50–$15.95 at dinner. AE, MC, V.
   Open: Sun–Thurs 11am–11pm, Fri–Sat 11am–1am.
Across the street from the Sheraton-Landmark is this fine little restaurant. Although it uses a mural of Vietnamese fishermen as its logo, fish is not a highlight of its menu. The food is great nevertheless, especially the curries and salad rolls. There are plenty of vegetarian dishes and combination meals, with brochettes—pork, chicken, beef, lamb, and seafood—a big favorite. You'll find another branch in Vancouver: in Kerrisdale at 41st Avenue and West Boulevard.

HEIDELBERG HOUSE, 1164 Robson St., near Bute St. Tel. 682-1661.
   Cuisine: GERMAN. **Reservations:** Recommended Sat–Sun evenings. **Bus:** 8.
$ **Prices:** Full dinner $8–$11. AE, DC, MC, V.
   Open: Daily 10am–midnight.
Like a Bavarian chalet in the middle of Robsonstrasse, the Heidelberg House is a cozy, dimly lit, wood-paneled establishment with Black Forest murals and stags' heads on the walls. Come for lunch, when there's an all-you-can-eat buffet for just $7.25, or dinner, to try the famous schnitzels and Apfelstrudel.

PENNY LANE BISTRO & CAFE, 1025 Robson St. Tel. 689-1888.
   Cuisine: INTERNATIONAL. **Bus:** 8.
$ **Prices:** $3.95–$10.95 per dish. AE, DC, DISC, ER, MC, V.
   Open: Daily 11:30am–1:30am.

This restaurant/lounge really isn't British, but the Beatles certainly were! You'll hear their music before you see the establishment—"She Loves You" and "Yellow Submarine" descend from a second-floor balcony over Robsonstrasse. The ambience is dedicated to the Fab Four: Even the menu is shaped like a record jacket and liberally spiced with John Lennon–style humor. There are salads, burgers, and other standard fare, but the specialties of the house are meat or fish schnitzels and a C-food (seafood) hot pot.

ROOSTER'S QUARTERS, 836 Denman St., at Haro St. Tel. 689-8023.
   Cuisine: CHICKEN. **Bus:** 8.
$ Prices: $6–$9 per dish. AE, MC, V.
   Open: Mon–Fri 11:30am–11pm, Sat–Sun noon–11pm.
When mealtime rolls around, you need only look for the lines in the streets to find this French-Canadian chicken eatery. Amid prints of Montréal scenes, you'll discover superb Québec-style barbecued chicken, crispy on the outside, melt-in-your-mouth tender on the inside. Quarter and half chickens are served with french fries, cole slaw, and a soft bun.

SAIGON, 1500 Robson St., at Nicola St. Tel. 682-8020.
   Cuisine: VIETNAMESE. **Bus:** 8.
$ Prices: Main courses $6.95–$16. AE, DC, MC, V.
   Open: Sun–Thurs 11am–11pm, Fri–Sat 11am–midnight.
Large and tastefully plain, the Saigon has no Asian imprint except in the general atmosphere. The only decorations are sprigs of foliage above the low, soft, rattan-shielded lamps. The portions of food are generous and the service is fast and courteous. Although there are all kinds of meat and seafood dishes on the menu, vegetarians will be especially pleased with the choices offered. There's an extensive list of beers, wines, and liqueurs.

SEA LEVEL BISTRO, 1795 Beach Ave. Tel. 669-2225.
   Cuisine: INTERNATIONAL. **Reservations:** Recommended.
Bus: 8.
$ Prices: $6.95–$12.95 per dish. AE, ER, JCB, MC, V.
   Open: Sun–Thurs 11:30am–10:30pm, Fri–Sat 11:30am–midnight.
The lower level of the English Bay Café (see above) is a popular meeting place for West End sophisticates. The cuisine is upscale but lighter and offered in somewhat smaller portions than upstairs. There are finger foods, salads, sandwiches, and pastas, as well as lamburgini (a ground-lamb burger), salmon burger, and Mexicali fettuccine. Parking is free at lunch, $4 (valet) in the evening.

SETTEBELLO, 1133 Robson St., near Thurlow St. Tel. 681-7377.
   Cuisine: LIGHT ITALIAN. **Bus:** 8.
$ Prices: $5.95–$11.95 per dish. AE, DC, ER, MC, V.
   Open: Daily 11:30am–midnight.
When the sun is out, this may be the most popular place for the Robsonstrasse shopping set to enjoy a light meal and a glass of chianti—it's the roof-deck patio of the Umberto Menghi restaurant. Salads, pasta, and finger foods like calamari and breaded zucchini are popular, but the individual brick-oven pizzas are best. Tell the server what you want, from seafood to salsiccia (spinach and chile peppers).

SOUVLAKI PLACE, 1181 Denman St., near Beach Ave. Tel. 689-3064.

   Cuisine: GREEK. **Bus:** 8.

$ **Prices:** $4.25–$6.50 per dish. No credit cards.

   Open: Daily 11:30am–11pm.

This is where English Bay beachgoers flock for souvlaki, the skewered lamb-and-vegetable dish with the incredibly inviting aroma. There's a handful of tables inside the unlicensed diner, but if the weather cooperates, patrons often take their food across Beach Avenue and stretch their legs in the grass or the sand. A very tasty falafel is also available.

WON MORE, 1184 Denman St., near Davie St. Tel. 688-8856.

   Cuisine: SZECHUAN. **Bus:** 8.

$ **Prices:** Main courses average $10. No credit cards.

   Open: Dinner only, daily 4–10:30pm.

The hot-and-spicy cuisine of China's Szechuan province holds sway at this small second-floor eatery. The down-home Chinese hospitality consists of a three-wok kitchen in the front window and steaming plates being rushed to crowded tables. The Kung Pao chicken (with the red chiles) is superb, and the moo shu pork is memorable.

3. EAST OF DOWNTOWN

EXPENSIVE

THE HART HOUSE, 6664 Deer Lake Ave., Burnaby. Tel. 298-4278.

   Cuisine: WEST COAST/CONTINENTAL. **Reservations:** Required. **Bus:** 131, 132, or 144 to Sperling Ave. **Directions:** Take the Kensington South exit off Trans Canada Hwy. 1, turn left on Canada Way, right on Sperling Avenue, and then make an almost immediate right onto Deer Lake Avenue.

$ **Prices:** Appetizers $3.95–$7.95; main courses $6.95–$11.95 at lunch, $9.95–$19.95 at dinner. AE, DC, ER, MC, V.

   Open: Lunch Mon–Fri 11:30am–2:30pm; dinner daily 5:30–10pm; brunch Sun 10:30am–2:30pm.

There's an Old English country charm about this 1910 Tudor Revival-style mansion on the shore of Deer Lake in suburban Burnaby. An elegant residence until 1979, its 3½ acres of grounds—once known as Rosedale Gardens—were visited by flower lovers from across Canada. (This setting is now popular for weddings: One is scheduled every Saturday a year in advance.) Local government offered the mansion to Hollywood for the filming of several movies until it was renovated as this fine restaurant in 1988. The house has a flat-roofed central square tower, step gables, and leaded-glass windows. Inside, the walls display historical photos of the families who once lived here. Ask for a tour of the three-story house after (or before) dinner.

The menu, heavy on wild game and local seafood, changes seasonally. Look for such appetizers as steamed clams and homemade pâté. Outstanding entrées include halibut steak, grilled and topped with baby shrimp and lemon-cream sauce; quail stuffed and roasted with fresh herbs; and Alberta prime rib of beef with Yorkshire pudding. For dessert, consider bread pudding with warm whiskey sauce, or honeydew melon in ginger-lemon syrup with meringue. Free parking.

MODERATE

THE CANNERY, 2205 Commissioner St., near Victoria Dr. Tel. 254-9606.

> **Cuisine:** SEAFOOD. **Reservations:** Recommended. **Bus:** 7 to Victoria Drive. **Directions:** From downtown, head east on Hastings Street, turn left on Victoria Drive (two blocks past Commercial Drive), and then right on Commissioner Street.
>
> **$ Prices:** Appetizers $4–$7; main courses $12–$20. AE, DC, DISC, MC, V.
>
> **Open:** Lunch Mon–Fri 11:30am–2:30pm; dinner daily 5:30–10:30pm.

Sometimes fish just tastes better when it's eaten on the docks, within sight of the vessels that hauled it in and carried it to shore. With its panoramic view of industry along Burrard Inlet's southeastern shore, the Cannery re-creates the mood of canneries that dotted the British Columbia coastline a century ago. The tin roof, rustic beams, and barn-board interior show off a collection of lobster pots and other fishing artifacts.

Those in-the-know order their seafood cooked West Coast style on the restaurant's 1,000° mesquite grill. But if you want your salmon (or whatever else happens to be fresh) baked or poached, pan-fried or barbecued, just ask. Sautéed scallops and prawns, Nova Scotia lobster, Alaskan smoked black cod, king crab legs, and bouillabaisse are other delectable choices. The Cannery is a five-time B.C. gold medalist for its wine list. Free parking.

THE PINK PEARL, 1132 E. Hastings St., near Clark Dr. Tel. 253-4316.

> **Cuisine:** CANTONESE/MANDARIN. **Reservations:** Recommended for dinner (not accepted for dim sum). **Bus:** 14, 20, or 21.
>
> **$ Prices:** Three main dishes (for two people) about $35; dim sum lunch about $20 for two. AE, DC, MC, V.
>
> **Open:** Dim sum daily 9am–2:30pm; dinner Sun–Thurs 5–9:30pm, Fri–Sat 5–10:30pm.

Vancouver's largest Chinese restaurant has the distinctive air of the dim sum parlors of Hong Kong's Nathan Road. Arrive in the middle of the day at this theater-size 650-seat establishment and you'll find yourself dodging dozens of cart-pushers shuttling steaming bamboo baskets of finger . . . er . . . chopstick food from table to table. Despite its huge capacity, you may still have to wait for a table on the weekend. Evenings are somewhat less frenetic, and you may be able to enjoy watching the live seafood tanks near the doors.

Fruits of the sea highlight the menu here, and the preparations include the unusual as well as the traditional. Stuffed blue crab shells and fillet of sole sautéed with snow peas are two of the best offerings. If you're in the mood for fresh shellfish (abalone, clams, geoducks, oysters, or scallops), crustaceans (shrimp, crab, or lobster), or fish (you name it), you'll probably find it here. Parking is free.

RUBINA TANDOORI RESTAURANT, 1962 Kingsway, at Victoria Dr. Tel. 874-3621.

Cuisine: INDIAN. **Reservations:** Recommended. **Bus:** 19, 20, or 21.

$ Prices: Appetizers $2.25–$13.95; main courses $7.25–$14.95; full meals (for two) $35–$64. AE, DISC, ER, MC, V.

Open: Dinner only, Mon–Sat 5–11pm.

Here's another restaurant with a less-than-attractive exterior but wonderful cuisine. Located on one of the more unsightly stretches of the unsightly Kingsway, the Rubina—like many Indian restaurants—entices diners with its front counter of take-out sweets and snack items. Inside, amid the Asian tapestries and artworks, is an elegant restaurant that runs the gamut of Indian cuisine: tandoori and Moghul dishes from the north, Tamil curries and sambhars from the south, Kerala seafood, Gujerati-style vegetarian, Bombay vindaloos, and Punjabi favorites.

Many diners prefer the oven-baked tandoori dishes, which (as the restaurant's name indicates) are the specialty of the house. Others like the curries (try the fish masala) or vegetarian meals. If you're not familiar with Indian desserts, here's the place to sample them. Personally I prefer those made without rosewater. On-street parking.

SZECHUAN CHONGQING RESTAURANT, 2495 Victoria Dr., at Broadway. Tel. 254-7434.

Cuisine: SZECHUAN. **Reservations:** Recommended. **Bus:** 9, 20, or 21.

$ Prices: Three main dishes (for two people) $25–$40. AE, ER, MC, V.

Open: Mon–Thurs 11am–3pm and 5–10pm, Fri 11am–3pm and 5pm–midnight, Sat 11am–midnight, Sun 11am–10pm.

Ensconced in a converted fast-food franchise, this restaurant is a prime example of why you shouldn't judge a book by its cover. The owners have paid minimal attention to the building's exterior and have given the interior a quiet once-over. What matters, however, is the food: Many believe that this restaurant produces the best Szechuan cooking in western Canada. Indeed, the owners are natives of that southwestern Chinese province and their dishes are hearty and spicy.

Two frequently recommended offerings are Tan Tan noodles, a thick soup with peanuts, dried shrimp, garlic, and red chili peppers; and shredded chicken or beef, served with a hot brown sauce on a bed of crispy spinach. For the more adventurous, the camphor-smoked duck is superb. Parking is free.

TOMMY O'S OFF BROADWAY, 2590 Commercial Dr., near Broadway. Tel. 874-3445.

Cuisine: NORTHERN ITALIAN. **Reservations:** Recommended. **SkyTrain:** Broadway. **Bus:** 9 or 21.

$ Prices: Appetizers $4–$8; main courses $9.25–$16.95. AE, DC, ER, MC, V.

Open: Mon–Sat 11:30am–11pm; Sun brunch 10am–3pm, dinner 5–11pm.

This bright trattoria is actually owned by an Irishman, Tommy O'Brien, who long ago discovered that he preferred pasta to potatoes. Marble and brass, as well as white tile and carved pine create an elegant setting.

It is widely believed that the fettuccine Alfredo here is the best in Vancouver, but the other pastas aren't far behind. Made fresh each day in the open kitchen, the pastas can be combined with various sauces to produce 16 or more different dishes. The cioppino is superb, with lobster and other fresh seafood in a clam broth. Or try the rack of lamb, the veal scaloppine, or the barbecued baby back ribs. On-street parking.

BUDGET

NEW SEOUL, 1682 E. Broadway, at Commercial Dr. Tel. 872-1922.
   Cuisine: KOREAN. **Bus:** 9, 20, or 21.
$ Prices: Three dishes (for two people) $18–$25. MC, V.
   Open: Mon–Sat 11am–11pm, Sun and holidays 3–11pm.
Cook your own dinner on top of your table: That's the concept behind what may be the city's best Korean eatery. Every table has a small gas burner for cooking marinated strips of beef, pork, chicken, or prawns. And since you're in Seoul, you won't want to miss Korea's favorite appetizer—kim chee, a cold, intensely spicy pickled cabbage dish.

VONG'S KITCHEN, 5989 Fraser St., at E. 44th Ave. Tel. 327-4627.
   Cuisine: NORTHERN CHINESE. **Reservations:** Recommended. **Bus:** 8.
$ Prices: Three dishes (for two people) $14–$30. No credit cards.
   Open: Dinner only, Wed–Sat 5–9:30pm, Sun 4:30–9pm.
Tiny and crowded, with simple Formica tables and steamed-up windows, Vong's may be Vancouver's favorite Asian hole-in-the-wall. The fact that it's not licensed to serve alcoholic beverages and requires payment in cash seems to attract even more people to its jade chicken and atomic rice. Ask about Tommy Vong's cooking classes and recipes.

4. SOUTH OF DOWNTOWN

EXPENSIVE

BISHOP'S, 2183 W. Fourth Ave., at Yew St. Tel. 738-2025.
   Cuisine: PACIFIC NORTHWEST. **Reservations:** Required. **Bus:** 4 or 7.
$ Prices: Appetizers $5.50–$8.95; main courses $10.50–$13.95 at lunch, $12.50–$22.95 at dinner. AE, DC, MC, V.
   Open: Lunch Mon–Fri 11:30am–2:30pm; dinner Mon–Sat 5:30–11pm, Sun 5:30–10pm.
Many Vancouverites regard John Bishop as the ultimate host. He personally greets all diners with a warm and gracious welcome, escorts them to their table in his small but elegant restaurant, and introduces them to a catalog of fine wines and what he describes as "contemporary home-cooking." Bright, stunning Jack Shadbolt abstracts dot the walls and menu covers, and taped light jazz provides the background sounds, giving the establishment a distinctively arty feel. The decor is candlelight and white linen, the service impeccable.

The menu changes from time to time, but certain time-honored items remain. Popular starters include herb-crusted goat cheese in red-pepper coulis or penne with tomatoes, rosemary, and chorizo. Entrées may include steamed mussels with champagne and chervil; grilled scallops with citrus fettuccine; lamb cooked with fresh plums, cherries, and clover honey; and charcoal-grilled fillet of beef with horseradish and Dijon mustard. Desserts? Try the papaya flan in macadamia crust, or the sweet that this city raves about—Death by Chocolate. With port, of course. Valet parking is available.

MALINEE'S, 2153 W. Fourth Ave., between Arbutus and Yew Sts. Tel. 737-0097.

Cuisine: THAI. **Reservations:** Recommended. **Bus:** 4.

$ Prices: Appetizers $4.75–$9.75; three main dishes with rice (for two people) $35–$60. AE, MC, V.

Open: Lunch Mon–Fri 11:30am–2:30pm; dinner Sun–Thurs 5:30–10pm, Fri–Sat 5:30–11pm.

Two former *farang* (white foreigners) returned to North America from Bangkok and brought with them a gourmet chef, Kem Thong. Together, they opened Malinee's, a restaurant truly a step above others of its kind in both menu and service. Amid the greenery, neoclassical Thai paintings, and batik tablecloths are attentive servers in handsome black-and-white outfits. Malinee's is to other Thai inns what a fine French restaurant is to a bistro.

Lovers of spicy Thai food who are used to curries, lemongrass, coconut milk, and chili-peanut sauces will find those here, but much more besides. A meal for four might start with stir-fried clams or steamed mussels, chicken saté, spring rolls, and fried cashews. Follow that with a lemon-shrimp soup (tom yum kung), tenderloin of beef marinated in soy and garlic with fresh coriander (nua ga tiam), chicken cashew in red curry (kai pad pangali), vegetables, and rice (to reduce the heat). Don't miss the special house curry of squid, shrimp, and mussels stir-fried in coconut milk with green and red chilies. Try a tropical fruit—jackfruit or rambutan—with mango or coconut ice cream to finish. Street parking.

MONK McQUEEN'S, upstairs at 601 Stamps Landing, False Creek. Tel. 877-1351.

Cuisine: SEAFOOD/CONTINENTAL. **Reservations:** Recommended. **Bus:** 50 or (in summer) catch the Aquabus water taxi from Granville Island public market. **Directions:** From the 900 block of West Sixth Avenue, turn north onto Moberly Road, which ends at Stamps Landing.

$ Prices: Appetizers $4.50–$8.75; main courses $12.50–$20; fixed-price menus $14–$18 at lunch, $22–$32 at dinner. AE, DC, ER, MC, V.

Open: Lunch daily 11:30am–2pm; dinner daily 5:30–11pm.

I visited Monk McQueen's the night the Rolling Stones performed at B.C. Place stadium. From the restaurant's outside terrace, I could see the arena's billowy dome directly across False Creek, framed by the downtown Vancouver skyline. I could feel the pulsing rhythms; I could clearly hear each word Mick Jagger sang, which (I later learned) was more than most concert attendees could say. What's more, I did so in a spacious, relaxed atmosphere. Monk McQueen's—built on pilings in False Creek—is actually two restaurants: McQueen's, the fine-dining establishment, and Monk's Oyster Bar, a ground-floor bistro (see my recommendation, below). McQueen's has a peaked, skylit roof and wrap-around windows that offer full advantage of the view. In summer there's live music and dancing during the dinner hours on Friday and Saturday.

The fare is quite varied, with such starters as smoked duck soup, baked orzo, pan-fried calamari, and potato-anchovy-caper salad. The choice of entrées includes B.C. salmon fillet with grilled or braised baby leeks, steamed Queen Charlotte crab with ginger aioli, and Icelandic scampi broiled with saffron sun-dried tomato beurre blanc. Carnivores will find steaks and other meats, as well as fresh fowl or game. Full four-course dinner menus are good value for big eaters. Valet parking.

MULVANEY'S, 1535 Johnston St., Granville Island. Tel. 685-6571.

Cuisine: CAJUN. **Reservations:** Recommended. **Bus:** 51.

$ Prices: Appetizers $3.95–$7.95; main courses $9.95–$19.95. AE, DC, ER, MC, V.

Open: Lunch (in the downstairs Créole Café only) Mon–Fri 11:30am–3:30pm; dinner Sun–Thurs 5:30–10pm, Fri–Sat 5:30–11pm; brunch Sun 11am–2pm.

This turn-of-the-century New Orleans–style restaurant was already flourishing when Granville Island was still an industrial wasteland. Mulvaney's was an act of courage that paid off—its owner believed that quality would prevail regardless of surroundings. Now that the "island" has blossomed into a popular attraction, this Cajun cantina can claim pioneer status. It's beautifully situated, overlooking a tranquil waterway, and the decor is a smart melange of swathed fabrics and rampant greenery. Adjacent to Granville Island's theater complex, Mulvaney's offers dinner-theater packages and dancing Thursday through Saturday nights.

The menu is pure Bourbon Street. Oysters Bienville, blackened prawns, and shrimp rémoulade are among the appetizers; there are outstanding soups like Cajun crab and sweet corn chowder, and tomato and fresh basil. The entrées, which guarantee a bit of tang for the tongue, include rack of lamb Lafayette topped with a Créole herb crust; West Coast jambalaya Jackson; Cajun cioppino; and halibut St. Charles, mesquite-grilled with a sauce of artichoke hearts, lemon, tomatoes, and white wine. Mulvaney's courtyard—the Créole Café—is open for lunch. Valet parking is available on Friday and Saturday.

PAPILLOTE FISH AND GAME HOUSE, 195 W. Broadway, at Columbia St. Tel. 876-9256.

Cuisine: SEAFOOD/GAME. **Reservations:** Recommended. **Bus:** 9.

$ Prices: Appetizers $4.50–$7.95; main courses $14.95–$22.95 at dinner. AE, MC, V.

Open: Lunch Mon–Fri 11:30am–2pm; dinner daily 5–10pm.

At this restaurant there's a beautiful view of the city and mountains, romantic piano music plays every night, and diners can sit either in a cozy fireplace-warmed room or a skylit sunroom. In either place, you'll always find a fresh rose on the table. But that's not why folks keep coming back to the Papillote—it's the menu that attracts them.

Nowhere else in Vancouver can diners find the incredible selection of fish and game offered here. In the seafood category, you'll find all the standards—salmon and snapper, scallops and clams—as well as dishes from other regions: John Dory from New Zealand, Arctic char from the Northwest Territories, goldeye from Lake Manitoba, barracuda, cabrilla, Hawaiian ono, and an additional three dozen-odd finny fellows (subject to availability, of course). And in the game category, how about Florida alligator? Colorado wild boar? Alberta buffalo? Yukon reindeer? B.C. pheasant? There's on-street parking.

TOJO'S RESTAURANT, 777 W. Broadway, at Willow St. Tel. 872-8050.
    Cuisine: JAPANESE. **Reservations:** Recommended; required for the sushi bar. **Bus:** 9.
$ **Prices:** Full dinners $10.50–$99.50 per person. AE, DC, MC, V.
    Open: Dinner only, Mon–Sat 5–11pm.

This stylish and ultramodern upstairs establishment might be consid-ered Vancouver's ultimate sushi bar. Its owner and chef, Hidekazu Tojo (call him "Tojo-san"), is renowned in local culinary circles for his inventiveness in sushi-making. He keeps his sushi bar small, no more than 10 seats, which enables him to banter with guests while molding fresh seafood and vegetables into memorable morsels.

There's more to Tojo's than the sushi bar. Whether you sit at a table or in a tatami room, you can choose to dine on *robata* (grilled) specialties, tempura, teriyaki, or his own version of nouvelle Japanese. Many dishes are seasonal. How much you pay depends on what kind of delicacies you choose: Omakase dinners, the chef's specialty, start around $25 per person, but the sky's the limit. Street parking.

MODERATE

ALMA STREET CAFE, 2505 Alma St., at W. 10th Ave. Tel. 222-2244.
    Cuisine: NOUVELLE/VEGETARIAN. **Reservations:** Recom-mended. **Bus:** 10 or 22.
$ **Prices:** Appetizers $3.25–$8.95; main courses $9–$14. AE, MC, V.
    Open: Mon–Thurs 7:30am–11pm, Fri 7:30am–midnight, Sat 8am–midnight, Sun and holidays 8am–10pm.

⭐ "Eclectic" might be a good word to describe the menu offerings of this neighborhood restaurant. The restaurant combines an interest in natural foods with a blend of Asian and West Coast cuisine in what owner Stephen Huddart describes as "a marriage of East and West." There are changing exhibits of photography or fabric art on the walls and modern jazz performances every Wednesday through Saturday night from 8 to 11:30pm. Huddart himself is no ordinary man—he's a former broadcast journalist and ethnomusicologist working in Latin America.

The menu changes daily. Some dishes to look for: Boston bluefish chowder, black-bean tortilla soup, warm scallop-and-ginger salad, grilled tofu-and-vegetable stir-fry, and a shrimp-avocado-artichoke-heart sandwich. Breakfast favorites include chocolate croissants, muesli and granola, and various egg dishes. There's an espresso bar, and the café is fully licensed. Parking is available in an adjacent pay lot.

THE AMOROUS OYSTER, 3236 Oak St., near W. 16th Ave. Tel. 732-5916.
    Cuisine: SEAFOOD. **Reservations:** Recommended. **Bus:** 17.
$ **Prices:** Appetizers $2.50–$6.95; main courses $9.50–$15.95. AE, ER, MC, V.

Open: Lunch Mon–Fri 11:30am–2:30pm; dinner Mon–Sat 5:30–11pm, Sun 5–10pm.

Seafood lovers find themselves as happy as clams inside this homey little pearl, whose decor resembles that of a European chalet. Blue tablecloths and curtains accent the natural-wood interior, and there are fresh flowers. The chalkboard menu features creative cooking (by Australian chef Sue Adams) in the West Coast, French, and Mediterranean styles.

As the name implies, oysters are a specialty. You can order them prepared in any of at least a half dozen different ways daily, including the angels on horseback and green-chili pesto. Combination plates are also available, and oyster chowder is a favorite among regulars. Entrées may include salmon dijonnaise, fettuccine and clams, tourtière, and zarzuela (a Spanish-style bouillabaisse). There's a carefully chosen wine list that features a "wine of the week." The amaretto cheesecake is an excellent dessert. Street parking.

BRIDGES, 1696 Duranleau St., Granville Island. Tel. 687-4400.

Cuisine: WEST COAST/SEAFOOD. **Reservations:** Recommended for upstairs. **Bus:** 51.

$ Prices: Upstairs, appetizers $3.95–$8.95; main courses $10–$22.95. Downstairs, main courses $5–$12. AE, ER, MC, V.

Open: Upstairs, dinner only, daily 5:30–10:30pm. Downstairs, breakfast 8:30–11:30am; lunch/dinner daily 11:30am–1am.

To your left is the Burrard Bridge. To your right, the Granville Bridge. In between, adjacent to the famous Granville Island Public Market on the island's west end, is this immense yellow structure, home of three distinct restaurants. Diners can choose among the formal elegance of the main dining room, the relaxed bistro ambience of the wine bar, or the even more relaxed pub, where fishing enthusiasts regale each other with tales of the one that got away. On the vast garden terrace overlooking False Creek—an extremely popular place on balmy summer evenings and weekend afternoons—diners order from the informal bistro menu.

The food is as fresh and as tasty as market produce, which most of it is. The dining room offers primarily nouvelle preparations of local and imported fish and game; the bistro menu specializes in pastas and finger foods. Parking is in an adjacent lot.

MONK'S OYSTER BAR, downstairs at 601 Stamps Landing, False Creek. Tel. 877-1351.

Cuisine: SEAFOOD. **Reservations:** Recommended. **Bus:** 50.

Directions: See Monk McQueen's, above.

$ Prices: Appetizers $3–$8.95; main courses $7.95–$13.50 at lunch, $12.95–$17.95 at dinner; fixed-price menus $13.50–$15.50 at lunch, $16.50–$22 at dinner. AE, DC, ER, MC, V.

Open: Mon–Fri 11:30am–10pm, Sat 11am–11pm, Sun 11am–10pm.

The ground floor of Monk McQueen's (see above) is an informal bistro-style restaurant specializing in seafood and tapas. Resembling a black-marble-and-neon New Orleans warehouse, it has an open grill in the center of the room surrounded by the oyster bar.

Most diners start with something from the oyster bar, like an oyster slider with vodka or tequila, then move on to something hot and spicy, such as Szechuan seafood stir-fry, blackened red snapper, or chicken jambalaya. Monk's also has good charcoal-broiled New York steaks; fresh fish are suggested on a weekly list. Valet parking available.

ORESTES' RESTAURANT, 3116 W. Broadway, at Balaclava St. Tel. 732-1461.
 Cuisine: GREEK. **Reservations:** Recommended. **Bus:** 10 or 22.
$ Prices: Appetizers $2.95–$9.95; main courses $4.95–$9.95 at lunch, $9.95–$16.95 at dinner. AE, DC, ER, MC, V.
 Open: Lunch daily 11:30am–4:30pm; dinner Sun–Wed 4:30–10pm, Thurs–Sat 4:30pm–midnight.

Melodic Greek music wafts through the rafters as a belly dancer, dripping with coins, glides past the tables. Although this taverna is large (it can seat 225 people), there are turnaway crowds on weekends—and on Thursday night, when scores of boisterous regulars from the surrounding Greek neighborhood drop in. With rooms on several levels, Orestes' decor varies from white plaster with sky-blue trim to a skylit courtyard with louvered windows, to rooms with hardwood floors and pillows on the benches. There's outdoor dining in summer, when the front doors open out and portions of the roof slide open.

Aficionados of Greek food know these appetizers: calamaraki, dolmades, spanakopita, oktapothi, hummus. They're all delicious! The avgolemono soup and Greek salad are good starters for those less familiar with Greek cuisine. Souvlaki kebabs of lamb, beef, chicken, pork, prawns, and salmon are roasted over an open fire and come with potatoes and vegetables. The moussaka and chicken-okra casseroles are superb, as are the prawns tourkolimano. Free parking.

PICASSO CAFE, 1626 W. Broadway. Tel. 732-3290.
 Cuisine: INTERNATIONAL. **Reservations:** Recommended. **Bus:** 10.
$ Prices: Appetizers around $3–$5; main courses $5.25–$10.95 at lunch, $8.95–$15.95 at dinner. No credit cards.
 Open: Lunch Mon–Fri 11:30am–2:30pm; dinner Tues–Fri 5:30–8pm, Fri–Sat 5–9pm; open for snacks between lunch and dinner.

Here's a worthwhile venture: on-the-job dining room and chef training for 12 youths, through the auspices of the Option Youth Society. Not only do the kids get paid for learning, but all the proceeds benefit the society's efforts. Pablo Picasso himself would have been pleased. Framed prints by many of Vancouver's finest artists hang on the walls of this garden-style café.

The food is surprisingly good and quite creative. A tasty and filling dinner might start with a hummus or Brazilian black-bean chowder, followed by snapper en papillote or salmon-on-a-raft (fillet of salmon on a whole-wheat bun). Lunches include sandwiches like "the Woodstock," with fresh veggies, mushrooms, and sprouts on eight-grain bread with herb yogurt. For dessert, there are unusual "heirloom recipes": tomato-soup cake, cardamom-beet cake, and molasses licorice pie. Street parking.

SANTA FE CAFE, 1688 W. Fourth Ave., at Pine St. Tel. 738-8777.
 Cuisine: SOUTHWESTERN. **Reservations:** Recommended; required on weekends. **Bus:** 4.

$ Prices: Appetizers $3.50–$7.95; main courses $5.50–$8.50 at lunch, $6.95–$16.95 at dinner. AE, MC, V.

Open: Lunch Mon–Fri 11:30am–2:30pm; dinner Sun–Thurs 5:30–10:30pm, Fri–Sat 5:30–11pm.

Like this restaurant's namesake city, the Santa Fe Café is a haven for local artists. Changing exhibits of their work are displayed on the walls; budding artists, meanwhile, are encouraged to be creative on the paper table coverings.

Southwestern food fanatics can certainly have their appetites satisfied here. There's corn and seafood chowder for starters, pan-fried linguine with jalapeños, southwestern-style crêpes, home-made canneloni, and a brilliant seafood chili con queso (made with fish, prawns, and scallops). Chef Kerry Lee's Asian roots are evident in such dishes as warm wild-mushroom salad, Chinese black beans, Oriental spicy lamb, chicken clay pot, and numerous sautés. Since there's no freezer here, everything's fresh, and the portions are unusually generous. On-street parking.

ZEPPO'S TRATTORIA, 1967 W. Broadway, near Maple St. Tel. 737-7444.

Cuisine: NOVELLA ITALIAN. **Reservations:** Required. **Bus:** 10.

$ Prices: Appetizers $3.95–$7.95; main courses $5.95–$10.95 at lunch, $7.50–$16.95 at dinner. AE, MC, V.

Open: Lunch Mon–Fri 11:30am–2:30pm; dinner daily 5:30–11pm.

A dynamic menu, exceptional food, moderate prices, great service— what more could a gourmet ask? How about music? An upbeat piano bar—sometimes jazz, sometimes classical—creates a near-perfect atmosphere for fine Italian food at Zeppo's Wednesday through Saturday nights. The decor is simple, a rose-colored interior with lime trim; and seating is limited to about 60 diners on a raised hardwood dais.

The menus change weekly. A choice of antipasto plates recently offered cold capicolla, bocconcini, olives, eggplant, and prawns, as well as hot shrimp in phyllo, duck sausage, oysters, snails, scallops, and squid. Stracciatella soup is a favorite of many regulars. Zeppo's features 10 pastas, including potato gnocchi in a rich meat sauce, and veal and spinach cannelloni. There's fresh seafood, such as grilled Hawaiian mahi mahi with ginger and lime; and meat or fowl plates like lamb shank on polenta. Parking is on the street or in an adjacent pay lot.

BUDGET

ATHENE'S, 3618 W. Broadway, at Collingwood St. Tel. 731-4135.

Cuisine: GREEK. **Reservations:** Recommended. **Bus:** 10 or 22.

$ Prices: Appetizers $3.95–$6.95; main courses $8.25–$11.95. AE, ER, MC, V.

Open: Daily 11:30am–11pm.

The atmosphere is pure Mediterranean: tile floors, bright white walls, classic vases set into niches, greenery spilling over the trellises that serve as room dividers. Greek music sets the mood for spanakopita (spinach pie), dolmades (stuffed grape leaves), oktapothi (pickled octopus with capers), calamari, moussaka, and other delicacies. Try the arni psito (lamb shoulder). The full bar features Greek wines like retsina, and liquors, such as ouzo.

DUTCH PANNEKOEK HOUSE, 3192 Oak St., at 16th Ave. Tel. 876-1913.

Cuisine: DUTCH PANCAKES. **Bus:** 9 or 17.
$ Prices: $3.45–$7.75 per dish. MC, V.
Open: Mon–Fri 8am–2:30pm, Sat–Sun 8am–3pm, holidays 9am–2pm.

This was the first restaurant of its type in North America, introducing the Dutch version of the French crêpe. The pannekoek is a solid meal: In fact, the house offers 36 varieties, from bacon, mushroom, and cheese, to apple, ginger, and strawberry with whipped cream—all of them platter size. You may encounter other Dutch Pannekoek Houses in the Vancouver area: It's a growing chain.

EARL'S, 1601 W. Broadway, at Fir St. Tel. 736-5663.

Cuisine: INTERNATIONAL. **Bus:** 9 or 10.
$ Prices: Appetizers $3.50–$7.95; main courses $5.95–$13.95. AE, MC, V.
Open: Sun–Thurs 11:30am–midnight, Fri–Sat 11:30am–1am. Parking: Free.

There are 12 Earl's restaurants in Greater Vancouver; this location is one of the more accessible. In this contemporary, relaxed atmosphere with wicker chairs, tragically hip penguins meander through an oversize menu that offers nachos and chicken wings, salads and sandwiches, pastas and stir-fries. The bar is big on margaritas and specialty cocktails. Free parking.

Other branches (close relatives) are Broadway Earl's, 901 W. Broadway (tel. 734-5995); Earl's On Top, downtown at 1185 Robson St. (tel. 669-0020); and Earl's Tin Palace, 303 Marine Dr., North Vancouver (tel. 984-4341).

FOGG N' SUDS, 3293 W. Fourth Ave., at Blenheim St. Tel. 73-BEERS.

Cuisine: INTERNATIONAL. **Bus:** 7.
$ Prices: Appetizers $1.75–$5.95; main courses $5.95–$9.95. AE, MC, V.
Open: Daily 11:30am–midnight.

The flagship of a growing chain of restaurants occupies a semi-basement room near Kitsilano. It's named in part for Phileas Fogg (of *Around the World in 80 Days*), but the "Suds" take priority here: Canada's largest beer list has some 250 brews from 36 countries. (Customers get passports stamped for each new beer they consume.) The menu is also worldly: American hamburgers, Mexican nachos, Italian pastas, Japanese stir-fries, Greek calamari.

There's another Fogg n' Suds in the West End, at 1393 Robson St., at Jervis St. (tel. 683-BEER); also on West Broadway near Cambie (tel. 87-BEERS); and in Burnaby and Victoria.

HEAVEN & EARTH INDIA CURRY HOUSE, 1754 W. Fourth Ave., near Burrard St. Tel. 732-5313.

Cuisine: INDIAN CURRIES. **Reservations:** Recommended.
Bus: 4.
$ Prices: $7.75–$13.95 per dish. AE, DC, MC, V.

Open: Dinner only, Sun–Thurs 5–10pm, Fri–Sat 5–11pm.

Curry is not, as many Americans choose to believe, a yellow powder that comes out of a spice container. The word may refer to any blend of spices, though cardamom, cumin, and turmeric are common ingredients. This restaurant makes it right, in dozens of different ways (and different heat levels). The name is apt: There's a dark, earthy atmosphere here, but the food is heavenly. The dishes are typical of both southern and northern India, with about an equal choice of meat or vegetarian plates.

ISADORA'S COOPERATIVE RESTAURANT, 1540 Old Bridge St., off Cartwright St., Granville Island. Tel. 681-8816.

Cuisine: WEST COAST. **Reservations:** Recommended for groups of six or more. **Bus:** 50 or 51.

$ **Prices:** Appetizers $2.75–$6.95; main courses $6.25–$12.95; kids' menu $4.75. MC, V.

Open: Mon–Fri 7:30am–9pm, Sat–Sun 9am–10pm. **Closed:** Mon in winter. Parking: Free.

This is the only restaurant in Vancouver that will offer you part-ownership (at $100 a share) along with a meal, should you be inclined to invest in Isadora's philosophy of community support. Most patrons, however, are content to pay low prices for hearty family-style cuisine. Appetizers include vegetarian nutcakes and seafood Danika—a Scandinavian-style ceviche of fresh seafood marinated with fresh dill and juniper. Salads are imaginative and delicious, and the range of entrées is wide enough to suit any palate. Try the Khatsah'lano burger (a salmon fillet on bannock with cranberry chutney) or perhaps the Malaspina chicken (stuffed with shrimp, crab, and cream cheese in a chili-cream sauce). For dessert, the pear gingerbread and German double-chocolate cheesecake are excellent. Isadora's is wheelchair-accessible; there's also a small children's play area and a children's menu.

LALIBELA ETHIOPIAN CUISINE, 2090 Alma St., at W. Fifth Ave. Tel. 732-1454.

Cuisine: ETHIOPIAN. **Reservations:** Recommended. **Bus:** 7.

$ **Prices:** $6.95–$11.95 per dish. AE, DC, MC, V.

Open: Dinner only, Tues–Sun 5–11pm.

The cuisine of this northeastern African land has been called "the ultimate finger food." The title fits—you won't get a spoon, fork, or knife here. Instead, your plate will be dominated by a large millet pancake called injera bread. On and around it will be a smörgåsbord of foods like doro (chicken tips) in a sauce of mushrooms, onions, and red peppers; zilzil (beef) with a hearty red berbere sauce; gomen wot (a vegetable stew of cabbage, carrots, potatoes, and hot green peppers); and misir wot (a spicy lentil stew).

MONTRI'S THAI RESTAURANT, 2611 W. Fourth Ave., at Trafalgar St. Tel. 738-9888.

Cuisine: THAI. **Reservations:** Recommended. **Bus:** 4 or 7.

$ **Prices:** Appetizers $5.50–$7.50; main courses $6.50–$10.95. AE, MC, V.

Open: Dinner only, daily 5–10:30pm.

At first you might feel a twinge of conscience, dining at a restaurant next door to a powerlifting gym and across the street from a fitness center. But the fresh, light, and spicy cuisine at Montri's can quickly erase any feelings of guilt. The Thai dishes here are authentic since the ingredients are flown in from Bangkok. But bowing to Western tastes, the chefs will adjust the heat content to suit individual preferences. For an appetizer, consider the larb gai (ground chicken marinated with lime juice, cilantro, and spices) or tod mun (fish cakes blended with prawns, chile curry, green beans, and spices). Then choose from a variety of salads; traditional noodle and rice dishes; chicken, pork, beef, seafood, and vegetarian entrées; and special hot curries. No sugar or MSG are used in cooking. Street parking.

THE NAAM RESTAURANT, 2724 W. Fourth Ave., near MacDonald St. Tel. 738-7151.
   Cuisine: VEGETARIAN. **Bus:** 4 or 22.
$ **Prices:** Appetizers $1.50–$5.50; main courses $3.95–$8.25. MC, V.
   Open: Daily 24 hours.

Vancouver's oldest natural-foods restaurant never closes. Located in the heart of Kitsilano, this 70-seat, rustic eatery is an institution. The food is not only good for you, it's really good. The salad bar charges per 100 grams (about three ounces). Light entrées include spinach enchiladas, pita sandwiches, and tofu burgers; for dinner, spaghetti, vegetable-and-tofu-teriyaki stir-fries, and macrobiotic specials. There's a breakfast menu as well as lots of spice teas and fruit drinks. Lest you think vegetarians are too pure, there are pizzas, cakes and pies, beer and wine.

SODAS, 2278 W. Fourth Ave., near Vine St. Tel. 731-7618.
   Cuisine: INTERNATIONAL. **Bus:** 4.
$ **Prices:** Main courses $1.95–$8.95. AE, MC, V.
   Open: Mon–Sat 8am–11pm, Sun 11am–11pm.

This Kitsilano diner delivers a bit of whimsy. Among the burger selections, look for the hamburger sundae (a meat patty smothered with vanilla ice cream, hot fudge, whipped cream, and chopped nuts, topped with a cherry). Or how about that beer milkshake? Nobody ever orders these things, but they're good for a chuckle. The CD jukebox plays Aaron Neville, Dion, and Chuck Berry; the *real* menu selections are "sodalicious" and they include satays, kebabs, and fajitas, as well as burgers and hot dogs.

Sodas has two other locations: 375 Water St., in Gastown (tel. 683-7632), and 4497 Dunbar St., not far from the University of British Columbia (tel. 222-9922).

WOODLANDS NATURAL RESTAURANT, upstairs at 2582 W. Broadway, at Trafalgar St. Tel. 733-5411.
   Cuisine: VEGETARIAN. **Reservations:** Recommended for Atrium. **Bus:** 9.
$ **Prices:** Atrium, appetizers $1.50–$5; main courses $6.50–$7.50. Buffet, lunch $4–$6, dinner $5–$8. MC, V.
   Open: Mon–Fri 7am–10pm, Sat–Sun 8am–10pm.

A sign at the entrance of Ratana and Arran Stephens' second-floor establishment greets the "Friends of Woodlands." It *is* a friendly place, featuring burled wooden posts and plenty of greenery. Guests serve themselves from an extensive vegetarian buffet. Most items cost a flat $1.25 per 100 grams (about three ounces); choices may include bean-and-lentil salad, curried potatoes, samosas, spinach pie, peas and paneer (homemade cheese), basmati rice, and tofu béarnaise. Desserts and beverages are individually priced: There's chocolate-hazelnut cake or fresh fruit flan, natural fruit seltzers, beer or wine, and spiced Indian tea. Full table service is offered in a separate dining room—The Atrium—where menu choices might include vegetarian sushi rolls or Camembert puff pastry followed by the "eight jewels clay pot"—braised lotus root, water chestnuts, baby corn, mushrooms, fresh veggies, and tofu, served in a sizzling clay pot with brown rice.

5. NEAR THE AIRPORT

VERY EXPENSIVE

LA BELLE AUBERGE, 4856 48th Ave., Ladner. Tel. 946-7717.
   Cuisine: FRENCH. **Reservations:** Required. **Bus:** 601. **Directions:** From Vancouver, drive south on Hwy. 99 to the first exit past the George Massey Tunnel; proceed southwest on River Road, turn left on Elliot Street, and then right on 48th Avenue; La Belle Auberge is about four blocks ahead, on the left.
$ Prices: Appetizers $5–$52; main courses $14.95–$43.95; menu gastronomique $45. AE, MC, V.
   Open: Dinner only, daily 6pm–midnight.

A French country inn deserves to be in the country. So chef *sans pareil* Bruno Marti established his kitchen in Ladner, a sleepy bedroom suburb a 40-minute drive from downtown Vancouver. The Swiss-German could be successful anywhere he chooses. Twice, in 1984 and 1988, he led Canadian teams to gold-medal performances in the international culinary Olympics, and he's received nearly every accolade available to a chef, including the B.C. Chef of the Year award in 1989. Here, in this Fraser River Delta fishing community, he has taken over a historic home and made it a point of pilgrimage for gourmets on both sides of the border. It's an ideal stop for those heading for (or arriving from) Victoria or Vancouver Island on the Tsawwassen ferry.

If you insist, you can stick with the traditional menu. You can start with escargots de Bourgogne or lobster bisque à l'Armagnac; proceed to a half duckling in quince sauce, milk-fed veal with prawns, or entrecôte au poivre flambéed with brandy. But if you really want to know why Marti is regarded as a culinary master, try the *menu gastronomique*. In other words, leave your meal entirely in his hands. "People who come to dine, not just to eat, deserve the best I have," Marti says. After your eight-course meal is over, your only regret will be that you can't savor just one more bite.

6. ON THE NORTH SHORE

EXPENSIVE

SALMON HOUSE ON THE HILL, 2229 Folkestone Way, West Vancouver. Tel. 926-3212.

Cuisine: WEST COAST. **Reservations:** Recommended. **Directions:** Take 21st Street exit off Hwy. 1 West, go through the stop-signed intersection, then turn right at the crest of the hill.

$ Prices: Appetizers $3.95–$7.95; main courses $12.95–$19.95. AE, MC, V.

Open: Lunch Mon–Sat 11:30am–2:30pm; dinner daily 5–10pm; brunch Sun 11am–2:30pm.

S This famous Native Canadian–style seafood establishment, high on a hill overlooking West Vancouver, is high on the list of places where locals like to take out-of-town guests. Every table in the multilevel room has a spectacular panoramic view, looking directly across Burrard Inlet and Stanley Park to the downtown skyline. Rough cedar paneling and a variety of Native Canadian artifacts, such as masks and totems, give the restaurant a look of authenticity.

Fresh salmon, barbecued over green alderwood to give it a subtle smoky flavor, is the house specialty. B.C. prawns, Alaska black cod, and salmon wonton are other items of note; landlubbers can satisfy their palates here as well with tasty lamb, chicken, and beefsteak offerings. Free parking.

SEVEN SEAS SEAFOOD RESTAURANT, at the foot of Lonsdale Ave., North Vancouver. Tel. 987-3344.

Cuisine: SEAFOOD. **Reservations:** Recommended. **SeaBus:** Lonsdale Quay. **Bus:** 246.

$ Prices: Appetizers $3.50–$7.95; full dinners $15–$42; buffet $29.75. AE, DC, ER, JCB, MC, V.

Open: Dinner only, Tues–Sun 5–10:30pm. **Closed:** Holidays and one week (for dry-dock maintenance) every other winter.

Until 1958, the *Seven Seas* plied the waters of the Burrard Inlet, carrying passengers between downtown Vancouver and North Vancouver. A year after the ship's permanent retirement, Diamond Almas and his father purchased it and converted it into a floating seafood restaurant. Almas and his own son, Mathew, now operate the business. It still looks much as it did three decades ago—reminiscent of a white hatbox with a neon sign on top—but the fish is as fresh and good as ever.

Nowhere in greater Vancouver is there a greater choice of seafood dishes. The best way to enjoy them is at the Seven Seas' famous 65-dish hot-and-cold seafood buffet. The standard salmon, halibut, and oysters are here, of course, prepared in several different ways; but it's the more unusual dishes that make this buffet a delight: octopus in basil, scallops in saffron cream, baked Fraser River sturgeon, Scottish pickled herring, pan-fried squid, smoked eel, curried crab, shrimp jambalaya, and more. Parking is free.

MODERATE

CAFE ROMA, 60 Semisch Ave., at Esplanade, North Vancouver. Tel. 984-0274.

Cuisine: ITALIAN. **Reservations:** Recommended for large parties. **SeaBus:** Lonsdale Quay. **Bus:** 246.

$ Prices: Appetizers $3.95–$9; main courses $6.25–$10 at lunch, $10.95–$16.95 at dinner. AE, MC, V.

Open: Lunch Mon–Fri noon–2:30pm; dinner Mon–Thurs 5:30–10pm, Fri–Sat 5:30–11pm, Sun 5:30–9:30pm.

A casual family charmer, Café Roma is owned by Antonio Corsi, a well-known name in North Shore restaurant circles (see the Corsi Trattoria, below). Decor heavy in the Italian national colors—red, white, and green—won't let you forget what country you're in as you peruse the lengthy menu, featuring 30 pastas, some of them old-country favorites; calzone; and numerous fish and meat dishes, including excellent halibut and scaloppine. Free parking.

CORSI TRATTORIA, 1 Lonsdale St., North Vancouver. Tel. 987-9910.
> **Cuisine:** ITALIAN PASTA. **Reservations:** Recommended. **SeaBus:** Lonsdale Quay. **Bus:** 246.
> **$ Prices:** Appetizers $4.95–$8.95; main courses $7.95–$11.95 at lunch, $10.50–$16.75 at dinner. AE, DC, MC, V.
> **Open:** Lunch Mon–Fri noon–2pm; dinner daily 5–10:30pm.

Back in Italy, the native land of the Corsi brothers, a trattoria is the place to go for pasta. The Corsi Trattoria—at the foot of Lonsdale Street, across from Lonsdale Quay—is a long way from Rome, but don't let that stop you. The old-country family of Mario (of the Park Royal Hotel) and Antonio (of the Café Roma, above) has run several trattorias, so the brothers know their stuff.

There are a couple dozen pastas on the Corsi menu, made fresh daily from semolina, flour, and eggs. They include rotoli (stuffed with veal, spinach, and ricotta) and trenette (with smoked salmon, cream, olives, and tomatoes). Consider the "For Italians Only" spaghetti trasteverini, with chicken, black beans, garlic, hot peppers, and olive oil; and l'abbuffatta ("the feast"), an enormous meal of four pastas, salad, lamb, veal, prawns, zabaglione, and espresso. There's free parking in the evening.

BUDGET

FRANKIE'S INN, 59 Lonsdale Ave., near 1st St. Tel. 987-3811.
> **Cuisine:** FAMILY STYLE. **SeaBus:** Lonsdale Quay. **Bus:** 246.
> **$ Prices:** $1.95–$5.25 per dish. No credit cards.
> **Open:** Mon–Fri 9am–8:30pm, Sat 9am–3:30pm.

An obvious favorite among budget travelers, here's a simple café where full roast-beef dinners and steak-and-eggs breakfasts cost about $5. Japanese dishes, such as tempura and sukiyaki, are also on the menu.

THE TOMAHAWK BARBECUE, 1550 Philip Ave., at Marine Dr., North Vancouver. Tel. 988-2612.
> **Cuisine:** FAMILY STYLE. **Bus:** 242 or 246.
> **$ Prices:** $2.50–$12 per dish. AE, MC, V.
> **Open:** Mon–Thurs 8am–10pm, Fri–Sat 8am–11pm, Sun 8am–9pm.

Some people think that the touristy Tomahawk, hiding behind its roadside totem poles, is the prototype for every kitschy Native American–theme restaurant in North America. Dating from the halcyon days before the Great Depression, it has developed a reputation for more than frivolity. In fact, locals line up here for the huge, low-priced breakfasts. And at least one Canadian magazine rated the hamburgers as the nation's best. Free parking.

7. GASTOWN/CHINATOWN

MODERATE

JAPANESE DELI, 381 E. Powell St., at Dunlevy St. Tel. 681-6484.
    Cuisine: JAPANESE. **Reservations:** Not required. **Bus:** 4 or 7.
$ Prices: Full meals $4.95–$35; fixed-price meal $8.95 at lunch, $11 at dinner. No credit cards.
    Open: Mon 11:30am–3pm, Tues–Fri 11:30am–8pm, Sat–Sun 11:30am–6pm.

Japantown isn't what it was before the World War II relocation of Japanese citizens. After being released from internment camps, they scattered to the four winds; consequently, Vancouver no longer has a distinct Japanese community. But this stretch of Powell Street is where the annual festivals take place, where a Buddhist temple and several interesting stores are located, and where you'll find this small and unobtrusive storefront. It seems to appeal mainly to Asian families and young counterculture types; for example, it catered for David Bowie when he serenaded Vancouver.

The budget beauty of the Japanese Deli is that there's a set price for all you can eat. Most guests dig into the tempura and the nigiri and maki sushi with a vengeance. It's good, and you don't have to stop till you're full. Wash it down with beer or sake. Street parking.

KILIMANJARO, 332 Water St. Tel. 681-9913.
    Cuisine: EAST AFRICAN/INDIAN. **Reservations:** Recommended. **Bus:** 1 or 50.
$ Prices: Appetizers $3.95–$8.95; main courses $13.95–$23.95. AE, DC, DISC, ER, MC, V.
    Open: Lunch Mon–Fri 11:30am–4pm; dinner daily 5:30–11pm.

Anyone who saw the movies *Gandhi* or *Mississippi Masala* knows that Africa, bordering the Indian Ocean as it does, has a sizable East Indian population. Like any transplanted cuisine, Indian cooking has undergone various changes in East Africa. Amyn Sunderji's restaurant in Gastown's Le Magasin mall exploits those unique tastes in this Nairobi-style setting, complete with tribal masks and batiks on the walls.

The recipes come from up and down the East African coast: Kenya, Zanzibar, and Mozambique; inland to Uganda, Zaire, and Zimbabwe; and well offshore to Madagascar and Mauritius. You can start with mitabaki, spiced crab wrapped in phyllo pastry; or soopu ya samaki unguja, a fish-and-coconut soup with leeks and celery. For a main course, try masala marlin (spiced blue marlin); trout tukutuku, baked with green mangoes and tamarind; prawns piripiri, with garlic butter, lime juice, paprika, and Congo peppers; matoke na nyama, plantains steamed in banana leaves, topped with groundnut sauce and served with a beef stew; or chicken moambe, cooked in hot peppers, palm oil, and garlic. The Kilimanjaro is fully licensed; you may need to drink something to put out the fire. On-street parking.

LE RAILCAR, 106 Carrall St., north of Water St. Tel. 669-5422.

Cuisine: FRENCH/CONTINENTAL. **Reservations:** Recommended. **Bus:** 1 or 50.

$ Prices: Appetizers $3.95–$6.95; main courses $6.95–$10.95 at lunch, $9.95–$18.95 at dinner. AE, DC, ER, MC, V.

Open: Lunch Sat–Sun 11:30am–2:30pm; dinner daily 5:30–10pm. **Closed:** Sun in winter.

A retired Canadian Pacific railcar rests unobtrusively beside the tracks half a block north of Water Street. The ancient Pullman conceals an elegant restaurant with inch-thick mahogany walls, brass fittings, rosewood furniture, and Tiffany wine cabinets.

Executive chef Brendon Cowell prepares his own sauces and pastries daily and insists on using ingredients as close to "alive" as can be (the mussels served at 6pm may have been delivered by the fishmonger at 5pm). Daily specials might include such starters as a tri-leaf (green, red, romaine) market salad mixed with homemade nachos. The extensive menu selection includes petoncles de l'été (scallops marinated in a coriander/rice-wine vinaigrette) served with summer fruit, poulet à la moutarde (grilled breast of chicken served over a bed of Dijon-cream sauce), filet de rouget (fillet of red snapper with banana-coconut-curry sauce), and blackened Louisiana catfish served with fresh basil. Dessert offerings might include banana cheesecake served with a dollop of whipped cream in a swirl of apricot-raspberry sauce. Street parking.

NEW DIAMOND RESTAURANT, 555 Gore Ave., between Keefer and Pender Sts. Tel. 685-0727.

Cuisine: CANTONESE. **Reservations:** Recommended for dinner. **Bus:** 19 at Main.

$ Prices: Three main dishes (for two people) $25–$40 at dinner; dim sum (for two) about $15 at lunch. MC, V.

Open: Breakfast/lunch Thurs–Tues 7:30am–3pm; dinner Thurs–Tues 5–10pm.

A longtime favorite among the several dozen restaurants in Chinatown, this large second-floor dim sum parlor is nondescript except for the golden dragon that adorns one whole wall. Come for lunch, when dim sum carts wheel their exotic selections (ever try stuffed duck's feet or steamed pig's blood with chives?) from table to table. The fresh-fish list is a good place to look for dinner: The crab preparations—for instance, with white (coconut) sauce—are superb.

NOODLE MAKERS, 122 Powell St. Tel. 683-9196.

Cuisine: CHINESE. **Reservations:** Recommended. **Bus:** 4 or 7.

$ Prices: Appetizers $3.95–$13.95; main courses $9.50–$27.95. AE, DC, ER, MC, V.

Open: Lunch Mon–Fri 11:30am–2pm; dinner daily 5–10pm.

Vancouver's Chinatown at the turn of the century was considerably different than it is today. For one thing, the gods and spirits were taken much more seriously. Buildings were constructed according to laws of geomancy, fierce-looking guardians were painted on merchants' doors, and joss sticks (incense) were offered at the family shrine—all as protection against evil forces. Those traditions are still maintained at this surprising restaurant, founded in the late 1960s by four very modern noodle makers: an architect, a chemical engineer, a mechanical technologist, and a China-educated historian. Inside, a giant paper lion hovers above four different dining levels. The lowest level houses 19th-century artifacts brought by early Chinese immigrants; another level features a waterfall and a pond where carp and goldfish are fed live shrimp by hand twice nightly.

You won't need a fortune teller to let you know how tasty the food is. Modern adaptations of traditional favorites work well here. Try one of these house specials: Noodle Makers Treat (poached salmon with ginger and soy sauce), Ocean Clouds (a scallop, crabmeat, and water chestnut combination), Seagods' Claypot (fish, prawns, oysters, scallops, and abalone in a Chinese claypot), Banana cornish hen (braised and smothered in banana sauce), or Emperor's Filet (marinated filet with ginger/green-onion or spicy sardare sauce). The restaurant does not use monosodium glutamate (MSG). Street parking available.

UMBERTO AL PORTO, 321 Water St. Tel. 683-8376.
    Cuisine: ITALIAN. **Reservations:** Recommended. **SkyTrain:** Waterfront. **Bus:** 1 or 50.
$ **Prices:** Appetizers $4.25–$7.50; main courses $9.95–$18.50. AE, DC, ER, MC, V.
    Open: Lunch Mon–Fri 11:30am–4pm; dinner Mon–Sat 4–11pm.

Many people seek out a good Italian restaurant for the scaloppines and parmigianas. In Vancouver, they come to Al Porto for the pasta and the wine. Located in the basement of a touristy mall on the west side of Gastown, this bright, colorful restaurant boasts what may well be the city's largest wine cellar. Amateur and professional oenologists are invited to visit the cavernous cellar and select a vintage from voluminous listings, divided regionally.

As for the pastas—well, there's agnolotti, cannelloni, lasagne, linguine, penne, rigatoni, spaghetti, tortellini, and my favorite, fettuccine con salmon affumicato (smoked salmon). You can have scaloppine, if you prefer; try it ai carciofi (with an artichoke-lemon sauce). There's good seafood and other main courses as well. There's a pay parking lot next door.

BUDGET

AL FORNO, 103 Columbia St., at Water St. Tel. 684-2838.
    Cuisine: ITALIAN/PIZZA. **Bus:** 1 or 50.
$ **Prices:** $6–$14.95 per dish. AE, MC, V.
    Open: Lunch Sun and Tues–Fri 11:30am–2pm; dinner Sun and Tues–Thurs 5–11pm, Fri–Sat 5pm–12:30am.

"The furnace" is indeed the focus of this corner favorite: a huge, wood-burning, brick oven that bakes pizzas and calzones the way you always heard they could be made. The oven keeps the entire place toasty on rainy winter evenings.

BROTHERS RESTAURANT, 1 Water St., at Carrall St. Tel. 683-9124.
    Cuisine: FAMILY STYLE. **Reservations:** Recommended, especially on weekends. **Bus:** 1 or 50.
$ **Prices:** Appetizers $2.95–$7.95; main courses $4.95–$7.95 at lunch, $6.95–$12.95 at dinner. AE, DC, JCB, MC, V.
    Open: Mon–Thurs 11:30am–10pm, Fri–Sat 11:30am–midnight, Sun 11:30am–9pm.

A Franciscan monastery atmosphere, complete with staff in friars' robes, provides a warm ambience that especially appeals to families and older folks. The main offerings are pastas, burgers, chowder, and light continental dishes, but there is now a sushi and oyster bar. Children get balloons and their own menu. A bistro lounge featuring wine casks and sushi and oyster bar caters primarily to young adults; the adjoining Punchlines comedy theater arranges joint promotions, and you can easily put together dinner/show packages.

INDIA VILLAGE, 308 Water St. Tel. 681-0678.

Cuisine: INDIAN. **Bus:** 1 or 50.

$ Prices: $2.50–$8.95 per dish. AE, DC, MC, V.

Open: Daily 11:30am–11pm.

Across the street from the old Gastown steam clock and up the steps of an old building is this casual, fully licensed restaurant. South Asian art and peacock feathers adorn the walls, ceiling fans re-create a colonial mood, and ragas play softly in the background. The food—even meat and chicken curries—is mild enough for almost any palate. You might start with samosas or mulligatawny soup, then order a tandoori dish (chicken, lamb, or fish), and accompany it with a mango lassi. There are numerous vegetarian specials.

OLD SPAGHETTI FACTORY, 53 Water St. Tel. 684-1288.

Cuisine: ITALIAN/PASTA. **Reservations:** Accepted only for parties of six or more. **Bus:** 1 or 50.

$ Prices: Appetizers $2.35–$4.50; main courses $5.75–$7.45 at lunch, $6.95–$11.85 at dinner. AE, MC, V.

Open: Mon–Thurs 11:30am–10pm, Fri–Sat 11:30am–11pm, Sun 11:30am–9pm.

Since Gastown is one of Vancouver's havens for antique shoppers, it shouldn't surprise anyone to see the collection that has been assembled in this old coffee- and tea-packing plant. Every kind of contraption you could imagine seems to be here—old street lamps, fine Tiffany glass, a penny farthing cycle mounted on a wall, and a 1904 B.C. electric trolley car that's now part of the restaurant's seating area. You can enjoy New York steak, veal à la parmigiana, green-and-gold fettuccine, or Mama Pulosi's secret lasagne; but most folks come for the spaghetti, prepared in nine different ways.

THE ONLY [FISH & OYSTER CAFE], 20 E. Hastings St., near Carrall St. Tel. 681-6546.

Cuisine: SEAFOOD. **Bus:** 8, 14, 20, or 21.

$ Prices: $5.25–$11.95 per dish. No credit cards.

Open: Mon–Sat noon–7pm.

This skid-row eatery is a Vancouver institution: pan-fried fish so fresh you can almost see the fins still wiggling, savory Manhattan-style clam chowder bubbling in the pot. Alcohol is not served, and public washrooms are not available, but lines form outside at mealtime, so be forewarned.

ON ON TEA GARDEN, 214 Keefer St. Tel. 685-7513.

Cuisine: CANTONESE. **Reservations:** Recommended. **Bus:** 8 or 19.

$ Prices: Three dishes (for two people) $18–$32. MC, V.

Open: Tues–Thurs 11am–9pm, Fri–Sat 11am–10pm, Sun 4–9pm.

★ Former Prime Minister Pierre Trudeau helped establish the fame of this Chinatown restaurant when he used it during his secret courtship of Margaret more than 20 years ago. In fact—except for the autographed photos of such regular customers as Bill Cosby, Burt Lancaster, Angie Dickinson, Christopher Lloyd, and the late Sammy Davis, Jr. on the walls—the restaurant's decor is pretty ordinary, with Formica furnishings and friendly waiters. The stir-fried scallops with vegetables (beans, asparagus, carrots, onions, and water chestnuts) are fabulous. The hot-and-sour soup is very good, as are the garlic prawns. This is one of the few Chinatown eateries where you can get such Americanized victuals as chop suey and egg foo yung.

PHNOM PENH RESTAURANT, 244 E. Georgia St., near Main St. Tel. 682-5777.
   Cuisine: CAMBODIAN. **Bus:** 8 or 19.
$ **Prices:** $4.50–$10.75 per dish. DC, MC.
   Open: Wed–Mon 10am–9:30pm.
Cambodian cooking strikes a cautious balance between the delicate Vietnamese and the more aggressively spicy Thai cuisine. This family restaurant offers western Canada's best of the genre. Tasteful artistic renderings of the ancient capital of Angkor adorn the walls, Khmer dolls are suspended in glass cases, and subdued lighting is a welcome departure from the glaring fluorescence of many other Chinatown budget establishments. Some of the dishes are also interesting departures. The hot-and-sour soup, stocked with prawns and spiced with lemongrass, contains bits of pineapple and slices of water-lily root. Entrées include chicken and beef specialties; adventurous diners might finish with a fruit-and-rice pudding. A small list of beers is available.

CHAPTER 6

WHAT TO SEE & DO IN VANCOUVER

Vancouver is a fascinating city with a multitude of major attractions. Many of them involve the city's spectacular scenery or its multicultural and multiethnic character. You should try to sample both.

SUGGESTED ITINERARIES

IF YOU HAVE TWO DAYS Spend your first day getting to know the central city area. After breakfast, get a perspective on Vancouver from Harbour Centre or Canada Place, then follow the walking tours of Gastown and downtown (see Chapter 7), including the Vancouver Art Gallery. Enjoy lunch at a Robsonstrasse café, then a sunny afternoon at Stanley Park (be sure to visit the world-acclaimed Vancouver Aquarium while you're there). If it's rainy, visit the museums suggested in the three-day itinerary.

Since Vancouver is surrounded by the natural beauty of the Canadian West Coast, your second morning is a good time to enjoy the great outdoors. Savor the view from Grouse Mountain, above North Vancouver, then spend some time at Capilano Canyon Regional Park, with its famous suspension bridge. Return to Vancouver for a late lunch in Chinatown or Granville Island, and spend the afternoon exploring one or both of these communities.

IF YOU HAVE THREE DAYS Spend your first two days as outlined above.

In the morning of Day 3, go to one or more of the Vanier Park museums on the south shore of English Bay: the Vancouver Museum for history, the Gordon Southam Observatory and H. R. MacMillan Planetarium, the Vancouver Maritime Museum, and the *St. Roch* National Historic Site. Have lunch at one of the many fine restaurants along West Fourth Avenue or Broadway, then head west to the campus of the University of British Columbia, where you can spend the afternoon at the UBC Museum of Anthropology, famous for its West Coast tribal artifacts, and the botanical gardens.

IF YOU HAVE FIVE DAYS OR MORE Spend your first three days as suggested above.

If you have more time, one day should be reserved for a ride north to Squamish on the Royal Hudson steam train and a return cruise aboard the MV *Britannia* through spectacular Howe Sound. Your itinerary should also include Queen Elizabeth Park and the VanDusen Garden, the Burnaby Village Museum, Science World B.C. at the former Expo '86 site, and the Italian, Greek, and East Indian communities. Dine at least once at a restaurant specializing in West Coast cuisine, enjoy a theatrical or symphonic performance, and attend a seasonal sports event, such as ice hockey or Canadian football.

If you have additional time, you can spend it at numerous mountain and seaside parks, the ski resort town of Whistler, and Fraser River Valley attractions such as Fort Langley and Harrison Hot Springs.

1. THE TOP ATTRACTIONS

STANLEY PARK

One of the world's great urban parks is just a 15-minute walk west of Vancouver's central business district. Named for the Canadian governor-general who dedicated it in 1889 (thanks to the conservationist vision of the Vancouver City Council), Stanley Park is a 1,000-acre promontory of forest land that juts like a mushroom into the middle of the Burrard Inlet. Almost completely surrounded by water, it's lush with Douglas fir, red cedar, and hemlock, and is home to myriad birds and small mammals. It's crisscrossed by dozens of trails, some of them made long ago by Native Canadians, and surrounded by a 6½-mile seawall that attracts scores of cyclists, joggers, and pedestrians (and their dogs). It also has two lakes, three major restaurants, and numerous beaches, playgrounds, and picnic areas, as well as other attractions.

The park is most easily approached from Beach or West Georgia Street. Drivers must enter on Georgia since traffic through the park is one-way counterclockwise. Avoid driving during rush hours, however. This is the only road across the Lions Gate Bridge to North and West Vancouver. Be sure to have enough change for parking.

The two-hour walk around the seawall is the best way to get a feel for the park and orient yourself to Vancouver's remarkable geographical setting. Most attractions are on the eastward-pointing finger of the park, closest to downtown and Coal Harbour. Detour to the left at the **Vancouver Rowing Club** to discover a monument to Lord Stanley: **Malkin Bowl,** site of summer "Theater Under the Stars"; and, beyond that, rose gardens. Another path leads to Stanley Park's major indoor attractions: the **Vancouver Aquarium** and two **zoos,** one specifically for children (see "Cool for Kids," below).

The promenade passes the **Royal Vancouver Yacht Club** and the **Deadman's Island** naval reserve training base. On the left, **Brockton Oval,** a cricket pitch and cinder jogging track, has public showers and changing facilities. Near Brockton Point is a cluster of late 19th-century **totem poles** and dugout canoes carved by the Kwakiutl and Haida. Close to the two-mile mark of the walk, a marine statue entitled *Girl in a Wet Suit* somewhat resembles *The Little Mermaid* in Copenhagen. There's a children's water playground, a miniature railway, and pony rides on the left.

From this point, expect more wilderness and fewer human-made points of interest. At three miles, **Prospect Point,** the peninsula's northernmost extremity, looks toward West Vancouver across the First Narrows from a 200-foot clifftop; the Prospect Point Café here is a popular restaurant. As the view shifts toward Vancouver Island, look for **Siwash Rock,** a legendary site to Native tribes. Another restaurant, the Teahouse, is at **Ferguson Point.** At five miles, **Second Beach** has a saltwater swimming pool. Then the park opens up near **Lost Lagoon,** a former swamp inhabited by Canada geese and rare trumpeter swans. (Tell the kids to bring breadcrumbs.) Nearby are a pitch-and-putt golf course, tennis courts, shuffleboard, and lawn bowling.

VANCOUVER AQUARIUM, Stanley Park. Tel. 682-1118 or 685-3364.

This exhibition of aquatic wildlife is world-famous. The third-largest aquarium in North America claims to have some 8,000 marine species. Outdoors are the new Arctic Canada, North Pacific, and Northwest Coast exhibits. In the Max Bell Marine Mammal Centre, visitors can observe the underwater activities of killer and beluga whales, sea otters, and harbor seals. The aquarium staff regularly provide live descriptions, interpreting the whales' actions as they occur. There are no set times for these presentations, since whale behavior is as unpredictable as human behavior.

Elsewhere in the aquarium, two galleries depict local marine life, while two others deal with tropical animals. The Sandwell North Pacific Gallery re-creates the B.C. coastline with creatures great and small, like the giant octopus and anemones. The adjacent Rufe Gibbs Hall focuses on freshwater life.

Temperatures are kept a little warmer in the H. R. MacMillan Tropical Gallery, with its colorful, beautifully delicate fish, as well as sea turtles and sharks. The Graham Amazon Gallery transports visitors to the South American jungle with a complete exhibition of flora and fauna, from exotic birds and primates to crocodiles and piranhas.

The Clamshell Gift Shop, one of Vancouver's best places to buy souvenirs, has handcrafts and books. The aquarium also has a theater and research laboratories.

Admission: $8.50 adults, $7.25 seniors and students, $5.25 children 5–12, free for children under 5, $22 families.

Open: Labor Day–June, daily 10am–5:30pm; July–Labor Day, daily 9:30am–8pm. **Bus:** 19; "Around the Park" bus Apr 15–Oct, weekends and holidays only.

STANLEY PARK ZOO, Stanley Park. Tel. 681-1141.

This modest zoo has a somewhat limited collection of foreign and native Canadian animals—otters, seals, penguins, monkeys, snakes, and tropical birds. If you want to see animals and can't get south to Seattle's Woodland Park Zoo or Tacoma's Point Defiance Zoo, this one will have to do. However, the zoo is undergoing a revitalization program: Some animals, like polar bears, are being phased out, while a new emphasis is being given to B.C. wildlife and conservation education. Nearby is a fine **Children's Zoo** where youngsters can cuddle up to domesticated baby animals—goats, rabbits, and llamas. Also in the vicinity is a Kangaroo House of Australian creatures.

Admission: Public zoo, free; children's zoo, $2 adults, 95¢ children and seniors, $4 families.

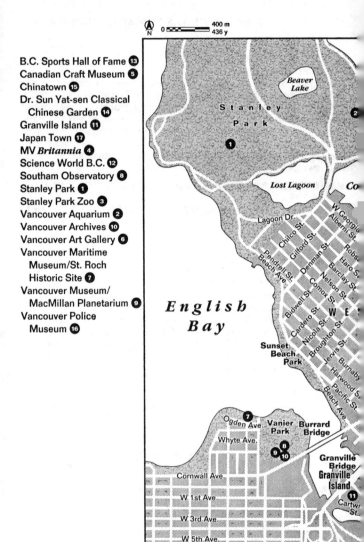

B.C. Sports Hall of Fame ⑬
Canadian Craft Museum ⑤
Chinatown ⑮
Dr. Sun Yat-sen Classical
  Chinese Garden ⑭
Granville Island ⑪
Japan Town ⑰
MV *Britannia* ④
Science World B.C. ⑫
Southam Observatory ⑧
Stanley Park ①
Stanley Park Zoo ③
Vancouver Aquarium ②
Vancouver Archives ⑩
Vancouver Art Gallery ⑥
Vancouver Maritime
  Museum/St. Roch
  Historic Site ⑦
Vancouver Museum/
  MacMillan Planetarium ⑨
Vancouver Police
  Museum ⑯

Open: Public zoo, daily 10am–dusk (9pm latest). Children's zoo, May–Sept, daily 11am–4pm; Oct–Apr, Sat–Sun 11am–4pm. **Bus:** 19; "Around the Park" bus Apr 15–Oct, weekends and holidays only.

MUSEUMS

GORDON SOUTHAM OBSERVATORY, 1100 Chestnut St., Vanier Park. Tel. 738-2855.

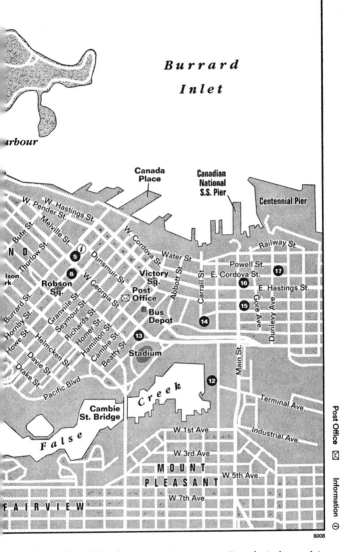

Burrard

Inlet

rbour

Canada Place

Canadian National S.S. Pier

Centennial Pier

W. Hastings St.
W. Pender St.
Melville St.
Bute St.
Thurlow St.
N D
son rk
Robson Sq.
Dunsmuir St.
W. Georgia St.
W. Cordova St.
Water St.
Victory Sq.
Post Office
Bus Depot
Abbott St.
Carrall St.
Railway St.
Powell St.
E. Cordova St.
E. Hastings St.
Gore Ave.
Dunlevy Ave.
Burrard St.
Granville St.
Seymour St.
Richards St.
Homer St.
Hamilton St.
Cambie St.
Beatty St.
Hornby St.
Howe St.
Helmcken St.
Davie St.
Drake St.
Pacific Blvd.
Stadium

⑤ ⑥ ⑰ ⑯ ⑮ ⑭ ⑬ ⑫

Creek

Cambie St. Bridge

Main St.
Terminal Ave.
Industrial Ave.

W. 1st Ave.
W. 3rd Ave.
False
MOUNT
PLEASANT
W. 5th Ave.
W. 7th Ave.
FAIRVIEW

Post Office ⊠   Information ⊖

6008

The only public observatory in western Canada is housed in a small building beside the museum-planetarium complex. There's no charge to go in and listen to an astronomer—a volunteer from the British Columbia Space Sciences Society—explain how to operate the Zeiss telescope, with its interchangeable filters, to view the sun, moon, planets, and stars.

Public programs and workshops are held throughout the year for all ages. Probably the most popular are the "Shoot the Moon" photography sessions on full-moon nights, when patrons with 35mm single-lens reflex cameras can take their own pictures of the Earth's satellite.

Admission: Free.

Open: Fri–Sun noon–5pm and 7–11pm (weather and volunteer staffing permitting); there are occasional unannounced closures, so telephone before your visit. **Bus:** 22.

H. R. MACMILLAN PLANETARIUM, Vanier Park. Tel. 736-3656.

This planetarium, one of North America's finest, was given to the City of Vancouver by a local industrialist. In the second-floor theater of the Vancouver Museum/Planetarium complex, viewers recline in comfortable armchairs with plush headrests and gaze at the Milky Way on the dome above them. A Zeiss star projector and hundreds of special-effects devices take the viewer on a dramatic trip through time and space—to search for other worlds or to look in-depth at the night sky. The shows are entertaining and educational for all ages.

Adolescents and young adults especially enjoy the spectacular laser sound-and-light shows at night. Using a combination of planetarium special effects, surround-sound, and laser imagery, the productions feature the music of world-famous rock groups (in 1992, these included U2 and Led Zeppelin). Buy your ticket in advance and arrive early for a seat; latecomers are not admitted.

Astronomy-related art or photography exhibits are on display in the upper gallery, outside the doors to the planetarium.

Admission: $5 adults, $3 seniors and children under 18, $12.75 families; laser shows, $7 per person.

Open: July–Labor Day, daily; Labor Day–June, Tues–Sun and most holidays; since the schedule varies, call 736-3656 for showtimes. **Directions:** See the Vancouver Museum, below.

MUSEUM OF ANTHROPOLOGY, University of British Columbia, 6393 NW Marine Dr. Tel. 822-5087, or 822-3825 for a recording.

This masterpiece of specialized architecture, designed by Arthur Erickson after a traditional Native cedar house, holds the world's finest collection of the artifacts of Canada's West Coast tribes. The Great Hall is an awesome showcase of totem poles, houseposts, bentwood boxes, and other massive works of art—much of it from the period before white settlement. Windows 45 feet tall look out on the Point Grey cliffs, where a simulated Haida tribal village, with more totem poles and longhouses, hangs over the Strait of Georgia.

There were many tribes along this coast—Haida, Tsimshian, Kwakiutl, and Salish, to name a few—but their cultures were similar (see "History, Geography, and People" in Chapter 1). The totemic designs carved on poles, houseposts, masks, and other media usually depicted their clans or the legendary creatures after which they were named: Raven, Eagle, Bear, Whale, Otter, or Frog.

Totemic art is very much alive in contemporary Native Canadian art. There is no better example than the prominently displayed yellow-cedar sculpture *Raven and the First Men,* designed and carved by Haida artist Bill Reid, which depicts the legends of his own tribe. An enormous stylized raven stands stoically atop a giant clamshell, as perhaps half a dozen tiny men try to force their way out.

The expressions on the men's faces range from fear and confusion to stubborn insistence.

Jewelry and sculpture in gold, silver, bone, and argillite—a jet-black stone mined only in B.C.'s Queen Charlotte Islands—make up the Walter and Marianne Koerner Collection of Native arts. There are also fine displays of ceremonial masks and baskets.

There's more to the museum than Native culture. The traditions of Asia and the Pacific, along with many parts of Africa and Latin America, are well represented in arts and crafts, notably fine collections of masks and textiles. The entire permanent collection is displayed in glass-topped storage drawers; information on all objets d'art is available in computer-produced data books.

Guided and self-guided tours are available, the latter either with a rented cassette deck and tape or with the museum's excellent guidebook. There's a small but excellent gift shop, specializing (of course) in Native crafts, opposite the ticket booth. Sunday-afternoon concerts, evening lectures, youth programs, changing exhibits, and other special events keep the museum a stimulating venue throughout the year.

Admission: $5 adults, $2.50 seniors and students, free for children under 6, free for everyone Tues; $12 families.

Open: Tues 11am–9pm, Wed–Sun 11am–5pm. **Closed:** Dec 25–26. **Bus:** 42 direct; 4 and 10 go from downtown to the central campus.

VANCOUVER ART GALLERY, 750 Hornby St., Robson Square. Tel. 682-5621.

✪ The former provincial courthouse is, in a way, a collaboration between British Columbia's two most famous architects. Originally built in neoclassical style in 1911 by Francis Rattenbury (who also designed Victoria's Empress Hotel and Legislative Buildings), its somber chambers and corridors were transformed into bright exhibit halls in 1983 by Arthur Erickson. Impressive Greek columns and stone lions still greet the visitor, but inside, a new glass-topped dome permits natural light to enter the spacious rotunda and four floors.

Temporary exhibits feature contemporary Canadian and international painters, sculptors, photographers, and video artists, especially from British Columbia and East Asia. The permanent collection includes European and North American masters, including Pablo Picasso, Marc Chagall, Francisco Goya, Georges Braque, Thomas Gainsborough, and John Constable, plus Canada's Group of Seven, whose landscapes exerted an important influence on the nation's art in the 1920s and 1930s.

Don't miss the Emily Carr Gallery, where the work of British Columbia's most famous artist is displayed. A native of Vancouver Island, Carr captured the mystery and power of the coastal rain forests and their Native inhabitants in the early 1900s. Before her death in 1945, Carr bequeathed 157 paintings and drawings to the people of B.C. Private donations have expanded the collection further.

The Children's Gallery, off the main lobby, has changing exhibits (with an educational emphasis) of interest to youngsters. Hard-core art-lovers may want to visit the research library (in the former law library), with its hundreds of art magazines, thousands of books, catalogs from countless other museums around the world, and files on contemporary Canadian artists. The Gift Shop, one of Vancouver's best bets for buying souvenirs, carries books on Emily Carr and reproductions of her art. Hungry? Try the Gallery Café, overlooking the Sculpture Garden.

Free guided tours are led by museum docents at least twice each weekday. Check the schedule at the gallery's information desk.

Admission: $4.25 adults, $2.50 seniors and students, free for children under 12, free for everyone Thurs after 5pm.

Open: Mon–Wed and Fri–Sat 10am–5pm, Thurs 10am–9pm, Sun and holidays noon–5pm. **Closed:** Tues Oct–May (gift shop and café remain open). **SkyTrain:** Granville. **Bus:** 3, 8, 15, or 17.

VANCOUVER MUSEUM, 1100 Chestnut St., Vanier Park. Tel. 736-4431, or 736-7736 for 24-hour recorded information on programs and exhibits.

The Coast Salish people once had a village on the tip of land that juts into English Bay between the Burrard Street Bridge and Kitsilano Beach. Today, the carefully manicured parkland is the site of this oddly shaped museum, whose roof resembles the cone-shaped traditional northern Native woven-cedar-bark hat.

Beneath the roof is Canada's largest civic collection—one that traces the history of Vancouver and the Lower Mainland from prehistoric to modern times. The same building also houses the H. R. MacMillan Planetarium (see above).

The Vancouver Museum has rotating permanent displays and temporary exhibitions. Wing A focuses on Native prehistory and culture, from 8,000 years ago to the arrival of the white settlers. Wing B deals with the growth of the city from 1750 to the early 20th century. Highlights include life-size replicas of a Hudson's Bay Company trading post, the steerage portion of an immigrant ship, an 1887-vintage Canadian Pacific railroad car, and reconstructed rooms from Victorian and Edwardian homes. Wing C includes the Briggs Collection of Japanese jade and ivory, plus major visiting shows—often Pacific Rim–related. All told, the museum's collection includes more than a million artifacts and specimens, but you can't see them all in a single visit!

The Museum Gift Shop sells modern Native Canadian jewelry, weavings, and prints, as well as history books and standard souvenirs. The museum restaurant serves lunch and snacks overlooking English Bay.

Admission: $5 adults, $2.50 seniors and children (seniors free on Tues), free for children under 5; $10 families. Combined admission with Maritime Museum (see "More Attractions," below), $8 adults, $4 seniors and children, free for children under 5; $16 families.

Open: May–Sept, daily 10am–9pm; Oct–Apr, Tues–Sun 10am–5pm. **Bus:** 22; then walk three blocks south on Cornwall Avenue. **Boat:** Granville Island Ferry from Vancouver Aquatic Centre (Beach Avenue at Thurlow Street), Sat–Sun and holidays 10am–5pm, every 15 minutes.

NORTH VANCOUVER

CAPILANO CANYON REGIONAL PARK, 3735 Capilano Rd., North Vancouver. Tel. 985-7474.

This 15-acre park may be the nearest place to downtown

Vancouver that enables you to feel that you're a world away—in the midst of a primeval rain forest. Douglas firs and red cedars tower like skyscrapers over the wild Capilano River as it pours through a deep canyon to the Burrard Inlet. A famous suspension bridge stretches across the river near the south end of the park, and a salmon hatchery near its northern end replenishes the stock of spawning coho and chinook that turn the stream's waters nearly red from July through October.

The **Capilano Suspension Bridge** may be a tourist trap, but it's a spectacular one. Stretching 450 feet across, at 230 feet above the canyon floor, this swinging wood-and-wire rope bridge gives you a phenomenal feel for the beauty of the natural setting. You'll see tiny people on paths weaving through the forest, shrouded by the mists of a 200-foot waterfall; kayakers and canoeists can sometimes be seen battling the rapids below. (Because the bridge is on privately owned property in the park, there's an admission charge. At Lynn Canyon Park on the eastern edge of North Vancouver, there's a similar but less famous suspension bridge that's 10 feet higher—and free.)

Adjacent to the bridge are a restaurant, outdoor barbecue area, Native carving display, and the Trading Post—Vancouver's largest souvenir and gift shop. Guided forestry and anthropology tours begin here.

More energetic visitors, however, are delighted to wander the **Capilano trails** on their own. A series of well-maintained trails, with steps to aid walkers on the more precipitous sections, flank the river on either side. It's 4½ miles down to the Burrard Inlet at the Lions Gate Bridge, but only about a mile upstream to Cleveland Dam, behind which **Capilano Lake** preserves Vancouver's freshwater supply.

About a quarter mile below the dam, on the east side of the river, is the **Capilano Salmon Hatchery.** About two million salmon eggs are hatched here each year. There's no admission charge; outdoor displays explain the salmon's remarkable life cycle as you watch the fish in various stages of development swimming in glass-fronted tanks.

Admission: Park, free. Suspension bridge, $5.50 adults, $4.95 seniors, $4 students, $2 children 6–12, free for children under 6.

Open: May–Sept, daily 8am–dusk; Oct–Apr, daily 9am–5pm. **Closed:** Christmas Day. **Bus:** 246 to Ridgewood/Capilano.

GROUSE MOUNTAIN RESORT, 6400 Nancy Greene Way, North Vancouver. Tel. 984-0661.

A 100-passenger aerial tramway, known as the Superskyride, whisks visitors in just eight minutes (four minutes during ski season) to a 3,700-foot elevation, near the top of Grouse Mountain. The views of the city and harbor are magnificent.

The chalet at the top is a base for walking on paved paths or hiking on well-trodden trails. You can opt for a helicopter tour or a chair-lift ride to the mountain's 4,100-foot peak, a frequent site for major hang-gliding competitions. The Theatre in the Sky features *Our Spirit Soars,* a multimedia show about Vancouver and Haida Indian folklore. Logger sports can be seen periodically in the summer; there are even pony rides and an adventure playground for the kids.

The Grouse Nest Restaurant (tel. 986-6378) is popular for a

romantic dinner or Sunday brunch; the cost of the trip up is included with the meal.

For details on winter sports, see "Skiing," in "Sports and Recreation," later in this chapter.

Admission: $13.95 adults, $11.95 seniors, $8.95 students, $5.95 children 6–12, free for children under 6.

Open: Daily 10am–10pm. **Bus:** 246 to Edgemont/Ridgewood, then transfer to no. 232.

MV *BRITANNIA*, Harbour Ferries, No. 1 North foot of Denman St., Coal Harbour. Tel. 688-7246, 687-9558, or toll free 800/663-1500.

Most visitors like to combine the Royal Hudson excursion (see below) with a one-way journey to or from Squamish aboard this cruise vessel. Following the coast through Howe Sound, it offers a different perspective on the same magnificent view seen by rail travelers. The boat has two seating levels, both with large windows, and a sun deck on top. (Especially in the spring and fall, when the temperature may be a little warmer, it may be wiser to return by boat.) It also has a snack bar. Shuttle buses operate between the boat and rail terminals to return travelers to their own vehicles when the day's excursion is over.

Admission: Round-trip fares for train and boat, $45 adults, $40 seniors and students, $15 children 5–11, free for children under 5. Reservations are essential, at least 48 hours in advance.

Open: First week of June to mid-Sept, Wed–Sun with departures at 9:30am, returning at 4:30pm. **Bus:** 19 (Stanley Park bus; board on Pender Street) or "Royal Hudson Special" ($2; $1 seniors). Hotel pickup by Grayline for $5 (tel. 681-8687) or First Tours (tel. 688-7240).

ROYAL HUDSON STEAM TRAIN, B.C. Railways, 1311 W. 1st St., at Pemberton Ave., North Vancouver. Tel. 631-3500, 68-TRAIN, or toll free 800/663-1500 in western North America.

The last operating survivor of 65 steam trains that served Canada half a century ago, this beautifully restored iron horse runs most summer days on the B.C. Rail line from North Vancouver to the logging town of Squamish, 40 miles north. En route, it skirts the rugged coastline of Howe Sound, introducing travelers to some of the most dramatic landscape in North America. Wild streams thread their way through lush evergreen forests, then tumble from cliffs into the green waters, themselves speckled with islands and fishing boats.

B.C.'s *Royal Hudson,* Engine no. 2860, is the only steam locomotive in North America that has daily scheduled service on the main line of a major railroad. Restored from its heyday and immaculately maintained, the locomotive pulls nine coaches on the two-hour trip to Squamish. Another Hudson steam engine pulled King George VI and Queen Elizabeth more than 7,500 miles across Canada, from Québec City to Vancouver, in 1939, thereby earning the designation "Royal" for all Hudson locomotives.

Royal comfort is part of the experience today: There's full refreshment and bar service, as well as an on-board gift and souvenir stand. Live narration is provided. There's a layover of about 1½ hours in Squamish to give travelers time for lunch and sightseeing—the mountains here are spectacular—before the *Royal Hudson* returns to North Vancouver.

Admission: Round-trip fares, $28.50 adults, $24 seniors and students 12–18, $7 children 5–11, free for children under 5. Discount fares available at the beginning and end of the season, and on Thurs. Reservations are recommended, 48 hours in advance.

Open: First week of June to mid-Sept, Wed–Sun, departing North Vancouver at 10am, returning at 4pm. **Bus:** "Royal Hudson Special" departs Vancouver Bus Terminal, Cambie and Dunsmuir Streets, at 9am; picks up along Georgia Street at Granville, Burrard, and Denman Streets, en route to the B.C. Railway terminal ($2; $1 seniors). **Directions:** Cross the Lions Gate Bridge, turn right on Marine Drive for about half a mile, and then right on Pemberton Avenue.

2. MORE ATTRACTIONS

MUSEUMS

B.C. SPORTS HALL OF FAME AND MUSEUM, B.C. Place Stadium, Gate A, Robson St., at Beatty. Tel. 687-5523.

This museum—a high-tech, hands-on tribute to sports and athletics in British Columbia life—traces the history and development of 68 sports in the province, sometimes by means of soundtracks dramatizing great moments. Visitors can experience the "miracle mile" and the Hall of Champions, compete in the Olympics, and climb a rock face. The hall boasts one of the greatest collections of trophies and medals assembled anywhere, along with photos, equipment, and personal mementos of B.C.'s most famous athletes. A permanent exhibit features every provincial athlete who has won an Olympic medal since 1912. There is an on-site gift shop.

Admission: $3 adults, $1.50 seniors and students.

Open: Daily 10am–6pm. **SkyTrain:** Stadium. **Bus:** 15.

B.C. SUGAR MUSEUM, B.C. Sugar Refinery, Rogers St., Port of Vancouver. Tel. 253-1131.

The growth of the refinery closely parallels the historical growth of Vancouver. This theme is emphasized in old photographs and a 25-minute documentary film. There are also interesting displays of a plantation locomotive and sugar-making equipment dating from 1715.

Admission: Free.

Open: Mon–Fri 9:30am–3:30pm. **Bus:** 4 or 7; then walk two blocks north from East Hastings Street.

CANADIAN CRAFT MUSEUM, 639 Hornby St. Tel. 687-8266.

Canada's first national museum devoted exclusively to crafts features both the traditional and the contemporary. On exhibit are works in wood, clay, glass, fiber, and metal by both domestic and foreign artisans. There's an excellent gift shop. The museum opened on Granville Island as the Cartwright Gallery, and then moved in 1992 to its present location off a secluded courtyard in Cathedral Place, a new downtown office tower.

Admission: $2 adults, $1 seniors and students; free the first Thurs of each month.

Open: Mon–Sat 9:30am–5:30pm, Sun noon–5pm (first Thurs of each month 9:30am–8pm). **SkyTrain:** Granville. **Bus:** 3, 8, 15, or 17.

HASTINGS SAWMILL STORE MUSEUM, 1575 Alma St., Jericho Beach Park. Tel. 228-1213.

Vancouver's first general store, floated to this site from its original location on Burrard Inlet, is loaded with the type of items that it might have contained 120 years ago. It's charmingly cluttered with 19th-century clothing, furniture, Native baskets, and photographs, as well as smaller goods such as nails and mustache cups.

Admission: By donation.

Open: June to mid-Sept, daily 10am–4pm; the rest of the year, Sat–Sun 1–4pm. **Bus:** 4, 7, or 42.

SCIENCE WORLD BRITISH COLUMBIA, 1455 Quebec St., at Terminal Ave. Tel. 687-8414 or 687-7832.

Housed in what used to be the World Expo Centre, this fascinating cross between a museum, a laboratory, and a laser-light show provides a series of hands-on experiences. On your way through, you can touch a tornado, lose your shadow, blow square bubbles, walk inside a camera, and step on sound waves. You can also see a zucchini explode when zapped with a charge of 80,000 volts, stroll through the interior of a beaver lodge, compose music on an electric guitar, and run your hands through magnetic liquids—among other things. There's a cafeteria and gift shop, geared to science-lovers, of course.

The complex also houses the **Omnimax Theatre** (tel. 875-OMNI), with the largest screen of its kind in the world. A huge domed auditorium presents special films that seem to include the audience as part of the action. Call for presentation times and current productions. Separate tickets are required.

Admission: $7 adults, $4.50 seniors and students, free for children under 3; additional charge for Omnimax film.

Open: Sun–Fri 10am–5pm, Sat 10am–9pm. **SkyTrain:** Main. **Bus:** 3, 8, or 19.

VANCOUVER ARCHIVES, 1150 Chestnut St. Tel. 736-8561.

Next door to the Vancouver Museum, the archives has a huge collection of historical documents dating from the city's founding.

Admission: Free.

Open: Mon–Fri 9:30am–5:30pm. **Directions:** Same as for the Vancouver Maritime Museum, below.

VANCOUVER MARITIME MUSEUM, 1905 Ogden Ave., Vanier Park. Tel. 737-2211.

Perched on the banks of English Bay, this museum documents Vancouver's historical ties to the sea. Galleries recall the 18th-century European explorers, the city's growth as a port city, and the modern fishing industry. There are numerous naval exhibits, including a full-size replica of a modern tugboat's wheelhouse.

The highlight of the museum is the *St. Roch* **National Historic Site** (tel. 666-3201). This Royal Canadian Mounted Police patrol boat, a two-masted ketch, was the first sailing vessel to navigate the Northwest Passage (from west to east), in 1944. Free guided tours are conducted by Environment Canada, Parks. Admission is included with entrance to the Maritime Museum.

Outside, extending into English Bay, is **Heritage Harbour,** the home of restored heritage vessels, traditional craft of foreign lands, visiting tall ships, and many special maritime events.

Admission: $5 adults; $2.50 seniors, students, and children; $10 families. Combined admission with the Vancouver Museum (see "Museums" in "The Top Attractions," above), $8 adults, $4 seniors and children, free for children under 5; $16 families.

Open: Daily 10am–5pm. **Closed:** Mon Sept–Apr. **Bus:** 22; then walk four blocks south on Cornwall Avenue. **Boat:** Granville Island Ferry from Vancouver Aquatic Center (Beach Avenue at Thurlow Street), Sat–Sun and holidays 10am–5pm, every 15 minutes.

VANCOUVER POLICE MUSEUM, 240 E. Cordova St., at Main. Tel. 665-3346.

The city police depict their century-long history in permanent displays of weapons, counterfeiting equipment, and gambling paraphernalia seized during raids.

Admission: Free (donations accepted).
Open: Mon–Fri 11:30am–4:30pm.

UNIVERSITY OF BRITISH COLUMBIA

One of Canada's largest universities (40,000 students), UBC has a breathtaking setting on Point Grey, overlooking the Strait of Georgia and English Bay, surrounded by beaches and dense forests.

UBC has numerous attractions that are open to visitors: its Museum of Anthropology (see "Museums" in "The Top Attractions," above), botanical gardens (see "Parks and Gardens," below), the world's largest nuclear cyclotron, a geological museum, geophysical and astronomical observatories, various research centers open to public tours, and a wide range of cultural and sports facilities.

Free campus tours are offered May to September, Monday through Friday at 10am and 1pm; the rest of the year, by appointment. Specific questions and requests should be directed to the **Community Relations Office,** UBC, Vancouver, BC V6T 1W5 (tel. 604/822-3131).

Information on the university's **farming and forestry research centers** can be obtained from the UBC Community Relations Office (tel. 822-3131), in the Old Administration Building, Main Mall and Memorial Road. The **Fine Arts Gallery, Frederic Wood Theatre,** and **UBC School of Music** share student work with the public (see Chapter 9, "Vancouver Nights"); and the university's aquatic, tennis, and winter-sports centers are open for public use (see "Sports and Recreation," below). Miles of hiking trails wind through the University Endowment Lands, which buffer the campus from the rest of the city.

M. Y. WILLIAMS GEOLOGICAL MUSEUM, Geological Sciences Centre, Stores Rd., Gate 6. Tel. 822-5586.

About 4.5 billion years of mineral and fossil history are on display, including the skeleton of an 80-million-year-old lambeosaurus dinosaur.

Admission: Free.

Open: Mon–Fri 8:30am–4:30pm. **Bus:** 10, 41, or 42.

TRI-UNIVERSITY MESON FACILITY [TRIUMF], 4004 Wesbrook Mall, south of W. 16th Ave. Tel. 222-1047.

This world-class nuclear-physics research laboratory is operated jointly by UBC, the University of Victoria, Simon Fraser University in Burnaby, and the University of Alberta. Its cyclotron, with a maximum energy of 520 million electron volts, operates 24 hours a day at least 80% of the year. The tour is not suitable for children under 13 or those with heart pacemakers.

Admission: Free.

Open: 75-minute tours, May–Aug, Mon–Fri at 11am and 2pm; Sept–Apr, on Wed and Fri at 1pm. **Bus:** 41.

UBC ASTRONOMICAL OBSERVATORY AND UBC GEOPHYSICAL OBSERVATORY, Main Mall, Gate 1. Tel. 822-2802.

These side-by-side facilities welcome public visits. The star-gazing section is open most clear Saturday nights (other nights by appointment). The geophysical section offers tours to explore (among other things) earthquake probability and magnetic storms.

Admission: Free.

Open: Astronomical observatory, Sat 8pm–midnight; both observatories, by appointment year-round. **Bus:** 4, 10, 41, or 42.

PARKS & GARDENS

B.C. PARKWAY.

This 50-acre linear park follows the SkyTrain route 12 miles from Main Street to New Westminster Station. The 7-Eleven Bicycle Path and John Molson Way jogging path are the connecting links among 32 city parks. En route, there are also children's adventure playgrounds, theme gardens, floral displays, heritage plazas, and an International Mile of Flags.

Admission: Free.

Open: Daily 24 hours. **SkyTrain:** All stops from Main Street east.

DR. SUN YAT-SEN CLASSICAL CHINESE GARDEN, 578 Carrall St., near Pender. Tel. 689-7133 or 662-3207.

This $5.3-million masterpiece behind the Chinese Cultural Centre opened for Expo '86 as the first full-scale classical garden ever created outside China. Modeled after Ming Dynasty (1368–1644) gardens, it was designed by a team of 52 experts from the city of Suzhou, who spent a year on the project.

Initially, Westerners may find it sparse in vegetation, but the Chinese consider plants to be just one-fourth of a garden's serene yet ever-changing appeal. They seek a philosophical yin-yang balance of small and large, light and dark, soft and hard, flowing and immovable. This garden's elements, most of which were imported from China (in 950 crates), include massive rocks (convoluted limestone, prized as natural sculptures) and numerous buildings—pavilions, terraces, covered walkways, and lookout platforms, each unique in design. Reflecting pools of water and carefully tended plants—pine, bamboo, plum, and flowering shrubs—complete the picture.

The gift shop offers an excellent selection of Chinese artifacts, including ceramics and scroll paintings, and books on culture and history.

Admission: $3.50 adults; $2.50 seniors, students, and children; free for children under 6; $7 families.

Open: May–Aug, daily 10am–7:30pm; Sept–Apr, daily 10am–4:30pm. **Bus:** 19.

NITOBE MEMORIAL GARDEN, 6565 NW Marine Dr., Gate 4, University of British Columbia. Tel. 822-6038.

Like a Zen sanctuary, this authentic 2.4-acre garden behind UBC's Asian Centre offers visitors a meditative escape from the surrounding campus bustle. Those who visit often remark on the almost timeless harmony of the changing seasons. The lake waters reflect delicate cherry blossoms in the early spring, the colorful leaves of maples in the fall, and numerous bridal gowns in the summer. Arched bridges wind past stone lanterns and through immaculately maintained woods to a traditional teahouse.

Admission: $2 adults, 50¢ seniors and students, free for children under 6, free for everyone on Wed.

Open: Daily 10am–dusk. **Closed:** Sat–Sun Oct 10 to mid-March. **Bus:** 10 or 42.

QUEEN ELIZABETH PARK AND BLOEDEL CONSERVATORY, Cambie St., at W. 33rd Ave. Tel. 872-5513.

Two former Oak Ridge stone quarries have been converted into this 133-acre civic arboretum with a domed floral conservatory in its midst. The park's eastern slope is a living museum that contains every major species of tree and shrub native to coastal British Columbia, plus a handful of foreign specimens. A rose garden, 20 tennis courts, and a pitch-and-putt golf course share the grounds.

The Bloedel Conservatory is a triodetic Plexiglas dome, 70 feet high and 140 feet in diameter, that harbors a tropical environment. Within are 500 varieties of plants from jungle and desert, more than 100 free-flying tropical birds, and streams and ponds filled with colorful koi (Japanese carp). A plaza with lighted fountains and covered walkways surrounds the conservatory, located atop Little Mountain—at 500 feet, this is the highest point within the Vancouver city limits. There are fine views from the café and gift shop.

Admission: $2.85 adults, $1.40 seniors and children, $5.70 families.

Open: Summer, Mon–Fri 9am–8pm, Sat–Sun 10am–9pm; winter, daily 10am–5pm. **Closed:** Christmas Day. **Bus:** 15.

UBC BOTANICAL GARDEN, 6250 Stadium Rd., near SW Marine Dr. and W. 16th Ave., Gate 8, University of British Columbia. Tel. 822-4208.

This garden, established in 1916 as the first university botanical garden in Canada, has numerous components in its 70 acres. They include the B.C. Native Garden, featuring specimens from the coastal woodland and peat bog to the dry interior; the E. H. Lohbrunner Alpine Garden, displaying mountain flora from around the world; the

Food Garden, with fruits, vegetables, and edible plants grown on espaliers; the Physick Garden, a re-created 16th-century garden of medicinal herbs, laid out around a sundial; and the Asian Garden, with an outstanding collection of magnolias, rhododendrons, and blue Himalayan poppies.

Admission: $3.75 adults, 75¢ seniors and students, free for children under 6.

Open: Daily 10am–dusk. **Bus:** 41.

VANDUSEN BOTANICAL GARDEN, 5251 Oak St., at W. 37th Ave. Tel. 266-7194.

One of the city's largest botanical gardens, with 55½ acres, occupies the site of an abandoned golf course in the well-to-do Shaughnessy district. The garden is unique in that plants are arranged according to their ecological niche or botanical relationship: Pathways and wooden bridges lead visitors through various geographical zones.

The garden contains one of Canada's most extensive collections of ornamental plants, including spring bulbs, rhododendrons, summer annuals, and heathers. There's also an Elizabethan-style hedge maze and a children's topiary garden. In the Alma VanDusen Garden, colorful perennials thrive around meandering streams and across the meadows. Numerous sculptures are situated around the grounds.

From Sprinklers Restaurant you can enjoy lovely views of downtown Vancouver and the North Shore mountains. The garden also has a popular gift shop.

Admission: $4.50 adults, $2.25 seniors, students, and children; $9 families. Half price Oct 15–Mar 29.

Open: Daily 10am–dusk. **Closed:** Christmas Day. **Bus:** 17.

ETHNIC COMMUNITIES

Vancouver's largest and best-known ethnic area, **Chinatown,** is covered in Chapter 7, "Strolling Around Vancouver."

GREEKTOWN, W. Broadway between MacDonald and Alma Sts.

To casual visitors, the most notable feature of this part of Vancouver is the proliferation of Greek restaurants, all of which seem to boast the Aegean blue and white of their nation's flag. But look again: There are food stores, selling olive oil, phyllo dough, feta cheese, grape leaves, and fresh squid. There are bakeries, with delicious honey-sweet pastries like baklava. There are *kaffenion,* men-only social clubs housed in billiard parlors and coffeehouses. There are jewelers, urging patrons to buy "evil eyes" to ward off misfortune and "worry beads" to chase away anxiety. And there's **Minerva Greek Imports,** 2924 W. Fourth Ave., Vancouver's best source of woolen sailors' hats, wooden wine gourds, baptismal candles, coffee-making *briki,* and cassettes of Greek music, from bouzouki instrumentals to Melina Mercouri.

St. George's Orthodox Church, West 31st Avenue and Arbutus Street, is the focal point for this deeply religious community. Visitors are welcome to drop in and admire the church's art and architecture, particularly its sacred icons. (Women should not wear slacks or shorts.) Sunday services are in Greek, with lots of incense-burning and chanting. The **Greek Community Centre** (tel. 266-7148) is next door to the church.

Easter is the biggest holiday of the year, and it's celebrated with full spiritual devotion, but to the general public, the **Greek Days** in late June may be of greater interest. West Broadway is blocked to traffic from noon to early the next morning for street dancing and general feasting.

JAPAN TOWN, Powell St. and Dunlevy Ave.

Once the focus of a sizable community, this area was more Japanese prior to World War II, when Japanese-Canadians were sent to internment camps. Today, Vancouver's Japanese are scattered throughout the metropolitan area, although they return en masse to Oppenheimer Park for O-Bon dances in July and the annual **Japanese Festival** in August.

The **Vancouver Buddhist Church** is on the corner of Jackson Avenue opposite the park. Several small shops, on Powell Street west to Gore, include the Japanese Deli (see Chapter 5, "Vancouver Dining").

LITTLE ITALY, Commercial Dr., between Venables St. and E. Broadway.

Since most Italian-Canadians came from the poorer southern regions of Italy, Neapolitan and Sicilian styles tend to predominate in Vancouver's Italian community. Commercial Drive doesn't have the "grit" of Little Italy in New York, but it has dozens of charming shops, a wonderfully relaxed atmosphere of large awnings over shaded sidewalks, and plenty of streetcorner gossip.

Italians love to eat and dress well. The restaurants here attract crowds with antipasti, pastas, and homemade gelati (Italian ice creams). The grocery stores sell dozens of varieties of fresh and dried pasta, cheeses, and cured meats; other shops specialize in one or another of these foods. The cafés, which serve the best espresso in town, double as men's social clubs and often exclude women. Italian tailors and leather importers are well represented on the Commercial Drive strip.

The **Italian Cultural Centre**, 3075 Slocan St. (tel. 430-3337), is well east of Little Italy on the Grandview Hwy. It provides family services, hosts Italian movies and concerts, and offers a library of art books donated by the Italian government. **Carnevale,** the Italian Mardi Gras, is celebrated at the center every year with two days of eating and dancing. During **Italian Days** in late June or early July, several blocks of Commercial Drive are cordoned off for shopping, feasting, and merrymaking.

PUNJABI MARKET (LITTLE INDIA), Main St., between E. 49th and E. 51st Aves.

Greater Vancouver's 65,000 East Indians have their largest community in the city's southeastern quadrant. Here on Main Street is a two-block stretch of shops that sell nearly everything you might find in New Delhi: silk saris, gold bangles, religious icons, Punjabi-language videos and cassette tapes, traditional musical instruments, and so forth. Grocery stores have huge bins of spices and dried vegetables for curries and other dishes; rosewater-sweet gulab jamun and other taste-tempters fill the front counters of such restaurants as the Himalaya and the Bombay Sweet Shop.

These streets are jammed during traditional Sikh festivals such as **Baisakhi,** which takes place on a Saturday in mid-April. A cast of thousands parades through the cheering Main Street throngs about midday. Most other Saturdays, there are colorful 11am weddings at the Arthur Erickson–designed **Khalsa Diwan Gurudwara Temple,** 8000 Ross St., at SW Marine Drive (tel. 324-2010); visitors are welcome with advance notice. It's a tremendous cultural experience, one that doesn't end until you share a fiery vegetarian lunch with the wedding party in the temple basement!

NEARBY ATTRACTIONS

BURNABY

BURNABY ART GALLERY, 6344 Deer Lake Ave., Century Park, Burnaby. Tel. 291-9441.

A heritage building just a short stroll from the Burnaby Village Museum, the gallery specializes in 20th-century art.

Admission: $2 adults, free for children.

Open: Tues–Fri 9am–5pm, Sat–Sun and holidays noon–5pm (first Thurs of each month 9am–8pm). **Bus:** 120, 131, or 132.

BURNABY VILLAGE MUSEUM, 6501 Deer Lake Ave., Century Park, Burnaby. Tel. 293-6501.

Here's a living, open-air museum that takes history seriously and makes it fun. Spread across this five-acre plot is a typical Lower Mainland community, circa 1890–1925. Its 30-plus buildings have been transplanted from other sites or reconstructed. There's a church, school, general store, residential log cabin, pharmacy, dentist's office, Chinese herbalist, photography studio, barbershop, and more. The steam-powered sawmill, blacksmith shop, and printing press are fully operational. A miniature steam train (for kids) and turn-of-the-century ice-cream parlor are enchanting. Guides in period costumes are well informed. The village offers old-time crafts and baking demonstrations throughout the year.

Admission: $4.65 adults, $3.25 seniors and students, $2.50 children 6–12, free for children under 6; $12 families.

Open: Apr–Sept, daily 11am–4:30pm. **Closed:** Oct–Mar, except for Thanksgiving and Christmas. **Bus:** 120, 131, or 132.

Directions: Take the Kensington Avenue exit from Hwy. 1.

SIMON FRASER UNIVERSITY, Gaglardi Way, Burnaby Mountain, Burnaby. Tel. 291-3210.

This modern institution atop 1,200-foot Burnaby Mountain has a commanding view of the Lower Mainland. When it opened in 1965, its stunning architecture won acclaim for Vancouverite Arthur Erickson. Among campus attractions, the **Museum of Archeology and Ethnology** (tel. 291-3325) has fine native displays. It's open May to August, Monday through Friday from 10am to 4pm and on Saturday and Sunday from noon to 3pm; September to April, some evenings; admission is free. The **University Art Gallery** (tel. 291-4266) has an excellent collection of Inuit art. It's open on Monday from noon to 6pm and Tuesday through Friday from 9am to 4pm; admission is free.

Open: Free campus tours with student guides, daily July–Labor Day, hourly 10:30am–3:30pm; rest of year, one-hour tours by appointment. **Bus:** 135, 144, or 145. **Directions:** Head east seven miles on Hastings Street, turn right on Sperling Avenue, and then left on Curtis Street; Curtis becomes Gaglardi Way and climbs the mountain to SFU.

RICHMOND & THE AIRPORT AREA

FANTASY GARDEN WORLD, 10800 No. 5 Rd., Richmond. Tel. 277-7777.

There are two parts to this tourist-oriented complex, once owned by former British Columbia Premier Bill Vander Zalm. The botanical garden features stunning seasonal displays: 200 varieties of tulips and 1,000 rhododendrons in spring, a dazzling show of roses and other annuals in summer. It also has a biblical garden with Christian scenes, a children's farm with rides and animals, exotic aviaries, a wedding chapel, a carillon, and a gazebo teahouse.

The European Village—unmistakable from the highway, with its profile of old-world facades—has 20 restaurants and shops that sell Scottish tartans, German bratwurst, French lace, Swiss chocolates, Scandinavian woolens, English pub ales, and so forth. European street entertainment is performed weekends and summer weekdays in the cobblestone plaza.

Admission: European Village, free; garden, $6 adults, $4.50 seniors, $3.50 students, $2.50 children, free for children under 6.

Open: Hours vary seasonally. **Bus:** 403, then transfer to no. 404 or 405. **Directions:** Take the Steveston Hwy. exit from Hwy. 99 south.

GROCERY HALL OF FAME, 6620 No. 6 Rd., Richmond. Tel. 669-2214.

If you enjoy studying the transformation of the Morton Salt girl during this century, if you appreciate the differences in Coca-Cola's logo over the decades, and if you recall the Campbell's Soup kids with affection, then this little storefront museum is for you. There's shelf after shelf of packages, tins, and advertising, plus a future store shelf for the year 2010.

Admission: Free.

Open: Sat 9am–noon.

GUAN YIN CHINESE BUDDHIST TEMPLE, 9160 Steveston Hwy., Richmond. Tel. 274-2822.

Perhaps the best example of traditional Chinese religious architecture in North America, this rather ostentatious structure has golden porcelain tiles and flying dragons on its rooftop. Climb the granite stairway, past guardian marble lions and an enormous incense burner; remove your shoes, then reverently enter the main worship hall.

Directly ahead are three golden images of the Buddha, to which chants are delivered in ceremonies at 10:30am each Saturday. To his right is an enormous sculpture of Guan Yin, goddess of mercy, with her thousand arms and heads. Behind are funeral tablets to deceased ancestors and written requests for assistance from beyond. The temple has a bonsai garden, small museum, resource library, gift counter, and a chapel where you shake sticks and have your fortune told (in Chinese). Inquire about lectures and meditation classes.

Admission: Free; donations appreciated.
Open: Daily 10am–5pm; prayer ceremony, Sat at 10:30am. **Bus:** 403. **Directions:** Take the Steveston Hwy. exit off Hwy. 99 south.

REIFEL BIRD SANCTUARY, 5191 Robertson Rd., West-ham Island, Delta. Tel. 946-6980.

This 850-acre estuary marsh at the mouth of the south fork of the Fraser River is claimed by the B.C. Wildlife Society to be a crucial wetland. Countless thousands of migratory birds, traveling the Pacific Flyway, land here to rest and feed. Myriad others spend the winter in this protected habitat, and still other species make this a year-round home, nesting and rearing their young here in late spring and summer. In all, more than 230 species have been identified, some of them extremely rare—like the Temminck's stint and the spotted redshank. The sanctuary has an observation tower, picnic tables, washrooms, and two miles of trails. You're likely to find the greatest activity in the fall, the least in midsummer.

Admission: $3.25 adults, $1 seniors and children.
Open: Daily 9am–4pm. **Directions:** Take the Tsawwassen exit (Hwy. 17) off Hwy. 99 south, turn west on 48 Avenue through Ladner, where it becomes River Road West; turn right on Westham Island Road across the river and follow it to the end; the sanctuary is five miles west of Ladner.

STEVESTON

Established as a Japanese fishing village around the turn of the century, this quaint harbor community makes a great day trip from Vancouver, especially on a Saturday or Sunday morning. Arrive soon after dawn, when fishers from all over the Fraser River delta region congregate at **Government Wharf** to sell seafood directly from their boats. It's hectic—and fascinating.

Afterward, drop by the tiny **Steveston Museum,** on the top floor above the post office (Moncton Street at First Avenue) to see a photographic history of old Steveston and a number of Japanese artifacts. A few blocks east on Moncton is the **Dojo** (martial-arts center), a traditional-style building that draws the province's 300 best masters in judo, kendo, and other disciplines. It's open to visitors on Sunday. There are several Japanese grocery stores and a couple of outstanding fish-and-chips shops—**Dave's** and the **Steveston Seafood House**—on Moncton Street.

You can get to Steveston on bus no. 402. Or take the Steveston Hwy. exit west off Hwy. 99 south, travel 4½ miles west to No. 1 Road, turn left for half a mile, then right onto Moncton Street.

ON THE NORTH SHORE

LYNN CANYON PARK, Park Rd., North Vancouver. Tel. 987-5922.

The **Lynn Canyon Suspension Bridge,** originally built in 1912, may be even more thrilling than the one in Capilano Canyon. At 225 feet it's only half as long, but its height of 240 feet above Lynn Canyon is 10 feet higher than the bridge at Capilano. There's lots of hiking in the heavily wooded 300-acre park and reserve. (Sly Stallone fans take note: Most of *First Blood* was filmed here.) The park's **Ecology Centre** presents films and slide shows on various aspects of natural history. Staff members lead frequent walking tours.

Admission: Free.
Open: Daily dawn–dusk. **Bus:** 228 or 229; then walk five blocks west on Lynn Valley Road. **Directions:** Take Lynn Valley Road northeast off Hwy. 1, continue 1½ miles to Park Road, and turn right.

LYNN HEADWATERS REGIONAL PARK, Lynn Valley Rd., North Vancouver. Tel. 432-6350.

An inaccessible wilderness until the mid-1980s, this park features a network of hiking trails with some mountain views.
Admission: Free.
Open: Daily dawn–dusk. **Directions:** Follow those given for Lynn Canyon Park (above), but continue up Lynn Valley Road approximately four miles.

MOUNT SEYMOUR PROVINCIAL PARK, Mt. Seymour Rd., North Vancouver. Tel. 986-2261.

Offering a view to match that of Grouse Mountain, Mount Seymour rises 4,767 feet above the Burrard Inlet's Indian Arm. The road winds through ancient stands of fir, cedar, and hemlock to a cafeteria and gift shop at a height of 3,300 feet. From there, a chair lift—heavily used by skiers in winter—climbs to alpine meadows, and a hiking trail goes straight to the summit. On clear days, you can see Washington State's snowcapped Mount Baker to the south.
Admission: Park, free; chair lift, $5 adults, $2.50 children under 12.
Open: Park, daily 7am–11pm. Chair lift, July–Aug, daily 11am–5pm; Sept–Oct, Sat–Sun 11am–5pm. **Bus:** 211. **Directions:** Cross Second Narrows Bridge on Hwy. 1 west, take Exit 22 and go east on Mt. Seymour Parkway for three miles, then north on Mt. Seymour Road.

NORTH VANCOUVER MUSEUM AND ARCHIVES, 333 Chesterfield St., North Vancouver. Tel. 987-5618.

Exhibits feature North Vancouver history, shipbuilding, and Native Canadian artifacts. Extensive archives contain about 6,000 photographs.
Admission: By donation.
Open: Museum, Wed and Fri–Sun noon–5pm, Thurs noon–9pm; archives, Wed–Fri 9:30am–12:30pm and 1:30–4:30pm.
SeaBus: Lonsdale Quay. **Bus:** 242.

PRESENTATION HOUSE GALLERY, 333 Chesterfield Ave., North Vancouver. Tel. 986-1351.

This art gallery emphasizes photography by local, national, and international artists.
Admission: $2 adults, $1 seniors and students; free for everyone on Fri.
Open: Wed and Sat–Sun noon–5pm, Thurs–Fri noon–9pm.
SeaBus: Lonsdale Quay. **Bus:** 242.

HORSESHOE BAY

This picturesque cove at the foot of Howe Sound is best known as the staging area for ferries to Nanaimo (on Vancouver Island),

Langdale (on the Sunshine Coast), and Bowen Island. But it's a lovely small community in its own right, with numerous shops, waterfront restaurants, and a designer brewery, **The Troller.** Horseshoe Bay is a good place to rent a boat for a day of salmon fishing in Howe Sound.

To get here, take bus no. 250. By car, take Hwy. 1 west, eight miles from Lions Gate Bridge.

3. COOL FOR KIDS

By now you've already discovered a handful of good ideas for sights the kids will enjoy, but if you're staying more than a few days with the children, you won't want to be without Daniel Wood's *Kids! Kids! Kids! in Vancouver* (Douglas & McIntyre).

In **Stanley Park** (see "The Top Attractions," above), younger children won't want to miss the children's zoo, miniature railway, and playgrounds. The whole family will enjoy the Vancouver Aquarium, Stanley Park Zoo, Lost Lagoon, and a drive (or a walk) around the Seawall.

In **Vanier Park,** get the family interested in the stars at the H. R. MacMillan Planetarium in the Vancouver Museum (see "The Top Attractions," above), and let them board a real icebreaker, the *St. Roch,* in the Vancouver Maritime Museum (see "More Attractions," above).

Science World B.C. (see "More Attractions," above) on the old Expo '86 site, is a hands-on experience guaranteed to change children's view of the world.

The **Burnaby Village Museum** (see "Nearby Attractions" in "More Attractions," above) will appeal to even the least scholarly child because of the way it makes history fun (especially the old-fashioned ice-cream parlor). Some youngsters will enjoy the totem poles and other Native Canadian artifacts in city museums; others may prefer the natural beauty of the botanical gardens.

In **North Vancouver,** kids will love crossing the suspension bridges at Capilano Canyon or Lynn Canyon Parks.

A walk through **Chinatown** may be an adventure in a different world. The strange sights (like barbecued ducks hanging in shop windows), smells (for example, in a herbalist's shop), and sounds (such as fireworks during a dragon dance) are immensely exciting to many youngsters, and Chinese toys are thought-provoking.

One of Granville Island's biggest attractions for youngsters is the **Kids Only Market,** 1496 Cartwright St., beside the access road to the island; open in summer, daily from 10am to 6pm (closed Monday the rest of the year). Various fun activities are scattered up and down its two stories. The 16 shops here cater to children (and indirectly to their parents) with toys, books, records, clothes, food, and even computers! Nearby, the **Children's Water Park and Adventure Playground** lets you relax while the kids release some energy. If they get wet or dirty, you can use the changing facilities in Isadora's restaurant.

If your children love sports, check out the activities in "Sports and Recreation," later in this chapter.

Here are some other suggestions just for kids:

LA FETE COLOMBIENNE DES ENFANTS, 12840 16th Ave., Suite 202, Surrey. Tel. 535-1311.

Both French-speaking children and children who speak French only in the classroom will enjoy this unique festival. With all the entertainment and events staged in Canada's "other official language," La Fête takes place at a different site each year, for example, the seaside community of White Rock, historic Fort Langley, or Vancouver's Science World.

Admission: No charge at site; performances, about $8.

Open: Usually held the last weekend in Apr; phone for exact dates and times.

MAPLEWOOD FARM, 405 Seymour River Place, North Vancouver. Tel. 929-5610.

This five-acre farm, operated by the North Vancouver Parks Department, has a large number of domestic animals and birds for petting. There are two main visiting areas: "Goathill" and "Rabbitat." If you happen to be in town Memorial Day weekend, don't miss the annual Sheep Fair; the Farm Fair is held in mid-September.

Admission: $1.50 adults, $1 seniors and children; $4.50 families.

Open: Tues–Sun and holidays 10am–4pm. **Bus:** 211 or 214.

PLAYLAND, Exhibition Park, Hastings and Cassiar Sts. Tel. 255-5161.

A traditional Midwest-style amusement park, Playland has 40 rides, including Canada's largest wooden roller coaster. You'll find clowns, a midway where you can test your strength or intelligence, and, of course, lots of hot dogs and cotton candy.

Admission: $5 adults, $2 children; rides priced individually. All-day pass (including admission), $17.95 adults, $13.95 children (does not include some adult rides).

Open: Apr–Sept; hours vary seasonally. **Bus:** 10 or 14.

VANCOUVER CHILDREN'S FESTIVAL, Vanier Park, 1100 Chestnut St. Tel. 280-4444.

If you're in town with kids, don't, under any circumstances, miss this! A performing arts celebration for the younger set, the festival features Canadian and foreign artists in music, dance, theater, mime, and puppetry productions. In past years, the cultures of Japan, China, Spain, and Zimbabwe have been represented, together with that of North America.

Admission: No charge at site; performances, $2.70–$6.45.

Open: Third week of May. **Bus:** 22; then walk three blocks south on Cornwall Avenue. **Boat:** Granville Island Ferry from Vancouver Aquatic Centre.

4. ORGANIZED TOURS

Many travelers prefer the comfort of letting someone else handle their sightseeing arrangements—they like to relax and not worry about transportation, admissions, timing, or narration. Listed below is a selection of the many tours available.

BUS TOURS

Gray Line of Vancouver, 900 W. Georgia St., Suite 108, Vancouver, BC V6C 2W6 (tel. 604/682-2877, or toll free 800/663-0667), offers Vancouver city tours lasting 3½–4 hours, at a cost of $28 for adults, $25 for seniors, and $17 for children. Tours depart April to October, daily at 9:30am and 1:45pm; November to March, daily at 9:30am.

Pacific Coast Lines, 150 Dunsmuir St. (tel. 662-7575), offers three major tours:

"Introduction to Vancouver" tours depart May to September, daily at 9:30am. They last 1¾ hours and cost $18 for adults, $16 for seniors, $9 for children 5–11.

The "Vancouver Grand City Tour" lasts 3½ hours, departs daily at 1:45pm (and also at 9:30am in July and August), and costs $28 for adults, $25 for seniors, $14 for children 5–11.

The "Majestic North Shore Tour" departs May to September, daily at 1:45pm. It lasts 4 hours and costs $38 for adults, $35 for seniors, $19 for children 5–11.

In addition, Pacific Coach Lines also offers two combination tours: The 5¾-hour "Introduction to Vancouver and Majestic North Shore Tour" departs May to September, daily at 9:30am, charging $50 for adults, $45 for seniors, $22.50 for children 5–11; and the 3-hour "Vancouver and Majestic North Shore Tour" departs May to September, daily at 9:30am, and costs $25 for adults, $20 for seniors, and $12.50 for children.

Operated by the **Vancouver Trolley Company,** 2650 Slocan Ave., Vancouver, BC V5M 4E9 (tel. 604/255-2444; fax 604/251-5923), these natural-gas-powered, enclosed, tire-driven replicas of turn-of-the-century Vancouver streetcars run every half hour on a 90-minute circuit of Vancouver's major sights, including Stanley Park, Science World, and Queen Elizabeth Park. April to October, the "trolleys" can be boarded at any of 17 stops en route, daily from approximately 9am to 6pm. The cost is $17 for adults, $15 for seniors and students. Tickets are good all day.

BOAT TOURS

1st Tours, Harbour Ferries, 1782 W. Georgia St., Vancouver, BC V6G 2V7 (tel. 604/688-7246, or toll free 800/663-1500), operates a 1½-hour "Paddlewheel Harbour Tour" aboard the MVP *Constitution.* This tour departs mid-May to mid-September, daily at 9:30am, 11:30am, 1:30pm, and 3:30pm, and costs $15 for adults, $12 for seniors and students, $10 for children 5–11.

Fraser River Tours, 19252 119th Ave., Suite 8, Pitt Meadows, BC V3Y 2K4 (tel. 604/272-9187 or 465-4859), operates a 6-hour "Pitt River Tour" which departs in summer at 10am three days a week (depending on demand) from New Westminster Quay. The cost of $39 for adults, $35 for seniors, $26 for children 5–12, includes a buffet lunch.

If you want to see wildlife, there's also a "Sea Lion Tour" lasting 1 hour and 40 minutes. It departs from Steveston, Richmond, in April and May, depending on the sea lion migrations. The cost is $16 for adults, $14 for seniors, $9.50 for children 5–12.

Gray Line Water Tours, 399 W. Sixth Ave., Suite 200, Vancouver, BC V5Y 1L1 (tel. 604/681-8687), presents a 2-hour "Harbour Cruise Tour," departing July to mid-September, daily at 9:30am and noon. The charge is $25 for adults, $22 for seniors, and $13 for children.

From mid-May to late September, the **SS *Beaver* Steamship Company,** 554 Cardero St., Barbary Coast Yacht Basin, Vancouver, BC V6G 2W6 (tel. 604/682-7284), operates a 5-hour "Indian Arm Adventure Tour," at a cost of $49.95 per person, including lunch.

During these same months there's also a 4-hour "Sunset Dinner Cruise," departing daily at 6:30pm. The charge of $49.95 per person includes a buffet meal on English Bay.

AIR TOURS

Vancouver Seaplane Adventures, Harbour Air, on Waterfront Street between Canada Place and the Westin Bayshore Hotel (tel. 688-1277), offers five seaplane flightseeing tours: the "Vancouver Panorama," lasting 30 minutes and costing $60 per person; the "Sunshine Coast Dinner Flight," lasting 75 minutes and costing $80 per person; a "Glaciers and Alpine Lakes" tour, taking 75 minutes, at $150 per person; a 2½-hour "Alpine Lake Picnic" for $140 per person, which includes an hour of flightseeing and a 1½-hour luncheon; and the "Fiords and Fishing Villages" tour, lasting 1¼ hours and costing $150 per person.

Vancouver Helicopter Tours, 455 Commissioner St. (tel. 683-HELI), offers the 20-minute "Greater Vancouver Scenic Tour," for $80 per person; the 45- to 50-minute "North Shore Discoverer," at $165 per person; and the 1¾-hour "Coastal Mountain Odyssey," for $290 per person, which includes a 10-minute stop on a glacier.

Heli-tours from the top of Grouse Mountain include: the "Crown Mountain Tour" for $30 per person, and the "Lions Peak Tour" for $60 per person.

5. SPECIAL & FREE EVENTS

Vancouver starts the year with one of its biggest events: **First Night,** a New Year's Eve performing arts festival that closes the streets of downtown. Admission to the shows, held at a variety of sites, is a $5 button. Tens of thousands of revelers are convinced anew each year that they can have a good time without getting drunk: No alcohol is served. The following morning, thousands of hardy folks show up at icy English Bay for a **Polar Bear Swim.** (They probably resolve thereafter never to enter such cold water again.)

In late January or early February, the Chinese community launches its lunar year—be it the Year of the Horse, the Dragon, or whatever—with a noisy parade through the streets of Chinatown. Formally this **Chinese New Year** celebration lasts two weeks—from new moon to full moon.

Come summer, the **Vancouver Sea Festival** draws throngs to the shores of English Bay for about four days in mid-July. Highlights include a parade along Beach Avenue, the city's biggest pyrotechnic display, and the finish of the Nanaimo-to-Vancouver bathtub race. There's no charge for the festivities, including numerous open-air concerts.

The **Pacific National Exhibition** (tel. 253-2311), the 10th-largest fair in North America, runs for 17 days in late August and early September, concluding on Labor Day. There's something for everyone here, from big-name entertainment to a demolition derby, livestock demonstrations to logging competitions, fashion shows to a frenetic midway. Adults and teenagers pay $7.50 admission, seniors pay $4.25, children 6–12 are charged $3, and tots get in free.

A complete list of major annual events in Vancouver and vicinity appears in Chapter 2, "When to Go."

6. SPORTS & RECREATION

As you might expect of a city that's sports-crazy enough to have a provincial hall of fame to honor its heroes in 68 different pursuits, Vancouver offers a wide choice of spectator and participatory sports.

SPORTS

Tickets for professional sports events can be purchased from the **Vancouver Ticket Centre** (tel. 280-4444), which has branches in major malls and department stores throughout the city; tickets can also be ordered by phone and charged to a major credit card.

BASEBALL   The **Vancouver Canadians** (tel. 872-5232), a California Angels farm club, play a 144-game schedule in the AAA Pacific Coast League, which is one step below the major leagues. Home games are at Nat Bailey Stadium, 33rd Avenue at Ontario Street, adjacent to Queen Elizabeth Park. The season begins in April and continues to early September. Games are Monday through Saturday at 7:05pm on Sunday at 1:30pm, and on Wednesday at 12:15pm; tickets to see future big-league stars cost no more than $7.50 for box seats, $5 for the covered grandstand, and $3 for kids. The Angels, Seattle Mariners, Montréal Expos, and Toronto Blue Jays sometimes play preseason major-league exhibition games here in late March or early April.

The **University of British Columbia** and **Simon Fraser University** have teams that compete against other major Canadian schools. Secondary schools and younger children also have leagues.

BASKETBALL   The **University of British Columbia** competes against other Canadian universities in men's and women's basketball with international rules. Burnaby's **Simon Fraser University** plays in NAIA Division 1 competition against four-year colleges in Washington and Oregon. The SFU men's and women's teams have been especially strong in recent years.

CRICKET   This slow-moving British sport, which vaguely resembles baseball, is played every weekend from late April to September. Brockton Oval at Stanley Park is the site of regular Saturday and

Sunday matches between amateur clubs in the B.C. Cricket Association.

FOOTBALL The **B.C. Lions** (tel. 585-3323) plays a 20-game schedule in the Canadian Football League. Home games are at B.C. Place Stadium. The season runs from late June into November, with the Grey Cup league championship game played in late November. Home games start at 7:30pm (8:10pm if televised)—usually on Tuesday or Thursday in July and August, then on Saturday beginning in mid-September. Tickets cost $15 (end zone) to $30 (midfield).

Canadian football differs a bit from its American cousin. The field is 10 yards longer, for instance, and the teams have only a three-down offense; thus the emphasis is on passing.

Both **UBC and SFU** have teams. SFU plays NAIA ball against small colleges in Washington and Oregon (with U.S. rules).

HORSE RACING "The Track" at **Exhibition Park** (tel. 254-1631) is the site of thoroughbred racing from mid-April to mid-October. Post times are 6:30pm on Wednesday and Friday, and 1:30pm on weekends and holidays. There are full clubhouse ($5.25) and covered grandstand ($3.25) facilities, as well as an excellent restaurant.

As soon as the racing season ends in Vancouver, the trotting season gets under way at the **Cloverdale Raceway,** 6050 176th St. (tel. 576-9141), in suburban Cloverdale, about 25 miles southeast of Vancouver. There's harness racing here from October to April, with post times at 7pm on Wednesday and Friday, and at 1pm on Saturday, Sunday, and holidays. The raceway has a 3,300-seat glass-enclosed grandstand, licensed clubhouse, and cafeteria.

ICE HOCKEY The **Vancouver Canucks** (tel. 254-5141) play an 80-game schedule in the National Hockey League. Home games are at Pacific Coliseum in Exhibition Park. The regular season runs from October through March, with playoffs for the championship's Stanley Cup extending into May or June. Home games begin at 7:35pm on weekdays, 5:05pm on Saturday, and 7:05pm on Sunday, with a handful of 2:05pm Sunday and holiday games. Tickets cost $15–$30.

Since hockey is Canada's unofficial national sport, there's fierce competition at every level, from the youngest juniors through colleges and semipro leagues.

LACROSSE Canada's official national sport is played from May through August at various locations, including Renfrew Community Park, West Point Grey Park, and Hastings Community Centre Park. The top local league is the Western Lacrosse Association. Contact the **B.C. Lacrosse Association** (tel. 294-2122) for information.

RODEO The **Cloverdale Rodeo** (tel. 576-9461), one of North America's largest, takes place the third full weekend of May at the Lower Fraser Valley Exhibition Grounds, 6050 176th St., Cloverdale. Competitors from all over the continent vie for prize money in such events as bronco and bull riding and calf roping.

RUGBY Another British sport with a strong following in British

Columbia, rugby is played from mid-September to April at more than a score of parks in metropolitan Vancouver. Clubs play one another in their association, including the **Vancouver Rugby Union** (tel. 988-7660) and the **B.C. Rugby Union** (tel. 737-3065). UBC and SFU have teams of their own.

SOCCER   The semiprofessional **Vancouver 86ers** (tel. 299-0086) play a full season of games at Swangard Stadium, Kingsway and Patterson Avenue in Burnaby, from May to September. Games are typically scheduled for 7:30pm on Sunday; tickets are $14 for adults, $10 for seniors and students.

Both UBC and SFU have teams.

RECREATION

Living close to the mountains and the shore, Vancouver residents are especially interested in sports and outdoor activities. The following list includes only a few of the activities that may interest Vancouver visitors. An umbrella agency for amateur sports—**Sport B.C.,** 1367 W. Broadway, at Hemlock (tel. 737-3000)—can probably put you in touch with your favorite sport in a matter of minutes. In addition to those mentioned above and below, Sport B.C. can offer connections to archery, badminton, boxing, curling, fencing, field hockey, figure and speed skating, gymnastics, handball, horseshoe pitching, judo, kendo, rowing, shooting, softball, table tennis, track and field, triathlon, volleyball, water polo, waterskiing, weight-lifting, wrestling, and more.

Those who need appropriate equipment for any sport can probably get it from **Recreational Rentals,** with locations at 2560 Arbutus St. (at Broadway) in Kitsilano (tel. 733-7368), and 4411 No. 3 Road in Richmond (tel. 273-9176).

BALLOONING   **Fantasy Balloon Charters** in suburban Langley (tel. 736-1974) offers silent early-morning and evening flights in the shadow of Washington's imposing Mount Baker. Trips cost $165 for adults and children are charged $1 per pound if they don't displace an adult passenger. The trip includes champagne, hors d'oeuvres, and souvenirs. Departures are from the Langley Airport at 7am and again two hours before sunset.

BEACHES   Perhaps because they experience so many rainy days each year, Vancouverites love to sunbathe. Some escape to Hawaii or Mexico for a few weeks in winter, but in summer they soak up the hot sun on sandy B.C. beaches. And many people swim, although the water temperature doesn't exceed 65°F (18°C) even in midsummer.

Most accessible to downtown are the beaches at Stanley Park. **Second Beach,** beside the playground at the southwest corner of the park, has a shallow, unheated pool that children enjoy. **Third Beach,** a bit more isolated, is on the west side of the park near the Teahouse Restaurant. There is no First Beach—unless you bestow that honor upon the beautiful, sandy **English Bay Beach** along Beach Avenue outside of the park, opposite the English Bay Café.

On the south shore of the bay, **Kitsilano Beach** (tel. 731-0011) has a huge, modern saltwater pool heated to 78°F (25°C). Located off Cornwall Avenue opposite Vine Street, it's shallow at one end for kids and deep at the other end for advanced swimmers. It's open from Victoria Day (late May) to Labor Day, on weekdays from 7am to 8:45pm and on weekends from 10am to 8:45pm; admission is $2.85 for adults, $1.40 for seniors and children, $1.80 for children 6–12; maximum for families is $5.70.

West of "Kits" Beach is a string of beaches extending several miles west, then south around Point Grey and the University of British Columbia. First and largest is **Jericho Beach,** which begins at the end of Alma Street off Point Grey Road. **Locarno Beach** is next, between Discovery and Tolmie Streets off NW Marine Drive; then comes **Spanish Banks,** farther along Marine Drive.

Adventurous souls who continue all the way around Point Grey to the place where the cliffs drop rapidly from the UBC campus will encounter **Wreck Beach,** where college students come *au naturel* to soak up rays on every square inch of their bodies.

At the north foot of the Lions Gate Bridge, **Ambleside Park** has a three-quarter-mile sandy beach facing the Burrard Inlet entrance to Vancouver Harbour. It's popular among North Shore residents.

From June through August, lifeguards are on duty at Second Beach, English Bay Beach, Kitsilano Beach, Jericho Beach, Locarno Beach, and Spanish Banks.

BICYCLING Bike paths around Stanley Park and along the south shore of English Bay at Kitsilano and Jericho beaches are especially popular with cyclists. In addition, the 7-Eleven Bicycle Path follows B.C. Parkway along the SkyTrain route from Main Street to the New Westminster Station, linking 32 parks en route.

There are about 20 places in the Vancouver area where you can rent bikes. Close to the 5.6-mile seawall loop is **Stanley Park Rentals,** 676 Chilco St. (tel. 681-5581), with bikes for $5–$7 per hour (tandem bikes for $9 per hour). Half- and full-day rates are also available (mountain bikes rent for $21 for four hours and $28 for all day).

The **Bicycling Association of British Columbia** has a hotline (tel. 731-7433) for information on group rides and other upcoming events.

For competitors, the **Gastown Grand Prix** takes place on July 1 through downtown over several cordoned-off streets. And on Labor Day weekend, the **Tour de White Rock Cycle Race** follows a route near the U.S. border south of Vancouver.

BOATING Numerous operators have vessels for charter rental, bareboat or skippered, for periods of a few hours to several weeks. In central Vancouver, the Coal Harbour area near the Westin Bayshore Hotel and Granville Island are the best places to look. Horseshoe Bay, west of West Vancouver, and Richmond's Fraser River shoreline, near the international airport, also have major docks.

Delta Charters, 3500 Cessna Dr., Richmond (tel. 273-4211), at the Delta River Inn, has weekly bareboat rates (for vessels 32–58 feet), ranging from $1,800 to $4,000 during high season (June 11 to September 16), 20% off in low season.

Pacific Quest Charters, 1521 Foreshore Walk, Granville Island (tel. 682-2161), has sailboats (27–44 feet) and powerboats (32–42 feet). They sleep 4–10 people. Rental rates during peak season (July 27 to September 7) are $179–$625 daily, $1,053–$3,675 weekly; 15% discounts April 17 to July 26 and September 8 to October 12, 20% discounts October 13 to April 16. The skipper's fee is $125 per day.

Other operators with full charter services are **Bayside Yacht Charters,** Box 17-554, Cardero St., Coal Harbour (tel. 681-2442), and **Westin Bayshore Yacht Charters,** 1601 W. Georgia St. (tel. 682-3377).

Sailors can listen to a taped marine forecast by calling 270-7411. Those unfamiliar with local waters, or unsure of their own skills, can enroll in courses at the **Blue Orca Sailing School,** 1818 Maritime Mews (tel. 683-6300).

CANOEING/KAYAKING Within the Vancouver city limits, False Creek and the shores of English Bay provide good waters for paddling. (Burrard Inlet is not recommended because of heavy harbor traffic and hazardous currents in the First and Second Narrows.) Indian Arm, a 19-mile-long semi-wilderness inlet that defines the eastern boundary of North Vancouver, is a suggested alternative for those who are more adventurous. There are numerous large glacial lakes east of Vancouver. Novices may prefer Deer Lake, a quiet park in central Burnaby.

Rentals are available from **Recreational Rentals** (see above); **Ecomarine Ocean Kayak,** 1668 Duranleau St., Granville Island (tel. 689-7575), for False Creek and English Bay; **Deep Cove Canoe and Kayak Rentals,** Deep Cove (tel. 929-2268), for Indian Arm; and **Deer Lake Boat Rentals,** 2148 Franklin St., Burnaby (tel. 255-0081), for Deer Lake.

DIVING Because of the long, protected coastline, British Columbia and adjacent Washington State have some of the most accessible and safest scuba diving in the world. In fact, Canada's first undersea park, **Telegraph Cove** in Howe Sound, is an easy trip from Vancouver. All told, there are more than two dozen recommended dive locations in Howe Sound and Indian Arm. **Lighthouse Park,** at the northern entrance to Burrard Inlet, is reputed to have the most interesting seascape and widest variety of marine life in the Vancouver area.

Information, equipment, and diving courses are available from **The Diving Locker,** 2745 W. Fourth Ave., Vancouver (tel. 736-2681).

FISHING The Vancouver area offers anglers a choice between world-class freshwater or saltwater fishing. Rainbow and cutthroat trout, char, kokanee, and whitefish are found in southwestern B.C. lakes and rivers, and huge sturgeon have been taken from the Fraser River. Saltwater varieties include all species of salmon (chinook, coho, pink, sockeye, and chum), halibut, ling cod, rockfish, and snapper.

You need a license to fish in British Columbia if you're 15 or older (for tidal waters) or 16 or older (for freshwater or nontidal waters). The regulations change frequently, as dictated by fish conservation studies, so you should check the current rules in the annual B.C. Fishing Regulations Synopsis. No license is required for catching shellfish, though size restrictions apply.

The **B.C. Department of Fisheries** (tel. 666-0383 during office hours) has a 24-hour phone line during spring, summer, and fall (tel. 666-2268). It gives pertinent recorded information, including openings, closings, and restrictions; where the big ones are hitting; and what lures they're hitting on.

Numerous fishing operators have charters available.

GOLF The "sport of kings" is played year-round in Vancouver, except when snow covers the fairways or rain makes the greens too soggy.

There are five public courses in the city. Most accessible to downtown may be the **University Golf Club,** 5185 University Blvd. (tel. 224-1818), a 6,560-yard par-71 course. It has a beautiful new clubhouse with a big pro shop and locker rooms, the Thunderbird Bar and Grill for dining, a sports TV lounge, and 280-car parking.

Leading private clubs, most of which have reciprocal privileges with other North American clubs, include the **Capilano Golf and Country Club,** 420 Southborough Dr., West Vancouver (tel. 922-9331); **Marine Drive Golf Club,** West 57th Avenue and SW Marine Drive (tel. 261-8111); **Point Grey Golf and Country Club,** 3350 SW Marine Dr., at Blenheim Street (tel. 266-7171); **Seymour Golf and Country Club,** 3723 Mt. Seymour Pkwy., North Vancouver (tel. 929-2611); and **Shaughnessy Golf and Country Club,** 4300 SW Marine Dr., at Kullahun Drive (tel. 266-4141).

HIKING This sport is everywhere: All you need is a good pair of walking shoes. Most visitors start in Stanley Park or at one of the numerous large provincial and regional parks in the North Shore Mountains—Cypress, Capilano River, Lynn Headwaters, Mount Seymour, Belcarra, Burke Mountain, and Golden Ears. There are literally hundreds of miles of trails. For information about provincial parks, call the **Ministry of Parks** (tel. 929-1291); for local regional parks, call the **Greater Vancouver Regional Parks District** (tel. 432-6350).

If you're looking for trail information or would like to join a group hike, contact **Vancouver Natural History Society,** at 1367 W. Broadway (tel. 737-3057).

HUNTING License fees for non-Canadian residents to carry firearms are steep—$155.15 to hunt all game. (It's only $22.45 for residents of Canada.) Species licenses required for the following animals cost nonresidents about six times the cost for Canadians (tax included): black bear ($107), grizzly bear ($535), caribou or cougar ($160.50), white- or black-tailed deer or Queen Charlotte deer ($80.25), elk or moose ($160.50), mountain goat ($214), mountain sheep ($428), and bobcat, lynx, wolverine, or wolf ($26.75). Specific requirements should be studied in the annual "B.C. Hunting and Trapping Regulations Synopsis," or call the **B. C. Environment, Lands and Parks Office** (tel. 604/582-5231).

ICE SKATING Right in downtown Vancouver, **Robson Square** offers free skating from November to early April on its central rink. But there's no skate rental here; you'll have to bring your own. Other rinks that do rent skates include the **West End Community Centre,** 870 Denman St., at Nelson (tel. 689-0571), open October through March; **Britannia Community Centre,** 1661 Napier St., off Commercial Drive (tel. 253-4391); **Kerrisdale Arena,** 5760 East Blvd. (tel. 261-8144); and the **UBC Thunderbird Winter Sports Centre,** 6066 Thunderbird Blvd. (tel. 822-6121), with public skating and casual hockey September to April (hours are usually 8:30am to 4pm, but phone ahead).

MOUNTAINEERING   Mountains are one thing there's no shortage of in this corner of British Columbia. Neither is there a lack of mountaineers and rock climbers. Experts know where to go; one of their favorite ascents is the Chief, a stark wall that looms above the town of Squamish at the head of Howe Sound.

Beginning and intermediate climbers can take courses, and experts can bone up on local knowledge, with the assistance of the **Federation of Mountain Clubs of B.C.,** 1367 W. Broadway (tel. 737-3053). Backpacking trips to interior British Columbia are also organized here.

PARASAILING   **Aquila Para-Sail,** 167 E. Osborne Rd., North Vancouver (tel. 984-4333), offers parasailing adventures 500 feet above the city.

RIVER RAFTING   Although a score of streams in British Columbia attract whitewater enthusiasts, two are of special interest to short-term Vancouver-area visitors: the Chilliwack River, 65 miles east of the city, and the Thompson River, 160 miles northeast. Both have Class II to IV rapids, making them accessible to rafting newcomers but exciting to veterans as well. Rates are typically in the $59–$69 range, per person, for half-day runs, with full-day trips up to $85. Overnight trips cost about $175. Young children (under 10) are usually not accepted. The season may extend from April to October, with most rafting done between June and August.

Action River Expeditions, 5389 SE Marine Dr., Burnaby (tel. 437-6679), runs 12–14 different B.C. rivers, with trips lasting 1–18 days. **Hyak River Expeditions,** 1958 W. Fourth Ave., Vancouver (tel. 734-8622), has Chilliwack and Thompson River runs and full-week journeys. **Kumsheen Raft Adventures,** 281 Main St., Lytton (tel. 604/455-2296, or toll free 800/482-2269), focuses on the Thompson and Fraser, at whose junction they are based.

RUNNING   Jog anywhere you like. **Stanley Park** is a particular favorite of locals. For longer outings, consider **John Molson Way,** a gift of Molson Brewery B.C. Ltd. as part of its 200th-anniversary celebration in 1986. This track follows the 12-mile SkyTrain route from Main Street to the New Westminster station, crossing 32 neighborhood parks en route.

SAILBOARDING   Better known as windsurfing, this new sport—which combines surfboard and sail—has become extremely popular in Vancouver. Beginning, intermediate, and advanced instruction is offered by **Windmaster,** at Denman and Pacific Streets, at the English Bay Beach House (tel. 685-7245), and **Windsure Windsurfing School,** 1300 Discovery St., at Jericho Beach (tel. 224-0615). Instruction packages include board rentals and wet suits.

Sailboards are not allowed at the mouth of False Creek near Granville Island, between the Granville and Burrard Bridges.

SAILING   Lessons are offered by **Cooper Boating Center,** 1620 Duranleae St. (tel. 687-4110), and the **Sea Wing Sailing School,** 1815 Mast Tower (tel. 669-0840). Many boat charter operators also have sailboats available for rent by experienced sailors. The inland waters here are a joy for those with know-how.

SKIING There are seven major ski areas within easy driving distance of Vancouver, but the area everyone talks about is **Whistler/Blackcomb.**

The two mountains flanking the world-class resort village of Whistler, 75 miles north of Vancouver on Hwy. 99, have been rated by *Ski* magazine as one of North America's most popular ski resorts, second only to Vail, Colorado, in recent years. Whistler Mountain, established as a ski area in the mid-1960s, boomed in the 1980s with the opening of Blackcomb—whose one-mile vertical drop is the highest serviced vertical of any ski area on the continent.

There are more than 1,500 hotel and luxury condominium units at the base of the lifts, along with dozens of restaurants and shops. Whistler Village is a year-round resort.

Whistler Mountain has a 5,006-foot vertical and 53 marked runs, serviced by one high-speed gondola, eight chairs (three high-speed), and five other lifts and tows. Helicopter skiing makes accessible another 100-plus runs on nearby glaciers.

Blackcomb has a 5,280-foot vertical and 91 marked runs, serviced by 10 chairs (four high-speed) and three other lifts and tows. Year-round skiing is possible on Blackcomb Glacier.

For more information on these areas, contact the **Whistler Resort Association,** 4010 Whistler Way, Whistler, BC V0N 1B4 (tel. 604/932-3928 or 685-3650 or toll free 800/WHISTLE or 800/944-7853; or 604/932-4222 or 685-3650 for reservations). For a snow resport, call 604/687-6761 or 932-4191 for Whistler, 604/932-4211 for Blackcomb.

Three areas in the North Shore Mountains are readily visible from metropolitan Vancouver—especially after dark, when their lights are on for night skiing. **Grouse Mountain,** 6400 Nancy Greene Way, North Vancouver, BC V7R 4K9 (tel. 604/984-0661), overlooks the Burrard Inlet from 4,100 feet above sea level. It has a 1,200-foot vertical and 13 groomed runs, serviced by a tramway, four chairs, and five other lifts and tows. For a snow report, call 986-6262.

Also on the North Shore, **Mount Seymour,** Mt. Seymour Rd., North Vancouver, BC V7G 1L3 (tel. 604/986-2261), has a 1,350-foot vertical with 20 groomed runs, serviced by four chairs and one tow. For a snow report, call 986-3444.

Cypress Bowl, P.O. Box 91252, West Vancouver, BC V7V 3N9 (tel. 604/926-5612), has a 1,750-foot vertical with 23 groomed runs, serviced by four chairs and one tow. For a snow report, phone 926-6007.

Farther east, a two-hour drive up the Fraser Valley, is **Hemlock Valley,** P.O. Box 7, Site 2, Rural Route 1, Agassiz, BC V0M 1A0 (tel. 604/797-4411 or 524-9741). This family-oriented area has a 1,200-foot vertical, with 30 runs serviced by three chairs and one tow. It also has night skiing. Overnight packages are offered in conjunction with Harrison Hot Springs. For a snow report, call 520-6222.

Manning Park Resort, Manning Provincial Park, BC V0X 1R0 (tel. 604/840-8822), is more of a wilderness experience than the other areas, offering equal alpine and nordic opportunities. For downhillers, it has a 1,400-foot vertical, with 20 runs serviced by two chairs and two other lifts and tows. For a snow report, phone 733-3586.

All southwestern B.C. areas offer rental packages.

Cross-country skiers will find 19 miles of track-set trails and 120 miles of wilderness trails at Manning Park. Mount Seymour has about 16 miles of nordic trails; Hemlock, about 20 miles.

Whistler Resort itself has only about 16 miles of trails, but the **Mad River Nordic Centre,** south of Whistler, has 38 miles of groomed trails equipped with warming huts and a nordic ski school.

At Cypress Bowl, the **Hollyburn Ridge** nordic center has 16 miles of groomed and set track, including 3 miles lit for night skiers.

SWIMMING   There are two great year-round indoor facilities in Vancouver. Both have 50-meter Olympic-size heated pools, with separate teaching pools, diving tanks, saunas, whirlpools, and exercise gyms. The **Vancouver Aquatic Centre,** 1050 Beach Ave. (tel. 665-3424), at the foot of Thurlow Street on False Creek, and the **UBC Aquatic Centre,** on University Boulevard (tel. 822-4521), next to the Student Union Building, have varying hours for public swimming and changing charges, so it's best to call ahead. There are also pools downtown at the **YMCA** and at the **YWCA** (women only), as well as the **South Slope YMCA,** 282 W. 49th Ave., at Alberta Street (tel. 324-2261).

TENNIS   When the sun is shining, especially in spring and summer, Vancouverites are on the courts in force. There are some 250 public courts around the city, but you may still have to wait in line for playing time on weekends and in the evening. After all, they're nearly all free.

Stanley Park has the largest number of courts in the city—21, including 17 near the Beach Avenue entrance and 4 more by Lost Lagoon. There are another 20 courts at **Queen Elizabeth Park** and 10 more at **Kitsilano Beach Park.** The **UBC Tennis Training Centre,** on Thunderbird Boulevard (tel. 822-2505), has 10 outdoor and 4 indoor courts. The cost is $10 per hour if you wish to reserve, or take your chances and play free if no one else has reserved. After dark, you can use the lit public courts at the **Langara Campus** of Vancouver Community College, on West 49th Avenue, between Main and Cambie Streets.

WATER SPORTS   There are a number of family-fun water-sports centers around the Lower Mainland.

The **Canada Games Pool and Fitness Centre,** 65 E. Sixth Ave., New Westminster (tel. 526-4281), has a giant water slide, water games like rope swings and an overhead trolley, an enormous Jacuzzi, and a 5,000-square-foot fitness facility. It's open year-round: Monday through Friday from 6:30am to 10:30pm and on Saturday and Sunday from 8:45am to 10:30pm.

The **Newton Wave Pool,** 13730 72nd Ave., Surrey (tel. 594-7873), has two water slides, a three-foot-wave generator, and assorted fitness equipment. It's open on Monday, Tuesday, and Thursday from noon to 4pm and 6:45 to 10pm; on Friday from noon to 9pm; and on Saturday and Sunday from 11am to 9pm. Admission is $5.65 for adults, $4.25 for youths 13–18, $2.80 for seniors and children 6–12, $2.25 for preschool children 2–5, and free for children under 2. Family rates available.

Splashdown Park, 4799 Hwy. 17, Tsawwassen (tel. 943-2251), is a recreational complex with half a dozen interwoven water slides of the ever-popular twister and tube (and twister-tube) varieties, plus smaller and wider slides for the more timid. There are also picnic tables, hot tubs, mini-golf, a video arcade, concessions, and so forth. It's adjacent to the B.C. Ferry terminal to Vancouver Island. Open May 30 through the summer.

CHAPTER 7

STROLLING AROUND VANCOUVER

1. DOWNTOWN
2. GASTOWN
3. CHINATOWN
4. GRANVILLE ISLAND

Strolling around Vancouver enables you to sample the diversity, sophistication, and historic character of this multicultural city. To get you started, here are four Walking Tours through areas of the city that I particularly enjoy.

WALKING TOUR 1 — DOWNTOWN

Start: Harbour Centre.
End: Harbour Centre.
Time: 3 hours to all day, depending on the time you spend eating, shopping, and sightseeing at various locations.
Best Times: Any weekday when it's not raining, especially in summer.
Worst Times: Any day when it *is* raining.

1. **Harbour Centre,** 555 W. Hastings St., between Seymour and Richards (tel. 689-0421), offers an observation deck 553 feet above street level with a breathtaking 360° panorama of the entire Vancouver area. Telescopes and explanatory plaques assist viewers, and there's a 1,000-image, 12-minute multimedia show, *Once in a World Vancouver,* about the city and its people. It's open June to September, daily from 8:30am to 10pm; October to May, daily from 10am to 8pm. Admission is $5.35 for adults, $3.75 for seniors, students, and children. Take the glass "Skylift" elevator. A revolving restaurant, the Top of Vancouver, is one floor above the observation deck.

   Exit Harbour Centre by its Cordova Street (north) doors. Across the street, just to the west, is:

2. **The Station.** Formerly the Canadian Pacific Railway station, it has been completely restored to its original Beaux Arts style and is now the Waterfront terminal of the SkyTrain light-rail system and the SeaBus to North Vancouver. There are numerous shops and cafés on the ground level, with three floors of offices above.

   Next door to the west is:

3. **Granville Square,** a 32-story office tower. Beyond, extending into Burrard Inlet, are the unmistakable sails of:

4. **Canada Place.** Built as the Canada Pavilion for the Expo '86 world's fair, Canada Place has quickly become as much a trademark of Vancouver as Australia's Sydney Opera House, which it vaguely resembles. Five 80-foot-tall fiberglass sails give

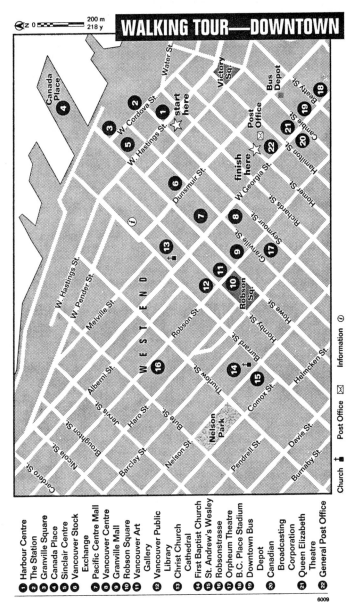

WALKING TOUR—DOWNTOWN

Church ✝   Post Office ☒   Information ⓘ

6009

the structure the appearance of a clipper ship leaving port. From inside, the sails create a unique skylight over the impressive Prow Restaurant (see Chapter 5, "Vancouver Dining") and an entry hall that boasts a unique collection of Native quilts and totem poles. An indoor concourse has several international fast-food outlets and souvenir shops.

Some 43 descriptive plaques along the outdoor **Promenade into History** encourage visitors to make self-guided tours around Canada Place—while learning about Vancouver's history. Free guided tours are also offered daily from 9am to 5pm from the information booth (tel. 688-TOUR) on the downtown side of the complex.

The complex also houses the **Vancouver Trade and Convention Centre,** with three levels, 21 meeting rooms, a 16,700-square-foot ballroom, a main exhibition hall of 94,000 square feet, and a meeting capacity for 11,000 people; the **World Trade Centre** office complex, including the Asia Pacific Foundation; the luxurious 505-room **Pan-Pacific Hotel** (See Chapter 4, "Vancouver Accommodations"); and the **Cruise Ship Terminal,** which berths up to four ships at a time (200 sailings a year) during the summer season. Nearly all of these ships ply the Inside Passage route to Alaska. Adjacent is the **Waterfront Centre** (tel. 691-1991), with a new world-class hotel that sits atop an underground dining and shopping complex.

You'll also see the **CN Imax Theatre** (tel. 682-IMAX), home of the giant five-story screen for travel, nature, and technology-oriented movies. Other types of films are also shown, such as *Top Gun* or *The Rolling Stones at the 'Max.* There are daily matinees on the hour from noon to 3pm, and evening features at 7 and 9:15pm. Matinee admission is $6.25 for adults, $5.25 for seniors and students, $4.25 for children; evening admission is $7.50 for adults and students, $4.50 for seniors and children.

On leaving Canada Place, venture south on Howe Street. At the corner of Hastings is the:
5. **Sinclair Centre,** 757 W. Hastings St. (tel. 666-4483). This unique restoration of four early 20th-century structures houses a variety of shops, services, and federal government offices. It's best-known tenants are Leone and Plaza Escada, exclusive retailers of imported European clothing (see Chapter 8, "Vancouver Shopping").

Hastings and West Pender Streets, which parallel the Sinclair Centre to the south, are at the heart of Vancouver's financial district. Here you'll find a score of national and international banks as well as the:
6. **Vancouver Stock Exchange.** The VSE's Visitors Centre (tel. 643-6590 or 689-3334) is at Granville and Dunsmuir Streets; open Monday through Friday, it offers self-guided tours and video presentations from 6am to 4pm.

Adjacent to the stock exchange is the:
7. **Pacific Centre Mall** (tel. 688-7236), which covers three full blocks between Pender and Robson, and Howe and Granville Streets. Downtown Vancouver's largest underground shopping mall, it comprises 200 stores, numerous fine eating places, banks, and other services. From the glass-domed atrium of the Four Seasons Hotel, a three-story waterfall splashes into a pool surrounded by fountains. Eaton's, one of the city's two largest department stores, extends into the mall at Granville and Georgia Streets. The other, The Bay (the Hudson's Bay Company), is catercorner; its basement is a part of the:
8. **Vancouver Centre** (tel. 684-7537), a smaller mall adjoining the Pacific Centre (see Chapter 8, "Vancouver Shopping").

The six-block stretch of Granville Street from Hastings to Nelson is a pedestrian mall; the only vehicles allowed on the street are buses. This northern end of the:

9. **Granville Mall** focuses on shopping; the southern two blocks, below Robson, are a bit tawdry, with numerous theaters, video arcades, and pawnshops that appeal to a young street-smart set.

Exit Pacific Centre or Granville Mall onto Robson Street. On the south side of the street, between Howe and Hornby, is:

10. **Robson Square** (tel. 661-7373), widely considered to be the town center because it houses B.C. government offices and the law courts, designed by famed architect Arthur Erickson, at its Nelson Street end. This extensive development also has an underground Media Centre for lectures, exhibitions, films, and concerts; an ice-skating rink; a food court (with cheap and tasty fast food); and other facilities. Tourism British Columbia has an office here.

Directly opposite, on Robson Street, are the former courts, now rehabilitated as the splendid:

11. **Vancouver Art Gallery** (tel. 682-4668) (see "The Top Attractions" in Chapter 6).

One block west on Burrard Street, at Robson, the main branch of the:

12. **Vancouver Public Library** (tel. 665-2287) has frequent author readings, and historical photos are on display. A three-month library card will cost you $20 ($15 is refundable when you turn it in).

Some of the city's most magnificent early 20th-century stone churches are north and south of here on Burrard Street. A full block north, at the corner of Georgia, is:

13. **Christ Church Cathedral** (Anglican Church of Canada). Three blocks south, on opposite sides of Nelson Street, are the:

14. **First Baptist Church** and

15. **St. Andrew's Wesley** (United Church of Canada).

West of Burrard, several blocks of Robson Street have a distinctly European ambience with their high-fashion boutiques, trendy restaurants, and gift and novelty shops. Although the street signs don't say so, this stretch is best known as:

16. **Robsonstrasse.** This is where you can dine on bratwurst or coquilles St-Jacques, sip espresso or buy English breakfast tea, nibble Swiss chocolates or Belgian waffles, buy last weekend's London *Times,* check out the latest sexy lingerie, or have your hair done by a European-trained coiffeur/coiffeuse. (See Chapter 8, "Vancouver Shopping.")

If you get caught up in the Robsonstrasse whirlwind, you may want to end your downtown walking tour here. Otherwise, reverse direction and proceed east on Robson Street. One block past Granville, and half a block south on Seymour, is the eclectic but elegant:

17. **Orpheum Theatre,** built in 1926. Now the home of the Vancouver Symphony Orchestra (see Chapter 9, "Vancouver Nights"), this 2,800-seat theater was built for the Chicago-based Orpheum vaudeville circuit. Plan to return for a performance so that you can see the interior—the Spanish arches, travertine walls, and remarkable plasterwork ceiling.

Continue east on Robson for another five blocks, where it ends at:

18. **B. C. Place Stadium** (tel. 669-2300 or 661-7373). Some call this $126-million inflated-dome stadium a "giant spaceship";

one of my journalist friends refers to it as "the marshmallow in bondage" because of the white fiberglass roof, kept aloft by fans and restricted by cables. Opened in 1983, the 60,000-seat stadium is the home of the B.C. Lions (Canadian Football League). Numerous trade shows and one-time sporting events are held here, and it's the primary venue for big-time concerts. Guided, pre-arranged one-hour tours are offered for groups of 10 or more, when the stadium is not in use. Admission is $3.50 for adults, $2 for seniors, students, and children.

In front of the stadium is the **Terry Fox Monument,** honoring a modern Canadian hero from suburban Port Coquitlam. As a 19-year-old cancer victim, in 1980–81 Fox ran more than halfway across Canada on an artificial leg, raising money for cancer research until the disease forced him to quit and eventually took his life.

Leave the stadium and walk north on Beatty Street one block to Georgia Street. Turn left. On your right is the:

19. Downtown Bus Depot. A block ahead on your left is the western headquarters of the:

20. Canadian Broadcasting Corporation. Opposite the CBC on Hamilton Street is the:

21. Queen Elizabeth Theatre, a modern venue for theater and operas.

Facing the theater and catercorner from the CBC is the:

22. General Post Office (tel. 662-5725). Stamp collectors will be attracted to its excellent Philatelic Centre, open Monday through Friday from 8am to 5pm.

To return to your starting point, walk one block west, to Richards, then three blocks north to Harbour Centre.

WALKING TOUR 2 — GASTOWN

Start: Harbour Centre.
End: Harbour Centre.
Time: Approximately 1 hour, not counting time for browsing in shops.
Best Times: Any sunny day.
Worst Times: Any rainy day.

Start at:

1. Harbour Centre, 555 W. Hastings St., between Seymour and Richards (for details, see Walking Tour 1, above).

Cross Cordova Street, turn right (east), and take the left-hand fork onto Water Street, and you'll be in Gastown. Vancouver was founded here in 1867; it became incorporated but then was inadvertently razed in 1886, and later rebuilt with Victorian dignity. Eight decades later, having fallen into disrepair, Gastown was scheduled for the wrecking ball. But in 1971 the British Columbia government designated it a heritage area, launching the renovation that has made Gastown a charming (if touristy) district of shops, restaurants, nightclubs, and cobbled streets shaded by trees and imitation old-time gaslamps.

The first building on your left is:

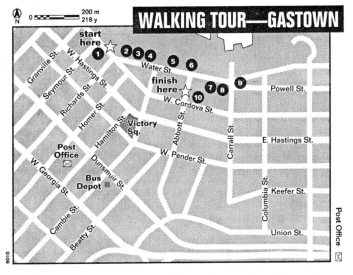

① Harbour Centre
② The Landing
③ Inuit Gallery
④ Gastown Steam Clock
⑤ The Courtyard
⑥ Fish-head Water Fountain
⑦ Gaoler's Mews
⑧ Maple Tree Square
⑨ Hotel Europe
⑩ Blood Alley Square

2. **The Landing,** 375 Water St. (tel. 687-1144), a restored 1905 Klondike gold-rush warehouse that has been converted into an exclusive shopping and office complex with a fine restaurant.

   A couple of storefronts farther, duck into the:

3. **Inuit Gallery,** 345 Water St. (tel. 688-7323), a virtual museum of Native Canadian art and artifacts (see Chapter 8, "Vancouver Shopping").

   At the corner of Cambie Street, pause to study the:

4. **Gastown Steam Clock,** framed in bronze, the only one of its kind in the world. Powered by an underground steam system that also heated adjoining buildings, it has a glass window that enables passersby to observe its works. The clock shrilly whistles the Westminster Chimes' theme every 15 minutes and noisily spews steam on the hour.

   There are a number of interesting shops on the next couple of blocks, including Native Canadian crafts and antique outlets. Check out:

5. **The Courtyard** arcade, 131 Water St.; the tiny:

6. **Fish-head water fountain,** at the corner of Abbott Street; and:

7. **Gaoler's Mews,** 12 Water St., a little shopping center built around winding turn-of-the-century passageways.

   At the spot where Water, Carrall, Alexander, and Powell Streets converge is:

8. **Maple Tree Square,** the spiritual center of Gastown. This was probably the location of Capt. John Deighton's original Globe

Saloon. Legend holds that the Yorkshireman disembarked from a canoe in 1866, accompanied by his Native mistress, a dog, and a barrel of whiskey. The spirits and Deighton's natural gift of gab persuaded local sawmill workers to help him build the first structure of future Vancouver—his saloon. The river pilot's nonstop monologue earned him the nickname "Gassy Jack" and helped attract further development to the area, such as stores and a hotel. The town assumed Jack's nickname.

In 1970, a bronze statue of Gassy Jack standing on his whiskey barrel was erected in Maple Tree Square. It faces the:

9. **Hotel Europe,** 43 Powell St., an early 20th-century flatiron building that was once the city's most luxurious apartment house.

Heading back up Cordova Street from Carrall, pass:

10. **Blood Alley Square,** about half a block on the right. This dead-end alley not only provided a covert location for shady deals during Gastown's wild days but was the place where many business arrangements were terminally concluded.

You can return up Cordova from here about four blocks to your starting point at Harbour Centre.

WALKING TOUR 3 — CHINATOWN

Start: Chinese Cultural Centre.
End: Chinese Cultural Centre.
Time: About 2 hours, not counting time spent in the classical garden or the many fascinating shops.
Best Times: Early mornings, when the street markets are busiest.
Worst Times: After 5pm any day, when many shops are closed.

Vancouver's Chinatown is the largest in Canada and the second largest in North America after San Francisco's. (With the recent influx of Hong Kong immigrants boosting the Chinese population in the metropolitan area to nearly a quarter million, it may soon overtake San Francisco.) This traditional area is concentrated along Hastings, Pender, Keefer, and Georgia Streets from Carrall to Gore.

Start at the:

1. **Chinese Cultural Centre,** 50 E. Pender St., between Carrall and Columbia (tel. 687-0729), is a center for social services, community programs, and instruction in language, art, and t'ai chi; and it sponsors the annual Chinese New Year parade and related events. There are free changing public exhibits of local history and/or traditional culture in the multipurpose hall. The small bookstore will sell you an excellent, detailed walking-tour brochure of Chinatown for $1.25. Guided walking tours are available at $12 for adults and $8 for children.

Behind the CCC is the:

2. **Dr. Sun Yat-sen Classical Chinese Park and Garden,** 578 Carrall St. (tel. 662-3207). There's a small admission charge for the $6-million garden, but the adjacent park is free.

At the southwest corner of Carrall and Pender Streets, opposite the Cultural Centre, is the:

3. **Sam Kee Building,** 8 W. Pender St., listed in the *Guinness*

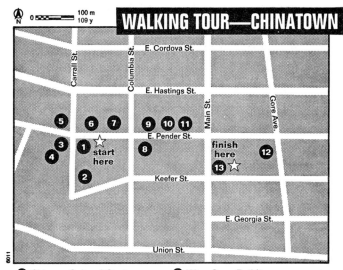

WALKING TOUR—CHINATOWN

- **1** Chinese Cultural Centre
- **2** Dr. Sun Yat-sen Classical Chinese Park and Garden
- **3** Sam Kee Building
- **4** Shanghai Alley
- **5** Chinese Freemasons' Building
- **6** Chinese Times Building
- **7** Wing Sang Building
- **8** Chinese Benevolent Association
- **9** Mon Keang School
- **10** Lee Building
- **11** Lung Kung Kong Shaw Building
- **12** Kuomintang Building
- **13** Ten Ren Tea & Ginseng Co.

Book of World Records as the narrowest building in the world. A two-story steel-framed building erected in 1913, its ground floor is 5 feet 10 inches wide. Bay windows on its second floor increase its width by 50%. An insurance agency is the current tenant.

Just west of this building is:

4. Shanghai Alley. Only three Chinese buildings still stand on this narrow lane, but during its early 20th-century heyday, this was the site of a public bath, theater, restaurants, pawnshops, stores, and residences.

Cross Pender Street, opposite the Sam Kee Building, and you will come to the:

5. Chinese Freemasons' Building (1901), 3 W. Pender St., which housed a society that helped finance Sun Yat-sen's 1911 Chinese Revolution.

Head east and you'll see the:

6. Chinese Times Building (1902), 1 E. Pender St., home of Chinatown's first newspaper. The community's first bank was in the:

7. Wing Sang Building, 51-67 E. Pender St. Constructed in 1889, this is Chinatown's oldest standing building. The shops on this block seem to have the best and lowest-priced selection of traditional crafts and other souvenirs.

Cross Columbia Street and you'll come to the:

8. Chinese Benevolent Association (1909), 108 E. Pender St., which provides welfare services throughout the community. Across the street is the:

9. **Mon Keang School** (1921), 123 E. Pender St., the first Canadian school to offer Chinese classes at the high-school level.
    Next door to the east is the:
10. **Lee Building** (1907), 127-133 E. Pender, which once concealed an opium factory.
    Another door east is the:
11. **Lung Kung Kong Shaw Building,** 135 E. Pender St., a newer building that displays traditional Chinese architectural details.

THE HEART OF CHINATOWN The intersection of Pender and Main Streets is the commercial heart of modern Chinatown. Throughout the community, you'll see countless restaurants, from Cantonese dim sum parlors to noodle houses to formal dining rooms. Keep an eye out for bakeries, where you can try moon cakes or bao (steamed buns with meat or sweet bean fillings). You can enjoy shopping for groceries like the Chinese do: Buy your fresh vegetables and "thousand-year-old" eggs from the sidewalk stands at one store, pick out a live eel or a preserved pressed duck from another. Everything is written in Chinese pictograms, so if you don't know what you're buying . . . guess. Life should be an adventure.

It's a different experience to venture into any of Chinatown's several herbalist shops. The dried sea horses, reindeer antlers, snakeskins, buffalo tongues, ginseng root, and other items on sale are remedies for various ailments. At the rear of each shop is a traditional doctor's office, where herbs and teas are prescribed in appropriate combinations.

Continue up Pender Street another block past Main, then turn right at Gore to the:

12. **Kuomintang Building,** 529 Gore St. Built in 1920, this was the western Canadian political headquarters of the Chinese Nationalist Party, which still retains power in Taiwan. Overseas politics were once of vital concern to Canadian Chinese.
    Turn right at Keefer, stopping into the:
13. **Ten Ren Tea & Ginseng Co.,** at the corner of Main, for a sample of their excellent ginger or jasmine tea.
    Then proceed north on Main, turn left (west) at Hastings, then left (south) on Columbia to the Cultural Centre, where you began. As you go, observe the architecture of Chinatown's traditional buildings. Most of them have recessed balconies, originally designed to help cool the interior of homes of steamy South China. Look for the use of various colors—red is associated with happiness and prosperity, blue and green with peace and fertility—as well as decorative carvings. The dragon motif, symbolic of royalty and longevity, is common.

WALKING TOUR 4 —— GRANVILLE
ISLAND

Start: Granville Island Information Centre.
End: Granville Island Information Centre (short tour) or Stamp's Landing on False Creek (long tour).
Time: About 2 hours, plus time to enjoy the public market and

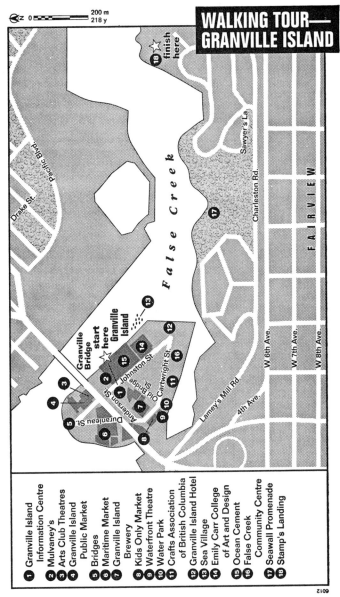

WALKING TOUR—GRANVILLE ISLAND

1. Granville Island Information Centre
2. Mulvaney's
3. Arts Club Theatres
4. Granville Island Public Market
5. Bridges
6. Maritime Market
7. Granville Island Brewery
8. Kids Only Market
9. Waterfront Theatre
10. Water Park
11. Crafts Association of British Columbia
12. Granville Island Hotel
13. Sea Village
14. Emily Carr College of Art and Design
15. Ocean Cement
16. False Creek Community Centre
17. Seawall Promenade
18. Stamp's Landing

artisans' galleries; allow an additional 30 minutes to 1 hour for the longer tour.

Best Times: Thursday in summer, when the Farmers' Market is in full swing.

Worst Times: Monday in winter, when the public market is closed.

What, in fact, is Granville Island? It's an adult entertainment center, with a hotel, eight restaurants and lounges, and three theaters. It's a place for the children, with a water park and Kids Only Market. It's a focus for the arts community, with numerous galleries and guilds as well as the Emily Carr College of Art and Design. It's an industrial center—the site of two large and several smaller factories. It's a market center, with a huge public market and dozens of independent merchants. It's a social entity, composed of a houseboat village, schools, a community center, and ferry terminals. Yet for all practical purposes, it's hardly more than a decade old.

Vancouver likes to think of the 38-acre promontory beneath the Granville Street Bridge as an "urban park." There's a remarkable story behind its development. Once a marshy tidal flat in False Creek, it was reclaimed for heavy industry in 1917 and became an ironworks and shipbuilding center during World War II. By the 1960s it had become an eyesore, plagued by rats and heaps of garbage.

In 1972 the federal government agreed to sponsor the island's redevelopment to the tune of $19.5 million. The goal was a multi-use facility—for industry and commerce as well as arts and entertainment. The planners kept the warehouse appearance of the island, with its tin and stucco sidings, false-fronted buildings, rail tracks, and seawall. They tied it together visually with canopies, streetworks, and bright colors. Although most of the visible work had been completed by 1979, the renovation is still continuing under federal management.

Getting There Driving on the island today presents no real problem, so long as you remember that the traffic flow is one-way counterclockwise. There's three-hour free parking from 7am to 7pm, and unlimited parking after 7pm—but because of the space restrictions, it's always somewhat limited. (If you're **driving** from downtown on the Granville Street Bridge, go right on West Fourth Avenue, then turn right onto Fir Street, right again onto West Second Avenue, and left onto Anderson Street.) Buses nos. 50 (Gastown–False Creek) and 51 (Broadway–Granville) do swings around the island.

You can also arrive by water aboard a miniature passenger ferry. **Granville Island Ferries** (tel. 684-7781) leave the Aquatic Center, beneath the Burrard Street Bridge at Beach Avenue, every five minutes daily from 7:30am to 8pm (later in summer); and there's an **Aquabus** (tel. 874-9930) from the Hornby Street Dock on False Creek.

Start your walking tour at the:
  1. **Granville Island Information Centre,** 1669 Johnston St. (tel. 666-5784), opposite the bus stop and near the public market. The Info Centre has an excellent museum-style exhibit and audiovisual presentation to explain Granville Island's history. Pick up an island map and special events calendar here.

Granville Island is a great place for strolling. Many of the buildings house art galleries and craft cooperatives, bookstores, bakeries, custom jewelers, and ship's chandleries. (Most businesses are open daily from 9am to 6pm.) Peek into some of the studios just west of the Info Centre and you may see artisans throwing potter's clay, weaving cloth, blowing glass, hammering gold, and so forth.

Across Johnston Street is:
  2. **Mulvaney's** restaurant (see Chapter 5, "Vancouver Dining") and, next door, the:

3. Arts Club Theatres (see Chapter 9, "Vancouver Nights"). The Aquabus terminal is adjacent to the theater.

Next comes the 50,000-square-foot:

4. Granville Island Public Market. All kinds of fruits and vegetables, meat and seafood, wine and cheese, crafts, flowers, and candy can be purchased here, and there's a seemingly endless series of international fast-food counters. Best of all is the people-watching. Every Thursday from June through September, there's a **Farmers' Truck Market** from 9am to 4pm. The public market is open year-round: daily from 9am to 6pm in summer, closed Monday (except public holidays) in winter.

At the end of Johnston Street are the Granville Island Ferry terminal and:

5. Bridges restaurant (see Chapter 5, "Vancouver Dining"). Turn sharply to the left and head south down Duranleau Street. There are more art studios on your left. On your right is the:

6. Maritime Market, where you can buy a yacht from a broker or order one custom-made from a boatbuilder, outfit it with help from a chandler and sailmaker, and sign up for sailing lessons to learn how to get around in it. You can even rent a kayak here from the **Ecomarine Ocean Kayak Centre** (tel. 689-7575).

Cross Anderson Street and head east on Cartwright Street. The first building on your left is the:

7. Granville Island Brewery (tel. 688-9927), British Columbia's most esteemed cottage brewer. No preservatives or chemicals are used in making their fine brews, which include cold Island Lager (a Bavarian-style pilsner), sweet, dark Island Bock, Island Light (pilsner), and Lord Granville Pale Ale. Free tasting tours are offered daily at 1pm and 3pm. You can buy eight-packs of lager or a variety of gifts year-round, Sunday through Thursday from 9am to 7pm and on Friday and Saturday from 9am to 9pm.

Opposite the brewery is the:

8. Kids Only Market, 24 shops and services oriented completely to the younger set. There are toy stores and clothing shops, rides and games, ice-cream stands, and even a day-care center.

Next door is the:

9. Waterfront Theatre (see Chapter 9, "Vancouver Nights"), whose adjunct Carousel Theatre schedules frequent youth-oriented shows.

REFUELING STOP   A few steps down Old Bridge Street is **Isadora's** (tel. 681-3748), a co-op restaurant that will please both children (clown-face pizza, honey-sweetened ice cream) and adults (organic sandwiches, light entrées, wine list).

There's an indoor play station and an outdoor:

10. Water Park, with movable water cannons to keep the youngsters happy and busy. (Changing facilities are available at Isadora's or the Community Center.)

Farther down Cartwright Street are the studio/galleries of the:

11. Crafts Association of B.C., Potters' Guild of B.C., and Arts Umbrella, with some 50 classes in all areas of the performing and fine arts for kids from preschool through high school.

Cartwright ends at the:

12. Granville Island Hotel (see Chapter 4, "Vancouver Accommodations") at the eastern edge of the island.

Directly north of the hotel is:

13. Sea Village, a neighborhood of elaborate floating homes. Also in the vicinity are architects' and attorneys' offices, and a computer learning center aboard the Granville Island Barge.

Two entities dominate Granville Island's north shore. They are the:

14. Emily Carr College of Art and Design, 1399 Johnston St. (tel. 687-2345), which has an open-air mall where you can view students' work in progress, and:

15. Ocean Cement, between the college and the public market, the island's largest still-operating industry.

By the time you've passed the cement plant, you're back at the Info Centre. To extend this tour, head back to the:

16. False Creek Community Center, adjacent to the Arts Umbrella on the southeast side of Granville Island. The center has facilities for all ages and outdoor public tennis courts. Follow the:

17. Seawall promenade down the south shore of False Creek, which is another award-winning urban redevelopment project. It's a 20-minute stroll through landscaped parkland to:

18. Stamp's Landing, just beyond a mixture of luxury town houses, apartments, and senior-citizen residences. At the east end of the promenade are the **False Creek Marina** and several fine restaurants, including Monk McQueen's (see Chapter 5, "Vancouver Dining").

CHAPTER 8

VANCOUVER SHOPPING

1. SHOPPING A TO Z
2. MARKETS

Shopping in Vancouver is fun. From trendy Robsonstrasse and Gastown to ethnic neighborhoods like Chinatown, a multitude of fascinating shops beckon, offering everything from the latest in European fashions to ancient Ming ceramics.

The cornerstones of Vancouver shopping are two department stores, The Bay (Hudson's Bay Company) and Eaton's. Their main outlets are across the street from one another at Granville and Georgia Streets, in the heart of downtown. Both are connected to major underground shopping malls, the Pacific Centre Mall and Vancouver Centre, with a combined total of more than 300 shops.

Another "don't miss" shop is Leone, an international fashion magnet in Sinclair Centre at 757 W. Hastings St., near Canada Place. This two-story shopping center has 31 stores and occupies four interconnected heritage buildings that have been restored in grand fashion.

SHOPPING AREAS Some of the most interesting shopping areas were described in Chapter 7, "Strolling Around Vancouver." In downtown Vancouver, **Robsonstrasse**—that portion of Robson Street between Burrard and Jervis Streets—has something of a European flavor because of its high-fashion boutiques, intriguing gift shops, and trendy restaurants. The shops and eating establishments of **Gastown,** the original 19th-century Vancouver, face tree-lined, brick-paved streets. In adjacent **Chinatown,** the markets, crafts shops, and restaurants could as easily be on the other side of the Pacific. On **Granville Island,** the imaginative mix of galleries, theaters, restaurants, specialty shops, and a public market make this one of the city's most popular destinations.

SHOPPING HOURS Thursday and Friday are the late shopping nights in downtown Vancouver. Normal shopping hours are 9am to 5:30pm Monday through Wednesday and Saturday from 9am to 5:30pm, on Thursday and Friday from 9am to 9pm, and on Sunday from noon to 5pm.

1. SHOPPING A TO Z

ANTIQUES

Antiques stores are found in three principal areas. Tourists like Gastown, but Vancouverites opt for South Granville Street, where elegant early British and Asian pieces can be found, or the lesser-known shops along Main Street south of Chinatown. The best prices are available at antiques auctions—but you have to know what you're bidding on. Try **Love's Auctioneers and Appraisers,** 1635 W. Broadway, at Fir Street (tel. 733-1157), on Wednesday at noon and 6pm, and on Thursday at 6pm; **Appleton Auctioneers,** 1238 Seymour St., between Davie and Drake Streets (tel. 685-1715), specializing in Native and Inuit art, every three or four weeks at 7pm with viewing the same day from noon to 7pm; or **Tyldesley's Ltd.,** 1339 Kingsway (tel. 874-4238), on Tuesday at 1pm, with viewing on Tuesday from 9am to 1pm.

ARTEMIS ANTIQUES LTD., 321 Water St., near Cordova, Gastown. Tel. 685-8808.

The specialty here is 18th- and 19th-century furniture, along with clocks, paintings, bronzes, art glass, and other objets d'art— including art nouveau and art deco articles. Open Monday through Saturday from 10am to 5pm and by appointment. Bus: 1 or 50.

FRANKIE ROBINSON ORIENTAL GALLERY, 3055 Granville St., near W. 16th Ave. Tel. 734-6568.

Bronzes, cloisonné, porcelain, textiles, Buddha images, prints, paintings, furniture, and other "mysteries" of the East are available here, as well as contemporary fine Asian art. Open Monday through Saturday from 10am to 5pm and by appointment. Bus: 20 or 401.

HAMPSHIRE ANTIQUES LTD., 3007 Granville St. Tel. 733-1326.

British wares are readily available here, including furniture, paintings, ceramics, and such items as clocks and barometers. Antiques, including golf items, can be found here. A library of antiques collectors' reference books is available for perusal. Hampshire also offers a generous antiques finder service, taking potential clients from their hotels or the airport to galleries of possible interest and then arranging shipment and delivery of any purchases. Open Tuesday through Saturday from 11am to 5pm (with extended hours in summer). Bus: 20.

UNO LANGMANN LTD., 2117 Granville St. (beneath the Granville Bridge). Tel. 736-8825.

Old masters of the 18th and 19th centuries and early 20th-century paintings are the forte of this outstanding gallery. Also on display are furniture, silver, porcelain, Oriental carpets, and West Coast Native Canadian art. Open Tuesday through Saturday from 10am to 5pm, on Monday by appointment. Bus: 20.

ART

There are fine galleries all over the city, but most knowledgeable people recommend South Granville (between 6th and 15th Avenues) for traditional oils and the studios of Granville Island for more contemporary works.

ALEXANDER HARRISON GALLERIES, 2932 Granville St., between W. 14th and 15th Aves. Tel. 732-5217.

Widely regarded as one of the city's outstanding galleries of traditional western art, this highly praised collection includes Canadian classics and local landscapes. Open Monday through Wednesday from 10am to 6pm, on Thursday and Friday from 10am to 9pm, and on Sunday from noon to 5pm. Bus: 20.

There's another branch at 2022 S. Park Royal Shopping Centre, in West Vancouver (tel. 926-2615).

BAU-XI GALLERY, 3045 Granville St., between W. 15th and 16th Aves. Tel. 733-7011.

This gallery is nationally renowned for the important new artists it has introduced over the years. Paul and Xisa Wong present the work of accomplished artists along with that of newcomers. Open Monday through Saturday from 9:30am to 5:30pm. Bus: 20.

FEDERATION GALLERY, 952 Richards St., near Nelson St. Tel. 681-8534.

This showcase of the Federation of Canadian Artists changes its exhibitions of acrylics, watercolors, oils, drawings, and other media every couple of weeks. Many of Canada's leading painters are represented. Open Tuesday through Friday from 10am to 4pm and on Saturday from 11am to 3pm. Bus: 15; then walk two blocks north.

GALLERY OF B.C. CERAMICS, 1359 Cartwright St., Granville Island. Tel. 669-5645.

Owned and operated by the Potters' Guild of British Columbia, this spacious facility has continuing shows of clay artists (including sculptors), most of whose designs are remarkably innovative. Open Tuesday through Sunday from 10:30am to 5:30pm. Bus: 51.

GALLERY SHOP, Vancouver Art Gallery, 750 Hornby St., at Robson St. Tel. 682-2765.

This is the place to come for fine art reproductions and art books, including the works of Emily Carr and other Canadian artists. Also represented are jewelry by B.C. designers and carvings by Native artisans. Open Monday through Wednesday from 10am to 5:30pm, on Thursday from 10am to 9pm, on Friday and Saturday from 10am to 5:30pm, and on Sunday from noon to 5:30pm. Bus: 8.

KENNETH HEFFEL FINE ART, 2247 Granville St., between W. Seventh and Eighth Aves. Tel. 732-6505.

This gallery has probably the finest private collection of Canada's acclaimed Group of Seven and their contemporaries. Another exhibition hall offers the work of current B.C. artists. Open Tuesday through Saturday from 10am to 6pm. Bus: 20.

BOOKS

Duthie Books and Blackberry Books have the most comprehensive collections, but if it's a bargain you're seeking, try the Book Warehouse, with outlets on Robsonstrasse and West Broadway.

For travel literature, check out **Voyager Books and Maps,** 722 Smithe St., downtown, and **The Travel Bug,** 2667 W. Broadway, Kitsilano.

Other specialty stores tend to be clustered near the University of British Columbia. They include **Banyen,** 2671 W. Broadway (back-to-nature, metaphysics); **Comicshop,** 2089 W. 4th St. (comics and fantasies); **Graffiti Books,** 3514 W. 4th St. (visual and performing arts); **Pink Peppercorn,** 2686 W. Broadway (cookbooks); **Siliconnections,** 3727 W. 10th St. (business and computers); **Vancouver Kidsbooks,** 3083 W. Broadway (children's); and **White Dwarf Books,** 4374 W. 10th St. (science fiction and astronomy).

BLACKBERRY BOOKS, 1663 Duranleau St., Granville Island. Tel. 685-4113 or 685-6188.

This bookstore stocks a broad selection of books on art, architecture, and cuisine. Open daily from 9am to 9pm.

Other branches are in Sinclair Centre, Suite 250, 757 W. Hastings St., at Granville Street (tel. 685-0833), and at 2206 W. Fourth Ave., at Yew Street, Kitsilano (tel. 733-1673), where paperback literature dominates. The Sinclair Centre branch is open Monday through Saturday from 9am to 6pm; the Kitsilano branch, daily from 9am to 9pm.

THE BOOK WAREHOUSE, 1150 Robson St., near Thurlow St. Tel. 685-5711.

Remainders are the mainstay here, but that translates into big savings (usually at least 20%) off the list prices of best-selling hardcovers and paperbacks. The selection is good and current. Open Monday through Thursday from 10am to 11pm, on Friday and Saturday from 9:30am to midnight, and on Sunday from 10am to 11pm. Bus: 8.

There's another branch at 632 W. Broadway, near Heather Street (tel. 872-5711), open the same hours. Bus: 15.

DUTHIE BOOKS, 919 Robson St., at Hornby St. Tel. 684-4496.

This is by far the city's largest—with some 20,000 volumes, many of them hardcover, on the main floor alone, and a separate "Paperback Cellar" down a spiral staircase. Whether you're looking for fiction or nonfiction, you'll probably find it here. The UBC off-campus outlet has a more academic emphasis. Open Monday through Friday from 9am to 9pm, on Saturday from 9am to 6pm, and on Sunday from noon to 5pm. Bus: 8 or 15.

There's another branch at 4444 W. 10th Ave., near Sasamat Street, West Point Grey (tel. 224-7012), which opens at 9:30am Monday through Saturday, but otherwise keeps the same hours.

CHINA & CRYSTAL

MILLAR & COE, 419 W. Hastings St., near Homer. Tel. 685-3322.

This store, established in 1912, offers customers a choice of some 1,200 china patterns, 300 crystal patterns, and 200 flatware styles, making it Canada's largest dealer. Waterford crystal, Wedgwood, Royal Doulton, and other famous names are available. There's also a wide selection of figurines and giftware. Open Monday through Thursday and on Saturday from 9:30am to 5:30pm, and on Friday from 9:30am to 8pm. Bus: 8, 10, or 20.

CRAFTS

Water Street in Gastown is the center for collectors of traditional Northwest Coast Native Canadian arts and crafts. These are always a hit among visitors. Look for woodcarvings (ceremonial masks, miniature totem poles, bentwood boxes, calabash bowls), jewelry (carved silver, gold, jade, and black argillite), weaving (including fine blankets), leatherwork, basketry, and carvings and sculptures of soapstone, whalebone, and walrus-tusk ivory. Always popular are Cowichan sweaters, hand-spun from undyed raw wool by Native peoples of Vancouver Island. Because they retain the sheep's natural lanolin and oils, they are resistant to rain and snow, and are especially long-wearing.

Two of the finest shops in the Vancouver area are the **University of British Columbia Museum of Anthropology gallery** and the **Capilano Trading Post,** at the Capilano Suspension Bridge in North Vancouver.

AUTHENTIC COWICHAN INDIAN KNITS, 424 W. 3rd St., North Vancouver. Tel. 988-4735.

Freda Nahanee's home-industry shop, on the North Vancouver Indian Reserve, offers its namesake sweaters from Vancouver Island as well as carved-silver Kwakiutl jewelry, Squamish woodcarvings, beaded leather moccasins, woven baskets, and other crafts. Open Monday through Saturday from 10am to 6pm, and some Sundays (phone ahead). Bus: 242.

HERITAGE CANADA, 356 Water St., Gastown. Tel. 669-6375.

Handcrafted silver and gold jewelry, original argillite carvings, Cowichan sweaters, moccasins, woodcarvings, and serigraph prints are among the goods available. Open Monday through Saturday from 10am to 6pm. Bus: 8 to Cordova Street.

Other branches are in Vancouver Centre (tel. 669-2447) and at Blackcomb Lodge, Whistler (tel. 932-4667).

HILL'S INDIAN CRAFTS, 165 Water St., near Cambie St., Gastown. Tel. 685-4249.

The second-floor gallery is a treasure trove of one-of-a-kind totem poles, ceremonial masks, bentwood boxes, animal plaques, Salish weavings, and other artifacts. They've all got price tags but they're not cheap. Downstairs, jewelry, moccasins, and other artworks are more reasonably priced. One of Vancouver's longest-established crafts shops, Hill's opened in 1946. Open daily from 9am to 9pm. Bus: 8 to Cordova Street.

IMAGES FOR A CANADIAN HERITAGE, 779 Burrard St., at Robson St. Tel. 685-7046.

Carvings in stone and wood by Native and non-Native artists are the focus of this fascinating gallery at the east end of Robsonstrasse. Inuit sculpture (in soapstone, whalebone, ivory, jade, and marble), Northwest Coast tribes' masks and jewelry, modern pottery and basketry, and original paintings and graphics are all included in the collection. Open Sunday through Thursday from 10am to 6pm, and on Friday and Saturday from noon to 5pm. Bus: 8.

INUIT GALLERY OF VANCOUVER, 345 Water St., Gastown. Tel. 688-7323.

Considered to have Canada's best collection of masterworks of Native Canadian art, this remarkable gallery should be on every visitor's "don't miss" list, whether you buy anything or not. Also displayed are masks and other artifacts from Papua New Guinea. Worldwide shipping is easily arranged. Open Monday through Saturday from 10am to 6pm, and on Sunday and holidays from noon to 5pm, and by appointment. Bus: 8 to Cordova Street.

DEPARTMENT STORES

THE BAY, 674 Granville St., at Georgia St. Tel. 681-6211.

The Hudson's Bay Company dates back more than three centuries, to a network of trading posts and forts established in the 1670s. The modern coast-to-coast chain is now known simply as "The Bay." The main downtown store, an imposing white structure with Greek columns, has seven levels of merchandise of all types. Many visitors buy a woolen Hudson's Bay point blanket, a true piece of Canadiana woven in England; its colorful stripes originally represented the number of beaver pelts taken in trade. English bone china can be found on the fifth floor, and the Okanagan Estate Wine Cellar is on the Vancouver Centre mall level. Open Monday through Wednesday from 9:30am to 6pm, on Thursday and Friday from 9:30am to 9pm, on Saturday from 9:30am to 5:30pm, and on Sunday from noon to 5pm. SkyTrain: Granville. Bus: 8, 10, or 20.

EATON'S, 701 Granville St., in the Pacific Centre Mall. Tel. 685-7112.

Vancouver's "other" huge department store is Eaton's. Its numerous fashion boutiques include styles from traditional to avant garde, among them the classic designs of Canadian Alfred Sung. You'll find fine china and crystal, kitchenware and gourmet foods, books and souvenirs, a Kids' World, three restaurants, a beauty salon, bakery, photo studio, florist, jeweler, optometrist, pharmacy, post office, shoe repair, ticket center, and travel agent. The seventh floor has a bargain annex with great deals on clothes, especially on children's and men's clothing. Open Monday through Wednesday from 9:30am to 6pm, on Thursday and Friday from 9:30am to 9pm, on Saturday from 9:30am to 5:30pm, and on Sunday from noon to 5pm. SkyTrain: Granville. Bus: 8, 10, or 20.

HOLT RENFREW, 633 Granville St., at Dunsmuir St., in the Pacific Centre Mall. Tel. 681-3121.

If The Bay is Vancouver's Macy's, then Holt Renfrew is its Saks Fifth Avenue. This elegant store has an upper level especially popular among the fashion-conscious for its classic designs, sportswear, and shoes. Naturally, it's got everything else a good department store should have as well. Open Monday through Wednesday from 9:30am to 6pm, on Thursday and Friday from 9:30am to 9pm, on Saturday from 9:30am to 5:30pm, and on Sunday from noon to 5pm. SkyTrain: Granville. Bus: 8, 10, or 20.

WOODWARD'S, 101 W. Hastings St., at Abbott St., Gastown. Tel. 684-5231.

This highly respected, family-owned local chain is a charming alternative to its fast-paced competitors. Of special interest to consumers are its Woodwynn bargain floors, offering great savings in dry goods, shoes, and other items. Open Monday through Thursday and on Saturday from 10am to 6pm, on Friday from 10am to 8pm, and on Sunday from noon to 5pm. Bus: 14, 20, or 21.

FASHIONS

Robsonstrasse has trendy mid-priced North American active wear. South Granville shops are more upscale, specializing in European imports. The department stores and shopping malls, of course, carry a wide variety of styles and price ranges.

Canada's best-known fashion designer is Alfred Sung. Other noted Canadian designers to look for are Simon Chang, Tom D'Auria, Susie Hayward, and Jean-Claude Poitras.

ALFRED SUNG OF TORONTO, 1143 Robson St., near Thurlow St. Tel. 687-2153.

Canada's most highly regarded fashion designer offers his creations for women at this exclusive shop on Robsonstrasse. The lines are clean, simple, and refined. Open Monday through Wednesday and on Saturday from 10am to 6pm, on Thursday and Friday from 10am to 9pm, and on Sunday from noon to 5pm. Bus: 8.

ARMADILLO, 3385 Cambie St., at W. 19th Ave. Tel. 873-2916.

Billing itself as a "designer discount boutique," Armadillo takes 50%-80% off the suggested retail prices of silks, cottons, woolens, and other fabrics from France, Italy, and Asia. Open Tuesday through Saturday from 10:30am to 5:30pm. Bus: 15.

BOBOLI, 2776 Granville St., at W. 12th Ave. Tel. 736-3458.

This elegant shop in the South Granville shopping district has exclusive designer clothing, shoes, and accessories for men and women. The owners travel to Italy four times a year to stock up on the latest in European fashions. Open Monday through Thursday from 9:30am to 6pm, on Friday from 9:30am to 9pm, and on Saturday from 9:30am to 5:30pm. Bus: 10, 14, or 20.

BRATZ, 2828 Granville St., at W. 13th Ave. Tel. 734-4344.

This is where the rich kids' parents shop—not only are the clothes for newborns to teenagers imported from Europe, but there's even a children's hair salon on the premises. Open Monday through Saturday from 9:30am to 5:30pm. Bus: 20 or 401.

CLUB MONACO, 1153 Robson St., near Thurlow St. Tel. 687-8618.

Men, women, and children can find more moderately priced Alfred Sung clothing here than at the designer boutique next door. The styles tend toward preppy. Open Monday through Wednesday and on Saturday from 10am to 6pm, on Thursday and Friday from 9am to 9pm, and on Sunday from 11am to 6pm. Bus: 8.

E. A. LEE, 466 Howe St., near W. Pender St. Tel. 683-2457.

The shop was founded in the 1920s, but E. A. Lee has modern European styles for 1990s executives—women as well as men—in cotton, cashmere, leather, and other fabrics are offered. Private consultations and same-day tailoring are among the many services provided. Open Monday through Saturday from 9am to 5:30pm. Bus: 10, 14, or 20.

EDWARD CHAPMAN, 833 W. Pender St., between Howe and Hornby. Tel. 685-6207.

This establishment, famous for traditional British woolens, celebrated its 100th anniversary in 1990. The main store in the financial district has a wide selection of men's and women's clothing and specialty items. Open Monday through Saturday from 9am to 5:30pm. Bus: 19.

There are branches in the Westin Bayshore Hotel, 1601 W. Georgia St. (tel. 685-6734), and in Oakridge Centre, 650 W. 41st Ave. (tel. 261-3223), featuring only men's fashions; and "Chappy's," at 2135 W. 41st Ave., Kerrisdale (tel. 261-5128), which is exclusively a women's store.

LEONE, in Sinclair Centre, 757 W. Hastings St., at Howe St. Tel. 683-1133.

Vancouver's trendiest high-fashion outlet is designed like a theater for patrons of the arts. A galleria stages the creations of well-known European designers, with clothing, footwear, leather goods, accessories, and fragrances. A cappuccino bar also offers light lunches. Open Monday through Friday from 9:30am to 6pm, on Saturday from 9:30am to 5:30pm, and on Sunday from noon to 5pm. SkyTrain: Waterfront. Bus: 8, 10, or 20.

MARK JAMES, 2941 W. Broadway, at Bayswater St., Kitsilano. Tel. 734-2381.

Men's and women's fashions, including many current European imports, are offered here at moderate prices. The inventory focuses on linens, silks, and natural cottons in summer, woolens in winter. Open Monday through Thursday from 10am to 6pm, on Friday from 10am to 9pm, on Saturday from 10am to 6pm, and on Sunday from 11:30 to 5:30pm. Bus: 10 or 22.

NETO, 347 and 359 Water St., at Cordova St., Gastown. Tel. 682-6424.

Men's and women's fashions of European design are manufactured here in Gastown. The line is noted for its colorful leather and lambskin items, but it also features woolens, linens, and silks, as well as matching shoes, handbags, and other accessories. Custom orders are welcomed. Neto ships all over the world. Open Monday through Thursday and on Saturday from 9:30am to 6pm, on Friday from 9:30am to 9pm, and on Sunday from noon to 5pm. SkyTrain: Waterfront. Bus: 8.

PEPPERMINTREE, 4243 Dunbar St., at W. 27th Ave., Dunbar. Tel. 228-9815.

This store has perhaps the largest stock of children's clothing, shoes, and accessories in Vancouver. Domestic and imported styles are moderately priced. There's a play area to occupy the kids while mom or dad shops. Open Monday through Saturday from 9:30am to 6pm, and on Sunday and holidays from 11am to 5pm. Bus: 22.

PRONTO, 2698 Granville St., at W. 12th Ave. Tel. 736-8751.

The merchandise here comes straight from Milan: men's and women's high-fashion Italian clothing, including leather goods and silk scarves. Open Monday through Saturday from 10am to 6pm. Bus: 20 or 401.

FOOD

Boxed salmon is probably the most popular gift item sold to visitors. Smoked or canned Pacific salmon, packed in a cedar box bearing a

Native motif, makes a wonderful gift for friends back home. Many gourmet specialty shops will even ship frozen fresh salmon to your home, timed for your return. Other good gift items include maple syrup (and maple sugar candy), B.C. honey, wild rice, and English teas and biscuits. You'll find all these and more, at the best prices, on the food floor of major department stores.

CHEENA B.C. LTD., 667 Howe St., near Georgia St. Tel. 684-5374.

This retail shop for souvenir gourmet foods packs smoked salmon for travel. Fish, beef jerky, chocolates, honey, and other items can be delivered to your hotel. Open Monday through Wednesday from 9am to 7pm, Thursday through Saturday from 9am to 9pm, and on Sunday from 9am to 6pm. SkyTrain: Granville. Bus: 401.

THE LOBSTERMAN, 1807 Mast Tower Rd., at Duranleau St., Granville Island. Tel. 687-4531.

Live lobsters, Dungeness crab, oysters, mussels, clams, geoduck, and scallops are kept in saltwater tanks holding more than 15,000 gallons. Lobster or crab can be cooked, on request, at no extra charge. Salmon and other fresh catches can be packed for travel. Open daily from 9am to 6pm. Bus: 51.

MURCHIE'S TEA & COFFEE, 970 Robson St. Tel. 662-3776.

This is the Vancouver institution for gourmet teas and coffees from around the world. Buy in bulk if you like. Seminars on tea and coffee can be arranged. Fine bone china, crystal, and giftware are also available. Open Monday through Wednesday and on Saturday from 9:30am to 6pm, on Thursday and Friday from 9:30am to 9pm, and on Sunday from noon to 5pm. Bus: 8.

There are also branches at 850 N. Park Royal Shopping Centre, West Vancouver; and in the Richmond Centre, Richmond.

SALMON VILLAGE, 779 Thurlow St., near Robson St. Tel. 685-3378.

Smoked salmon and caviar are the specialties of this gourmet food outlet just off Robsonstrasse. They will wrap and mail any item bought at their store. Open daily from 8:30am to 10pm. Bus: 8.

TEN REN TEA & GINSENG CO., 550 Main St., at Keefer St., Chinatown. Tel. 684-1566.

A variety of fine Chinese teas and tea sets are sold here, and samples are available in a corner tea ceremony. One wall of the shop is devoted to cases of ginseng root, an astringent medicinal herb that often sells for astronomical prices. Open daily from 9:30am to 6pm.

JEWELRY

The most interesting pieces are those crafted by Native artisans of silver, gold, British Columbia jade, or black argillite (a semiprecious stone mined only in the Queen Charlotte Islands).

HENRY BIRKS & SONS, 710 Granville St., at Georgia St. Tel. 669-3333.

This long-established jeweler offers traditional high-quality watches, clocks, diamonds and other stones, gold, silver, pearls, china, crystal, flatware, and handbags, as well as a variety of men's and women's gift items. Repairs are available on the premises. Open Monday through Wednesday from 9:30am to 6pm, on Thursday and Friday from 9:30am to 9pm, and on Saturday from 9:30am to 5:30pm. SkyTrain: Granville.

JADE WORLD, 1696 W. First Ave., at Pine St. Tel. 733-7212.

Three master carvers conduct free tours of the jade factory and carving studio. The tours conclude in the large gift shop, where a wide variety of jade is sold. Jade World mines the stone itself in northern British Columbia and keeps 100 tons in stock at all times! Open Monday through Friday from 8am to 4:30pm; appointments recommended for groups of 10 or more. Bus: 22; then walk one block west to Burrard and one block north at Cornwall.

SCANDINAVIA (CANADA) LTD., 648 Hornby St., near Georgia St. Tel. 688-4744.

Sterling-silver jewelry of Scandinavian design, most of it imported from Denmark, is offered in this exclusive shop. Stainless-steel flatware, crystal, glassware, and Danish teak accessories are also displayed. Open daily from 9:30am to 7pm. Bus: 242.

MALLS & SHOPPING CENTERS

EATON CENTRE METROTOWN, 4700 Kingsway, near Nelson Ave., Burnaby. Tel. 438-4700.

There are some 175 shops and services in this beautiful new development, just a few minutes from downtown Vancouver on the SkyTrain. Eaton's and two other department stores—Bretton's and the Real Canadian Superstore—anchor the mall, which features marble walkways, twin glass domes, and interior landscaping. Among the shops are 59 clothing stores, 17 shoe stores, and 26 food outlets. Open on Monday, Tuesday, and Saturday from 9:30am to 5:30pm, Wednesday through Friday from 9:30am to 9pm, and on Sunday from noon to 5pm. SkyTrain: Metrotown. Bus: 19.

HARBOUR CENTRE, 555 W. Hastings St., at Seymour St. Tel. 689-7304.

Forty-five specialty shops and a food market are located across the street from the Waterfront station. The Harbour Center Observation Deck affords an outstanding bird's-eye view of the city. Open Monday through Saturday from 10am to 6pm. SkyTrain: Waterfront.

THE LANDING, 375 Water St., at Cordova St., Gastown. Tel. 687-1144.

A new multipurpose development overlooking the waterfront, the Landing combines 19 retail outlets and an office complex. Fashion boutiques and restaurants predominate. The building dates back to 1905, when it was erected from Klondike gold-rush profits to serve as a warehouse. Open Monday through Wednesday and on Saturday and Sunday from 9:30am to 5:30pm, and on Thursday and Friday from 9:30am to 9pm. SkyTrain: Waterfront.

METROTOWN CENTRE, Kingsway, near Nelson Ave., Burnaby. Tel. 438-2444.

An 80-foot atrium covers 150 retail outlets and another 50

professional offices, anchored by Sears and Woodward's stores. A 100-store shopping center next door includes The Bay. Open on Monday, Tuesday, and Saturday from 9:30am to 5:30pm, Wednesday through Friday from 9:30am to 9pm, and on Sunday from noon to 5pm. SkyTrain: Metrotown. Bus: 19.

PACIFIC CENTRE MALL, 700 W. Georgia St., between Dunsmuir and Robson, and Howe and Granville Sts. Tel. 688-7236.

More than 200 shops and service outlets occupy this architectural delight—downtown Vancouver's largest mall. A skylit atrium connects it to the Four Seasons Hotel, and a three-story waterfall lends a playful feeling to the interior decor. Eaton's and Holt Renfrew department stores are here, as well as clothiers, jewelers, home furnishings stores, electronics stores, bookstores, gift shops, and three dozen family restaurants and fast-food outlets. There are also several banks and a theater complex. The mall is connected underground to Vancouver Centre, and directly linked to SkyTrain. Open Monday through Wednesday from 9:30am to 6pm, on Thursday and Friday from 9:30am to 9pm, on Saturday from 9:30am to 5:30pm, and on Sunday from noon to 5pm. SkyTrain: Granville.

PARK ROYAL SHOPPING CENTRE, Marine Dr. and Taylor Way, West Vancouver. Tel. 922-3211.

When the Park Royal opened in 1950, it was Canada's first shopping center. Today, it consists of two malls on opposite sides of Marine Drive. Together they house 190 stores and services, including three major department stores—The Bay, Eaton's, and Woodward's. There are also fashion stores, jewelers, children's stores, home furnishings and entertainment stores, sporting goods stores, a fitness center, 11 restaurants and 23 other food outlets, and numerous services. Open Monday through Wednesday from 10am to 6pm, on Thursday and Friday from 10am to 9pm, on Saturday from 9:30am to 5:30pm, and on Sunday from noon to 5pm. Bus: 250 or 253.

ROYAL CENTRE MALL, 1055 W. Georgia St., at Burrard St. Tel. 689-1711.

After a $10-million face-lift and expansion in 1989, this mall, which adjoins the Hyatt hotel, now boasts 47 shops and restaurants, plus a major cinema complex. It connects underground to the Burrard SkyTrain station. Open Monday through Thursday and on Saturday from 9:30am to 5:30pm, and on Friday from 9:30am to 7pm. SkyTrain: Burrard.

SINCLAIR CENTRE, 757 W. Hastings St., at Howe St. Tel. 666-4483.

Four city landmarks within a stone's throw of Canada Place and the Waterfront Station were elegantly restored by a federal grant and linked by a central court to create this upscale shopping center. The landmarks are the 1910 Post Office, the mosaic-tiled 1911 Winch Building, the 1913 Customs Examining Warehouse, and the art deco Federal Building, constructed in 1937. New Canadian citizens are still sworn in here on Monday and Friday. Sophisticated Leone (see "Fashions," above) is the flagship store of the complex, and there are 18 other shops, 12 food outlets and bistros, and art galleries on the atrium and mezzanine levels. Open Monday through Friday from 10am to 5:30pm (most stores), and on Saturday from 10am to 5pm. Closed: Public holidays. SkyTrain: Waterfront. Bus: 22.

VANCOUVER CENTRE, 650 W. Georgia St., between Dunsmuir and Georgia, and Granville and Seymour Sts. Tel. 684-7537.

The Bay anchors this complex of 120 shops and service outlets, which connects underground to the Pacific Centre at the Granville SkyTrain station. Open Monday through Wednesday and on Saturday from 9:30am to 6pm, on Thursday and Friday from 9:30am to 9pm, and on Sunday from noon to 5pm. SkyTrain: Granville.

SOUVENIRS

Shops selling T-shirts and Canada Place keychains are ubiquitous along major shopping streets like Robsonstrasse and in Gastown. However, the best prices and selections tend to be found at the major department stores.

TOYS

Handcrafted wooden toys from British Columbia's evergreen forests are handsome remembrances of a visit here. Check the selection at **Kids Only** on Granville Island or **Kids' Alley** at the Lonsdale Quay Market.

KABOODLES, 4449 W. 10th Ave., at Sasamat St., West Point Grey. Tel. 224-5311.

There's a little of everything for the children in this shop, from T-shirts to model dinosaurs. The staff is knowledgeable as to what's hot among today's kids. Open Monday through Thursday and on Saturday from 10am to 6pm, on Friday from 10am to 9pm, and on Sunday from noon to 5pm. Bus: 10.

KIDS ONLY, Cartwright and Anderson Sts., Granville Island. Tel. 684-0066.

This shop has a great selection of everything for kids. Open Monday through Thursday and on Saturday and Sunday from 10am to 6pm, and on Friday from 10am to 9pm. Bus: 51.

KINDERSPEL, 3039 Granville St., at W. 15th Ave. Tel. 254-0413.

Located on the sophisticated South Granville Street fashion strip, this store carries highbrow imports—European items, fragile Asian dolls, and top-of-the-line North American products. Older kids enjoy the computers and electronic games downstairs. Open Monday through Saturday from 9:30am to 5:30pm. Bus: 20 or 401.

WINDMILL TOYS, 2387 W. 41st Ave., near Vine St., Kerrisdale. Tel. 261-2120.

This may be the city's best toy store, especially in the moderate price range. All your kids' favorites—from Teenage Mutant Ninja Turtles to the latest versions of Barbie—are available, as well as many outstanding educational toys. A back room entertains children with a model train and giant stuffed animals. Open Monday through Friday from 9:30am to 9pm, on Saturday from 9:30am to 5:30pm, and on Sunday from noon to 5pm; closed holidays and Sunday on holiday weekends. Bus: 18 or 41.

WINE

For B.C. wines, including Cedar Creek and Mission Hill, check the wine shops in the department stores and public markets.

2. MARKETS

Five major public markets are easily reached from downtown Vancouver.

BRIDGEPOINT MARKET, 8811 River Rd., Richmond. Tel. 273-8500.

Like the New Westminster Quay Public Market, the Bridgepoint Market is located by the Fraser River. It's most easily reached by car, or if you're in the vicinity of Vancouver International Airport, it's an eight-minute cab ride away. Open Tuesday through Sunday and holiday Mondays from 9am to 6pm.

GRANVILLE ISLAND PUBLIC MARKET, Johnston St., Granville Island. Tel. 666-5784.

At this 50,000-square-foot market, all manner of fruit and vegetable, meat and seafood, wine and cheese, crafts, flowers and candy can be purchased, and there's a seemingly endless series of international fast-food counters. Best of all is the people-watching. From mid-June to September there's a farmers' truck market on Thursday from 9am to 6pm, depending on crops. Open daily from 9am to 6pm; closed Monday in winter, except public holidays. Bus: 51. Ferry: Granville Island Ferry or Aquabus across False Creek.

LONSDALE QUAY MARKET, 123 Carrie Cates Court, North Vancouver. Tel. 985-6261.

This colorful two-tier group of market vendors, specialty shops, and restaurants on North Vancouver's waterfront even houses a hotel! (See the Lonsdale Quay Hotel in Chapter 4.) The ground floor is the food floor—fresh produce, seafood, meat, bakery items, gourmet delicacies, wine, and a row of international fast-food outlets offering everything from burritos to pasta, sushi to espresso. The upper floor houses a variety of fashion stores, bookstores, gift shops, houseware outlets, and craft shops, as well as Kids' Alley—a number of children's shops offering toys, puppets, kites, clothing, and a special play area. Open Saturday through Thursday from 9:30am to 6:30pm, and on Friday from 9:30am to 9pm. SeaBus: Lonsdale Quay.

NEW WESTMINSTER QUAY MARKET, 810 Quayside Dr., New Westminster. Tel. 520-3881.

A scenic and cheap 25-minute ride on the Skytrain (B.C. Transit's clean and efficient rapid-transit rail service) will take you from downtown Vancouver to this nicely situated riverfront market. More than 80 businesses, including one major hotel (the Inn at Westminster Quay), occupy this two-level market on the Fraser River. There are food courts on both floors, along with produce and crafts enterprises. Open Saturday through Thursday from 9:30am to 6:30pm, and on Friday from 9:30am to 8pm. Skytrain: New Westminster station.

ROBSON PUBLIC MARKET, 1610 Robson St., at Cardero St. Tel. 682-2733.

A glass atrium soars over produce sellers and an international food fair in this contemporary market, whose design recalls that of London's Crystal Palace. You'll find French, Italian, Greek, Chinese, and Japanese food, plus grilled salmon, bagels, and stuffed pita bread. There are also housewares and leather-goods outlets, a video store, a florist, and a newsstand. Open daily from 9am to 9pm. Bus: 8.

CHAPTER 9

VANCOUVER NIGHTS

- **MAJOR CONCERT & PERFORMANCE HALLS**
1. **THE PERFORMING ARTS**
2. **THE CLUB & MUSIC SCENE**
3. **THE BAR SCENE**
4. **MORE ENTERTAINMENT**

Vancouver is an entertainment-oriented city, offering everything from highbrow culture such as theater, symphony, and dance to the less sedate pleasures of jazz or rock 'n' roll. Shows that closed on (or off) Broadway a couple of seasons ago may be big hits today in Vancouver. The Canadian West Coast's outstanding opera, symphony, and dance companies share stage time with touring troupes from all over North America and abroad. Jazz and rock music are big attractions; the city is on the touring itinerary of nearly every famous recording artist. In film, Vancouver has become known as "Hollywood North": A half dozen major U.S. network television programs are shot here, and the region is a popular venue for major California studio productions.

Full information on all major cultural events is available from the Vancouver Cultural Alliance **Arts Hotline,** 938 Howe St., in the Orpheum Theatre (tel. 684-2787). The office is open Monday through Friday from 9am to 5pm. Current listings can be found in the two daily newspapers, *The Sun* and *The Province;* a weekly newspaper devoted to arts and entertainment, *The Georgia Straight;* or another weekly, the *West Ender,* and the monthly *Vancouver* magazine.

Your best bet to learn about current entertainment events is to phone the Arts Hotline and ask where and how to get tickets. Many of the larger outlets don't maintain regular box office hours, since they prefer to let ticket brokers handle reservations and sales.

MAJOR CONCERT & PERFORMANCE HALLS

B.C. Place, 777 Pacific Blvd. S. (tel. 669-2300).

Orpheum Theatre, 884 Granville St., at Smithe Street (tel. 665-3069).

Pacific Coliseum, Renfrew Street, at Hastings Street (tel. 661-6773).

Queen Elizabeth Theatre, 649 Cambie St., at Dunsmuir Street (tel. 665-3050).

Vancouver East Cultural Centre, 1895 Venables St., at Victoria Drive (tel. 254-9578).

Vancouver Playhouse, Hamilton Street, at Dunsmuir Street (tel. 873-3311).

Tickets for most major events can be obtained at **TicketMaster** (Vancouver Ticket Centre), 1304 Hornby St. (tel. 280-3311, or 280-4444 to place credit/charge-card orders on American Express, MasterCard, or VISA). TicketMaster has 40 outlets in the greater Vancouver area, including all Eaton's department stores and major shopping malls.

Discount tickets are often available for midweek and matinee performances. Check with specific theaters or concert halls.

Throughout the summer, there's lots of free entertainment all over this lively city. Wherever people "hang out"—in places like Granville Island, English Bay Beach, Robson Square, and the Plaza of Nations on the former Expo '86 site—street buskers provide free music, mime, juggling, and other diversions. And numerous festivals bring outstanding artists in all fields to parks and performing arts centers at little or no charge.

1. THE PERFORMING ARTS

MAJOR CONCERT & PERFORMANCE HALLS

B.C. PLACE, 777 Pacific Blvd. S. Tel. 669-2300.
Huge rock acts, like the Who and the Rolling Stones, play at this $126-million inflated-dome stadium. Opened in 1983, it has 60,000 seats. It's best known as a sports venue. The box office is open Monday through Friday from 9am to 4:30pm. SkyTrain: Stadium.

Tours lasting 1–1½ hours are given for groups of 10 or more only. The cost is $3.50 for adults, $2.75 for seniors and students, and $2 for young children.

Admission: Ticket prices vary depending on the performance.

ORPHEUM THEATRE, 884 Granville St., at Smithe St. (stage door entrance on Seymour St.). Tel. 665-3069.
Built in 1927 during the age of vaudeville, the Orpheum has hosted a veritable hall of fame of the entertainment world, from Bob Hope to Marilyn Monroe, Igor Stravinsky to Louis Armstrong. But it took a citizens' campaign during the 1970s to save the theater from the wrecking ball. The City of Vancouver bought the building, restored it to its Roaring '20s splendor, and made it the home of the Vancouver Symphony Orchestra. Many concerts and musical events are held here. Visitors take note of the ornate theater's gilt ornamental plasterwork, painted domed ceiling, crystal chandeliers, and Wurlitzer organ. Box office hours vary. SkyTrain: Granville; then walk two blocks north. Bus: 8, 10, or 20.

Group tours are given by appointment only (tel. 684-2787), at $2 per person.

Admission: Tickets, symphony $14–$40, with discounts for students and seniors; ticket prices for other events vary.

PACIFIC COLISEUM, Renfrew St., at Hastings St., in Exhibition Park. Tel. 253-2311.
Located on the grounds of the Pacific National Exhibition, the old

coliseum hosts many big-name concerts when it's not scheduled for Vancouver Canucks hockey, pro wrestling, or other big sporting events. You won't find the Stones here, but performers like James Taylor and Fine Young Cannibals have drawn sellout crowds. The box office is open Monday through Friday from 9:30am to 5pm and before events. Bus: 14 or 21.

Admission: Ticket prices vary depending on the performer, but usually run around $30.

QUEEN ELIZABETH THEATRE, 649 Cambie St., at Dunsmuir St. Tel. 665-3050 for information.

The focal point of Vancouver's performing arts, the Q.E. is a beautiful and expertly designed 2,800-seat theater. Broadway musicals, grand opera, ballet, symphony, drama, rock, recitals, and touring theatrical productions have all appeared here. The huge stage complex also includes the smaller Vancouver Playhouse (see below). The box office, at 543 W. Seventh Ave., at Cambie Street, is open Monday through Friday from 9:30am to 4:30pm. SkyTrain: Stadium. Bus: 242.

Admission: Ticket prices vary depending on the performance, but may run $5–$45.

ROBSON SQUARE MEDIA CENTRE, 800 Robson St., at Howe St. Tel. 660-2830.

This ultramodern showcase-cum-exhibition area contains two theaters and an outdoor stage for almost everything from pop concerts and dance performances to avant-garde theatricals and ethnic cultural events. The box office is open Monday through Friday from 8am to 5pm; also at other times depending on the scheduled event. Bus: 8.

Admission: Ticket prices vary depending on the performance; often free.

VANCOUVER EAST CULTURAL CENTRE, 1895 Venables St., at Victoria Dr. Tel. 254-9578.

This converted early 20th-century church is probably the most adaptable performing-arts space in Vancouver. On any given night, the VECC may host sophisticated adult or light children's theater, classical music recitals or folk performances, jazz dance or ballet. Internationally known artists frequently perform at this 280-seat venue. A lounge opens one hour before shows. Bus: 20 or 21.

Admission: Ticket prices vary depending on the performance. Reservations are recommended; all seats are general admission.

VANCOUVER PLAYHOUSE, Hamilton St., at Dunsmuir St. Tel. 665-3050 for information, 873-3311 for tickets.

This 650-seat theater is the home of the Vancouver Playhouse Company, the city's leading resident company. It presents six major productions during its October-to-May season. A recent season included classics by William Shakespeare, George Bernard Shaw, and Noël Coward, as well as several contemporary productions, including one by Canadian playwright Dan Needles (*Letter from Wingfield Farm*). In winter, the stage hosts the Dance Centre subscription series of classic and contemporary dance. The box office, at 543 W. Seventh Ave., at Cambie Street, is open Monday through Friday from 9:30am to 4:30pm. SkyTrain: Stadium.

Admission: Tickets, $29 adults midweek, $35 weekends; discounts for students and seniors available.

THEATER

ARTS CLUB THEATRE, 1585 Johnston St., Granville Island. Tel. 687-1644.

Vancouver's most active theater is actually two. The 425-seat Granville Island Mainstage, established in 1979 in a former industrial warehouse on False Creek, presents major dramas, comedies, and musicals from Shakespeare to Neil Simon, *Steel Magnolias* to the punk-rock classic *Angry Housewives*. (The adjoining Backstage Lounge has live entertainment after weekend performances.) The Arts Club Revue Stage, next to the Granville Island Public Market, offers an intimate, cabaret-style showcase for small productions, late-night improvisation, and musical revues like *Ain't Misbehavin'* and *A Closer Walk with Patsy Cline.*

The box office is open Monday through Saturday from 10am to 7pm. Bus: 51 (Granville Island); or 8, 10, or 20 (and walk one block west of Seymour, at Davie Street).

Admission: Tickets, $18–$24.50, with discounts for students and seniors.

BACK ALLEY THEATRE, 751 Thurlow St., at Robson St. Tel. 688-7013.

The raison d'être of this intimate downtown theater is "theater sports"—a unique form of improvisational theater performed weekend nights by the Vancouver Theatresports League. Quirky, satiric, and often hilariously funny, it features two opposing teams of five actors wrestling without scripts over theatrical themes. A referee, three judges who award points, and fanatical audiences complete the picture (the comedy is not sexist or abusive). Improvisational comedy is on Monday and Thursday at 8pm; Theatresports, on Friday at 9 and 11pm, and on Saturday at 7 and 11pm. There's an "open stage" on Sunday at 7pm. Bus: 8.

Admission: $10 adults Tues–Thurs, $12 Fri–Sat; $8 students Tues–Thurs, $10 Fri–Sat; $2 Sun; $5 Mon. Seating is first-come, first-served.

FIREHALL ARTS CENTRE, 280 E. Cordova St., Gastown. Tel. 689-0926.

This 125-seat theater, occupying (since 1975) Vancouver's original Firehouse No. 1, is the home of three innovative companies: the Firehall Theatre Co., the Touchstone Theatre, and Axis Mime. All are noted for their experimentation and originality. Dance events and concerts are also held here. The box office is open Tuesday through Friday from 5pm until show time, on Saturday from 6:30pm until show time, and on Sunday from 5:30pm until show time. Bus: 8.

Admission: Ticket prices vary with the performance (usually $12–$15); discounts for seniors and students.

FREDERIC WOOD THEATRE, Gate 4, University of British Columbia. Tel. 822-2678.

UBC students put on five or six productions from September to November and January to March. During a recent season, plays by

Charles Dickens, George Büchner, James Reaney, and Brian Friel shared the stage with the musical *Cabaret*. There's also a summer season of lighter material. The Dorothy Somerset Studio offers a venue for more intimate plays. The box office is open Monday through Friday from 8:30am to 4:30pm. Bus: 10.

Admission: Tickets, $10 adults, $7 students; summer season, all seats $10.

THEATRE UNDER THE STARS, Malkin Bowl, in Stanley Park. Tel. 687-0174.

From mid-July to mid-August, on nights without rain, professional-amateur productions of popular musicals are performed at Stanley Park's Malkin Bowl bandshell. This is an outdoor event—be sure to bring a blanket. The box office is open Monday through Saturday beginning at 7pm, with curtain time at 8:30pm, weather permitting. Bus: 8.

Admission: Tickets, $15 adults, $9 seniors and children.

VANCOUVER LITTLE THEATRE, Heritage Hall, 3102 Main St., at E. 15th Ave. (enter from the back alley). Tel. 876-4165.

Serious dramas by new Canadian playwrights, as presented by a variety of professional companies, share the stage with controversial classics, such as *Screwtape* (based on C. S. Lewis's novel) and Caryl Churchill's *Vinegar Tom*. The box office opens 30 minutes before show time, but show times vary. Bus: 3.

Admission: Ticket prices vary; usually $7–$12, with discounts for seniors and students.

WATERFRONT THEATRE, 1412 Cartwright St., Granville Island. Tel. 685-6217.

Granville Island's "other" major theater complex, the Waterfront is the home of the New Play Centre, which sponsors hit-or-miss original works by B.C. playwrights; the Carousel Theatre, which offers family entertainment; and various other companies that have no permanent home of their own. Sometimes shows that succeed at the Arts Club or Vancouver Playhouse theaters move here if they are preempted by other scheduled productions. The Waterfront also hosts script-development workshops, readings, and new play festivals.

The box office is open Monday through Friday from 9am to 5pm; show times vary. Bus: 51.

Admission: Ticket prices vary, but are usually in the $12 range.

OPERA

VANCOUVER OPERA, 1132 Hamilton St. Tel. 682-2871.

Four lavish productions are presented between late October and early May each year at the Queen Elizabeth Theatre, with English supertitles projected above the stage so viewers can follow the dialogue. Works—which often feature international stars—range from traditional classics (Bizet's *Carmen,* Verdi's *La Traviata*) to 20th-century standards (Lehar's *The Merry Widow,* Stravinsky's *The Rake's Progress*) to esoteric modern productions. The Vancouver Opera Association is celebrating its 34th season in 1993–94.

Admission: Tickets, $24.60–$72.95; no discounts for students or seniors.

ORCHESTRAL & CHORAL MUSIC

FESTIVAL CONCERT SOCIETY, 3737 Oak St. Tel. 736-3737.

This association sponsors a Coffee Concert series every Sunday at 11am, September through June, at the Queen Elizabeth Theatre. The one-hour concert may be classical, jazz, folk, dance, theater, or opera, but it's always pleasant and relaxing. Babysitting is provided free. The box office opens on Sunday at 10am.

Admission: Tickets, $5.

UNIVERSITY OF BRITISH COLUMBIA SCHOOL OF MU-SIC, Recital Hall, Gate 4, 6361 Memorial Rd. Tel. 822-3113.

UBC presents eight faculty and guest-artist concerts between September and November, January and March, often featuring renowned performers. The box office is open Monday through Friday from 8:30am to 4:30pm.

Admission: Tickets, $13 adults, $7 seniors and students.

VANCOUVER BACH CHOIR, 5730 Seaview Rd., West Vancouver. Tel. 921-8012.

This 150-voice ensemble, generally considered to be Vancouver's top amateur choir, presents five major concerts a year at the Orpheum Theatre, one of which is a Christmas season sing-along performance of Handel's *Messiah*. The group has won several international competitions.

Admission: Ticket prices vary depending on the performance and venue.

VANCOUVER CANTATA SINGERS, 5115 Keith Rd., West Vancouver. Tel. 921-8588.

This semiprofessional mixed choir of 40 voices specializes in performances of early music. Past schedules have included works by Brahms, Stravinsky, and Handel, as well as choral music from eastern Europe. The season usually includes three programs (November, December, and March) in different venues.

Admission: Tickets, $20 adults, $15 seniors and students.

VANCOUVER CHAMBER CHOIR, 1254 W. Seventh Ave. Tel. 738-6822.

Western Canada's only professional choral ensemble, the Chamber Choir presents a six-concert main series annually at the Orpheum Theatre. When it's not touring internationally or recording, the group also performs a chamber music series at Ryerson United Church, 2195 W. 45th Ave., at Yew Street.

Admission: Tickets, Orpheum series, $16–$32 adults, $14–$27 students and seniors.

VANCOUVER NEW MUSIC SOCIETY, 207 W. Hastings St. Tel. 874-6200.

Seven annual concerts, featuring the work of contemporary composers, are presented at the Vancouver East Cultural Centre between September and April. The society features innovative groups, sometimes in conjunction with dance or film, and avant-garde foreign composers.

Admission: Tickets, $14 adults, $10 students.

VANCOUVER SOCIETY FOR EARLY MUSIC, 1254 W. Seventh Ave. Tel. 732-1610.

This group's focus is medieval, Renaissance, and baroque music, performed on instruments of the period. Concerts are held at varied locations, including the UBC Recital Hall and St. Andrew's Wesley Church, 1012 Nelson St. The society's annual highlight is the Festival of Early Music, which draws musicians from all over North America to UBC in July and August.

Admission: Tickets, UBC, $14 adults, $8.50 seniors and students; informal concerts, $5 adults, $4 seniors and students.

VANCOUVER SYMPHONY ORCHESTRA, 601 Smithe St. Tel. 684-9100, or 876-3434 for ticket information.

The city's acclaimed, extremely active orchestra presents as many as a dozen concerts a month in a wide variety of series and recitals. There's the Masterworks series of great classical works; Air Canada Favourites, featuring varied themes like Russian composers; Tea & Trumpets, with modern classics and ethnic music; VSO Pops, often including show tunes and other contemporary favorites; and a children's series. If that's not enough, a summer concert series takes the orchestra all over the Lower Mainland, from White Rock and Cloverdale on the U.S. border to Blackcomb Mountain at Whistler. It usually performs at the ornate Orpheum Theatre.

Admission: Tickets, $12.75–$38 adults; reduced rates for students and seniors.

DANCE

Vancouver has a surprising number of new, relatively unknown contemporary dance companies. Watch the media for performance dates or check with the **Dance Centre** (tel. 872-0432), a nonprofit group that provides information on dance in the city. Many local troupes participate in the Discover Dance gala evening at the Vancouver Playhouse, or in the annual Dancing on the Edge Festival at the Firehall Arts Center in September.

In addition to the groups noted below, look for the **Judith Marcuse Dance Company** (tel. 985-6459) and the **Karen Jamieson Dance Company** (tel. 872-5658).

ANNA WYMAN DANCE THEATRE, 1705 Marine Dr., West Vancouver. Tel. 926-6535.

Vancouver's best-known professional contemporary dance troupe is bold, colorful, and aggressively theatrical, with a worldwide following: Its entire tour in China was sold out. Try to catch a free outdoor appearance in late summer at Granville Island or Robson Square. The indoor and touring season concludes in March.

Admission: Tickets for indoor performances, $15–$17.

BALLET BRITISH COLUMBIA, 502-68 Water St. Tel. 669-5954.

This major troupe, founded in 1986, performs at the Queen Elizabeth Theatre. Its repertoire ranges from classical ballet to contemporary works. Ballet B.C. also hosts visits by the National Ballet of Canada, the Royal Winnipeg Ballet, the Pacific Northwest Ballet of Seattle, Les Ballets Jazz de Montréal, and other touring groups.

Admission: Tickets, $15.50–$40 adults; senior and student discount usually about 20%.

2. THE CLUB & MUSIC SCENE

NIGHTCLUBS & CABARETS

BIG BAM BOO CLUB, 1236 W. Broadway, at Alder St. Tel. 733-2220.

Situated in a renovated dance hall dating from the 1930s, this popular club features a large, wood-sprung dance floor surrounded by lots of greenery. Between Top 40 sets by live bands, DJs spin CDs. Expect crowds, especially on weekends. The big, boisterous main floor contrasts sharply with the smaller, quieter upstairs lounge where $7–$8 will buy you a plate of sushi as you enjoy a more intimate piano bar with an adjacent dance floor. An ever-changing variety of "special" evenings are featured, including a "ladies night" on Wednesday. Drinks run about $4.50. The club is open on Monday from 9pm to 2am and Tuesday through Saturday from 8pm to 2am. Bus: 9 or 10.

Admission: $3 Mon–Tues, $5 Wed–Thurs, $7 Fri–Sat.

COMMODORE BALLROOM, 870 Granville St., at Smithe St. Tel. 681-7838.

After a $1-million facelift, this longtime institution (built in 1929) is probably Vancouver's number-one cabaret. Major rock, rap, jazz, blues, reggae, and other performers are booked here in a continuous stream. Ice-T and Body Count, Queen Ida and the Bon Temps Zydeco Band, the Violent Femmes, the Pixies, and Al DiMeola all performed during one recent four-week stretch. Up to 1,000 patrons can squeeze into the Commodore, which has four bars, six video screens, and a suspended wooden dance floor sprung with railway car springs, rubber tires, and horsehair. Drinks are in the $5 range. The club is open most nights from 8pm. Bus: 8, 10, or 20.

Admission: Varies depending on the performer.

86 STREET MUSIC HALL, Plaza of Nations, 750 Pacific Blvd. S., at Cambie St. Tel. 683-8687.

A high-tech cabaret on the old Expo '86 site, this club consistently features outstanding local, national, and international acts—including, for instance, Vancouver's own Bryan Ferry, Toronto's Tragically Hip, Australia's Hoodoo Gurus, and American jazz innovators Hiroshima. 86 Street seats 850. Drinks average $4.75. Open Wednesday through Saturday from 7pm to 2am. SkyTrain: Stadium.

Admission: Wed–Thurs no cover charge; Fri–Sat $7, more for major artists; Sun–Tues closed; advance tickets may be purchased from TicketMaster.

SOFT ROCK CAFE, 1925 W. Fourth Ave., at Cypress St., Kitsilano. Tel. 736-8480.

The attraction here is dancing and dining in a comfortable, upscale atmosphere. Diners can sup on steaks, seafood, or pasta (dinners run $7.95–$14.95) while listening to top local or North American rock acts (no heavy metal here!), then work off their meal on the dance floor beneath the stage. Nondiners appreciate the café's elaborate seafood and martini bar and the breezy patio. Drinks begin at $3.50. The café is open on Tuesday and Wednesday from 6pm to midnight, and Thursday through Saturday from 3pm to 1am. Live music is presented Tuesday through Saturday from 9:30pm to 1am. Bus: 4.

Admission: Varies depending on the performer.

COMEDY CLUBS

PUNCHLINES COMEDY THEATRE, 15 Water St., at Carrall St., Gastown. Tel. 684-3015.
Jay Leno, Howie Mandel, and other famous comedians have performed at this club—albeit before they became truly "big." Tuesday is Amateur Night. Wednesday nights there are comedy "jams," featuring improvisational troupes such as the No Name Players. Stand-up comics take the stage on weekends. Drinks run $3. The box office is open Monday through Friday from noon to 4pm (closed Saturday and Sunday). Doors open at 8pm. Show time in summer (May to September) is 9:30pm on Wednesday and Thursday, 9:30 and 11:30pm on Friday and Saturday; on Tuesday at 8:30pm all year; winter shows begin 30 minutes earlier.

Admission: $3.50 Tues, $6.50 Wed–Thurs, $9.65 Fri–Sat.

YUK YUK'S KOMEDY KABARET, Plaza of Nations, 750 Pacific Blvd. S., at Cambie St. Tel. 687-LAFF (687-5233).
Leading Canadian and American stand-up comics perform at this club on the Expo '86 site. Amateurs take the stage on Wednesday nights. Drinks run $4.75. Show times are Wednesday and Thursday at 9pm, and Friday and Saturday at 9 and 11:30pm. SkyTrain: Stadium.

Admission: $3 Wed, $6 Thurs, $10 Fri–Sat (tax included).

JAZZ, BLUES & FOLK

Jazz is big in Vancouver—in fact, it has its own "hotline." The **Coastal Jazz and Blues Society** (tel. 682-0706) offers full information on all current and upcoming jazz events, including dates, times, and ticket prices.

In June the **du Maurier International Jazz Festival** is held at venues all over Vancouver, and in July the **Vancouver Folk Festival** takes place. Both feature free performances in addition to paid-admission events.

ALMA STREET CAFE, 2505 Alma St., at W. 10th Ave. Tel. 222-2244.
Ethnomusicologist Stephen Huddart's eclectic neighborhood eatery (see Chapter 5, "Vancouver Dining") is one of the best places in the city to catch modern jazz performers, including many of the best from eastern Canada or United States. Drinks run $3.75; entrées, $8.95–$14.95 (reservations recommended). The café is open Monday through Thursday from 8am to 11pm, on Friday from 8am to midnight, on Saturday from 9am to midnight, and on Sunday and

holidays from 9am to 11pm. There's music Wednesday through Saturday from 8 to 11:30pm. Bus: 10 or 22.

Admission: Free (cover only for special performances).

BLARNEY STONE, 216 Carrall St., between Powell and Cordova Sts., Gastown. Tel. 687-4322.

This Irish pub-cum-nightspot has a relaxed and rollicking atmosphere for those who like St. Patrick's Day every day—for example, the irreverent, full-throated ballads of a traditional Dublin band. You don't have to know the steps to join the lively crowd on the dance floor. Drinks average $4; meals, $10–$16. Open Tuesday through Saturday from 5pm to 2am; music starts at 9pm. Bus: 8.

Admission: $5 (free for diners).

CAFE DJANGO, 1184 Denman St., at Davie St. Tel. 689-1184.

This café offers a great view of English Bay, a fine, multicultural menu, and some wonderful talent. Soloists, such as Jim Byrnes (also an actor on the TV series "Wiseguy"), play Monday through Wednesday, with jazz trios and quartets showcased Thursday through Saturday. Well-known performers have included Herb Ellis, Paul Brady, Viveza, and Charlie Hayden. The café is open daily for lunch from 11am to 3pm, and for dinner (main courses run $10–$17) from 5pm to midnight. Music begins at 8:30pm or 9pm most nights; there is often classical music during weekday lunches, Gospel music for Sunday brunch. Bus: 8.

Admission: Free (cover only for special performances).

CARNEGIE'S, 1619 W. Broadway, near Fir St. Tel. 733-4141.

Top local and touring artists in both traditional and modern jazz perform at this popular bar and grill from 9pm to 1am. The atmosphere resembles an upscale English pub, with rich wood furnishings and fine upholstery. Dinner entrées run $7.95–$13.95. Open Monday through Saturday from 11:30am to 1am. Bus: 10.

Admission: $6 minimum; no cover.

GLASS SLIPPER, 185 E. 11th Ave., at Main St. Tel. 877-0066.

This showcase for the Coastal Jazz and Blues Society and the New Orchestra Workshop offers contemporary and improvised jazz in an intimate, informal, inexpensive setting. Located downstairs from the Cinderella Ballroom, it's open on Wednesday and Thursday from 9pm to 2am, on Friday and Saturday from 8:30pm to 2am, and on Sunday from 9pm to midnight. Bus: 3.

Admission: $5; more for special acts.

HOT JAZZ CLUB, 2120 Main St., at E. Fifth Ave. Tel. 873-4131.

Dixieland, swing, and big-band sounds blast from the instruments of local and visiting musicians at this casual club. At this writing, two big bands play on alternate weeks. There's a full bar (drinks run $3.50) and a fairly large floor for free-form dancers. Open on Wednesday from 8pm to midnight and on Friday and Saturday from 8:30pm to 1am. Bus: 8 or 19.

Admission: $6 members, $8 guests; more for special acts.

YALE HOTEL, 1300 Granville St., at Drake St. Tel. 681-YALE or 681-9253.

When it comes to seeing and hearing gritty-voiced blues greats like Clarence "Gatemouth" Brown, John Hammond, or Charlie Musslewhite, it's somehow appropriate that the venue should be in a somewhat seedy neighborhood. This late 19th-century hotel fits the bill. It's a spot for hardcore blues-lovers: "We don't like to vary too much from the real stuff," says owner Jim Tortyna. Drinks average $4.50. Open Monday through Friday from 11:30am to 1:30am, on Saturday from 1:30pm to 1:30am, and on Sunday from 2pm to midnight; there's music Monday through Saturday from 9:30pm, and jam sessions on Saturday and Sunday from 3pm. Bus: 8, 10, or 20.

Admission: Sun–Wed no cover charge, Thurs–Sat usually $5–$7.

ROCK MUSIC

Like most major cities, Vancouver has no shortage of places to listen and dance to live rock bands. The following are some of the most popular:

THE BIG EASY, 1055 Homer St., near Helmcken St. Tel. 682-4171.

A large nightclub with a huge dance floor, the Big Easy features a house band that plays upbeat contemporary rock. You'll have unobstructed views of the dance floor from the comfortable couches that line the walls beneath intriguing Indonesian art. Thursday is "Ladies Night," featuring a male dance revue. Visiting bands are showcased once a month. Drinks run $4.35. Open Tuesday through Saturday from 8pm to 2am. Bus: 8, 10, or 20; then walk three blocks west on Granville Street.

Admission: $2 Tues–Wed; $4 for men Thurs (after 10pm only), free for women; $6 Fri–Sat.

RAILWAY CLUB, 579 Dunsmuir St., at Seymour St. Tel. 681-1625.

Attracting a nonyuppie, nonhippie, non-heavy-metal, generally proletarian clientele, here's a place where you can enjoy a pub-style weekday lunch, sip a quiet afternoon drink, or boogie to outstanding bands at night. Rustic in atmosphere, this upstairs establishment has a quieter conversation lounge separated from the dance floor and stage by a long wooden bar. Bands like the Secular Atavists, the Cranium Miners, and Bob's Your Uncle—all with strong local followings—perform nightly. There's jazz on Saturday from 3 to 7pm. Drinks begin at $3.75. Open Monday through Friday from noon to 2am, on Saturday from 2pm to 2am, and on Sunday from 4pm to midnight. SkyTrain: Granville.

Admission: $2 members, $5 guests ($10 membership requires a member's endorsement).

RICHARD'S ON RICHARDS, 1036 Richards St., between Nelson and Helmcken Sts. Tel. 687-6794.

If there's any one club that can be considered Vancouver's "in" place, it's Richard's. Attracting a well-dressed young professional crowd that likes to "network," the festive atmosphere includes four bars, a laser-lighting system, and live soft-rock bands that begin nightly at 9:30pm. A semicircular mezzanine balcony overlooks the main dance floor. Drinks average $4.75. Open Monday through Saturday from 7pm to 2am and on Sunday from 7pm to midnight (from 8pm in winter). Bus: 8, 10, or 20; then walk two blocks west on Granville.

Admission: $3 Mon, $4 Tues–Wed, $5 Thurs, $7 Fri–Sat, free Sun.

ROXY, 932 Granville St., between Smithe and Nelson Sts. Tel. 684-ROXY (684-7699).

The emphasis here is on "classic rock" of the '50s, '60s, and '70s presented by live bands. The atmosphere is casual and fun—Tom Cruise–clone bartenders straight out of *Cocktail,* weekly theme parties (often with vacation giveaways), old-time movies, and a Wednesday "Student Night." Drinks run $3.95. Open Monday through Saturday from 7pm to 2am and on Sunday from 7pm to midnight. Bus: 8, 10, or 20.

Admission: $3 Mon–Wed, $5 Thurs, $6 Fri–Sat, free Sun.

TOWN PUMP, 66 Water St., near Abbott St., Gastown. Tel. 683-6695.

One of Vancouver's favorite social spots, this Gastown club attracts top local and national acts to its casual, antique-filled premises. Patrons can enjoy a full-menu restaurant and piano lounge (open from 5 to 9pm) before the loud music and dancing begin. The drink menu ($4 average) features a large number of imported beers. Open Monday through Friday from noon to 2am, on Saturday from 7:30pm to 2am (earlier in summer), and on Sunday from 7:30pm to midnight. Bus: 8 to Cordova Street.

Admission: Varies depending on the performer.

COUNTRY

BOONE COUNTY CABARET, 801 Brunette Ave., Coquitlam. Tel. 525-3144.

Many of the Vancouver area's best country-and-western night-spots are in such suburban Lower Mainland towns as Surrey, Langley, and Abbotsford. This one, not far off Trans-Canada Hwy. 1, is among the closest to the city and among the most popular. Drinks run $4.05. Free dance lessons are offered at 8pm on Monday, Tuesday, and Thursday. It's open Monday through Saturday from 8pm to 2am. Bus: 151.

Admission: Free Mon–Thurs, $3.25 Fri–Sat.

CHEYENNE SOCIAL PUB, in the Lynnwood Hotel, 1515 Barrow St. (Main St. at Mountain Hwy.), North Vancouver. Tel. 988-6161.

This North Shore watering hole has live country music Thursday through Saturday nights. Among its regular performers are such local favorites as Cactus Club, Underground Outlaws, and the Hotshots. Drinks go for $3.85. Open Monday through Friday from 11am to 1am, on Saturday from noon to 2am, and on Sunday from 11:30am to midnight. Bus: 210 or 239.

Admission: Free.

JR COUNTRY CLUB, in the Sandman Inn, 180 W. Georgia St., near Cambie. Tel. 681-2211.

Downtown Vancouver's leading country nightclub, this establish-ment features leading Canadian bands playing in the rustic atmos-phere of the Old West. Radio station CJJR broadcasts from here and plays popular records between live sets. The club offers free lessons in line-dancing on Monday and Wednesday and in two-stepping on Tuesday. Drinks are $4.15. Open Monday through Thursday from 8pm to 1:30am and on Friday and Saturday from 7pm to 1:30am. SkyTrain: Stadium. Bus: 242.

Admission: Free Mon–Thurs, $4 Fri–Sat.

DISCOS

GRACELAND, 1250 Richards St., between Davie and Drake Sts. Tel. 688-2648.

One of Vancouver's more bizarre nightspots, Graceland bears little or no resemblance to Elvis's Memphis mansion. A very outré establishment appealing to modern counterculturalists, it offers high-energy "industrial" dance music appropriate for a warehouse space. This is definitely *not* a Top 40 establishment. Wednesday is reggae night. Drinks run $3.95. Open Tuesday through Saturday from 9pm to 2am. Bus: 8, 10, or 20; then walk two blocks west at Granville Street.

Admission: Cover charge varies (usually $3–$7).

LUV-A-FAIR, 1275 Seymour St., at Davie St. Tel. 685-3288.

"Outrageous" might be the best word to describe this disco. The usual crowd here ranges from acrylic mohawks to drag queens to zoned-out college students. It features a great dance floor, an outstanding sound system, and imported European new-wave music and rock videos. Drinks average $3.75. Open Monday through Saturday from 9pm to 2am and on Sunday from 9pm to midnight. Bus: 8, 10, or 20; then walk one block west on Granville.

Admission: $3 Mon–Tues, $2 Wed–Thurs, $6 Fri–Sat, free Sun.

SHAMPERS, Coast Plaza at Stanley Park, 1733 Comox St., at Denman St. Tel. 688-7711 or 684-6262.

The West End's most popular disco, Shampers also has a piano bar. Monday through Thursday you can enjoy the piano bar from 9:30pm to midnight. Friday and Saturday night has disco only, from 9pm. The evening menu features pasta. Drinks run $4.25. Open Monday through Thursday from 4:30pm to 12:30am, on Friday and Saturday from 4:30pm to 2am, and on Sunday from noon to midnight. Bus: 8.

Admission: Sun–Thurs no cover charge, Fri–Sat $4.

3. THE BAR SCENE

Looking for quiet conversation or perhaps a game of darts? There are many fine neighborhood pubs throughout Vancouver and the Lower Mainland. And many of them feature live music on certain nights; licensing laws, however, require them to close by midnight on weeknights.

BIMINI, 2010 W. Fourth Ave., near Maple St., Kitsilano. Tel. 738-2714.

At this immensely popular pub with two seating levels, patrons come to mingle and converse, watch sporting events on TV, or listen (but not dance) to small bands. Drinks run $4. Open Monday through Friday from 11am to midnight, on Saturday from 11am to 1am, and on Sunday from noon to midnight. Bus: 4.

CHECKERS, 1755 Davie St., at Denman St. Tel. 682-1831.

At this friendly bar in the West End, patrons can either sit near the bandstand where the music is often classic rock, or withdraw to a less noisy corner for conversation. The decor is black-and-white, like a checkerboard. Food is also served. Drinks go for $4.35. Open Monday through Saturday from 11am to 2am and on Sunday from 11am to midnight. Bus: 8.

DARBY D. DAWES, 2001 MacDonald St., at W. Fourth Ave., Kitsilano. Tel. 731-0617.

A favorite among university students, Darby's inviting English pub atmosphere is the venue for live entertainment Tuesday and Thursday through Saturday nights. Drinks are $4. Open Monday through Thursday from 11:30am to midnight, and on Friday and Saturday from 11:30am to 1am. Bus: 4.

DOVER ARMS, 961 Denman St., at Nelson St., West End. Tel. 683-1929.

Another neighborhood pub of the English variety, this one attracts the literati from the densely populated West End—near Stanley Park and English Bay Beach. Drinks average $3.80. Open Monday through Saturday from 10am to midnight and on Sunday from 11am to midnight. Bus: 8.

THE ELEPHANT WALK PUB, 1445 E. 41st. Ave., at Knight St., Kensington. Tel. 324-1400.

A bit off the beaten track, this is an essential watering hole for pub-lovers. The pub is decorated with lots of brass and wood, and has comfortable furnishings. It's a place where the working class and students rub shoulders and enjoy it. Drinks go for $3.80. Open daily from 10am to midnight. Bus: 22.

HERITAGE HOUSE HOTEL, 455 Abbott St., at Pender St., Gastown. Tel. 685-7777.

One of the city's popular gay bars; the lounge and pub on the main floor attract both men and women. Downstairs, there's a lesbian bar open Tuesday through Saturday; only women are admitted on Wednesday and Friday. Drinks run $3.60. Open Monday through Saturday from 11am to 1am and on Sunday from 11am to midnight. Bus: 19.

THE JOHN B NEIGHBOURHOOD PUB, 1000 Austin Ave., at Le Bleu St., Coquitlam. Tel. 931-5115.

Voted Greater Vancouver's number-one pub, this establishment 14 miles east of downtown offers "businessmen's lunches" at noontime and pub dinners from 5 to 8pm daily. It has a piano bar, nightly dance music, and a satellite TV for sports events. The pub stocks 20 local and imported beers and handmade draft cider. Patrons can enjoy a large no-smoking fireplace area and garden patio. There's a dress code after 7pm. Drinks are $3.95. Open Monday through Saturday from 11am to 1am and on Sunday from 11am to midnight. Bus: 152.

THE ODYSSEY, 1251 Howe St., near Davie St. Tel. 689-5256.

A big dance club for Vancouver's sizable gay population, the Odyssey offers live entertainment every Tuesday and Wednesday night. A DJ spins records the rest of the week. The patio is open in warm weather. Drinks go for $3.75. Open Monday through Saturday from 9pm to 2am and on Sunday from 9pm to midnight. Bus: 8

Admission: Free Sun–Mon and Wed–Thurs, $2 Tues, $3 Fri–Sat.

THE RUSTY GULL, 175 E. 1st St., at St. Andrew's Ave., North Vancouver. Tel. 988-5585.

Barely three blocks from Lonsdale Quay, this is a bar for gourmet beer drinkers. It has 13 brews on tap, mostly from local cottage producers. There's frequent live entertainment. Drinks run $4.20–$5.50. Open daily from 10am to midnight. SeaBus: Lonsdale Quay.

STAMP'S LANDING, 610 Stamp's Landing, False Creek. Tel. 879-0821.

The yachting crowd, especially those who live on their boats in the False Creek Marina, pack into this pub adjacent to Monk McQueen's restaurant. There's never a dull moment. Drinks are $4. Open daily from 11am to midnight. Bus: 50; then walk a quarter mile south on West Sixth Avenue.

---

4. MORE ENTERTAINMENT

MOVIES

Vancouver has become not only the western capital of Canada's film industry, but also something of a northern outpost for U.S. film producers. At least half a dozen major-network television programs are filmed here, including "The Commish," "Street Justice," and "MacGyver" (now in syndication), and a growing number of major studios are setting movies in and around the city. Some insiders have dubbed Vancouver "Hollywood North."

Wherever movies are shot, of course, they are also screened. Vancouver has a great many cinemas, especially along a one-block strip of Granville Mall between Robson and Smithe Streets. The two biggest cinema groups are:

Famous Players, with 10 theaters (tel. 681-4255). The downtown theaters are the Capital 6, 820 Granville St. (tel. 669-6000), and the Vancouver Centre, 620 W. Georgia St. (tel. 669-4442).

Cineplex Odeon, nine theaters (tel. 687-1515). The downtown theaters are the eight-cinema Granville Theatre complex, 855 Granville St. (tel. 684-4000), and the Royal Centre complex, 1055 W. Georgia St., at Burrard (tel. 669-9791).

Ticket prices are normally about $8 for adults, with student and senior discounts. Sometimes there are reduced prices for matinee performances, costing about $4.50.

There are several second-run double- and triple-feature cinemas in Vancouver, including the **Paradise Theatre,** 919 Granville St.

(tel. 681-1732), with three films for $2.50; the **Hollywood Theatre,** 3123 W. Broadway, Kitsilano (tel. 738-3211), with two films for $3.25; and the **Denman Place Discount Cinema,** on Comox at Denman (tel. 684-2202), with three films for $2.

Foreign, art, and "cult" films tend to be the domain of these theaters:

FESTIVAL CINEMAS Festival Cinemas operates the **Starlight Cinema,** 935 Denman St. (tel. 689-0096); the **Park Theatre,** 3440 Cambie St. (tel. 876-2747); and the **Varsity Theatre,** 4375 W. 10th Ave. (tel. 222-2235). These three offer first-run, foreign-language, independent, art, and issue-oriented films.

Admission for nonmembers is $8 for adults ($4 on Tuesday) and $4 for seniors and children under 14; members pay $5 for adults and $3 for seniors and children under 14. On Sunday, students pay $4.

PACIFIC CINEMATHEQUE This theater, at 1131 Howe St., between Helmcken and Davie Streets (tel. 688-FILM or 688-3456), is for serious movie buffs only, please. Important foreign films are shown as part of a series, together with outstanding but unknown North American features. This is also the headquarters cinema for the Vancouver Film Festival, held every September and October here as well as at the Hollywood, Park, Starlight, Varsity, Ridge, and University of British Columbia theaters.

Admission is $5 for adults, $4 for seniors and students. Double features cost $1 extra. Annual membership is $5. Bus: 4, 10, or 20 to Granville Street.

RIDGE THEATRE The Ridge, at 3131 Arbutus St., at W. 16th Ave., Arbutus Ridge (tel. 738-6311), is where you're likely to catch the first Vancouver release of a Cannes Film Festival award winner, a new uncut print of an old classic, an unpublicized rock-music movie, or a sensational underground sleeper. This theater has installed the city's first induction-loop system for hearing-impaired persons.

Admission to first-run films is $6 for adults and $3 for seniors and children under 13; for double features, it's $4 for adults and $2 for seniors and children under 13. Seniors are admitted free on Monday. Bus: 18.

GAMBLING CASINOS

During the past few years government regulations have changed to permit public gambling in British Columbia—with certain restrictions, to be sure. The use of dice is still banned, ruling out many games of chance. The law also stipulates that no gaming room can have more than 15 tables, that bets are limited to a maximum of $5, and that a percentage of all proceeds must go to charity.

As a result, Vancouver boasts a sprinkling of perfectly legal casinos scattered throughout the city and the suburbs. None of them provides a floor show or other diversion, and the decor is usually modest and devoid of glamour.

Here are a couple:

GREAT CANADIAN CASINO, in the Holiday Inn, 2477 Heather St., at W. Broadway. Tel. 872-5543.
The largest Vancouver-area casino with several branches around the Lower Mainland, this casual establishment features blackjack, roulette, and sic-bo. It's open daily from 6pm to 2am. Bus: 9.

ROYAL DIAMOND CASINO, 1195 Richards St., at Davie St. Tel. 685-2340.

Informal and very friendly, the Royal Diamond is within easy walking distance of most downtown hotels. Its games include blackjack, roulette, and Canadian craps. It's open daily from 6pm to 2am. Bus: 8, 10, or 20; then walk two blocks west at Granville Street.

CHAPTER 10

GETTING TO KNOW VICTORIA

1. ORIENTATION
2. GETTING AROUND
● **FAST FACTS:**
VICTORIA

Victoria, it is said, is "more English than the English." British Columbia's provincial capital and second-largest city (population about 300,000) continues to have a colonial ambience that is largely absent from Vancouver, its cosmopolitan cousin across the Strait of Georgia.

Here, the venerable Parliament Buildings and the Empress Hotel both face the magnificent natural harbor. Flower baskets line the streets, and colorful gardens make the spring and summer seasons especially joyful. The climate is milder—and drier—than Vancouver's. Perhaps best of all, the city is amazingly easy to get around, especially for those who enjoy walking.

1. ORIENTATION

ARRIVING

There are three principal ways to reach Victoria—by air, by sea, or by land. Most visitors prefer the marine connection.

BY PLANE

THE AIRPORT The **Victoria International Airport** is about 16 miles (26km) north of downtown, adjacent to Sidney near the northern tip of the Saanich Peninsula. For airport information, call 363-6600.

Three major **airlines**—Air Canada, Canadian, and Horizon—provide Victoria with direct connections to Seattle, Vancouver, Calgary, Edmonton, Saskatoon, Winnipeg, and Toronto.

Numerous provincial commuter airlines also serve the city, including several with floatplanes that land in Victoria's Inner Harbour many times daily. Among them are Air B.C. (tel. 604/382-9242) and Harbour Air (tel. 604/688-1277), both from Vancouver, and Lake Union Air (tel. toll free 800/826-1890), from Seattle.

Helijet Airways (tel. 604/382-6222 in Victoria, 604/273-1414 in Vancouver) has helicopter service between downtown Vancouver and Victoria up to 20 times daily on weekdays, four times daily on weekends. The fare is $115 one-way, $230 round-trip.

The Victoria International Airport Customs office (tel. 604/363-6644) is open daily from 8am to midnight. Revenue Canada Customs & Excise (tel. 604/363-3531) is open 24 hours daily. For details on Customs regulations, see "Information, Entry Requirements, and Money" in Chapter 2.

GETTING INTO TOWN   From the airport, the four-lane Patricia Bay Hwy. (Route 17) speeds straight south into downtown Victoria. The **Airporter Shuttle Bus** (tel. 383-7311) covers the distance in about 30 minutes; buses leave every half hour from 5:25am to 11:55pm. The one-way fare is $12. A limited number of hotel courtesy buses also serve the airport.

The average **taxi** fare from Victoria International to downtown is about $40.

Several **car-rental firms** have desks at the airport with vehicles ready for drivers. They include Avis (tel. 604/656-6033), Budget (tel. 604/656-3731), Hertz (tel. 604/656-2312), and Tilden (tel. 604/656-2541). It's best to make reservations well ahead of time, especially during busy periods.

BY TRAIN

You could only arrive by train if you've taken a ferry from the British Columbia mainland to Nanaimo or Courtenay. Then you could board the **Esquimalt & Nanaimo Railway,** a service of VIA Rail Canada. Qualicum Beach is a favorite spot for many rail-traveling tourists on the island.

The train leaves Courtenay, about 130 miles (210km) northwest of Victoria, at 1:15pm daily, arriving in Nanaimo about two hours later, and completing the final half of the journey at 5:45pm. Trains leave Victoria daily at 8:15am, arriving in Nanaimo at 10:40am and in Courtenay at 12:50pm. One-way fare from Victoria to Nanaimo is $17.10 for adults, $15 for seniors and students, $8.55 for children 3–11; to Courtenay, one-way fare is $31.05 for adults, $27.80 for seniors and students, $16.05 for children. (Prices include the goods and services tax.)

Victoria's **E&N Station** is at 450 Pandora Ave., at the Johnson Street Bridge (tel. 604/383-4324, or toll free 800/561-8630 in Canada).

BY BUS

It's hard to imagine a bus terminal more centrally located than Victoria's. **Victoria Depot** (tel. 604/385-4411) is at 710 Douglas St., at the corner of Belleville Street, directly behind the Empress Hotel (between the new Victoria Conference Centre and the Royal British Columbia Museum).

Pacific Coach Lines (tel. 604/385-4411) operates between here and Vancouver—a 3½-hour trip, including the ferry portion (see below). Daily service is hourly from 6am to 9pm from June to mid-October; every two hours from 6am to 8pm from mid-October to March; times vary daily in April, May, and June, depending on the B.C. Ferries schedule.

Island Coach Lines (tel. 604/385-4411), with Seattle–Victoria–Vancouver Island runs, is also based here. **Gray Line** (tel. 604/385-5248) has daily service to and from Seattle, originating and terminating at the Victoria Depot.

BY CAR & FERRY

Because Victoria is on an island, those who drive to the city must first put their vehicle aboard a ferry. Three separate ferries serve the city: **B.C. Ferries** (tel. 604/386-3431 or 656-0757) has four routes across the Strait of Georgia from the British Columbia mainland. The most direct for Vancouver–Victoria travelers is the 24-mile Tsawwassen–Swartz Bay route. Though schedules change seasonally, 95-minute sailings through the Gulf Islands operate more or less continually between 7am and 9pm daily. Tsawwassen is a 30- to 40-minute drive south of Vancouver; Swartz Bay is about the same distance north of Victoria, a straight drive down the Patricia Bay Hwy.

Also appealing to many Vancouver–Victoria travelers is the Horseshoe Bay–Nanaimo route—a 30-mile, 95-minute run operating on a schedule similar to the Tsawwassen ferry's. Its mainland terminal is adjacent to West Vancouver; Nanaimo is 68 miles (110km) north of Victoria on Trans-Canada Hwy. 1.

Ferries also cross from Tsawwassen to Nanaimo. Known as the "Mid-Island Express," this two-hour crossing operates six times daily, from 5:30am to 11pm.

A fourth ferry route connects the Powell River, some 100 miles north of Vancouver, with Comox on Vancouver Island. Infrequently taken by tourists, it operates four times daily.

The fare on all three routes is the same: $5.50 per driver or adult passenger, $2.50 for children 5–11, $20 for a car, and from $29.50 for an RV.

Washington State Ferries (tel. 604/381-1551, or toll free 800/843-3779 in Washington) operate twice daily in summer, once daily September through May, between Anacortes, a 90-minute drive north of Seattle, and Sidney, a 30-minute drive north of Victoria. The trip (via Friday Harbor in Washington's San Juan Islands) takes about three hours; the fare (in U.S. dollars) is $31.25 for car and driver, $6.05 per passenger, in summer; $5 less for vehicles off-season. From Sidney—where boats arrive between 11:30am and noon every day year-round, and about 5:30pm as well in summer—the Patricia Bay Hwy. affords direct access to Victoria.

Black Ball Transport (tel. 604/386-2202) crosses the Juan de Fuca Strait between Victoria and Port Angeles on Washington's Olympic Peninsula. The ferry MV *Coho* runs four times daily from mid-May through September; twice a day, mid-March to mid-May and in October and November; and twice daily, December to mid-March. Fares (in U.S. dollars) are $24 for a car or RV and driver, $6 per adult passenger, $3 per child 5–11. The often-rough 22-mile (36km) trip takes about 1 hour 35 minutes. A bonus is that the boat docks right in Victoria's Inner Harbour, within 350 yards (300m) of the Empress Hotel.

Canada accepts all valid U.S. driver's licenses. Proof of insurance is required in the event of an accident (see "Health and Insurance" in Chapter 2). Make sure you have your vehicle registration with you. Wearing seat belts is mandatory in British Columbia.

BY SHIP

The *Victoria Express* (tel. 206/452-8088 or 604/361-9144) crosses the Juan de Fuca Strait from Port Angeles to Victoria in one hour. There are four trips daily in each direction, June 15 to September 8; and two trips daily, May 23 to June 14 and September 9 to October 31.

You can travel from the Seattle waterfront to Victoria's Inner Harbour aboard the *Victoria Clipper,* a 300-passenger, 130-foot water-jet-propelled catamaran. Attendants provide first-class food, beverages, and duty-free shopping services for travelers who don't want to leave their seats.

The trip to the Wharf Street terminal—near the Visitor's Information Centre—takes precisely 2½ hours. From early October to mid-May, the *Clipper* leaves Seattle at 8am and returns from British Columbia's capital city at 9:30pm. In the summer season, there are additional sailings, at 8:40am, 9:30am, and 3pm with additional departures from Victoria at 11:15am, 2:30pm, and 5:30pm. Summer fares for adults (in U.S. dollars) are $52 one-way, $85 round-trip; seniors pay $46 one-way, $75 round-trip; children under 12 are half price when accompanied by an adult. There are discounts for advance purchase.

For information and reservations, contact **Clipper Navigation** at 1000A Wharf St., Victoria, BC V8W 1T4 (tel. 604/382-8100), or at 2701 Alaskan Way, Pier 69, Seattle, WA 98121 (tel. 206/448-5000, or toll free 800/888-2535).

Featuring high-speed catamarans built by the same Norwegian company that crafted Clipper Navigation's vessels, **Royal Sealink Express** (tel. 604/687-6925 in Vancouver, 604/382-5465 in Victoria) operates a service connecting downtown Vancouver with downtown Victoria. In addition to impressive views of the cities and the islands between, Royal Sealink's facilities include a children's play area, on-board movies, telephones and fax machines, group seating, and a snack galley. Vessels are handicapped-accessible; bicycle racks are planned. The voyage takes 2½ hours.

The *Royal Sealink* departs from Vancouver daily, from the north foot of Granville Street, at 7am, 10am, 2:30pm, and 5:30pm. Victoria departures are from Wharf Street, in front of the Empress Hotel, at the same times. Summer one-way fares are $37 for adults, $31 for seniors, $19 for children 3–12, free for infants.

Future plans may include integrated scheduling and reservations with Seattle's Clipper Navigation and Amtrak rail service between Seattle and Vancouver. Service between Vancouver and Nanaimo (Vancouver Island) is also planned.

Gray Line Cruises (tel. 206/738-8099, or toll free 800/443-4552) operates the *Victoria Star* from Bellingham, Wash., daily from June 1 to October 15. The ship departs Bellingham at 9:30am and arrives in Victoria at 2pm (with a stop in Friday Harbor, San Juan Island).

For **Customs** information, see "Information, Entry Requirements, and Money" in Chapter 2. For specific questions, consult the **Victoria Harbourmaster** (tel. 604/363-3578 anytime) or the **Inner Harbour Customs Dock** (tel. 604/363-3330 from 8am to 4:30pm, 604/363-3339 after 4:30pm). **Revenue Canada Customs & Excise** (tel. 604/363-3531) is open 24 hours daily.

During the summer months, many cruise-ship companies also include Victoria on their itineraries for brief shore leaves.

TOURIST INFORMATION

The **Tourism Victoria Information Centre,** 812 Wharf St. (tel. 604/382-2127), is your single best source of tourist information. Located beneath the art deco tower on the Inner Harbour, across the causeway from the Empress Hotel, it's the province's largest information center. The staff offer assistance in planning sightseeing, transportation and tours, fishing and whale-watching charters, entertainment, and (perhaps most of all) accommodations. Visitors having trouble finding a place to stay can call the center's reservation hotline (tel. 604/382-1131, or toll free 800/663-3883 from throughout North America). The Information Centre is open daily: September to March, from 9am to 5pm; in May and June, from 9am to 8pm; and in July and August, from 9am to 9pm.

Tourism Victoria's executive offices are at 1175 Douglas St., Suite 710, Victoria, BC V8W 2E1 (tel. 604/382-2160).

Visitors planning trips outside of the immediate Victoria area—for example, elsewhere on Vancouver Island or to the Gulf Islands—can receive assistance from the **Tourism Association of Vancouver Island,** Bastion Square, Victoria, BC V8W 1J1 (tel. 604/382-3551; fax 604/382-3523).

CITY LAYOUT

Victoria sits on the extreme southeastern tip of Vancouver Island, the largest island on the Pacific coast of North America. Its spectacular doorstep is the Juan de Fuca Strait, a 15-mile-wide (24km) sleeve of the Pacific Ocean that separates the island from Washington's snow-capped Olympic Peninsula. The city lies much closer to the United States than it does to mainland Canada. But downtown Victoria doesn't face the open water of the strait. Instead, it nestles around its cozy Inner Harbour, which defines the central city's western edge.

Get your bearings from the **Empress Hotel,** the city's social focal point since the 1920s. This palatial grande dame is of such regality that you may get the impression that the town was built around her as an afterthought. Standing with your back to the hotel, you're looking across little James Bay at the **Inner Harbour,** a wonderful bustle of yachts, ferries, fishing boats, launches, and seaplanes.

On your left rises the green-domed stone majesty of the Parliament Buildings, housing the legislative apparatus of British Columbia. Just east of it, and south of the Empress, is the outstanding Royal British Columbia Museum. On your right, Government Street slices through Victoria's main shopping and entertainment area. This is **downtown** and **Olde Town,** a pair of tightly entwined districts—a mix of arcades, small squares, picturesque alleys, and wide commercial streets.

Farther to the north and east stretches what is known as **Greater Victoria,** more like a patchwork of townships and villages held together by parks and gardens. East lies **Oak Bay,** northeast the University of Victoria, and due north on the **Saanich Peninsula,** the enchanting Butchart Gardens, the airport, the town of **Sidney,** and the ferry terminal at **Swartz Bay.** West of downtown, across the Inner Harbour, is the industrial suburb of **Esquimalt,** and another 20 miles (32km) west, the seaside community of **Sooke.**

MAIN ARTERIES & STREETS **Government Street** is paralleled to its east by two major north-south thoroughfares—**Douglas Street** and **Blanshard Street.** Douglas, in fact, is seven miles long, extending from the Juan de Fuca Strait on the south shore of Victoria to the community of Saanich, four miles north of downtown. There, it becomes the Patricia Bay Hwy., which extends all the way to Swartz Bay.

To the west of Government Street, **Wharf Street** winds along the Inner Harbour shore as far as Market Square, a quaint shopping complex. A major city landmark between Government and Wharf Streets is Bastion Square, which is believed to occupy the site of Victoria's pioneer fort. It's located behind the Central Post Office on View Street.

Chinatown, with its center at **Fisgard Street** at Government, about eight blocks north of the Empress, marks the northern edge of Olde Town. It's actually so small that many locals call it "China Block." City government functions are located just east, on **Pandora Avenue.** Pandora (one-way west) and **Fort Street** (one-way east) are the main thoroughfares to the affluent suburb of Oak Bay. The Johnson Street Bridge, at the west end of Pandora, crosses the Inner Harbour to Esquimalt.

South of the Empress, Government and Douglas Streets are crossed by **Belleville Street,** a short but important thoroughfare that fronts James Bay. Along with adjacent Quebec Street, which parallels it a block to the south, it is the site of many Victoria hotels.

FINDING AN ADDRESS Victoria's streets are numbered from the city's southwest corner, near the Ogden Point Docks; the numbers increase as you go north and west. The numbers on Douglas Street, for example, begin with zero at Dallas Road (which weaves along the city's south coastline) and reach 3200 at Tolmie Street—the city's northern limit. Fort Street starts with its 500 block at Wharf Street, and reaches the 1900 block when it crosses the city line into Oak Bay. If you're following Government Street north from James Bay to Chinatown, you'll go from the 700 block to the 1700 block.

STREET MAPS Free, detailed street maps are available at the Tourism Victoria Information Centre. They're excellent, showing all streets in Victoria and arterials leading out of town. Stewart Maps & Guides publishes the best central-city map I've seen; Davenport's Greater Victoria map is excellent for getting around the Saanich Peninsula. Check for either at local bookstores.

2. GETTING AROUND

BY PUBLIC TRANSPORTATION

The buses of the **Victoria Regional Transit System (B.C. Transit)** operate about 18 hours each weekday (6am to midnight), with only slightly shorter hours on weekends. The system has 142 diesel-powered buses that carry 16 million people a year on 36 routes from Swartz Bay in the north to Sooke in the west. Information is available from a 24-hour automated "Busline" (tel. 382-6161).

Unless you're taking the bus well out of the city proper, you'll pay a **one-zone fare** of $1.25 for adults, 85¢ for seniors, students, and children. Two-zone fares are $1.75 and $1.25, respectively. Unlimited one-day **bus passes** are $4 for adults, $3 for seniors, students, and children, and can be obtained (along with schedules) from Tourism Victoria and dozens of merchants throughout the area.

Routes popular with tourists include no. 2 (Oak Bay), no. 5 (downtown, James Bay, Beacon Hill Park), no. 14 (Victoria Art Gallery, Craigdarroch Castle, University of Victoria), no. 24 (Anne

Hathaway's Cottage), no. 30 (James Bay night route from downtown), no. 61 (Sooke), no. 70 (Sidney, Swartz Bay), and no. 75 (Butchart Gardens).

Disabled persons can book door-to-door rides by calling 727-7811.

BY TAXI

Victoria has 33 separate cab companies, so you should never have long to wait. Outside of downtown, though, a phone call is a surer thing than a streetcorner wave. Try **Blue Bird Cabs** (tel. 382-4235) or **Crown Taxi** (tel. 381-2242).

Fares are reasonable: Within downtown, you can expect to travel for under $5, except during rush-hour traffic and during the wee hours, when you'll pay drivers double. Typical fare to the airport, 16 miles (26km) distant, is about $40.

Something a bit more upscale? Give a call to **Classic Limousine** (tel. 386-5466), which offers hourly rates.

BY CAR

Having a car in Vancouver can be a great convenience, despite that city's heavy rush-hour traffic. A car in Victoria, on the other hand, often seems superfluous. So much of the B.C. capital can be enjoyed on foot, after all!

CAR RENTALS   Some folks like to rent a car for one day to go to Butchart Gardens and other up-island attractions. If you're among them, consider **Budget Exotic Cars,** 2-635 Humboldt St. (tel. 604/383-1444), for an upscale Mazda Miata, Jaguar, or BMW. Rentals run $75–$250 per day.

Auto-rental firms represented in downtown Victoria include **Avis,** 843 Douglas St. (tel. 386-8468), **Budget,** 757 Douglas St. (tel. 386-3712), **Hertz,** 901 Douglas St. (tel. 388-4411), **Metro Lexus Toyota,** 625 Frances Ave. (tel. 386-3516), **Tilden,** 767 Douglas St. (tel. 386-1213), and **Victoria Nissan,** 3361 Oak St. (tel. 382-7227).

Joy Vacations, 2343 Hamiota St. (tel. 598-6001), has recreational vehicles, ideal for lengthy up-island excursions.

MOTORCYCLES & MOPEDS   Seasonal motorcycle and moped rentals are available at **Harbour Scooters,** 843 Douglas St. (tel. 385-2133), and **Budget Cycle-Time,** 727 Courtney St. (tel. 388-7874).

PARKING   All major downtown hotels have **parking lots** for guests, with varying daily charges. There's parking on Gordon Street at Broughton, View Street between Douglas and Blanshard, Johnson Street just west of Blanshard, Yates Street just north of Bastion Square, and at The Bay, Fisgard Street at Blanshard.

Metered **street parking** is in high demand downtown, and is strictly enforced (for this reason, you should carry a pocketful of Canadian coins). Unmetered parking on side streets may be a long trek from where you're headed. Read signs carefully: If you park in a designated rush-hour lane, you can expect to be towed.

DRIVING RULES   Driving rules are quite similar to those in the United States. Remember, though: You'll have to deal with the metric system. Speeds and distances are in kilometers and gas is sold by the liter. You're permitted to turn right on a red light after you've come to a full stop. Wearing seat belts is mandatory; children under 5 must be in car seats; helmets are compulsory for motorcyclists.

AUTO CLUBS   Members of the American Automobile Association (AAA) can get information and assistance from the **British Columbia Automobile Association,** 1075 Pandora Ave. (tel. 389-6700). They can provide emergency road service to AAA members (tel. toll free 800/663-2222).

BY BICYCLE

With Victoria's relatively flat terrain, two wheels can get you around the city very easily. Even the busiest city streets can be safely negotiated by cautious riders.

For seasonal rentals, check with **Budget Cycle-Time,** 727 Courtney St. (tel. 388-7874), or **Harbour Scooters,** 843 Douglas St. (tel. 384-2133).

ON FOOT

As previously stated, Victoria is a marvelous walking city. Stroll where you will; if you need suggestions, see Chapter 14, "Strolling Around Victoria." An early-morning or dusk-hour stroll around the Inner Harbour shoreline is particularly recommended.

Wheelchairs and strollers can be rented from Budget Rent-a-Car, 727 Courtney St. (tel. 388-7874).

FAST   *VICTORIA*

For details on mail, restrooms, taxes, telephones, time, and tipping—and for additional information on many of the following topics—see "Fast Facts: Vancouver" in Chapter 3.

Airport   See "Orientation," above.

Area Code   Victoria's telephone area code is 604.

Babysitters   Major hotels can usually arrange babysitting service on short notice, though a day's advance notice is preferred.

Banks   Most banks are open Monday through Thursday from 10am to 3pm and on Friday from 10am to 6pm, although some are open later throughout the week.

Business Hours   Typical business hours are 8am to 5pm Monday through Friday, with a lunch break from noon to 1pm. Shop hours vary, but many stores are open Monday through Thursday and on Saturday from 9:30am to 5:30pm and on Friday from 9:30am to 9pm. Some may be open on Sunday in summer.

Business Services   Most major hotels offer secretarial, fax, and other services for a fee. Otherwise, B&B Secretarial Plus, 1248 Fort St. (tel. 381-2155), is well equipped.

Climate   Victoria, protected from southerly chinook breezes by Washington's Olympic Range, gets far less rainfall than Vancouver—just 26 inches annually, including less than 3 inches between May and August. More than a third of the rain falls in December and January. Average temperatures range from a balmy 72°F (22°C) in July to a chilly 43°F (6°C) in January. See "When to Go" in Chapter 2 for details.

Currency   See "Information, Entry Requirements, and Money" in Chapter 2 and "Currency" in "Fast Facts: Vancouver" in Chapter 3.

Currency Exchange   The Victoria Conference Centre Currency Exchange, 724 Douglas St. (tel. 384-6631), specializes in exchanging money.

Dentists   Major hotels may have a dentist on call. A dental-health center is the Cresta Dental Centre, 3170 Tillicum Rd., at Burnside Street (tel. 384-7711). Located a couple miles from downtown, it's associated with the Abacus Dental Centre at 14-1153 Esquimalt Rd. (tel. 386-3044).

Doctors   Hotels typically have a doctor on call. A doctor is on call 24 hours for consultation at 595-9200, and will make referrals where appropriate.

Drugstores   McGill & Orme, 649 Fort St. (tel. 384-1195), is open Monday through Friday from 8:30am to 8pm, on Saturday from 9am to 6pm, and on Sunday from 11am to 6pm; it has several dispensaries around the city, and has an emergency phone forwarding service. Shopper's Drug Mart, 1222 Douglas St. (tel. 384-0544), is open Monday through Wednesday from 7am to 7pm, on Thursday and Friday from 7am to 8pm, on Saturday from 9am to 6pm, and on Sunday from 10am to 6pm.

Electricity   As in the U.S., it's 110 volts, alternating current.

Emergencies   Dial **911** for fire, police, ambulance, and poison control.

Eyeglasses   Try London Drugs, 911 Yates St. (tel. 381-1113) and 1320 Douglas St. (tel. 386-7578); or Tru-Valu Optical, 1708 Douglas St. (tel. 386-6622). If you wear lenses, go to Nordic Contact Lenses, 1105 Pandora Ave. (tel. 389-1325).

Hairdressers   Many major hotels have their own salons, and there are others along stylish streets and in shopping arcades. Tourism Victoria recommends the Queen Victoria Inn, 655 Douglas St. (tel. 388-5912); Terry's Beauty Salon, 1207 Douglas St. (tel. 383-2334); and Margo Beauty Studio, 1644 Hillside Ave. (tel. 595-2424).

Holidays   See "When to Go" in Chapter 2.

Hospitals   The Fairfield Health Centre, 841 Fairfield Rd. (tel. 389-6300), is just three blocks east of the Empress Hotel. The Royal Jubilee Hospital, 1900 Fort St. (tel. 595-9200; emergency 595-9212), is also nearby, not far from Oak Bay. Victoria General Hospital, 35 Helmcken Rd. (tel. 727-4212; emergency 727-4181), is in the western suburb of View Royal. There's also Saanich Peninsula General Hospital, 2166 Mount Newton Cross Rd. (tel. 652-3911), about 13 miles (20km) north of the city, and the Queen Alexandra Hospital for Children, Finnerty Cove off Arbutus Road (tel. 477-1826).

Information   See "Orientation," above.

Language   English and French are the official languages of Canada. In British Columbia, English is the predominant language.

Laundry/Dry Cleaning   You can either leave your clothes with your hotel valet service and pay the price, or drop them off at Mr. One Hour Dry Cleaners, 1019 Cook St. (tel. 388-5058). There are also numerous self-service laundries around the city.

Liquor Laws   See "Fast Facts: Vancouver" in Chapter 3.

Lost Property   Consult the Victoria Police (tel. 384-4111). If you think it may have disappeared on public transportation, call B.C. Transit's lost-and-found line (tel. 382-6161).

Maps   You can get good city and regional maps from information centers, bookshops, automobile clubs, service stations, and even hotel desks.

Metric Measurements Canada uses the metric system of measurement. For a conversion chart, see the Appendix.

Newspapers The *Times-Colonist* is the city's daily newspaper. A broadsheet, it's published every morning, seven days a week, and is sold on newsstands and in many hotel lobbies. *Monday Magazine,* a weekly entertainment paper, comes out (wouldn't you know it?) on Thursday.

Photographic Needs London Drugs, 911 Yates St. (tel. 381-1113) and 1320 Douglas St. (tel. 386-7578), has an excellent camera department. For more specific requirements, including repairs, try City Photo Centre, 1227 Government St. (tel. 385-5633).

Police Dial 911 in emergency; property crime can be reported at 383-1313 in Victoria, 592-2424 in Oak Bay, 385-3311 in Saanich.

Post Office The main Victoria Post Office, 1230 Government St. (tel. 363-3142), occupies most of the block at the southwest corner of Government and Yates Streets. It's open Monday through Friday from 8am to 4pm. Merchants with the Canada Post symbol in their windows offer basic services Monday through Saturday. Remember to use Canadian postage stamps (48¢ for postcards or letters to the States), not the U.S. variety!

Radio and Television AM radio stations include 900 CJVI (classic rock), 1070 CFAX (easy listening), and 1200 CKDA (soft rock). FM stations include 98.5 CFMS (easy listening), 100.3 CKKU (album rock), and 102 CFUV (jazz, classical, alternative music).

CHEK (Channel 6), a Canadian network affiliate, is Vancouver Island's only broadcast television station; Rogers Cable (Channel 11) does community programming. Victoria viewers also receive all Vancouver and Seattle television broadcasts, including those of the Public Broadcasting System of the United States.

Religious Services The variety should suit nearly everyone's needs. Among places of worship within walking distance of most downtown hotels are Christ Church Cathedral (Anglican), 912 Vancouver St., at Quadra and Courtney (tel. 383-2714); Central Baptist Church, 833 Pandora Ave. (tel. 385-7786); Cathedral of St. Andrew (Roman Catholic), 740 View St. (tel. 388-5571); Grace Lutheran Church, 1273 Fort St. (tel. 383-5256); Glad Tidings Pentecostal Church, 1800 Quadra St. (tel. 384-7633); St. Andrew's Presbyterian Church, 680 Courtney St. (tel. 384-5734); and James Bay United Church, 511 Michigan St. (tel. 384-5821). Nearby are Charismatic, Eastern Orthodox, Evangelical, Methodist, Mormon, Nazarene, Seventh-Day Adventist, Unitarian, Unity, and other Christian denominations.

Major non-Christian places of worship near downtown include Congregation Emanu-El, 1461 Blanshard St. (tel. 382-0615); the Buddhist Dharma Centre of Victoria, 1149 Leonard St. (tel. 385-4828); and the Punjabi Akali Sikh Temple, 2721 Graham St. (tel. 386-1081).

Safety Whenever you're traveling in an unfamiliar city or country, stay alert. Be aware of your immediate surroundings. Wear a moneybelt and don't sling your camera or purse over your shoulder—wear the strap diagonally across your body. This will minimize the possibility of your becoming a victim of crime. Every society has its criminals. It's your responsibility to be aware and alert even in the most heavily touristed areas.

Shoe Repairs   Try Stevenson's Shoe Clinic, 714 Fort St. (tel. 383-8615), or a major department store.

Taxis   See "Getting Around," above.

Transit Information   See "Getting Around," above.

Useful Telephone Numbers   Royal Canadian Mounted Police (tel. 380-6161), Emotional Crisis Centre (tel. 386-6323), Sexual Assault Centre (tel. 383-3232), Poison Control Centre (tel. 595-9211), Help Line for Children (dial 0, zero, and ask for Zenith 1234), SPCA animal emergency (tel. 385-6521), Better Business Bureau (tel. 386-6348), Lawyer Referral Service (tel. 382-1415), B.C. road conditions (tel. 380-4997).

Water   You can drink the tap water everywhere.

Weather   See "Climate," above, and "When to Go" in Chapter 2. For current forecasts, call 656-3978; for a marine forecast, dial 656-7515; for an aviation forecast, call 363-6630.

CHAPTER 11

VICTORIA ACCOMMODATIONS

1. THE INNER HARBOUR

2. DOWNTOWN/OLDE TOWN

3. OUTSIDE THE CENTRAL AREA

Victoria has a wide choice of fine accommodations in all price ranges. They predominate in two areas: Most deluxe hotels nestle around the Inner Harbour at James Bay, while a high concentration of moderately priced motels flank Gorge Road, northwest of downtown. Accommodation standards are high, and visitors usually appreciate the little touches of England that are found in many of Victoria's hotels.

In this listing, I have organized accommodations first by geographic area and then by price.

PRICE CATEGORIES In general I have used four price categories, according to summer rates in standard rooms for two persons: "Very Expensive" ($175 and up a night), "Expensive" ($125–$175), "Moderate" ($85–$125), and "Budget" (under $85). *Prices are quoted in Canadian dollars* and do not include the 10% provincial sales tax; you will also be charged the 7% goods and services tax.

The listed rates are the officially quoted, or "rack rates," and do not take into account any individual or group discounts that may be available.

RESERVATIONS Reservations are always important, but are absolutely essential from June to September and during other holiday periods. If you arrive without a reservation and have trouble finding a room, call **Tourism Victoria** (tel. 604/382-1131, or toll free 800/663-3883). They will try to help, but you may have to settle for something several miles from downtown—perhaps out on the Saanich Peninsula.

BED-AND-BREAKFASTS If you find it difficult to get a hotel room, or if you prefer to stay in a bed-and-breakfast, the following agencies try to match visitors and hosts with similar interests:

All Season Bed & Breakfast Agency, Box 5511, Station B, Victoria, BC V8R 6S4 (tel. 604/655-7173).

Canada-West Accommodations Bed & Breakfast Registry, P.O. Box 86607, North Vancouver, BC V7L 4L2 (tel. 604/388-4620, or toll free 800/873-7976).

Garden City Bed & Breakfast Reservation Service, 660 Jones Terrace, Victoria, BC V8Z 2L7 (tel. 604/479-9999 or 479-1986).

All are members of the **British Columbia Bed & Breakfast Association,** 810 W. Broadway (P.O. Box 593), Vancouver, BC V5Z 4E2, an umbrella agency formed at the request of Tourism British Columbia to promote B&Bs and ensure quality control. Each member home is inspected for cleanliness, comfort, courtesy, and service to guarantee high standards. Numerous other B&Bs, unaffiliated with agencies, also are members of the provincial association.

Although B&B rates vary widely, they may begin as low as $30 single, $40 double, and may range up to $100 or more for special suites. Specify your preferred price range when making reservations. Fireplaces, Jacuzzi baths, and heated swimming pools are sometimes available in the higher price categories. Credit cards are usually accepted.

1. THE INNER HARBOUR

VERY EXPENSIVE

COAST VICTORIA HARBOURSIDE HOTEL, 146 Kingston St., Victoria, BC V8V 1V4. Tel. 604/360-1211, or toll free 800/663-1144. Fax 604/360-1418. 132 rms, 6 suites. A/C MINIBAR TV TEL **Bus:** 30 from Superior and Montreal.

$ Rates: May–Sept, $154–$174 single; $164–$184 double; Oct–Apr, $114 single or double; year round $300 suite. Children under 18 stay free in parents' room. AE, DC, ER, MC, V. **Parking:** Free, underground.

Located on Victoria's Inner Harbour south of Laurel Point, this new hotel offers easy access to whale-watching, fishing charters, and dinner cruises from a private marina. There are fine views from most rooms and suites. Some of the penthouse suites on two executive floors have extra-large balconies. Rooms are elegantly appointed with contemporary furnishings.

Dining/Entertainment: The intimate Blue Crab Bar & Grill offers West Coast cuisine in a waterfront setting. The menu features freshly caught Pacific salmon and local shellfish, and there's live entertainment on Thursday, Friday, and Saturday nights.

Services: 24-hour room service, complimentary downtown shuttle, laundry and dry cleaning service.

Facilities: Indoor/outdoor pool, health club, whirlpool, private marina, conference facilities for up to 150, no-smoking rooms and facilities for the handicapped.

THE EMPRESS, 721 Government St., Victoria, BC V8W 1W5. Tel. 604/384-8111, or toll free 800/828-7447 in the U.S., 800/268-9420 in Ontario and Québec, 800/268-9411 in other provinces. Fax 604/381-4334. 452 rms, 29 suites. MINIBAR TV TEL **Bus:** 5.

$ Rates: Early May to mid-Oct, $155–$210 single; $180–$235 double. Mid-Oct to early May, $104–$145 single; $129–$170 double. Year-round, from $325 suite. AE, CB, DC, DISC, ER, MC, V. **Parking:** $9 underground (24 hours), $15 valet.

In many regards, the Empress *is* Victoria. The crowning achievement of early 20th-century architect Francis Rattenbury, the stately, ivy-banked, graystone château on the Inner Harbour opened for business in 1908. Ever since, it has created the first impression of Victoria for anyone arriving by sea. Celebrities from Rudyard Kipling and the King of Siam to John Wayne and Bob Hope have stayed here, and Queen Elizabeth II has been a frequent visitor. In 1988–89, the hotel—a Canadian

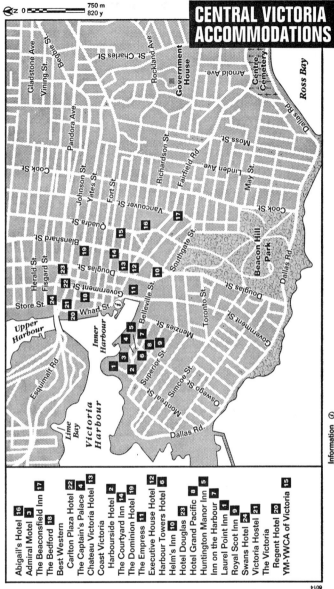

750 m
820 y

Ross Bay

Gladstone Ave.
Vining St.
Biggs St.
St. Charles St.
Rockland Ave.
Government House
Arnold Ave.
Centre Cemetery
Dallas Rd.

Pandora Ave.
Cook St.
Richardson St.
Fairfield Rd.
Moss St.
Linden Ave.
May St.
Cook St.

Johnson St.
Yates St.
Fort St.
Vancouver St.
Southgate St.
Beacon Hill Park
Dallas Rd.

Quadra St.
Blanshard St.
Herald St.
Fisgard St.
Douglas St.
Government St.
Belleville St.
Menzies St.
Toronto St.
Douglas St.
Government St.

Store St.
Wharf St.

Upper Harbour
Inner Harbour
Victoria Harbour
Lime Bay
Esquimalt Rd.

Superior St.
Simcoe St.
Oswego St.
Montreal St.
Dallas Rd.

Information ⓘ

Abigail's Hotel **16**
Admiral Motel **3**
The Beaconsfield Inn **17**
The Bedford **18**
Best Western
Carlton Plaza Hotel **22**
The Captain's Palace **4**
Chateau Victoria Hotel **13**
Coast Victoria
Harbourside Hotel **2**
The Courtyard Inn **14**
The Dominion Hotel **19**
The Empress **11**
Executive House Hotel **12**
Harbour Towers Hotel **6**
Helm's Inn **10**
Hotel Douglas **23**
Hotel Grand Pacific **8**
Huntington Manor Inn **5**
Inn on the Harbour **7**
Laurel Point Inn **1**
Royal Scot Inn **9**
Swans Hotel **24**
Victoria Hostel **21**
The Victoria
Regent Hotel **20**
YM-YWCA of Victoria **15**

Pacific property—closed for five months while undergoing a $45-million renovation. Its new lobby features a three-story-high ceiling supported by imposing pillars, a green Oriental carpet on a black marble floor, and a jade railing along the stairway to the mezzanine deck.

It's impossible to describe a typical guestroom—there are 96 different configurations. All have an appropriately Victorian appearance, with richly restored antique furnishings and special features such as balloon curtains. The more deluxe rooms have harbor views;

the more moderately priced face the new Victoria Conference Centre. In the renovation, eight cozy "Romantic Attic" honeymoon view suites were added; accessible only by a private stairway, they have love seats and four-poster canopy beds. The renovation also added rooms for the hearing-impaired, with a strobe-light alarm system.

Dining/Entertainment: There's sophisticated dining in the classically elegant Empress Dining Room, open daily for dinner. It offers finely crafted woodwork, custom-designed china table settings, and evening harp music. The spectacular Crystal Room, with its mirrored ceiling, serves brunch year-round and is open for other meals in the summer. More casual meals are served downstairs all day in the Garden Café, a contemporary bistro. The Bengal Lounge, with a curry lunch buffet Monday through Saturday, retains the ambience of British India. The hand-painted silk wall hanging and the canopied bar cooled by Indian punkah fans add to the atmosphere, along with live piano music in the summer. But the Empress is perhaps most famous for its afternoon teas: Seatings are four times daily, mid-September to mid-May, in the Tea Lobby, and eight times daily, mid-May to mid-September, in the art deco Palm Court, a '20s masterpiece with a Tiffany glass dome. Tea (with crumpets and scones, of course) runs $16.95 per person, and there's a dress code. Call for reservations.

Services: 24-hour room service (summer only), concierge, valet cleaning, secretarial service, massage service. Business-class guests get upgraded amenities, including continental breakfast.

Facilities: Indoor swimming pool, health club (with weight/exercise room, sauna, and whirlpool), shopping arcade (including Native art gallery, men's and women's clothing stores, chocolate and china shops); the adjoining Victoria Conference Centre has meeting/banquet space for up to 1,500 people.

HARBOUR TOWERS HOTEL, 345 Quebec St. (at Oswego St.), Victoria, BC V8V 1W4. Tel. 604/385-2405, or toll free 800/663-5896. Fax 604/385-4453. 99 rms, 86 suites. A/C TV TEL **Bus:** 30 to Superior and Oswego.

$ Rates: May–Sept, $160 single; $180 double; $220 one-bedroom suite; $275–$290 larger suite. Oct–Apr, $136 single; $156 double; $196 one-bedroom suite; $236–$500 larger suite. AE, CB, DC, ER, MC, V. **Parking:** Free, underground.

A look of simple elegance greets arrivals at the 12-story Harbour Towers, the headquarters hotel for the annual Victoria Jazz Festival. Light jazz music wafts year-round beneath the glass chandeliers of the marble-floored lobby. The natural lighting and soft colors give it a sort of Mediterranean appearance.

All rooms have floor-to-ceiling sliding windows, especially appreciated in rooms with a harbor view. The decor is primarily in beige hues, and every room has a vanity and clock radio; some have minibars. Suites have kitchens with two-burner stoves, microwave ovens, and small refrigerators. Seven deluxe penthouse suites even have fireplaces and stereo systems.

Dining/Entertainment: The Impressions Café serves three meals daily in a "California-style" art deco atmosphere. Steak and seafood dinners are in the $14–$18 range. The Lobby Lounge is open nightly.

Services: Room service (6:30am–1am), concierge (full-time in summer), courtesy van, babysitting service. "Royal Treatment" rooms include continental breakfast, upgraded amenities, minibar, hairdryer, vanity, newspaper, free local calls.

Facilities: Indoor swimming pool, sauna, whirlpool, beauty salon, gift shop, meeting space for up to 300, no-smoking rooms.

HOTEL GRAND PACIFIC, 450 Quebec St. (at Oswego St.), Victoria, BC V8V 1W5. Tel. 604/386-0450, or toll free 800/663-7550. Fax 604/383-7603. 126 rms, 24 suites. A/C MINIBAR TV TEL **Bus:** 30 to Superior and Oswego.

$ Rates: June–Sept, $165–$200 single or double; $190–$225 one-bedroom suite; $420 executive suite. Oct–May, $105–$140 single or double; $130–$165 one-bedroom suite; $360 executive suite. AE, CB, DC, ER, MC, V. **Parking:** Free.

Built like a turn-of-the-century French château, the Grand Pacific only opened its doors in 1989 but major renovations are already planned for 1994. For now, the hotel is an elegant but unpretentious showcase for its Canadian owners' collection of antiques and Asian art. It has two wings—an eight-story no-smoking West Wing, and a six-story East Wing.

The rooms feature rich wood decor and subdued color schemes with floral trim. Each has a balcony, two sinks (one in the vanity), and brass fittings in the bath. Junior suites have French doors separating the bedroom and sitting room, as well as a walk-through bath. Each executive suite features a marble bathroom floor, a double Jacuzzi, a fireplace, three balconies, and a wet bar.

Dining/Entertainment: The Dining Room seats 160 for three meals daily, including a buffet breakfast in the summer. Its pastel decor, big bay windows, and brass chandeliers will be retained when it's converted to a meeting space in a year or two. Trophy's Club & Bar offers light dining and a lounge with a piano bar.

Services: Room service, concierge, valet cleaning, courtesy limousine.

Facilities: Athletic club with 25-meter indoor pool, separate kids' pool, weight room, aerobics classes, racquet courts, sauna, whirlpool, massage therapist, equipment sales; fully equipped business center.

EXPENSIVE

THE CAPTAIN'S PALACE, 309 Belleville St. (at Oswego St.), Victoria, BC V8V 1X2. Tel. 604/388-9191. Fax 604/388-7606. 16 suites in two buildings. **Bus:** 5 to Belleville and Government.

$ Rates (including full breakfast): Apr 15–Oct 15, $110–$155 suite for one or two. Oct 16–Apr 14, $65–$110 suite for one or two. AE, DC, MC, V. **Parking:** Free.

This small Victorian hotel-restaurant, originally built in 1897 as the home of a prominent merchant and his family, has been restored and preserved in remarkably faithful fashion. From the foyer, with its hand-painted, ceramic-tiled fireplace and its rich wood paneling, to the crystal chandeliers hanging from frescoed ceilings, to the stained-glass windows and velvet tapestries, it's like a period museum. Even the staff is clad as liveried butlers or pinafored maids. Don't miss the $12,000, 1⁄12-scale dollhouse replica of this mansion in the second-floor sitting room!

Every suite is fully furnished with estate antiques, right down to the carpeted private baths. There are no elevators, of course, but the stairs add to the charm! Some rooms have harbor views; others feature private parlors.

Dining/Entertainment: Breakfast, lunch, afternoon tea, and dinner are served in several lovely ground-floor rooms. Dinner prices are in the $15–$20 range; oyster stew, Neptune's sole, Cornish game hen, and Yorkshire beef bites are among the favorites.

HOLLAND HOUSE INN, 595 Michigan St. (at Government St.), Victoria, BC V8V 1S7. Tel. or fax 604/384-6644.
10 rms. TV TEL **Bus:** 5 to Superior and Government.

$ Rates: May–Oct, $105–$175 single; $115–$180 double. Nov–Apr, $70–$135 single; $80–$145 double. AE, DC, MC, V.

Owned by noted avant-garde artist Lance Olsen, this impeccably clean and tidy home is a veritable fine-art museum. The work of Olsen, sculptor David Toresdahl, and other B.C. artisans is on display throughout the home. Located less than two blocks behind the Parliament Buildings, it isn't Dutch at all: The three-story manse surrounded by a white picket fence was built in 1934 by an Englishman named Holland.

All rooms are furnished with antiques, and have private baths, wood floors, and four-poster beds with goose-down comforters. Two have wood-burning fireplaces, but smokers are requested to use the outside balconies.

Dining/Entertainment: Gourmet breakfasts—the likes of German apple pancakes or baked eggs with Brie and ham—are served between 7 and 9am to the strains of classical music in the Gallery Lounge. Jazz is the order of the afternoon in the lounge.

Services: Room service.

Facilities: One handicapped-accessible room.

LAUREL POINT INN, 680 Montreal St., Victoria, BC V8V 1Z8. Tel. 604/386-8721, or toll free 800/663-7667. Fax 604/386-9547. 130 rms, 72 suites. A/C TV TEL **Bus:** 30 to Montreal and Superior.

$ Rates: May–Sept, $110–$130 single or double; $130–$195 junior suite; $245 bedroom suite; $495 full suite. Oct–Apr, $95 single or double; $130–$175 junior suite; $245 bedroom suite; $395 full suite. Children under 12 stay free in parents' room. Special midweek winter rates. AE, CB, ER, MC, V. **Parking:** Free.

A magnificent property surrounded by immaculately tended gardens, Laurel Point occupies a promontory that juts into the Inner Harbour where visiting vessels make their final turn toward downtown. The spacious hotel added a new 72-room wing and a spectacular Japanese garden in 1989. The Asian art influence persists throughout the hotel, especially in the sculpture and ceramics mounted in glass-enclosed nooks in the hallways.

The rooms—every one of which offers a harbor view from a small balcony—have a simple beauty not often seen in hotel rooms. Some might find the light maple decor and beige-and-cream color scheme stark; others will see in it a Scandinavian or perhaps a Shinto touch. There's a photo mural of historical Victoria on one wall. Especially notable is the deep marble bathtub.

Dining/Entertainment: The Café Laurel, an open lobby bistro with hanging baskets, wicker furniture, and antique cookware on its walls, serves three meals daily. Cook's Landing lounge has a nightly piano bar and large windows facing the harbor. The Sunday luncheon buffet was declared "Best in Victoria" by *Monday Magazine.*

Services: 24-hour room service, concierge, valet laundry.

Facilities: Indoor swimming pool, Jacuzzi, sauna, exercise bicycles, gift shop, meeting/banquet space for up to 250, no-smoking rooms and facilities for the handicapped.

MODERATE

ADMIRAL MOTEL, 257 Belleville St., Victoria, BC V8V 1X1. Tel. 604/388-6267. 18 rms, 11 suites. TV TEL **Bus:** 5 to Belleville and Government.

$ Rates: May–Sept, $69–$95 single; $69–$109 double; $79–$119 suite. Oct–Apr, $45–$69 single; $55–$69 double; $65–$79 suite. Additional person $6 extra. Off-season and weekly rates available. Children under 12 stay free in parents' room. AE, DISC, ER, MC, V. **Parking:** Free.

Overlooking the Inner Harbour and close to restaurants and shopping, the small, family-operated Admiral Motel is quiet and modern. The rooms are attractively decorated and comfortably furnished, all with refrigerators. Some have kitchens and can sleep up to six people. The owners are friendly and provide personal assistance with sightseeing. A guest laundry and car-rental desk are available.

HUNTINGTON MANOR INN, 330 Quebec St. (at Oswego St.), Victoria, BC V8V 1W3. Tel. 604/381-3456, or toll free 800/663-7557. Fax 604/381-3456, ext. 403. 65 rms, 50 suites. TV TEL **Bus:** 30 to Superior and Oswego.

$ Rates: May 15–Oct 15, $98–$130 single or double; $107–$168 suite. Oct 16–May 14, $67–$86 single or double; $100–$128 suite. Off-season rates include breakfast. AE, CB, DC, ER, MC, V. **Parking:** $3 per night, underground.

"Leave your laughter by the fire, ere you take the high road." That 18th-century message from a Cambridgeshire coach house sets the mood for this gracious inn, named for the hometown of Oliver Cromwell, England's "Lord Protector." Built in 1981, patterned after an Edwardian manor, it carries the atmosphere of a British hunting lodge with its antique-filled, tartan-carpeted lobby and rich wood appointments. The staff even wears red riding jackets.

Each blue-carpeted standard room has two double beds with lacy floral spreads, brass lamps and a clock-radio on the nightstands, an armoire with TV, a working desk, and standard amenities. The two-story Gallery Suites have bedroom lofts, gabled ceilings, air conditioning, and full kitchen facilities.

The Hunters Club Lounge has a fox-and-hounds decor and a big fireplace. The adjacent Royal Stables Restaurant is a full-service dining room, offering breakfast, lunch, and dinner, with dinner entrées in the $9–$20 range. Both valet laundry service and guest laundrette are available. Facilities include an indoor whirlpool and sauna, a car-rental desk, meeting space for up to 30, and no-smoking rooms.

INN ON THE HARBOUR, 427 Belleville St., Victoria, BC V8V 1X3. Tel. and fax 604/386-3451. 69 rms. TV TEL **Bus:** 5 to Belleville and Government.

$ Rates: May–Sept, $105–$115 single; $110–$120 double; $115–$125 twin. Oct–Apr, $63–$69 single; $66–$72 double; $69–$75 twin. Children under 12 stay free in parents' room. Winter discounts available. AE, DC, DISC, MC, V. **Parking:** May–Sept, $2 per night, Oct–Apr free.

This very friendly hotel opposite the MV *Coho* ferry terminal has a vaguely nautical theme in its decor. In the lobby is a scale model of HMS *Royal Sovereign,* a 17th-century English vessel; its restaurant and lounge are named for the HMS *Swiftsure,* the last of the tall sailing ships to serve duty in the Pacific (1882–90).

Half the rooms face the Inner Harbour, with fine views of the oceangoing activity. Standard units are in forest-green and floral prints, with standard furnishings and a step-up bathtub; 18 have kitchenettes, including a stove and refrigerator.

The Swiftsure Restaurant offers three meals daily, with dinners in the $12–$17 range. The handsome Swiftsure Lounge also serves light meals, and features late-night fondues. In summer, there's an outdoor barbecue.

Guest services include room service, valet laundry, a courtesy van, secretarial service, safe-deposit boxes, a banking machine, and postal services. There are also an indoor/outdoor swimming pool, sauna, whirlpool, and meeting space for up to 60.

ROYAL SCOT INN, 425 Quebec St. (between Menzies and Oswego St.), Victoria, BC V8V 1W7. Tel. 604/388-5463, or toll free 800/663-7515. Fax 604/388-5452. 28 rms, 150 suites. TV TEL **Bus:** 5 to Belleville and Government.

$ Rates: May 16–Oct 15, $89–$119 single or double; $109–$129 studio suite; $119–$195 one-bedroom suite; $209–$269 two-bedroom suite. Oct 16–May 15, $79–$89 single or double; $103 studio suite; $121–$205 one-bedroom suite; $205–$215 two-bedroom suite. Weekly and monthly rates. AE, ER, MC, V. **Parking:** Free.

A converted apartment house, the Royal Scot is a modern motel just half a block from the Parliament Buildings. In winter, it's favored by prairie province retirees escaping subzero climes. Standard room furnishings include walk-in closets, dressing tables, and VCRs (there's an in-house video rental). All suites have fully equipped kitchens. Less expensive suites have a room divider separating the bedroom from the living room; some have balconies. Luxury suites have separate bedrooms, with queen-size rather than double beds.

Piper's Restaurant, offering outdoor seating in summer, serves three meals daily plus high tea. Steak or seafood dinners run $9.25–$15.95. Room service is available, along with valet laundry, a guest launderette, and courtesy van. Local phone calls are free. There's also an indoor swimming pool, sauna, Jacuzzi, exercise room, gift/sundries shop, and video rental, plus meeting space for up to 55.

BUDGET

THE JAMES BAY INN, 270 Government St. (at Toronto St.), Victoria, BC V8V 2L2. Tel. 604/384-7151. Fax 604/381-2115. 50 rms (29 with bath). **Bus:** 5 or 30 to Government and Superior.

$ Rates: (including continental breakfast): $29–$47 single without bath; $48–$84 double without bath. Higher rates for rooms with bath. MC, V. **Parking:** Free, but limited.

An early Edwardian manor built in 1907, this budget favorite was the last home of famed painter Emily Carr, a Victoria native. Its lobby features Gay '90s decor. Rooms are newly renovated. Rib Tickler's restaurant serves three meals daily; the Unwinder is a well-patronized neighborhood pub.

2. DOWNTOWN/OLDE TOWN

EXPENSIVE

ABIGAIL'S HOTEL, 906 McClure St. (at Quadra St.), Victoria, BC V8V 3E7. Tel. 604/388-5363. Fax 604/361-1905. 16 rms. **Bus:** 1.

$ Rates (including full breakfast): Year-round, $110–$215 single or double. Midweek rates discounted about 30%. MC, V. **Parking:** Free.

A four-story, gabled Tudor building surrounded by a beautiful garden, Abigail's is the quintessential small European-style luxury inn. This friendly, no-smoking hotel is only a four-block walk east of the Empress, but it seems like another world.

The rooms seem made to order for honeymooners or other young lovers. Decorated in pastel colors, they have crystal chandeliers with dimmer switches, stained-glass windows, fresh flowers, and goose-down comforters. Most have either a private Jacuzzi or a deep soaking tub; some also have fireplaces and/or four-poster canopy beds. Maybe best of all, there's no TV (a few have radios) or telephone (there's a pay phone in the lobby). Once you're here, you've escaped from the "real" world. But be sure to check in before 10pm—that's when the doors are locked, and unless you already have your room key, you won't get in.

Dining/Entertainment: A filling breakfast is served in the sun room between 8 and 9am. There's an afternoon "social hour" from 4 to 7pm in the library, with mulled wine and snacks. The library's piano and games table are popular with guests.

Services: Concierge, complimentary umbrellas.

THE BEACONSFIELD INN, 998 Humboldt St. (at Vancouver St.), Victoria, BC V8V 2Z8. Tel. 604/384-4044. Fax 604/361-1905. 12 rms. **Bus:** 1 or 2.

$ Rates (including full breakfast): Year-round, $100–$215 single or double. MC, V. **Parking:** Free.

An impressively restored Edwardian mansion dating from 1905, this companion hotel to Abigail's was originally commissioned as a wedding gift. Named for the London hotel said to have been King Edward VII's lover's rendezvous, it's centrally located just two blocks from Beacon Hill Park. The Beaconsfield boasts rich mahogany paneling, antique furnishings on hardwood floors, and delicate stained-glass window trim. The cozy library has wall-to-wall books.

All rooms have private baths (most with Jacuzzis or soaking tubs), down comforters, and impressive antiques. Some also have fireplaces, but as at Abigail's, none has a television or phone, and no smoking is allowed. Every room is unique; Lillie's Room features a wood-encased and canopied clawfoot bathtub.

If there's a guest overflow, three Victorian rooms with fireplaces and Jacuzzis are available at the nearby Humboldt House, 867 Humboldt St., a secluded and romantic retreat under the same ownership. You may request the Humboldt House, but check-in takes place only at the Beaconsfield. Breakfast can be enjoyed at the Beaconsfield, or it can be discreetly delivered in a basket to Humboldt House.

Dining/Entertainment: A full breakfast is served daily in the sun room, and there's an afternoon social hour—offering port, sherry, fruit, and cheese—in the library. The library also has a games table.

Services: Concierge, complimentary umbrellas.

THE BEDFORD, 1140 Government St. (at View St.), Victoria, BC V8W 1Y2. Tel. 604/384-6835, or toll free 800/665-6500. Fax 604/386-8930. 40 rms. TV TEL **Bus:** 5.

$ Rates (including full breakfast and afternoon tea): May 7–Oct 1, $185 superior; $135 deluxe; $170 deluxe with fireplace. Oct 2–May 6, $145 superior; $105 deluxe, $140 deluxe with fireplace. AE, MC, V.

An elegant small hostelry in early 20th-century European style, this hotel in the heart of Olde Town is a real find. Built in 1930, it was formerly the Bastion Inn, but in 1987 and 1988 it was thoroughly gutted and renovated. Today, the colorful flowerpots on the ledges above Government Street can only hint at its true charm. The Bedford offers the classic British tradition of high tea in an atmosphere of old-world charm and understated elegance. Guests are encouraged to leave the children at home.

As with many older inns, the rooms vary considerably in size, shape, and decor. Most share a pastel color scheme with brass accents, stocked bookshelves, goose-down comforters, and luxurious amenities. A dozen have wood-burning fireplaces and sliding doors linking them to private Jacuzzis.

Dining/Entertainment: The Red Currant Restaurant serves three gourmet meals daily in summer, breakfast and lunch in winter, and afternoon tea year-round. Garrick's Head Pub has pub meals from 11am to 11pm every day in summer, Monday through Saturday in winter. The pub has a piano sing-along Thursday through Saturday nights, and locally brewed beer all the time.

Services: Concierge, valet laundry, free local phone calls, morning coffee and newspaper delivered to room, overnight shoe-shine.

Facilities: Meeting space for up to 75.

CHATEAU VICTORIA HOTEL, 740 Burdett Ave. (at Douglas St.), Victoria, BC V8W 1B2. Tel. 604/382-4221, or toll free 800/663-5891. Fax 604/380-1950. 60 rms, 118 suites. A/C TV TEL **Bus:** 2.

$ Rates: $97–$141 single or double; $141–$215 suite. Seasonal discounts offered. AE, CB, DC, ER, MC, V. **Parking:** Free.

This 18-story hotel was erected in 1975, on the former site of the "Bird Lady's" house. Victoria Jane Wilson lived in a big white manor on the hill above the Empress. When she died in 1949 at the age of 76, she bequeathed a substantial sum to assure the lifelong support of her beloved parrot, Louis. The loquacious bird continued to live in the house until his caretaker's death in 1966, at which time he was moved to a retirement home. Unsubstantiated rumors have it that he's still alive, and may be over 100 years old. In any case, his spirit (and his mistress's) are alive at the Chateau. A major renovation was completed here in 1990.

Two-thirds of the rooms are elegant one-bedroom suites, with curtained French doors that separate sitting room from bedroom. Every suite has a coffee-maker and a small refrigerator; some have kitchenettes. Impressionist lithographs hang on the walls, and Italian oak furnishings include a working desk, armoire, and a king-size bed or two queen-size beds. All rooms have balconies, full-length-mirror closets, and built-in hairdryers. Seven floors are for nonsmokers only.

Dining/Entertainment: The Parrot House Restaurant, with its magnificent views, is Victoria's only rooftop restaurant. It's open daily for breakfast and dinner. Victoria Jane's Lobby Lounge offers lunch and light dinners.

Services: Room service, concierge, valet laundry, airport transfer, courtesy van, secretarial services, babysitting referral.

Facilities: Skylit indoor swimming pool, whirlpool bath, business center, meeting space for up to 50, seven no-smoking floors.

SWANS HOTEL, 506 Pandora Ave. (at Store St.), Victoria, BC V8W 1N6. Tel. 604/361-3310. Fax 604/361-3491. 10 suites. **Bus:** 23 or 24.

$ Rates (including continental breakfast): Apr–Sept, $115–$135 suite for two. Oct–Mar, $69–$89 suite for two. Additional person $15 extra. AE, MC, V.

"I may be an ugly duckling now, but I'll soon be a swan!" Hans Christian Andersen's fable inspired the name given to this converted 1913 feed warehouse when historic preservationist Michael Williams decided to turn it into a hotel-restaurant-brewery complex in 1988. Today, it's one of Olde Town's best-known buildings. Buckerfield's Brewery produces half a dozen highly regarded British-style draft ales.

Swans can be classified a "boutique hotel"—small, friendly, and charming. Located on the tip of the Inner Harbour, Swans offers tastefully designed spacious suites (many are split-level with open lofts) with kitchens, separate dining areas, and living rooms. The two-bedroom suites are great for families, as they can accommodate up to six people comfortably. Original artwork and fresh flowers add to the pleasant atmosphere.

Dining/Entertainment: Swans Café is open for lunch and dinner daily; lunches are in the $6–$9 range while dinner entrées run $9–$19. The often-crowded pub serves a wide variety of pub snacks and traditional British ales brewed on the premises.

Services: Room service, guest laundry.

THE VICTORIA REGENT HOTEL, 1234 Wharf St. (near Yates St.), Victoria, BC V8W 3H9. Tel. 604/386-2211, or toll free 800/663-7472. Fax 604/386-2622. 15 rms, 33 suites. MINIBAR TV TEL **Bus:** 23 or 24 at the Johnson St. Bridge.

$ Rates: May 16–Oct, $135 single or double; $75–$195 one-bedroom suite; $285–$395 two-bedroom suite. Nov–May 15, $90 single or double; $135 one-bedroom suite; $185–$285 two-bedroom suite. Children under 16 stay free in parents' room. AE, DC, DISC, ER, MC, V. **Parking:** Free, underground.

When an optimistic developer started this building in the late 1970s, he foresaw it as the future Victoria convention center. That plan crumbled, so he converted it to a condominium hotel. Today, it consists in part of individually owned units, a few of which are permanent homes. The hotel, with its wedding-cake architecture, is unmistakable from the water, as it juts into the Inner Harbour.

The units include 15 rooms, 10 one-bedroom suites, 18 two-bedroom suites, and five deluxe three-bedroom executive and penthouse suites with fireplaces, stereo systems, and bedroom Jacuzzis. All units are very large. There are full kitchens in each suite, equipped with stove, refrigerator, toaster, stoneware, tables for four, even a dishwasher. All have king-size beds, working desks, clock radios, and serigraph art on the walls.

Dining/Entertainment: The Water's Edge Restaurant, on the ground floor, is a converted suite that actually extends into the water. It serves three meals daily in summer, breakfast and lunch only in winter.

Services: Guest laundry, morning newspaper, babysitting referrals, secretarial service.

Facilities: Boat charters, meeting space for 30.

MODERATE

BEST WESTERN CARLTON PLAZA HOTEL, 642 Johnson St. (at Broad St.), Victoria, BC V8W 1M6. Tel. or fax 604/384-5122, or toll free 800/663-7241. 66 rms, 8 suites. TV TEL **Bus:** 5.

$ Rates (including continental breakfast): June–Sept, $94 single; $104 double; $114 twin; $134 suite. Oct–May, $79 single; $89 double; $99 twin; $129 suite. Children under 12 stay free in parents' room. AE, DC, DISC, ER, MC, V. **Parking:** Free, underground.

Built in 1912 as the St. James Hotel, this heritage property has gone through many incarnations. The most recent began in 1989 when it was gutted and renovated to the tune of $1.5 million. Now a Best Western hotel, its rooms feature soft pastel decor and standard amenities and furnishings; 41 have fully equipped kitchens.

The Garden Café serves three meals daily except Sunday. Continental breakfast is served in the Island Bar and Lounge, off the lobby. Services include valet laundry, in-room coffee, and video rentals. There's an outdoor swimming pool, sauna, whirlpool, beauty salon, jeweler, gift shop, and meeting space for up to 80; a fitness club is under construction.

THE COURTYARD INN, 850 Blanshard St. (at Courtney St.), Victoria, BC V8W 2H2. Tel. 604/385-6787. Fax 604/385-5800. 64 rms. A/C TV TEL **Bus:** 1.

$ Rates: May–Oct 14, $80–$85 single; $85–$95 double. Oct 15–Apr, $60–$75 single or double. AE, DC, MC, V. **Parking:** Free, underground.

Across the street from the law courts, this two-story hotel is built around a paved garden courtyard that sparkles in summer with wildflower baskets and safari umbrellas. Rooms are colorfully appointed, all with standard furnishings and amenities, including well-lit vanities. The quietest rooms either face the courtyard or are on the upper floor, with double-glazed windows.

The Court dining room serves breakfast daily, lunch weekdays, and gourmet dinners ($7–$14) nightly except Sunday. The Chambers lounge offers burgers and pub meals at lunchtime in a club atmosphere of Olde English prints and china. The Old Bailey pub, in the basement, is authentically British: Visiting rugby and cricket players make it their headquarters. Guests have use of a coin-op laundry, indoor swimming pool, and sauna; there's meeting space for up to 80.

THE DOMINION HOTEL, 759 Yates St. (at Blanshard St.), Victoria, BC V8W 1L6. Tel. 604/384-4136, or toll free 800/663-6101. Fax 604/382-6416. 101 rms. TV TEL **Bus:** 10, 11, or 14.

$ Rates: May–Sept, $99 single; $114 double. Oct–Apr, $39.50–$44.50 single; $44.50–$49.50 double. Children under 16 stay free in parents' room. AE, DC, ER, MC, V. **Parking:** Free.

Victoria's oldest surviving hotel dates from 1876. Today it's a lovely family-oriented heritage property with rich woods, marble floors, brass trim, and red-velvet upholstery on antique chairs, following a $7-million restoration. Rooms have more modern appointments, but keep the flavor of times past with ceiling fans, brass lamps, and steam rooms. There are dozens of room types; all have been fully renovated in the past few years.

Central Park is an excellent gourmet restaurant, serving continental and nouvelle dinners in a turn-of-the-century atmosphere for $16–$25. The Lettuce Patch coffee shop offers three meals a day. The intimate Gaslight Lounge features carved solid-oak paneling, while the Barbary Coast Lounge is a bustling sports bar done in 19th-century San Francisco style. Room service and valet laundry are offered, and a health club is available for guest use.

EXECUTIVE HOUSE HOTEL, 777 Douglas St. (at Humboldt and Collinson Sts.), Victoria, BC V8W 2B5. Tel. 604/388-5111, or toll free 800/663-7001 in B.C. and the U.S. Northwest, 800/663-7563 elsewhere in Canada. Fax 604/385-1323. 94 rms, 85 suites. A/C TV TEL **Bus:** 2.

$ Rates: May–Sept, $78–$139 single or double; $159–$295 suite. Oct–Apr, 20%–50% less, depending on season and availability. AE, CB, DC, ER, MC, V. **Parking:** $2.

This luxury high-rise overlooking the Victoria Conference Centre is full of pleasant surprises. Starting with the cozy lobby with its unusual wood-and-metal chandelier hanging over a table adorned with fresh flowers, the ambience makes it feel like a transplanted piece of home.

The rooms are very spacious, from studios to one- and two-bedroom suites. Suites have kitchens with a stove and refrigerator, well-lit vanities, generous closet space, television with in-house movies, and balconies. Studios have small fridges and standard furnishings, including a desk. Pastel shades are a common thread in the decor. All rooms include complimentary tea and coffee.

Barkley's Grill Room rates as one of Victoria's finest restaurants, with steaks and seafood in the $15–$25 range for dinner. The restaurant has an airy colonial-manor atmosphere, with nautical prints on the walls. Adjoining is the Polo Lounge, its decor reflecting the sport it's named for. Caffè d'Amore offers California-Italian cuisine and serves three meals daily amid lots of greenery. It shares the floor with Bartholomew's Pub and Grill (featuring nightly entertainment), and Doubles Oyster Bar (a good place for a quiet drink). Both are local hot spots.

Guest services include room service, a concierge, a valet laundry, and courtesy pickup from the Inner Harbour. There's also a health spa (with an exercise room, Jacuzzi, steam room, sun bed, and beautician), as well as meeting space for up to 70.

HELM'S INN, 660 Douglas St., Victoria, BC V8V 2P8. Tel. 604/385-5767. Fax 604/385-2221. 43 units. TV TEL **Bus:** 30.

$ Rates: May 21–Oct 14, $85–$95 single or double; $125 suite. Oct 15–May 20, $48–$59 single or double; $69 suite. AE, DC, MC, V. **Parking:** Free.

This gaily painted motel, just half a block from the Royal B.C. Museum, is popular among budget watchers who like to stay close to the center of action. Twenty-seven of the spacious rooms have kitchen units, making them especially appealing to families. The interior decor is eye-catching: blue trim around peach-colored doors, purple carpets, and a big grandfather clock on the stairway. Morning coffee is served.

BUDGET

HOTEL DOUGLAS, 1450 Douglas St. (at Pandora Ave.), Victoria, BC V8W 2G1. Tel. 604/383-4157. Fax 604/383-2279. 67 rms (47 with bath). A/C TV TEL **Bus:** 1, 14, or 30.

$ Rates: Mid-May to mid-Sept, $50 single; $55 double; $60 twin; $65 triple. Mid-Sept to mid-May, $45 single; $50 double; $55 twin; $60 triple. Rooms sharing baths, $15 less. Children under 6 stay free in same bed with parent. MC, V.

This old brick building across the street from City Hall is clean and basic. Its small lobby has no seating, but there's a bar on one side, a coffee shop on the other. Regular rooms are adequately furnished with modern bathrooms and nondenominational religious texts framed on the walls.

VICTORIA HOSTEL, 516 Yates St. (near Wharf St.), Victoria, BC V8W 1K8. Tel. 604/385-4511. Fax 604/385-3232. 104 beds. **Bus:** 23 or 24 at the Johnson St. Bridge.

$ Rates: $12.50 International Youth Hostel members, $17.85 nonmembers. MC, V.

Located in the heart of Olde Town, this friendly youth hostel has everything the traveler really needs. Facilities include two kitchens (stocked with utensils) and a dining room, TV lounge with VCR, games room, common room, library, laundry facilities, and hot showers. Most beds are in dormitories separated by gender, but there are a couple of family rooms. There's a 2am curfew.

YM-YWCA OF VICTORIA, 880 Courtney St. (at Quadra St.), Victoria, BC V8W 1C4. Tel. 604/386-7511. Fax 604/380-1933. 31 beds. A/C **Bus:** 1.

$ Rates: $31 single; $46 double; Payment required in advance. MC, V.

Although the same building provides facilities for both sexes, the residence is *for women only*. A big brown-brick building with a spacious lobby and green leather settees, the Y has a cafeteria (closed on Sunday), a swimming pool, and a cozy TV lounge. There are shared bathrooms and pay telephones on each floor.

3. OUTSIDE THE CENTRAL AREA

VERY EXPENSIVE

OCEAN POINTE RESORT, 45 Songhees Rd., Victoria, BC V9A 8T3. Tel. 604/360-2999, or toll free 800/667-4677. Fax 604/360-1041. 222 rms, 28 suites. A/C MINIBAR TV TEL **Bus:** 24 to Colville.

$ Rates: May–Sept, $160–$200 single or double; $200–$650 suite. Oct–Apr, $150–$180 single or double; $175–$600 suite. AE, DC, ER, MC, V. **Parking:** $9 per day valet, underground.

The only major hotel on the north shore of the Inner Harbour, this new (1992) hotel offers European-style hospitality—including full spa services—and a wide range of sports options. Guestrooms are comfortable and tastefully furnished, and most have outstanding harbor views. The executive floor offers suites, a boardroom and lounge, and a fully equipped business center.

Dining/Entertainment: The Victorian Restaurant, with views of Olde Town and the Parliament Buildings, offers elegant West Coast cuisine. Options for casual dining include the Boardwalk Restaurant and Deli and the Boardwalk Brasserie.

Services: Room service, concierge, shuttle service, valet laundry, multilingual staff, activities coordinator, babysitting.

Facilities: Indoor/outdoor pool, health club, raquetball/squash and tennis courts, shops, children's playroom, European spa (with massage, hydrotherapy, aromatherapy, and hairstylist), car-rental desk, business center, conference facilities for up to 400, no-smoking rooms and facilities for the handicapped.

EXPENSIVE

OAK BAY BEACH HOTEL, 1175 Beach Dr., Victoria, BC V8S 2N2. Tel. or fax 604/598-4556. 46 rms, 5 suites. TV TEL **Bus:** 2.

$ Rates: Apr 15–Oct 15, $103–$128 standard single or double; $154–$188 deluxe single or double; $158–$220 junior suite; $265–$395 executive suite. Oct 16–Apr 14, $88 standard single or double; $128 deluxe single or double; $142–$198 junior suite; $238–$355 executive suite. AE, DC, ER, MC, V. **Parking:** Free.

This Elizabethan-style inn sits on the Haro Strait, 3½ miles (5.5km) east of downtown Victoria. Beautiful gardens extend to the shoreline; guests get an eyeful of Washington's San Juan Islands and snow-capped Mount Baker. The hotel is pure elegance, starting with the Grand Lobby—a huge living room with a century-old baby grand piano, priceless antiques, and a big fireplace. Every room is different; all boast pieces from hotelier Bruce Walker's personal antiques collection. Rooms are priced according to size and view. The third-story junior suites are impressive, with canopy beds, bay windows, and balconies facing the sea.

Dining/Entertainment: The elegant Tudor Room by the Sea serves three meals, including Sunday brunch, and afternoon high tea daily. Gourmet West Coast cuisine dinners run $14–$28. The Snug, a cozy English pub, serves light meals and desserts.

Services: Room service, valet laundry, morning coffee and newspaper, complimentary seasonal shuttle service.

Facilities: Cruises and charters aboard the hotel's private yachts, meeting space for up to 150.

MODERATE

THE BOATHOUSE, 746 Sea Dr. (RR 1), Brentwood Bay, BC V0S 1A0. Tel. 604/652-9370. 1 unit. TEL

$ Rates (including continental breakfast): $105 single or double. MC, V. **Parking:** Free.

Jean and Harvey Merritt's quaint bed-and-breakfast cottage is exactly what it claims to be: a converted boathouse, built on pilings in the Saanich Inlet, literally a stone's throw from the famed Butchart Gardens. It's rich in wildlife, including seals, herons, bald eagles, otters, and raccoons, and is a great spot for a romantic getaway.

The charming red cabin is reached down a long—make that *very* long—flight of stairs behind the Merritts' hillside home. Inside are a hideaway sofa bed, dining table, kitchen area with small refrigerator and toaster oven, gas furnace, and a reading alcove looking out on the floating dock. Full toilet and shower facilities are in a separate bathhouse a short way back uphill. All the makings for a delicious continental breakfast are provided the previous evening. Guests have use of a boat.

THE COACHMAN INN, 229 Gorge Rd. E. (at Washington Ave.), Victoria, BC V9A 1L1. Tel. 604/388-6611. Fax 604/388-4153. 59 rms, 12 suites. TV TEL **Bus:** 10.

$ Rates: July–Sept 15, $75–$95 single or double; $115 suite. May 16–June and Sept 16–30, $65–$85 single or double; $105 suite. Oct–May 15, $49–$69 single or double; $82 suite. Children under 12 stay free in parents' room. AE, DC, DISC, ER, MC, V. **Parking:** Free.

This conveniently located Gorge Road motel has friendly and attentive service. All rooms have outside entrances and about half have queen-size beds; 28 have fully equipped kitchens. There's ample closet space, along with standard furnishings and amenities. Horse-and-hounds pictures hang on the walls.

The Post House Restaurant serves three meals daily. Squire's Lounge offers pub fare, and has an outside deck for warm afternoons. It's a major venue for darts tournaments, including the National Darts Championship in mid-June. There's a coin-op guest laundry and seasonal shuttle service, as well as an indoor swimming pool, sauna, video-games room, and meeting space for up to 125.

RAMADA INN, 3020 Blanshard St. (near Finlayson St.), Victoria, BC V8T 5B5. Tel. 604/382-4400, or toll free 800/268-8998. Fax 604/382-4053. 123 rms, 3 suites. **Bus:** 30 to Mayfair Centre or 70 to Douglas Street.

$ Rates: May–Sept, $99 single; $105 double; $119–$129 suite. Oct–Apr, $83 single; $89 double; $105–$115 suite. Children under 18 stay free in parents' room. AE, DC, ER, MC, V. **Parking:** Free, underground.

Victoria's entry in the international Ramada chain is appealing to many for its location: adjacent to the Mayfair Shopping Centre, Victoria's largest mall, and across the street from city-maintained Topaz Park and tennis courts. The lobby is sparse but spacious, the rooms nicely appointed; 22 rooms have kitchenettes.

Redd's Roadhouse Restaurant has all-day casual dining; the menu includes burgers, chicken dishes, and other family fare. Its upper floor is Redd's Pub, popular as a sports bar. Room service and valet laundry are available, and there's an exercise room, Jacuzzi, sauna, gift shop, and hair salon, as well as meeting space for up to 250.

BUDGET

MAPLE LEAF INN, 120 Gorge Rd. E. (at Albany St.), Victoria, BC V9A 1L3. Tel. 604/388-9901. 64 rms. A/C TV TEL **Bus:** 10.

$ Rates: $44–$54 single; $48–$58 double. AE, MC, V. **Parking:** Free.

Like an alpine transplant, this inn resembles a chalet with a swimming pool, sauna, and sun deck. About half the units have their own kitchens (for just $10 extra). All have queen-size beds, or waterbeds on request. There's free morning coffee and a coin-op laundry.

UNIVERSITY OF VICTORIA, Housing and Conference Services, P.O. Box 1700, Victoria, BC V8W 2Y2. Tel. 604/721-8395. Fax 604/721-8930. **Bus:** 4 or 14.

$ Rates (including full breakfast): May–Aug, $30.50 single; $44.50 double. **Parking:** $2 per day. **Closed:** Sept–Apr.

Victoria's major university opens its dormitories to visitors for four summer months, when classes are not in session. All rooms have single or twin beds and basic furnishings. Bathrooms, pay phones, and TV lounges are on every floor; linens, towels, and soap are provided. Each building has a coin-op laundry. Guests may use campus cafeterias, dining rooms, and athletic facilities, including the swimming pool, weight room, and squash and tennis courts.

CHAPTER 12

VICTORIA DINING

1. **THE INNER HARBOUR**
2. **DOWNTOWN/OLDE TOWN**
3. **OUTSIDE THE CENTRAL AREA**

What is true of cuisine in Vancouver is likewise true in Victoria. British Columbia's capital city isn't quite as cosmopolitan as its larger cousin, but the variety of food is still impressive—and here, it often comes with an added touch of English hospitality. Afternoon high teas are more "the thing" in Victoria than in Vancouver.

The following restaurant listing is organized first by geographical area and then by **price range:** "Very Expensive" (entrées average more than $20 per person), "Expensive" ($15–$20), "Moderate" ($10–$15), and "Budget" (less than $10). *All prices are given in Canadian dollars.* There's no provincial tax on restaurant meals in British Columbia—just the 7% federal goods and services tax.

Restaurant hours vary. Lunch is typically from noon to 1pm; in the evening, British Columbians rarely dine before 7pm, later in summer. **Reservations** are recommended at most restaurants, and are essential at the most popular. They may not be accepted at some budget and even some moderately priced establishments, however.

1. THE INNER HARBOUR

EXPENSIVE

HARBOUR HOUSE RESTAURANT, 607 Oswego St., at Quebec St. Tel. 386-1244.
    Cuisine: CONTINENTAL. **Reservations:** Recommended. **Bus:** 30 to Superior and Oswego.
$ **Prices:** Appetizers $3.95–$7.50; main courses $11.75–$24.95. AE, MC, V.
    Open: May–Sept, lunch daily 11:30am–5pm; dinner daily 5–11:30pm. Oct–Apr, dinner only, daily 5–11:30pm.

Good traditional North American cooking in a friendly, upscale environment is the forte at the Harbour House, set beside Quadra Park just off Belleville Street. Owner Harry Loucas, originally from the eastern Mediterranean island nation of Cyprus, emphasizes service: In fact, he personally greets each arriving customer and thanks him or her on departure. Waiters in bow tie and cummerbund bustle past tables bedecked with white linen, candles, and fresh flowers, delivering impeccable service and pausing long enough to discuss the menu and international wine list—and events of the world—with guests.

The menu is divided about evenly between meats and seafoods. Diners might start with the restaurant's excellent spinach salad, then dine on the generous salmon au champagne, served with three

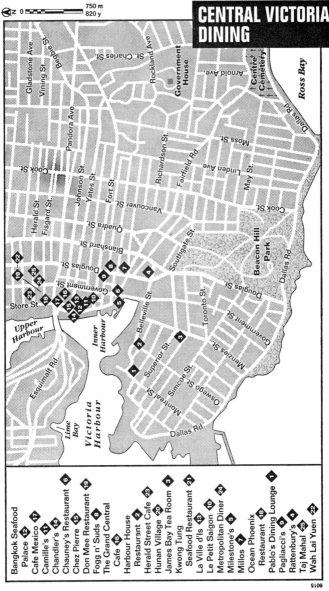

CENTRAL VICTORIA DINING

750 m
820 y

Gladstone Ave.
Vining St.
Begbie St.
St. Charles St.
Rockland Ave.
Government House
Arnold Ave.
Central Cemetery
Ross Bay
Dallas Rd.
Pandora Ave.
Cook St.
Johnson St.
Yates St.
Fort St.
Richardson St.
Fairfield Rd.
Moss St.
Linden Ave.
May St.
Cook St.
Herald St.
Fisgard St.
Vancouver St.
Quadra St.
Blanshard St.
Southgate St.
Beacon Hill Park
Douglas St.
Store St.
Government St.
Douglas St.
Belleville St.
Toronto St.
Dallas Rd.
Government St.
Upper Harbour
Inner Harbour
Esquimalt Rd.
Menzies St.
Superior St.
Simcoe St.
Oswego St.
Montreal St.
Victoria Harbour
Lime Bay
Dallas Rd.

Bangkok Seafood Palace ❷
Cafe Mexico ⓱
Camille's ⓭
Chandler's
Chauney's Restaurant ❻
Chez Pierre ⓯
Don Mee Restaurant ⓳
Fogg n' Suds ❽
The Grand Central Cafe ❹
Harbour House Restaurant ❷
Herald Street Cafe ㉓
Hunan Village ⓴
James Bay Tea Room
Kwong Tung
Le Petit Saigon
La Ville d'Ils
Metropolitan Diner ⓰
Milestone's ❺
Millos ❼
Ocean Phoenix Restaurant ⓲
Pablo's Dining Lounge ❶
Pagliacci's ❾
Rattenbury's
Seafood Restaurant ㉑
Taj Mahal ㉖
Wah Lai Yuen ㉒

5105

vegetables. Steak Stefanie (in a Grand Marnier sauce) is another favorite. On-street parking.

PABLO'S DINING LOUNGE, 225 Quebec St., at Pendray St. Tel. 388-4255.
  Cuisine: FRENCH. **Reservations:** Recommended. **Bus:** 30 to Montreal and Superior.
$ Prices: Appetizers $4.95–$8.95; main courses $13.95–$25. AE, MC, V.
  Open: Dinner only, daily 5pm to around 11pm.

Housed in a beautifully refurbished Edwardian home near Laurel Point, this restaurant is as famous for its food as it is for its Spanish coffee. It's served with the ritual showmanship patrons have come to expect from owner Pablo Hernandez, who came to Canada from Spain via London.

Seafood is a specialty; the paella valenciana is Victoria's best. If you've had enough marine bounty, go for the Saltspring rack of lamb, the chateaubriand forestière, or the marinated chicken tikka. Dessert and coffee are served with live entertainment Wednesday through Saturday nights. Parking is free.

BUDGET

JAMES BAY TEA ROOM, 332 Menzies St., at Superior St. Tel. 382-8282.
    Cuisine: ENGLISH. **Reservations:** Recommended. **Bus:** 5.
$ **Prices:** Lunches $4.25–$8.25; dinners $9.25–$11.25. MC, V.
    Open: Breakfast Mon–Sat 7–11:30am, Sun 8am–12:30pm; lunch Mon–Sat 11:30am–4:30pm; tea daily 1–4:30pm; dinner daily 4:30–9pm.

Portraits of Queen Elizabeth II and her father, King George VI, hang on the walls of this small white frame house behind the Parliament Buildings. It's English through and through. Hearty breakfasts, like eggs and kippers, are served daily. Lunch features steak-and-kidney pie, Welsh rarebit, and Cornish pasties. A dinner favorite is roast beef and Yorkshire pudding; nightly specials are priced no higher than $10.50. Afternoon tea includes scones with whipped cream and jam.

2. DOWNTOWN/OLDE TOWN

EXPENSIVE

CHAUNEY'S RESTAURANT, 614 Humboldt St., near Government St. Tel. 385-4512.
    Cuisine: CONTINENTAL. **Reservations:** Recommended. **Bus:** 5.
$ **Prices:** Appetizers $3.75–$8; main courses $15–$22 at dinner. AE, ER, MC, V.
    Open: Lunch Mon–Fri 11:30am–2:30pm; dinner daily 5–11pm.

Subdued luxury is the watchword at this near neighbor of the Empress. Swelling settees, soundless carpets, soft lighting, and a general air of total devotion to the pleasures of gastronomy, Mozart, and budding artists. The paintings and stained-glass windows represent the owner's commitment to promoting the city's artisans; the portraits of distinguished patrons are specially commissioned. Live classical entertainment is likewise presented by young Victoria musicians.

Though the art might sometimes be unacclaimed, the menu is very well established. Local seafood is carefully separated from imported delicacies. You can start with oysters Florentine and follow up with king crab Pernod. For dessert, try possibly the richest and most alcoholic baba au rhum on the island. There's a covered parking lot two blocks north at Gordon and Broughton Streets.

CHEZ PIERRE, 512 Yates St., at Wharf St. **Tel. 388-7711.**
   Cuisine: FRENCH. **Reservations:** Required. **Bus:** 23 or 24 to
   the Johnson St. Bridge.
$ Prices: Appetizers $5.75–$7.95; main courses $15.95–$19.95.
   AE, MC, V.
   Open: Dinner only, Mon–Sat 6pm to around 10pm.
In the very heart of Olde Town is this small, delightfully authentic
French eatery, a magnet for those who know about Gallic food and
the tourists they tell about it. Through the wrought-iron gates is an
atmosphere of charming French provincial decor. This is one of the
oldest restaurants in Victoria, according to owner Jean-Pierre Mer-
cier.

   The escargots are superb as an appetizer, while the rack of lamb
and the canard à l'orange (duck in orange sauce) continue to draw
rave reviews from patrons. B.C. salmon, Dover sole, and scallops
highlight the seafood list. Desserts are prepared fresh daily. There's a
parking lot at Yates and Langley Streets.

HOLYROOD HOUSE, 2315 Blanshard St., at Bay St. **Tel.
382-8833.**
   Cuisine: SCOTTISH. **Reservations:** Recommended. **Bus:** 6
   to Bay and Quadra.
$ Prices: Lunch $7.75; dinner $18; Thurs buffet $13.50; Sun
   brunch $13.50. AE, MC, V.
   Open: Lunch Tues–Fri 11:30am–2pm; dinner Thurs–Sun 5–
   9pm; brunch Sun 11:30am–2:30pm.
Named for the royal palace in Edinburgh, this unique baronial
building serves as the clubhouse of the Sons of Scotland and the
Caledonian Society. Though it was built only in 1957, it has an
atmosphere of medieval times—especially with its decor of Scottish
antiques and artifacts, among them the only known replica of a
13th-century Sir William Wallace sword. Authenticity carries to the
two dining rooms: The Scotia Lounge has a motif of highland
tartans; the Tartan Room (for nonsmokers) has a red tartan floor.

   Come here when you're hungry—service is buffet style, all-you-
can-eat. Savor the Scottish steak pie (without kidneys) or haggis, or
stick to a more North American regimen of international salads,
homemade soups, ham, turkey, roast beef, and salmon. Free parking.

LA VILLE D'IS, 26 Bastion Sq. Tel. 388-9414.
   Cuisine: BRETON. **Reservations:** Recommended. **Bus:** 5.
$ Prices: Appetizers $5.45–$7.45; main courses $4.95–$9.25 at
   lunch, $16.05–$22.45 at dinner. AE, DC, DISC, MC, V.
   Open: Lunch Mon–Sat 11:30am–2pm; dinner Mon–Sat 5:30–
   10pm.
An ancient Breton legend tells of a magical island city-
kingdom inundated 1,500 years ago by divine powers because
of royal debaucheries. The kingdom's name—and its rarely
experienced Breton cuisine—have survived at this intimate two-story
brick restaurant tucked away behind the Maritime Museum.

   Brittany native Michel Dutteau has preserved the seafood cuisine
of his homeland in such hors d'oeuvres as pâté aux moules (mussels)
and cotriade de Cornouailles (fish chowder); and entrées like lotte à
l'armoricaine (monkfish in garlic, cognac, and Mâcon wine) and
soufflé de homard (lobster soufflé with prawns). For non-lovers of fish,
there's a lapin chasseur (marinated rabbit in red-wine sauce). Chocolate mousse is a dessert favorite. Lunch specialties include seafood

vol-au-vent and crêpe crab Mornay. There's a covered parking lot at Yates and Langley Streets.

MODERATE

BANGKOK SEAFOOD PALACE, 1205 Wharf St., at Bastion Sq. Tel. 384-4899 or 384-0899.

Cuisine: THAI. **Reservations:** Recommended. **Bus:** 5.

$ Prices: Appetizers $5.95–$12.95; main courses $5.95–$8.95 at lunch, $9.95–$19.95 at dinner. AE, MC, V.

Open: Lunch Mon–Sat noon–2pm; dinner Mon–Sat 5–9:30pm.

"Authenticity" is the watchword at this establishment. Turn over the nickel/bronze cutlery and read "Thailand" on the handles. Walk past the bar and examine the transplanted Thai pedicab, seemingly waiting to transport passengers to the Far East.

Palates, too, await transportation to those culinary environs. Appetizers include shrimp spring rolls with spicy plum sauce, and tom yum talay, a hot-and-sour seafood soup. You can make quite a meal out of a "yum scallop" salad, pahd thai kung (rice noodles with prawns) and pla sam rot (deep-fried red snapper filet topped with the chef's special sauce). Most menu items are "asterisked" with one or two red chili peppers denoting degrees of spiciness; the waiter will inquire about your preference. Parking is free on the street or $1.25 at a nearby lot.

CAMILLE'S, 45 Bastion Sq. Tel. 381-3433.

Cuisine: CREATIVE CONTINENTAL. **Reservations:** Recommended. **Bus:** 5.

$ Prices: Appetizers $4.95–$5.95; main courses $12.25–$16.95. MC, V.

Open: Dinner only, Tues–Sat 5:30–10pm.

This find in the basement of Victoria's Old Law Chambers is a delightful and romantic experience. Tiffany-style lamps and wood partitions, accented by the original brick walls, create an atmosphere of mystery and intimacy.

The menu is more imaginative than mysterious. You might start with smoked salmon pinwheels with avocado and horseradish cream, or baked elephant garlic served with tawny port and cranberry chutney. Suggested entrées include grilled pepper steak with marsala-cream sauce; eggplant, spinach, and red pepper curry; and Portuguese pork tenderloin and clams baked with sherry, paprika, and caramelized apples. The homemade desserts are completely scrumptious. There's a parking lot at Langley and Fort Streets.

CHANDLER'S, 1250 Wharf St., at Yates St. Tel. 386-3232.

Cuisine: SEAFOOD. **Reservations:** Recommended. **Bus:** 23 or 24 to the Johnson St. Bridge.

$ Prices: Appetizers $3.95–$5.95; main courses $9.95–$18.95; oyster bar $4.95–$8.95. AE, DC, ER, MC, V.

Open: Lunch daily 11:30am–5pm; dinner Mon–Thurs 5–10pm, Fri–Sat 5–10:30pm, Sun 5–9:30pm.

⑤ You can't miss this building—its north wall is painted with an exquisite mural, depicting the orcas (killer whales) of the surrounding waters. Readers of *Best of Victoria* magazine voted it their favorite seafood restaurant. Originally a ship chandlery (thus the name), it has a sporty decor, with hardwood floors and green trim. Historic photos of the Port of Victoria hang on the walls, and easy-listening music plays continuously.

Full dinners are served upstairs, with entrées like barbecued tiger prawns, teriyaki salmon, and Caribbean lobster tail. But Shawkey's Raw Bar & Grill, a ground-floor oyster bar, seems to be crowded all the time. At least half a dozen different West Coast and East Coast oysters are offered daily, along with Dungeness crab, grilled halibut, steamed Manila clams, seafood Caesar salad, and specialty sandwiches (like the salmon croissant). There's a covered parking lot at Yates and Langley Streets.

DA TANDOOR, 1010 Fort St., near Vancouver St. Tel. 384-6333.

Cuisine: NORTHERN INDIAN. **Reservations:** Recommended. **Bus:** 1.

$ Prices: Appetizers $3.95–$7.95; main courses $6.95–$14.95; combination dinners $12.95–$17.95. MC, V.

Open: Lunch Tues–Fri 11:30am–2:30pm; dinner Tues–Sun 5–10:30pm.

An elaborately beautiful restaurant with a small dining patio in front, this one's near the east end of Antique Row. The interior gleams with ornamental copperware, in an aromatic atmosphere of spices and incense, with soft, melancholy sitar strains in the background and quietly impeccable service.

The menu is vast and takes some studying. There are cold and hot appetizers like shrimp pakora (marinated in yogurt and ginger), a hearty mulligatawny soup, and plates of Indian tidbits called samosas. Tandoori (oven-baked) dishes are the specialty, but the chicken curry with ground cashew nuts is also excellent, as is the saag gohst, a lamb preparation. Indian desserts include kulfi, a traditional ice cream. Street parking.

DON MEE RESTAURANT, 538 Fisgard St., Chinatown. Tel. 383-1032.

Cuisine: CANTONESE/SZECHUAN. **Bus:** 4, 10, or 14 to Douglas Street.

$ Prices: Three-course dinner (for two people) $22–$30. AE, DC, MC, V.

Open: Lunch Mon–Fri 11am–2:30pm, Sat–Sun and holidays 10:30am–2:30pm; dinner daily 5pm–closing.

A four-foot, gold-colored laughing Buddha, holding auspicious offerings of fruit in his upstretched arms, greets visitors at the foot of the stairs leading to this large and elegant room. Established in the 1920s, Don Mee's has updated its decor (lots of glass) and musical selections (modern jazz and pop), but still serves such tasty basic fare as dim sum, chop suey (13 kinds), sweet-and-sour spareribs, Szechuan-style seafood, and a special Cantonese "sizzling hot-iron plate."

THE GRAND CENTRAL CAFE, 555 Johnson St., opposite Market Sq. Tel. 386-4747.

Cuisine: CALIFORNIAN. **Reservations:** Recommended. **Bus:** 23 or 24 to the Johnson St. Bridge.

$ Prices: Appetizers $3.95–$7.50; main courses $7.95–$14.95 at dinner. MC, V.

Open: Lunch Mon–Sat 11:30am–2:30pm; dinner Sun–Thurs 5:30–10pm, Fri–Sat 5:30–11pm; brunch Sun 11am–2:30pm.

★ The best time to visit this spacious, elegant old brick structure is in summer, when the beautiful rear courtyard—with its classic fountain surrounded by flowering plants—is open for dining. Then the crowds come out for the splash of sunshine, just as they do in Monterrey.

That's what California style is all about: a little sun, a lot of choice. Pasta dishes are a specialty; they include pasta Carciofi (with marinated mushrooms, artichoke hearts, and red onions in olive-oil sauce, topped with feta cheese) and pasta Simone (with ginger, garlic, and prawns). Some diners prefer the chicken Rochambeau, the jambalaya, the tortilla sincronizade, or Pecos pescados—halibut in a pecan gratin. If you're still hungry, have a slice of key lime pie. For a "lighter" meal, enjoy the famous six-spice bread with the soup of the day: "If one's not enough, the next one's on us!" Street parking.

HERALD STREET CAFFE, 546 Herald St., near Government St. Tel. 381-1441.
   Cuisine: NOUVELLE/PASTA. **Reservations:** Required. **Bus:** 4, 10, or 14 to Douglas Street.
$ **Prices:** Appetizers $4.50–$7; main courses $5.50–$9 at lunch, $11.50–$17.95 at dinner. AE, ER, MC, V.
   Open: Lunch Wed–Sat 11:30am–3pm; dinner Sun–Wed 5:30–10:30pm, Thurs–Sat 5:30pm–midnight; brunch Sun 10am–3pm.

★ Exceptionally popular among young artistic types, this casual Olde Town restaurant, a block north of Chinatown, is in fact a gallery of local art—all of it for sale. But the beautiful fresh flower arrangements, potted palms, and hanging lamps wouldn't keep the intelligentsia—some in jeans, some in jacket and tie—coming if the food weren't also good.

The bistro is noted for its pastas—fettuccine, spinach linguine, canneloni, and others—made fresh daily and served many ways. Try it with steamed mussels in coconut milk, or with shrimp, puréed ginger, and roasted cashews. Other entrées include chicken sautéed with marinated black currants and blackberry cabernet, and a fish steamer (local whitefish with Cantonese black beans and vegetables, served with curried yogurt or creamy garlic). The wine list is a provincial gold-medal winner. On-street parking.

HUNAN VILLAGE, 546 Fisgard St., Chinatown. Tel. 382-0661.
   Cuisine: HUNANESE. **Reservations:** Not required. **Bus:** 4, 10, or 14 to Douglas Street.
$ **Prices:** Appetizers $3.95–$8.95; main courses $8.95–$12.95. AE, MC, V.
   Open: Lunch Mon–Sat 11am–4pm; dinner Mon–Sat 4–11pm, Sun 5–10pm.

The cuisine of the south-central Chinese province of Hunan is not intended for tender palates. Like that of its western neighbor, Szechuan, Hunanese food is quite spicy, but if it's prepared well, delicate flavors will still come through.

Here, in a room that has eschewed the ostentation of some Chinese designers for simple elegance, it *is* prepared well. Try the hot-and-sour beef or chicken, the braised rock cod, the harvest pork, or the kung pao shrimp. Street parking.

LE PETIT SAIGON, 1010 Langley St., near Fort St. Tel. 386-1412.

Cuisine: VIETNAMESE. **Reservations:** Not required. **Bus:** 5 to Douglas Street.

$ Prices: Appetizers $2.50–$6.95; main courses $4.95–$6.95 at lunch, $5.50–$14.95 at dinner. AE, MC, V.

Open: Lunch Mon–Sat 11am–2pm; dinner Mon–Thurs 5–9:30pm, Fri–Sat 5–10:30pm.

Vietnamese cuisine is a harmony of East and West—Chinese-inspired tempered by a century of French influence. Here, the light, subtle tastes are exquisitely done. Spring rolls, shrimp salad, brochettes, hot-and-sour seafood soup, shrimp on sugarcane, crêpes, lamb curry—you can't go wrong. A covered parking lot is next door.

METROPOLITAN DINER, 1715 Government St., between Fisgard and Herald Sts. Tel. 381-1512.

Cuisine: NOUVELLE. **Reservations:** Recommended. **Bus:** 4, 10, or 14 to Douglas Street.

$ Prices: Appetizers $3.85–$6.25; main courses $10–$19 at dinner. MC, V.

Open: Lunch Mon–Fri noon–2pm; dinner Sun–Thurs 5:30–11pm, Fri–Sat 5:30–midnight.

Talk about eclectic! But then, there are clues. The moment you enter, you'll realize that this is a stylish, upscale restaurant, not a diner; and Victoria isn't exactly a metropolis, either.

It's the menu—some describe it as a blend of California, the Continent, and the Far East—that has tongues wagging. How about a Castillo bleu cheese pizza with sliced green apple and caramelized onion? Charcoal-broiled chicken breast served with a sauce of mango chutney and brandied carrots? Prawns, scallops, and fresh fish sautéed with sweet peppers and fresh basil on a bed of julienned zucchini? It may raise eyebrows, but it all works. So do the delicious desserts, like the oddly named "chocolate bag." Street parking.

MILLOS, 716 Burdett Ave. Tel. 382-4422 or 382-5544.

Cuisine: GREEK. **Reservations:** Recommended. **Bus:** 2.

$ Prices: Appetizers $2.25–$17.95; main courses $4.25–$8.50 at lunch, $8.95–$18.95 at dinner. AE, DC, ER, MC, V.

Open: Lunch Mon–Sat 11:30am–4:30pm; dinner daily 4:30–11pm.

This windmill (*millos*) of fun is just half a block from the Victoria Conference Centre. Its white Mediterranean decor spills across five seating levels; there's a full mural of the Parthenon on one wall, Grecian urns with dried-flower arrangements against another, dolls and curios around a central fireplace. Three folk dancers invite the audience to join them weaving around the floor Friday and Saturday nights, and a belly dancer entertains an hour later (nightly in summer).

Owner George Mavrikos has seen to it that the food is genuine and the portions generous. The dolmades (stuffed grape leaves) and saghanaki (sharp cheese fried in butter and flambéed in brandy) are fine starters. Entrées include moussaka, lamb or halibut souvlaki, and kota kapama (a chicken casserole); non-Greek dishes are also on the menu, like baby back ribs and steaks. For dessert, consider yogurt with walnuts and honey. There's parking adjacent.

OCEAN PHOENIX RESTAURANT, 509 Fisgard St., Chinatown. Tel. 382-2828.

Cuisine: CANTONESE. **Reservations:** Not required. **Bus:** 4, 10, or 14 to Douglas Street.

$ Prices: Appetizers $5.25–$8.95; main courses $5.75–$25.95; three-course dinner (for two people) $18.50–$47.50. AE, ER, MC, V.

Open: Sun–Thurs 11am–10pm, Fri–Sat 11am–11pm.

It's unusual in North America to see the shrine of a Taoist god so prominently displayed in a restaurant, as it is here. Perhaps that's a good sign: No chef or server is likely to falter when they're being watched so closely.

One way to determine the quality of a Chinese restaurant is to see if it has shark's-fin or bird's-nest soup on the menu. Ocean Phoenix has both. It also has mashed winter melon and dry scallop soup, fish-maw soup with shredded chicken, duck-web hot pot, braised abalone with oyster sauce, crab in ginger and onions, and diced pork with walnuts. Talk about authentic! The restaurant, by the way, is handicapped-accessible. Park on the street or in the adjacent parkade.

PAGLIACCI'S, 1011 Broad St., near Broughton St. Tel. 386-1662.

Cuisine: ITALIAN/JEWISH. **Reservations:** Not accepted. **Bus:** 5 to Government Street or 30 to Douglas Street.

$ Prices: $8–$14 per dish. MC, V.

Open: Daily 11:30am–12:30am (light menu 3–6pm).

★ A happy and convivial mixture of Italian restaurant and New York nightclub, with possibly the most enthusiastic clientele in town, Pagliacci's is outrageously popular. Tables are so close together that you can spoon your neighbor's soup, and the vibes are so good that you hardly need the laid-on entertainment. The casual atmosphere here is perfect for people-watching. The bad news is that it's always crowded, and you may have to wait in line for the privilege; the good news is that people-watching's just as good in line! (When owner Howie Segal, a transplanted New Yorker, threw a party at Beacon Hill Park for his eatery's 10th anniversary, 25,000 people came!)

The food, perhaps surprisingly, is not secondary to the ambience. Delicious pastas and crêpes, and entrées like chicken marsala and veal parmesan, make zesty meals. Late-night arrivals often enjoy a cup of cappuccino and one of Pagliacci's melt-in-your-mouth desserts. There's a covered parking lot at Gordon and Broughton Streets.

RATTENBURY'S, 703 Douglas St., at Belleville St. Tel. 381-1333.

Cuisine: FAMILY STYLE. **Reservations:** Recommended at dinner. **Bus:** 5 or 30.

$ Prices: Appetizers $3.95–$7.95; main courses $5.95–$10.95 at lunch, $9.95–$17.95 at dinner. MC, V.

Open: Lunch daily 11:30am–4pm; dinner daily 4–10pm.

Housed in the south wing of the famed Crystal Gardens, and named for the architect who built the adjacent Empress Hotel, Rattenbury's might be construed as a relic. Quite the opposite is true: It's a modern, upscale restaurant, boasting a pleasant outdoor eating area where diners can watch the city stroll by.

Those outdoor seats are especially popular in summer, when barbecued salmon (marinated in pesto, grilled over charcoal) is the meal of choice. Anytime, Rattenbury's has such light lunchtime fare as homemade soups, papaya with shrimp salad, crêpes, quiche, and burgers; and gourmet dinners such as prime rib, steak Oscar, halibut Pacifica, and seafood Thermidor. There's also a children's menu. Dessert? Try the Nanaimo bars. There's parking in the Parkade at the Empress Hotel.

TAJ MAHAL, 679 Herald St., near Douglas St. Tel. 383-4662.

Cuisine: INDIAN. **Reservations:** Recommended. **Bus:** 4, 10, or 14 to Douglas Street.

$ Prices: Appetizers $2.95–$5.50; main courses $7.95–$15.95. AE, DC, MC, V.

Open: Lunch Mon–Fri 11:30am–2pm, Sat noon–2:30pm; dinner daily 5:30pm to about 10:30pm.

The domes and minarets of the exterior, while not exactly mimicking Shah Jahan's Agra tomb, hint at an exotic dining experience within—and that's what you get. It could be New Delhi, as servers in saris walk gracefully through a decor of imported Indian arts and crafts.

The food is superb: beef vindaloo, lamb biryani, fish masala, chicken tikka, mouth-watering tandoori dishes baked in a proper clay oven. There's also a menu for vegetarians. Everything is prepared according to the diner's palate: spiced mild, medium, hot, or very hot. For the latter category, you'd best be a native. Drink fresh mango juice or sweet lassi to refresh your palate throughout the meal and finish with an Indian dessert or chai (sweet, spiced Indian tea). There's a covered parking lot at The Bay, one block east.

BUDGET

CAFE MEXICO, 1425 Store St. Tel. 386-5454.

Cuisine: MEXICAN. **Bus:** 23 or 24 to the Johnson St. Bridge.

$ Prices: Appetizers $2.75–$15; main courses $4.95–$10.95. AE, DC, MC, V.

Open: Sun–Thurs 11:30am–11pm, Fri–Sat 11:30am–midnight.

A low-lit brick room decorated with lots of greenery and souvenirs from south of the (U.S.) border, this casual restaurant at Market Square is popular with a younger set. Salsa music plays not-so-softly in the background, while the kitchen serves up the usual fare of enchiladas, tacos, burritos, chiles rellenos, chimichangas, and fajitas. One dish worth requesting is vista del mar, a grilled flour tortilla topped with prawns and scallops in a wine-cream sauce, covered with melted cheese, avocado, and sour cream.

FOGG N' SUDS, 711 Broughton St., near Douglas St. Tel. 383-BEER.

Cuisine: INTERNATIONAL. **Bus:** 1, 2, or 5 to Douglas Street.

$ Prices: Appetizers $1.75–$6.50; main courses $5.95–$12.95. AE, MC, V.

Open: Mon–Sat 11am–1am, Sun 11am–11pm.

One of a growing chain of B.C. pub restaurants, Fogg n' Suds boasts an international menu: for example, American hamburgers, Mexican nachos, Italian pastas, Tokyo stir-fries, Greek calamari, and German schnitzel. The pub is named in part for Phileas Fogg (of *Around the World in 80 Days*), but the "Suds" take priority: Canada's largest beer list has some 250 brews from 36 countries. (Customers get "passports" stamped for each new beer they consume.) The Victoria restaurant is one of the chain's most elegant, with a rich wood decor.

KWONG TUNG SEAFOOD RESTAURANT, 548 Fisgard St., Chinatown. Tel. 381-1223.

Cuisine: DIM SUM/CANTONESE. **Bus:** 4, 10, or 14 to Douglas Street.

$ Prices: Three-course dinner (for two people) $13.50–$21. AE, MC, V.

Open: Lunch daily 11am–3pm; dinner Mon–Thurs 5pm–midnight, Fri–Sat 5pm–1am, Sun 5–10pm.

Just 26 steps above the rest of Chinatown, this spacious dim sum palace obviously believes in fortune and luck: The linen, hanging lanterns, and other trim are all symbolically red, and the placemats elucidate the Chinese zodiac. Luncheon diners enjoy dim sum, the Asian answer to petits fours; at dinnertime there's a good choice of the likes of garlic black-bean beef, scallops with pea pods, and oysters with ginger and onions—as well as chow mein, chop suey, and other San Francisco–style favorites.

MILESTONE'S, 812 Wharf St. Tel. 381-2244.

Cuisine: CALIFORNIAN. **Reservations:** Not required. **Bus:** 5.

$ Prices: Appetizers $3.50–$5.95; main courses $5.95–$9.95 at brunch, $5.95–$12.95 at dinner. AE, DC, MC, V.

Open: Brunch Mon–Fri 11am–4pm, Sat–Sun 10am–4pm; dinner Sun–Thurs 4–10pm, Fri–Sat 4–11pm.

This twin restaurant may have the best view to dine by in Victoria. Located on the Inner Harbour across Government Street from the Empress, it occupies the two lower floors of the same building as the Tourism Victoria Information Centre. The menu at the busy main establishment is eclectic and contemporary, with pastas, seafood, steak, ribs, and burgers. Beneath the main restaurant, the promenade café serves lighter fare in a casual atmosphere; in summer, the doors open wide to a 26-seat outdoor deck. Both restaurant and café have full bars.

PLUTO'S MESQUITE DINER, 1150 Cook St., at View St. Tel. 385-4747.

Cuisine: SOUTHWESTERN. **Reservations:** Recommended on weekend evenings. **Bus:** 5.

$ Prices: Appetizers $3.25–$6.95; main courses $6.25–$10.95; breakfast $4.45–$7.45. MC, V.

Open: Sun–Thurs 9am–11pm, Fri–Sat 9am–midnight.

Located in a converted gasoline station, Pluto's claims to have the "hottest foods from the coolest planet." The neon man-in-the-moon on the wall might even attest to that. In any case, if things get too hot, ceiling fans and large service-bay doors open to summer patio seating to keep things comfortable. Mesquite burgers, quesadillas, satays, mahi mahi, and vegetarian stir-fries are featured. Sharing the spotlight are some of the best desserts in this corner of the solar system—the Belgian chocolate cheesecake will send you to the moon. Folk singers perform Wednesday through Saturday evenings, with an open microphone on Thursday. Parking is free.

WAH LAI YUEN, 560 Fisgard St., Chinatown. Tel. 381-5355.

Cuisine: CANTONESE. **Bus:** 4, 10, or 14 to Douglas Street.

$ Prices: Three-course dinner (for two people) $11.50–$19.75. No credit cards.

Open: Tues–Sat 10am–9pm, Sun 10am–7pm.

This is a thoroughly local café—Formica tables, an open kitchen, no attempt at creating an atmosphere. There's no need: The food speaks for itself. One man's suggestion for a satiating meal: braised minced-beef soup, prawns with black-bean sauce, sweet-and-sour pork, tofu with mixed vegetables, and steamed rice.

3. OUTSIDE THE CENTRAL AREA

VERY EXPENSIVE

SOOKE HARBOUR HOUSE, 1528 Whiffen Spit Rd. (RR #4, Sooke, B.C. V0S 1N0). Tel. 642-3421. Fax 604/642-6988.

Cuisine: WEST COAST. **Reservations:** Required. **Bus:** 61.

$ Prices: Appetizers $6.50–$15; main courses $16–$28. AE, ER, MC, V.

Open: Dinner only, daily from 5:30pm (breakfast and lunch available to overnight guests only).

Victoria's finest restaurant isn't even in Victoria. It's 23 miles (37km) west near the seaside town of Sooke. Acclaimed as "the best restaurant in Canada" by the *Toronto Star,* the Sooke Harbour House offers diners a homey, romantic atmosphere, a spectacular view, and incomparable West Coast–style preparations of local seafood and organically farmed produce. A rambling white house on a bluff overlooking mile-long Whiffen Spit, the restaurant consists of a huge living room (with seating around a blazing fireplace in winter) and two adjoining rooms. Despite its acclaim, it's a come-as-you-are sort of place: Guests are encouraged to come in beach shorts or holiday casuals, if they choose.

Fredrica and Sinclair Philip, who opened Harbour House in 1979, buy from local fishermen and employ three full-time gardeners to help keep their large vegetable and herb patch thriving. The menu changes daily, according to available foods. My dinner at the Sooke Harbour House was as typical (and as satiating!) as any. My starter was shrimp bisque with roe; then abalone sautéed with pear butter and bronze fennel. My entrée of snapper and large shrimp was grilled with spinach, parsley, chives, and nasturtium crème fraîche, and served with beets, parsnips, and wild rice. I concluded with a salad of half a dozen local greens with a raspberry-hazelnut dressing, and a blackberry-and-riesling sabayon with coffee ice cream and hazelnut cookie.

The Philips also have an adjoining 13-room bed-and-breakfast inn. Every room has a different configuration and nature theme; furnishings and art are specially chosen or custom-designed. All rooms have fireplaces, private balconies, and phones; many have hot tubs or Jacuzzis. Rates—which include breakfast, lunch, and an evening decanter of port wine—are $145–$270, with two small rooms for $105 and $125. Parking is free.

EXPENSIVE

CHEZ DANIEL, 2524 Estevan Ave., near Heron St. (off Beach Dr.), Oak Bay. Tel. 592-7424.
  Cuisine: NOUVELLE FRENCH. **Reservations:** Recommended. **Bus:** 1.
$ Prices: Appetizers $5–$9; main courses $13.50–$24. MC, V.
  Open: Dinner only, Tues–Sat 5:30–10pm.

This tiny restaurant—10 tables in two rooms—is the personal domain of Daniel Rigollet, chef de cuisine and maître rôtisseur. There's a comfortable, intimate feeling here, enhanced by the classical music in the air.

Rigollet likes to experiment, based on whatever fresh ingredients are available, and he does so by keeping his recipes flexible. If they're fresh, start with mussels in a rich cream-and-chive sauce; otherwise, consider the consommé Germiny (with sorrel, cream, and egg yolk). Outstanding entrées include lamb with ginger in a cream sauce, duck with chestnuts and sea asparagus, salmon with vermouth and cream, and filet mignon à la moelle. The wine list has won top awards from *Wine Spectator* magazine and the Vancouver International Wine Festival. The desserts (including flambéed crêpes) are no less deserving. Parking is free.

THE LATCH RESTAURANT, 2328 Harbour Rd., Sidney. Tel. 656-6622.
  Cuisine: CONTINENTAL. **Reservations:** Recommended. **Bus:** 70 to Resthaven Drive.
$ Prices: Appetizers $4–$9; main courses $6.50–$10.50 at lunch, $15–$23 at dinner. AE, DC, ER, MC, V.
  Open: Lunch Tues–Fri noon–4pm; dinner daily 5pm to around 11pm; brunch Sun 11am–2pm. **Closed:** Labour Day, Christmas, and three days in Jan.

Five minutes from the Swartz Bay ferry terminal and a half hour from downtown Victoria, this timbered home is on a point of land extending into the Strait of Georgia. Built in 1926 as the private summer retreat of B.C. Lt. Gov. Walter Nichol, it was dubbed "The Latch" by guests who found that every door had been fitted with a latch in place of doorknobs. Today, the private drive leads through expansive gardens with glimpses of Tsehum Harbor and Sidney marinas.

The five dining rooms still have their original fir, beech, and cottonwood paneling. Three of the rooms are entirely private, and may be requested for no additional charge. Diners may start with Caesar salad, prepared tableside. Entrées are imaginative preparations of traditional favorites: Washington rack of lamb served with a ginger-herb demiglaze, breast of duck with a cranberry-orange chutney, or sautéed prawns with a smoked salmon and cream-cheese sauce. Homemade desserts, like Kahlúa torte and chocolate pâté, are served with coffee beside the fireplace in the cozy drawing room. Parking is free.

BUDGET

SIX MILE PUB, 494 Island Hwy. (Colwood exit), View Royal. Tel. 478-3121.
  Cuisine: ENGLISH PUB. **Bus:** 50.

$ Prices: $4.50–$7.50 per dish. ER, MC, V.
Open: Lunch daily 11:30am–2pm; dinner daily 6–9pm. Pub,
Mon–Sat 11am–1am, Sun 11am–midnight.

First opened in 1855 as the Parson's Bridge Hotel, this pub boasts the
longest-established liquor license in British Columbia. The current
building, erected in 1898, has a loyal local clientele. It has a dark
Tudor interior and an outdoor courtyard, and serves standard pub
fare as well as deli-style sandwiches. Free parking.

CHAPTER 13

WHAT TO SEE & DO IN VICTORIA

- **SUGGESTED ITINERARIES**
1. **THE TOP ATTRACTIONS**
2. **MORE ATTRACTIONS**
3. **COOL FOR KIDS**
4. **ORGANIZED TOURS**
5. **SPORTS & RECREATION**

There are three primary aspects to Victoria sightseeing: its parks and gardens, its British heritage (much of it reflected in historic homes and buildings), and its excellent museums. The chances are that you'll experience all of them each day.

SUGGESTED ITINERARIES

IF YOU HAVE ONE DAY Victoria has three essential sights, and today you'll want to see them all. Start with the sights, sounds, even smells, of the Royal British Columbia Museum, western Canada's finest. Cross Belleville Street to the Empress, the city's world-famous hotel, for lunch or (if you've reserved ahead) an early-afternoon tea. Then head north, up the Saanich Peninsula, to spectacular Butchart Gardens (you can travel there by city bus, tour bus, or private car). These gardens are so memorable, you may want to stay for dinner.

IF YOU HAVE TWO DAYS Spend Day 1 as outlined above. Then put on your walking shoes: Victoria is custom-made for walking.

On the morning of your second day, explore the Inner Harbour area, including the Parliament Buildings, the Royal London Wax Museum, the Undersea Gardens, and the Crystal Garden. Lunch at a restaurant or hotel café overlooking the bustle of boats on James Bay. Then head north on Government Street to spend the afternoon touring downtown and Olde Town, with their charming shops and attractions, such as the Maritime Museum (on Bastion Square) and Chinatown. See Chapter 14, "Strolling Around Victoria."

IF YOU HAVE THREE DAYS Spend Days 1 and 2 as outlined above.

On your third day, take the one-mile walk (via Antique Row) or a short bus ride (no. 11) out Fort Street to Craigdarroch Castle, the city's most remarkable Victorian mansion. Nearby is the Art Gallery of Greater Victoria, worth an hour's exploration. Then continue east to fashionable Oak Bay for lunch and the remainder of the afternoon. If you're driving, return along Beach Drive and Dallas Road for gorgeous seascapes across the Juan de Fuca Strait.

IF YOU HAVE FIVE DAYS OR MORE There's lots more to see and do in and around Victoria—heritage homes, small galleries, beautiful parks and gardens. But why not get out and discover Vancouver Island? Dive into the spectacular wilderness, hiking in Pacific Rim National Park or Strathcona Provincial Park, whale-watching from Tofino or Ucluelet, fishing at Port Alberni or Campbell River. Or go low-key and drive to the Native Heritage Centre, the British Columbia Forest Museum, lovely Lake Cowichan, and numerous parks and beaches.

For further information, contact the **Tourism Association of Vancouver Island,** 45 Bastion Sq., Victoria, BC V8W 1J1 (tel. 604/382-3551).

Another option: Ferry to B.C.'s Gulf Islands or Washington's San Juan Islands, all of them isolated jewels with quiet lifestyles.

1. THE TOP ATTRACTIONS

BUTCHART GARDENS, 800 Benvenuto Ave., Brentwood Bay, Central Saanich. Tel. 652-4422, or 652-5256 for a 24-hour recording.

These internationally acclaimed gardens on an arm of the Saanich Inlet, 13 miles (21km) north of Victoria, must not be missed. Comprising 50 acres of a 130-acre (53ha) private estate, they're considered one of the world's greatest horticultural achievements. It's hard to believe that they had their humble beginning in a limestone quarry.

Robert Butchart, a pioneer Canadian manufacturer of Portland cement, established a home on Tod Inlet in 1904. When he exhausted the limestone deposit near their house, his wife, Jenny, hatched a plan to relandscape the eyesore. Importing topsoil by horse and cart from nearby farmland, she slowly converted the quarry into a stunning showcase known today as the Sunken Garden. So impressed was Mr. Butchart that he populated the garden with birds—ducks, peacocks, and trained pigeons. The Butcharts added a Japanese Garden in 1908, an Italian Garden a few years later, and an English Rose Garden in 1929.

As the fame of the gardens grew, the Butcharts left the cement business and turned their house into an attraction of its own, with a bowling alley, indoor saltwater swimming pool, paneled billiard room, and self-playing Aeolian pipe organ. They named their estate Benvenuto, the Italian word for "Welcome." It now houses offices and the Dining Room restaurant.

The gardens today are owned and administrated by a Butchart grandson, R. Ian Ross. More than half a million visitors tour them each year. More than a million plants, in some 700 varieties, ensure uninterrupted bloom from March through October; in winter, the landscaping and shrubbery itself is awesome. Even then, there are plenty of blossoms in the Show Greenhouse.

From June through September, when the gardens are illuminated at night, there's evening musical entertainment every night but Sunday, plus Saturday-night fireworks. The gardens are also lit during the Christmas season (Dec 6–Jan 6).

Facilities include two restaurants: the formal Dining Room for gourmet lunches and dinners, and afternoon tea; and the family-oriented Blue Poppy, offering lunch and afternoon tea in the summer in a flower-filled greenhouse. The Coffee Bar serves snacks and beverages outdoors in summer. The Seed & Gift Store is one of the best spots in Victoria to find quality souvenirs. Wheelchairs, baby carts, cameras, and umbrellas are on loan to visitors.

Admission: Apr–Oct, $11 adults, $5.75 students 13–17, $1.50 children 5–12; Nov–Mar, $5 adults, $3 students, 50¢ children 5–12.

Open: Jan 7–Mar and Oct 16–Dec 6, daily 9am–4pm; Apr and Oct 1–15, daily 9am–5pm; May and Sept 16–30, daily 9am–6pm; June 1–15, daily 9am–7pm; June 16–Aug, daily 9am–10:30pm; Sept 1–15, daily 9am–9pm; Dec 6–Jan 6, daily 9am–10pm. **Bus:** 75.

ROYAL BRITISH COLUMBIA MUSEUM, 675 Belleville St., near Government St. Tel. 387-3701, or 387-3014 for a recorded announcement.

This outstanding museum documents the human and natural history of the province in a series of masterful displays.

Start with natural history on the second floor. Learn about fossil prehistory and regional landforms and vegetation. Then enjoy the vast and impressive dioramas—a coastal rain forest, a seacoast, and the Fraser River delta. Each presents typical flora and fauna of the ecozone; the seacoast exhibit even includes live tidepool dwellers.

The third-floor history section is a place to linger for hours. You'll work backward from the present day to Native Canadian prehistory, and it's a stunning journey! At the top of the escalator, you can compare artifacts from each decade since the 1920s. Then you enter the brick streets and wooden sidewalks of Old Town (1870–1920), a re-created townscape where you can see silent films at the Roxy Theatre, hear a train rumble through the Port Moody station, and smell the cinnamon in the baker's kitchen of the Grand Hotel. Late 19th-century industry is depicted in dioramas or working models of a farm, salmon cannery, sawmill, coal mine, and gold-sluicing operation. The reconstructed hull of Capt. George Vancouver's HMS *Discovery* is the centerpiece of the presentation on exploration and the fur trade.

Native Canadian history and culture take up the other half of the top floor. The exhibition starts with an audiovisual presentation and an exhibit explaining archeologists' methods of studying ancient cultures. Detailed displays, including some dioramas, portray aspects of the peoples' daily lives—highlighted by a sound-and-light show that makes cosmological myths come alive through masks. As you enter the gallery of coastal tribes' art, including totem poles and a longhouse, note the scale model of a Haida village—it took five years to create. Finally, you'll learn about the influence of European settlement on indigenous culture.

The 535-seat Newcombe Auditorium, on the ground floor, presents a marvelous series of evening programs that has included speakers such as Sir Edmund Hillary and scientist and TV personality Dr. David Suzuki. On the adjacent grounds, the Provincial Archives house a wealth of historical documents and photographs, Thunderbird Park hosts demonstrations of tribal totem-pole carving, and 19th-century St. Ann's Schoolhouse is open for inspection.

A tearoom (serving light meals) and an excellent gift shop are located on the main floor.

Admission: Two-day passes, $5 adults, $3 seniors and college students, $2 youths 6–18 and the disabled, free for children 5 and under; $10 families.

Open: May–Sept, daily 9:30am–7pm; Oct–Apr, daily 10am–5:30pm. **Closed:** Christmas Day. **Bus:** 5, 28, or 30.

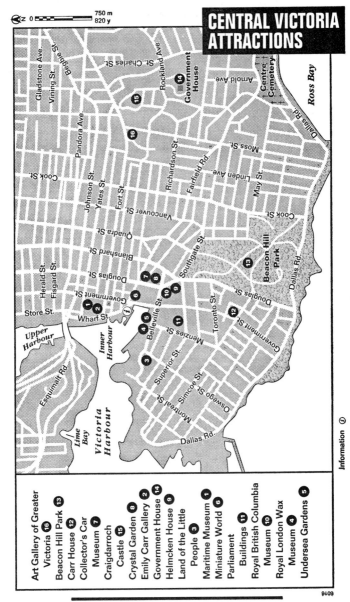

CENTRAL VICTORIA ATTRACTIONS

Legend:

- Art Gallery of Greater Victoria **16**
- Beacon Hill Park **13**
- Carr House **12**
- Collector's Car Museum **7**
- Craigdarroch Castle **15**
- Crystal Garden **8**
- Emily Carr Gallery **2**
- Government House **14**
- Helmcken House **9**
- Land of the Little People **3**
- Maritime Museum **1**
- Miniature World **6**
- Parliament Buildings **11**
- Royal British Columbia Museum **10**
- Royal London Wax Museum **4**
- Undersea Gardens **5**

2. MORE ATTRACTIONS

MUSEUMS & GALLERIES

ART GALLERY OF GREATER VICTORIA, 1040 Moss St., near Fort St. Tel. 384-4101.

Located in a historic mansion in the stately Rockland district, **the** gallery is one of the most important in Canada. Its six halls present permanent collections and temporary exhibits by leading Canadian contemporary artists, important North American and European artists from the 15th to the 20th century, and traditional and contemporary Asian artists. In particular, it houses an extensive collection of Japanese and Chinese art, featuring the only Shinto shrine on display in North America.

The gallery is a collector's piece in its own right. The 1889 Spencer Mansion is a Victoriana-lover's dream. Among its eccentricities is a fireplace faced with rare Minton tiles—each one telling part of the legend of King Arthur.

The Gallery Shop has fine art books and reproductions, while Art Rental and Sales offers original work by regional artists. Prior permission is required to take photographs.

Admission: $4 adults, $2 seniors and students, free for children under 12; free for everyone Thurs 5–9pm.

Open: Mon–Wed and Fri–Sat 10am–5pm, Thurs 10am–9pm, Sun 1–5pm. **Bus:** 10, 11, or 14.

COLLECTOR'S CAR MUSEUM, 813 Douglas St., at Humboldt St. Tel. 382-7180.

Sixty years of vintage automobiles are on display at this small museum behind the Empress. The sheer functional beauty of some of those Packards, Jaguars, Chryslers, and ancient Auburns makes some folks itch to get behind the wheels.

Admission: $5 adults, $4 seniors and AAA members, $3 children, free for children under 8.

Open: May–Oct, daily 9am–6pm. **Closed:** Sept–Apr. **Bus:** 4, 5, 27, 28, or 30.

EMILY CARR GALLERY, 1107 Wharf St., near Fort St. Tel. 384-3130.

Western Canada's most acclaimed artist was a Victoria native. This gallery preserves many of her works, including hundreds of her paintings of totem poles. She was renowned for capturing the early 20th-century lifestyles of coastal tribes.

Admission: $2 adults, $1 students, free for children under 12.

Open: May–Sept, Tues–Sun 10am–5:30pm; Oct–Apr, phone for hours. **Bus:** 5 to Fort and Government.

MARITIME MUSEUM, 28 Bastion Sq., at Langley St. Tel. 385-4222.

A wealth of artifacts and models connected with British Columbia's nautical history are on display here. They include a 36-foot dugout canoe; two famous vessels, the *Tilikum* and the *Trekka;* and various ship models, naval uniforms, photographs, journals, and other artifacts. The museum is housed in the former B.C. provincial courthouse, built in 1889.

Admission: $5 adults, $3 youths 12–17, $2 children 6–12, free for children under 6; 15% family discount.

Open: July–Aug, daily 9am–8:30pm; June and Sept, daily 9am–6pm; Oct–May, daily 9:30am–4pm. **Bus:** 5.

MINIATURE WORLD, 649 Humboldt St., at the Empress. Tel. 385-9731.

An unusual attraction, to say the least, Miniature World began in the late 1960s as the hobby of circus performers Don and Honey Ray.

Fascinated by miniatures, they bought them all over the world when they toured, and assembled them into lifelike dioramas when they got back home.

Today this lilliputian extravaganza in the basement of the Empress has more than 40 displays, depicting everything from historic battles to fairy tales, from the cross-Canada railroad to the world of Charles Dickens, and from an incredible 24-room dollhouse (right down to tiny Delft fireplace tiles) to a circus, with seven animated acts and a midway, that really works!

Admission: $6.50 adults, $5.50 youths, $4.50 children 5–11, free for children under 5; 10% family discount.

Open: June–Sept, daily 8:30am–10pm; Oct–May, daily 9am–5pm. **Bus:** 5, 27, 28, or 30.

ROYAL LONDON WAX MUSEUM, Belleville St., at Menzies St., Inner Harbour. Tel. 388-4461.

If you've never been to a wax museum, or even if you have, this one is fun. Wax figures of the rich and famous (as well as some poor and infamous) have been crafted at world-famous Tussaud's in London and transported here for display.

The cast includes British royalty, past and present (including Charles and Di); great composers, authors, inventors, and other intelligentsia; Storyland characters, among them Snow White and the Seven Dwarfs, Alice in Wonderland, and the Wizard of Oz; a Galaxy of Stars, including Elvis Presley and Marilyn Monroe with her petticoat blowing in the breeze; a Hall of Religion, with great spiritual figures of the ages; and the requisite Chamber of Horrors, a gruesome dungeon of guillotines and Algerian hooks, complete with sound effects.

The exit from the gift shop (don't get too enthusiastic here) leaves you in a parking lot. Circle to your right to return to the main entrance on Belleville Street.

Admission: $6.25 adults, $5 seniors, $5.25 youths 13–19, $3 children 6–12, free for children under 6; $21 families.

Open: May–Aug, daily 9am–9pm; Sept–Apr, daily 9:30am–5pm. **Bus:** 5, 27, 28, or 30.

HISTORIC SITES

CARR HOUSE, 207 Government St., at Simcoe St. Tel. 387-4697.

Situated just a couple blocks from Beacon Hill Park, this quaint 1860s house is notable as the 1871 birthplace of artist-author Emily Carr. Demonstrations and furnishings attempt to re-create her lifestyle. Administered by Victoria Heritage Properties.

Admission: $3.25 adults, $2.25 seniors and students, $1.25 children, free for children under 6. Combined admission to four Victoria Heritage Properties: $6.50 adults, $4.50 seniors and students, $2.50 children; $15 families.

Open: June–Sept, Thurs–Mon 11am–5pm; also for special Christmas events. **Closed:** Oct–May. **Bus:** 5 to Niagara Street.

CRAIGDARROCH CASTLE, 1050 Joan Crescent, near Fort St. Tel. 592-5323.

This splendid stone mansion on a low hill in the Rockland district was built in 1887–89 by Robert Dunsmuir, a Scottish immigrant who made a fortune in coal. He spared no expense on what was essentially a status symbol to announce—to all who cared to notice—that he was the richest and most important man in British Columbia. Dunsmuir died shortly before the house was completed; his widow, Joan, lived here until her death in 1908. Subsequently, it became a veterans' hospital and the seat of Victoria College, the school board, and a conservatory of music. In 1979, the Castle Society began to reconstruct the interior as it appeared in the Victorian age. The society has obtained many of the Dunsmuirs' original paintings and furnishings.

From the outside, Craigdarroch Castle—the name means "rocky oak place" in Gaelic—carries overtones of Dunsmuir's ancestral homeland. Heavy stonework of granite, marble, and sandstone has been shaped into a picture of Elizabethan chimneys soaring above Roman arches, corbeled turrets, and a French Gothic roofline. Within are four floors and 39 rooms with 18 fireplaces, each one different. The finest oak, walnut, mahogany, cedar, spruce, and other woods were used to panel the walls and ceilings, and to create the complicated parquet flooring. Throughout the castle, light is diffracted by art nouveau stained- and leaded-glass windows—one of North America's finest collections.

Admission: $5 adults, $4 students, free for children under 12.
Open: May–Sept, daily 9am–7:30pm; Oct–Apr, daily 10am–5pm. **Bus:** 11 or 14 to Fort Street.

CRAIGFLOWER FARMHOUSE, 110 Island Hwy., Admirals and Craigflower Rds., View Royal. Tel. 387-3067.

One of Vancouver Island's first farmhouses, this building was constructed in 1856. It has been painstakingly restored with many period furnishings from Scotland, home of its original owners. Staff in period costumes conduct demonstrations of crafts and lifestyles, many of them inviting visitor participation. Nearby, the Craigflower Colonial Schoolhouse, oldest standing school building in western Canada, has been restored to its 1855 appearance. Administered by Victoria Heritage Properties.

Admission: $3.25 adults, $2.25 seniors and students, $1.25 children, free for children under 6. Combined admission to four Victoria Heritage Properties: $6.50 adults, $4.50 seniors and students, $2.50 children; $15 families.
Open: June–Sept, Thurs–Mon 11am–5pm; also for special Christmas events. **Closed:** Oct–May. **Bus:** 14.

FISGARD LIGHTHOUSE NATIONAL HISTORIC SITE, 501 Belmont Rd., Colwood. Tel. 380-4662.

The first permanent light on the Pacific coast of Canada was built in 1860. It still guides vessels through the entrance to Esquimalt Harbour, principally to the navy base in Constance Cove on the opposite shore.

Admission: Free.
Open: Daily 10am–5:30pm. **Bus:** 50, then transfer to no. 52.

FORT RODD HILL NATIONAL HISTORIC PARK, 603 Fort Rodd Hill Rd., Colwood. Tel. 363-4662.

The fort on Rodd Hill was constructed between 1895 and 1900 to protect Royal Navy ships in Esquimalt Harbour against an attack from the sea. After the British garrison was withdrawn in 1906, it became a Canadian base and remained active for another 50 years.

Three separate batteries with gun emplacements make up the defense system.

Admission: Free.

Open: Daily 10am–5:30pm. **Bus:** 50, then transfer to no. 52.

HELMCKEN HOUSE, 675 Belleville St. Tel. 387-4697.

The oldest house in British Columbia open to the public, this 1850s residence of a pioneer doctor is a slice of upper-middle-class life 140 years ago. It contains period furnishings and Dr. Helmcken's medicine chest, a superb antiques collection brought from England in the colony's early days. The house is located adjacent to the Royal B.C. Museum, in Thunderbird Park. Administered by Victoria Heritage Properties.

Admission: $3.25 adults, $2.25 seniors and students, $1.25 children, free for children under 6. Combined admission to four Victoria Heritage Properties: $6.50 adults, $4.50 seniors and students, $2.50 children; $15 families.

Open: June–Sept, Thurs–Mon 11am–5pm; also for special Christmas events. **Bus:** 5, 27, 28, or 30.

POINT ELLICE HOUSE, 2616 Pleasant St., near the Bay Street Bridge. Tel. 387-4697.

British Columbia's largest collection of Victoriana—antiques and furnishings from three generations—are found in this beautiful home. It's surrounded by a magnificent garden, which includes roses planted in the 19th century and still blooming today. Administered by Victoria Heritage Properties.

Admission: $3.25 adults, $2.25 seniors and students, $1.25 children, free for children under 6. Combined admission to four Victoria Heritage Properties: $6.50 adults, $4.50 seniors and students, $2.50 children; $15 families.

Open: June–Sept, Thurs–Mon 11am–5pm; also for special Christmas events. **Closed:** Oct–May. **Bus:** 14.

PARKS & GARDENS

BEACON HILL PARK, between Southgate St. and Dallas Rd., Douglas and Cook Sts. Tel. 381-2532 or 361-0600.

Victoria's major city park covers 154 acres (62ha), stretching from just behind the Royal B.C. Museum south three-quarters of a mile to the Juan de Fuca Strait. Within it are groves of trees, gardens, wildflowers, trails, about a mile of pebble beach, and at least a half a dozen ponds—all of them wildlife sanctuaries. Notable among the trees are Garry oaks, unique to this coast of Vancouver Island. A lookout on top of Beacon Hill offers a marvelous view across the strait to Washington's Olympic Mountains. The park also contains what's said to be the world's tallest totem pole (128 ft./39m) as well as a children's farm, aviary, tennis courts, bowling green, putting green, cricket pitch, wading pool, playground, picnic area, and a memorial to Scottish poet Robert Burns.

Admission: Free.

Open: Daily dawn–dusk. **Bus:** 5.

CRYSTAL GARDEN, 731 Douglas St., at Belleville St. Tel. 381-1213.

A lush tropical garden in an all-season greenhouse, Crystal Garden is a fascinating example of adaptive reuse for historic preservation. Across the street from the Victoria Conference Centre, the structure was built in 1925 to hold the largest saltwater pool in the British Empire. Johnny Weissmuller once set a world swimming record here. Ballrooms hosted big-band dances here, and a promenade of flowers hosted many small exhibitions. Soaring maintenance costs forced closure in 1971, but a public outcry prompted the provincial government to invite restoration bids. Crystal Garden reopened about 1980 in its present form.

Today, 47 species of birds live under the glass roof in a garden filled with hundreds of rare and exotic trees, shrubs, and flowers. Flamingos and macaws roam freely; other species are in half a dozen aviaries. Better called a garden *and* a zoo, Crystal Garden has a family of pygmy marmosets, "the world's smallest monkeys," other primates, reptiles, tropical penguins, and a pair of wallabies fill out the menagerie. Colorful koi fish play in the waters of a stream that runs through the middle of the garden. Some endangered species are expected to be added to the collection in the future.

Afternoon tea is served daily on the promenade deck ($7.95 plus admission), and a mall of souvenir shops faces Douglas Street.

Admission: May–Oct, $5 adults, $3 seniors and children; $12 families. Nov–Apr, $3 adults, $2 seniors and children; $7.50 families.

Open: Daily 8am–5:30pm. **Bus:** 4, 5, 27, 28, or 30.

UNDERSEA GARDENS, 490 Belleville St., Inner Harbour. Tel. 382-5717.

A gently sloping stairway takes visitors to a glass-enclosed viewing area at the bottom of the Inner Harbour. There, at eye level, they see some 5,000 marine creatures feeding, playing, hunting, and mating. Among them are sharks, wolf eels, poisonous stonefish, flowerlike sea anemones, and salmon. The highlights are the underwater performances of scuba divers; the star of the show is a huge, ominous, but remarkably photogenic octopus.

Admission: $6 adults, $5.50 seniors, $4.50 students 12–17, $2.75 children 5–11, free for children under 5; $17.50 families.

Open: May–Sept, daily 9am–5pm; Sept–Apr, daily 10am–5pm. **Bus:** 5, 27, 28, or 30.

OTHER ATTRACTIONS

DOMINION ASTROPHYSICAL OBSERVATORY, 5071 W. Saanich Rd., Saanich. Tel. 363-0001, or 363-0012 for a recorded message.

Located atop Little Saanich Mountain just west of Elk Lake, about 10 miles (16km) north of Victoria, this observatory offers stargazers a stunning view of the universe on clear Saturday nights. The view from the top during the day is also worth the drive.

Admission: Free.

Open: Daily 8:30am–4:30pm. Observations Sat 7–11pm only. **Bus:** 74 (limited weekday-only runs).

ENGLISH VILLAGE, 429 Lampson St., near Wychbury, Esquimalt. Tel. 388-4353, or toll free 800/663-6106.

This authentic reproduction of an entire Elizabethan village— William Shakespeare's 16th-century Stratford-upon-Avon— includes the Olde England Inn hotel and restaurant. Shakespeare's birthplace has been replicated, along with the Plymouth Tavern, the Garrick Inn, Harvard House, God's Providence

House, and numerous other buildings, not the least of which is the Olde Curiosity Shoppe. Anne Hathaway's Cottage, the thatched, beamed, and shingled house of Shakespeare's wife, seems to be the main attraction, fully furnished with period antiques. The inn itself is a museum: The entry hall is replete with suits of armor, ancient weaponry, banners, and a huge copper-canopied fireplace. A fine restaurant serves teas and gourmet English food like Cumberland broth and rabbit pye (the original spelling).

Admission: $5 adults, $3 seniors and students 8–17, free for children under 8.

Open: Summer, daily 9am–9pm; winter, daily 10am–4pm. **Bus:** 24.

GOVERNMENT HOUSE, 1401 Rockland Ave., near Lotbiniere St. Tel. 387-2080.

The official residence of the lieutenant governor, who represents the British Crown in British Columbia, is not open to the public—but the grounds are! Lovers of parks and gardens find that the manicured lawns, flowering shrubs, and flower beds make a wonderful place for a stroll.

Admission: Free.

Open: Grounds only, daily dawn–dusk. **Bus:** 1.

PARLIAMENT BUILDINGS, 501 Belleville St., Inner Harbour. Tel. 387-3046.

Architect Francis Rattenbury designed and constructed these buildings in 1897, commemorating the diamond jubilee of Queen Victoria's reign. Lit in the evening by more than 3,000 light bulbs, the buildings are nearly as remarkable a landmark as the Empress hotel. Free tours of the complex—available in several languages, by request—are offered weekdays by reservation, except when the house is sitting.

The British Columbia legislature bears a certain resemblance to the British House of Commons, at least in the ceremonial trappings. The Speaker sits on a kind of canopied throne. He is escorted by a sergeant-at-arms. The symbol of his authority is a golden mace—now purely ornamental, but originally a very handy implement to use on the heads of obstreperous members who "disturbed the assembly."

Admission: Free.

Open: Mon–Fri 8:30am–5pm. **Bus:** 5, 27, 28, or 30.

ROYAL ROADS MILITARY COLLEGE, 2050 Sooke Rd., Colwood. Tel. 363-2000.

There may have been no reason for James Dunsmuir to one-up his late father, Robert Dunsmuir, who built Craigdarroch Castle in 1889. Nevertheless, early in the 20th century, James commissioned noted architect Samuel Maclure to build him a mansion to end all Victorian mansions. Completed in 1908, "Dunsmuir Castle" was indeed enormous—three times the size of Craigdarroch. The grounds, 650 acres at Hatley Park, 8 miles (13km) southwest of Victoria, were so extensive that a crew of over 100 maintained them. Today a military college has taken over Dunsmuir's home—sometimes called Hatley Castle—but the gardens and grounds are open to the public.

Admission: Free.

Open: Grounds only, daily 9:30am–4pm. **Closed:** Last two weeks of Aug and first week of Sept. **Bus:** 52, 53, or 61.

3. COOL FOR KIDS

In addition to the Land of the Little People (below), I have already made a few suggestions (most of them in "More Attractions," above) on how to entertain the children during your Victoria stay:

Beacon Hill Children's Farm, in Beacon Hill Park (see "Parks and Gardens") offers a petting zoo, pony rides, and other activities with young farm animals.

Crystal Garden (see "Parks and Gardens") has free-flying macaws and footloose flamingos that make it an exciting destination.

The animated circus at **Miniature World** (see "Museums and Galleries") is the icing on the cake for kids who have already marveled at the scenes of battles, the railroad diorama, the reborn fairy tales, and the great dollhouse.

The **Royal British Columbia Museum** (see "The Top Attractions") provides a fascinating learning experience. Children especially like the natural-history dioramas, the re-created Olde Town, the hull of Captain Vancouver's ship, and the sound-and-light show on Native Canadian myths.

Some children like the Storyland exhibit at the **Royal London Wax Museum** (see "Museums and Galleries"). Others prefer the Chamber of Horrors. You probably already know which one your kids will like best.

Undersea Gardens (see "Parks and Gardens") are a window into another world. Here, the youngsters can stare down a toothy wolf eel or gawk at a giant octopus.

If you're staying more than a few days with the children, you'll want to get your hands on a copy of *Kids! Kids! Kids! and Vancouver Island,* by Daniel Wood and Betty Campbell (Douglas & McIntyre).

LAND OF THE LITTLE PEOPLE, 321 Belleville St., Inner Harbour. Tel. 385-1735.

Laid out in a charming garden setting is a series of toy delights: a collection of dollhouses, a model railroad (you can run it yourself), an English village green, a pond with Japanese koi fish, a 1900s-style Main Street, and a superb model of London's Tower Bridge. In between are waterfalls, Japanese dwarf bonsai trees and shrubs, a wishing pond, and a Belgian chocolate factory.

Admission: $2.75 adults, $2 seniors and students 12–16, free for children under 12 with parent.

Open: May–Sept, daily 10am–7pm. **Closed:** Oct–Apr. **Bus:** 5, 27, 28, or 30.

4. ORGANIZED TOURS

Perhaps you're a traveler who prefers to let someone else handle your sightseeing arrangements. Transportation, admissions, timing, and narration are things you don't want to worry about. Listed below are several of the tours available:

Gray Line of Victoria, 700 Douglas St. (tel. 604/388-5248, or toll free 800/663-8390), offers bus tours of Victoria and the Butchart Gardens. The 1½-hour "Grand City Tour" costs $12 for adults and

$6 for children. The schedule varies by season, from departures every half hour from 9:30am to 7pm in midsummer to once daily (at 11:30am or 1:30pm) from November 29 to March 13.

The Butchart Gardens tour lasts 3 hours and costs $24.50 for adults, $20.50 for juniors, and $9.75 for children. The schedule varies by season, from departures every hour from 9am to 4pm in midsummer (with a dinner tour at 5pm and an evening tour at 7pm) to once daily (at 1:30pm) in early November and from mid-March to April 17 (no tours from mid-November to mid-March).

Other seasonal tours take in English Village, Marine Drive, Craigdarroch Castle, and lower Vancouver Island (including Chemainus and the B.C. Forest Museum).

Heritage Tours, 713 Bexhill Rd. (tel. 604/474-4332), offers tours of the city, Butchart Gardens, and Craigdarroch Castle in British Daimler limousines. Rates start at $62 per hour per vehicle—not per person. The limo can hold up to six adults.

The pedicabs or bicycle rickshaws operated by **Kabuki Kabs,** Unit 15, 950 Government St. (tel. 604/385-4243), can be found waiting in front of the Empress hotel on Government Street. Prices are negotiable (the company suggests $30–$40 per hour, but the drivers are free to set their own prices) and the cabs will take you "anywhere."

Since 1903, **Tallyho Tours,** 180 Goward Rd. (tel. 604/479-1113), has offered horse-drawn wagon tours of the city. The one-hour tour includes Beacon Hill Park, the waterfront, and heritage homes. The cost is $9.50 for adults, $6.50 for students, $5.75 for youths 13–18, and $4.75 for children under 12 if on a lap. Family rates are $26.50–$28.50. Tours leave June to August, every 15 minutes daily from 9:30am to 7pm; and in April, May, and September, every 20 minutes daily from 10am to 5:30pm. All tours start at the corner of Belleville and Menzies Streets.

Victoria Carriage Tours, 251 Superior St. (tel. 604/382-8509), offers horse-and-carriage tours around James Bay and Beacon Hill Park. The cost is $15–$60 per carriage (maximum of six adults per carriage) for 15–60 minutes. Tours start at the corner of Belleville and Menzies Streets.

5. SPORTS & RECREATION

SPORTS

The **XV Commonwealth Games** is sure to be one of the biggest sporting events in British Columbia in 1994. Second only to the Olympic Games in size, this international competition will be held August 18–28 at venues throughout the greater Victoria area. Events include track and field, gymnastics, cycling, boxing, badminton, shooting, swimming and more. For tickets and other information, contact the Victoria Commonwealth Games Society, P.O. Box 1994, Victoria, BC V8W 3M8 (tel. 604/380-1994).

The normal selection of competitive sports in Victoria is relatively small. The **University of Victoria** men's and women's basketball teams are consistent contenders for the Canadian national collegiate championship. Ice hockey, of course, is a major draw, especially the **Victoria Cougars,** who play a winter-long minor-league schedule in the Western Hockey League against teams from B.C., Alberta, Washington, and Oregon. The Cougars play from September to March at the Victoria Memorial Arena, Blanshard and Caledonia Streets. Games are at 7:30pm; call 604/361-0536 for tickets.

RECREATION

Victoria and Vancouver Island are tremendous places to be if you're an outdoors lover. The following listing can only provide a sampling of what's available.

BEACHES   In this Canadian sun belt, the most popular is **Willows Beach,** along the Esplanade in Oak Bay. It has a park with a playground and snack bar. A good approach is by Dalhousie Street, off Cadboro Bay Road. Other excellent beaches are at **Gyro Beach Park** on Cadboro Bay near the University of Victoria; **McNeill Bay** near Gonzales Point, Victoria's southeasternmost cape; and **Saxe Point Park** and **MacAulay Point Park,** both in Esquimalt.

The inland lakes have fine freshwater swimming, as well: Try **Elk Lake,** on Patricia Bay Road 7 miles (11km) north of downtown Victoria; and **Thetis Lake,** about 6 miles (10km) west. Be aware that at the latter, nude sunbathers often seek out secluded spots.

BICYCLING   This is a favorite way of getting around Victoria. A favored route for visitors is the 8-mile (13km) **Scenic Marine Drive,** following Dallas Road and Beach Drive along the city's south shore, then returning to downtown via Oak Bay Avenue. For rental locations, see "Getting Around" in Chapter 10.

BOATING   Numerous operators have vessels for charter hire, "bareboat" rental, or skippered rental, for periods from a few hours to several weeks. Check **Pedder Bay Marina,** Pedder Bay Drive, Metchosin (tel. 478-1771); and the **Brentwood Inn Resort,** 7172 Brentwood Dr., Brentwood Bay (tel. 652-3151).

Sailors can listen to a taped marine forecast by calling 656-7515. Those unfamiliar with local waters, or unsure of their own skills, might want to consult the **Horizon Yacht Centre,** 1327 Beach Dr., at Oak Bay Marina (tel. 595-2628), or the **Canadian Power Squadrons,** 28 Bastion Sq. (tel. 383-6677).

BUNGY JUMPING   Ever had the desire to dive off a 140-foot bridge, or wondered what it felt like to be a yo-yo? You can fulfill the craziest of urges at **The Bungy Zone** (tel. 604/753-5867), North America's only legally sanctioned bridge jump. At this writing, more than 25,000 leaps, including one airborne wedding, have taken place high over the Nanaimo River from a specially constructed steel trestle. Never have so many placed their trust in a rubber band. Should your nerve fail you (no accidents so far, by the way), it's still fun to watch others take the grand leap of faith. The Bungy Zone is a beautiful, scenic spot complete with picnic tables and forest walks.

Jumps cost $95 for your first leap of the day, $75 for the second (AE, MC, and V accepted). Youths 14–18 may jump with parental consent; children under 14 are not admitted. (The oldest jumper so far is 85.) The Bungy Zone is open daily 10am–4:30pm, year round. Reservations are recommended June through August. The Bungy Zone is located 41 miles (65km) north of Victoria, 8 miles (13km) south of Nanaimo, just off Hwy. 1. Visitors coming from the mainland specifically to jump may want to take the ferry directly to

Nanaimo, either from Tsawwassen (south of Vancouver) or Horseshoe Bay (north of Vancouver).

CANOEING/KAYAKING   The lakes and indented coastline of southeastern Vancouver Island are ideal for the paddle sports. Even more thrilling—for ocean kayaking, in particular—are the offshore Gulf Islands. A growing number of outfitters package trips for visitors. Some of the best are offered by **Gulf Island Kayaking,** 1050 Georgeson Bay, Galiano Island, BC V0N 1P0 (tel. 604/539-2442). The **Victoria Canoe and Kayak Club** (tel. 361-4238) can provide full information on how and where to get started.

DIVING   Both coasts of Vancouver Island have excellent diving. The strong tidal currents around the Gulf Islands, and farther south where the Strait of Georgia meets the Juan de Fuca Strait, create an ideal environment for rich and varied marine life, including abalone, scallops, sea cucumbers, forests of kelp, and much more. Along the coast of Pacific Rim National Park, west of Victoria, a stretch of sea known as "the graveyard of the Pacific" has literally dozens of shipwrecks, most from the late 19th and early 20th centuries. The Cousteau Society ranks Vancouver Island second (to the Red Sea) among the world's best diving destinations.

Information, equipment, and diving courses are available from the **Ocean Centre,** 800 Cloverdale Ave. (tel. 386-7528); and **Frank White's Scuba Shop,** 1855 Blanshard St. (tel. 385-4713).

FISHING   Vancouver Island has some of the best saltwater and freshwater fishing in the world. Many lakes are regularly stocked with rainbow and cutthroat trout and steelhead, while kokanee, char, brown trout, and trophy-size smallmouth bass are common. In the Victoria area, Elk and Beaver Lakes (8 miles/13km north via Patricia Bay Road) and Shawnigan Lake (39 miles/63km northwest via Hwy. 1 and Shawnigan Lake Road) are especially well stocked.

Saltwater fish include all species of Pacific salmon (chinook, coho, pink, sockeye, and chum), halibut, ling cod, rockfish, and snapper.

You need a license to fish in British Columbia if you're 15 (for tidal waters) or 16 (for freshwater or nontidal waters). Regulations change frequently, as dictated by fish conservation studies, so current rules should be checked in the annual B.C. Fishing Regulations Synopsis. No license is required for catching shellfish, though size restrictions apply.

The **B.C. Department of Fisheries** (tel. 387-9591 or 387-9737 during office hours) has a 24-hour phone line open spring, summer, and fall (tel. toll free 800/663-7867). It gives recorded information of interest to every angler: openings, closings, and restrictions; where the big ones are hitting and what lures they're hitting on.

Numerous fishing operators have charters available. Their packages typically include hotel pickup, fishing license, tackle, and a light lunch. Rates vary, but can typically run $90 per person per half-day charter.

GOLF   Golf seems tailor-made for Victoria. The mild climate, the Scottish-English heritage, and the rolling landscape combine to make this an extremely popular year-round sport for residents and visitors alike.

Public courses in or near the city include the **Cedar Hill Municipal Golf Course,** just 2 miles (3.2km) from downtown at

1400 Derby Rd. (tel. 595-3103), and the **Mount Douglas Golf Course,** 4225 Blenkinsop Rd. (tel. 477-8314), about 3½ miles (5.6km) away. The **Cordova Bay Golf Course,** at 5333 Cordova Bay Rd. (tel. 658-4444), northeast of downtown, is the area's newest, most widely acclaimed public course. Numerous other public courses are north, up the Saanich Peninsula, or west, toward Sooke.

Leading private clubs, which may have reciprocal privileges with other North American clubs, include the **Victoria Golf Club,** 1110 Beach Dr., Oak Bay (tel. 598-4321); the **Uplands Golf Club,** 3300 Cadboro Bay Rd., Oak Bay (tel. 592-7313); the **Gorge Vale Golf Club,** 1005 Craigflower Rd., Esquimalt (tel. 386-3401); and the **Royal Colwood Golf & Country Club,** 629 Goldstream Rd., Colwood (tel. 478-8331).

HIKING There are some fine trails in **Thetis Lake Park** and **Goldstream Provincial Park** near Victoria. But serious backpackers head to the huge 810-square-mile (2,100km²) **Strathcona Provincial Park** (200 miles/320km north of Victoria via Hwys. 1 and 19 to Campbell River, then west on Hwy. 28), or to **Pacific Rim National Park** (65 miles/105km west via Hwy. 14 to Port Renfrew).

Strathcona's Forbidden Plateau is speckled with alpine lakes, but the Pacific Rim's **West Coast Trail,** extending 48 miles (77km) from Port Renfrew to Bamfield, is the target of many experienced hikers. Established long ago as a lifesaving trail for shipwrecked sailors, it's rugged and often wet, and takes a week to hike from one end to the other at an average pace. Whales can frequently be seen from the trail. (Bamfield, at the trail's western terminus, is reached by ferry from Port Alberni).

Victoria's **West Coast Outdoor Recreation Society,** 1102 D'Arcy Lane (tel. 658-5139), provides a general information service to hikers planning to tackle the trail. The society also operates a "need-a-partner" computer data bank, and offers summer outings.

HUNTING See "Sports and Recreation" in Chapter 6 for information on hunting licenses and regulations in B.C.

ICE SKATING The most centrally located rink is the **Victoria Memorial Arena,** 1625 Blanshard St. (tel. 361-0538). Others are located at the **George R. Pearkes Recreation Complex,** 3100 Tillicum Rd. (tel. 388-6664); the **Oak Bay Recreation Centre,** 1975 Bee St. (tel. 595-7946); and the **Juan de Fuca Recreation Centre,** 1767 Island Hwy., Colwood (tel. 478-8384). Skates are generally available for rent.

SAILBOARDING This sport—which combines surfboard and sail—is better known as windsurfing. You may see occasional adventurers dodging boats on the Inner Harbour, but novices are usually advised to try **Elk Lake,** 8 miles (13km) north of Victoria, and experts are steered to **Lake Nitinat** in Pacific Rim National Park, some 100 miles (160km) northwest via Lake Cowichan.

Beginning and advanced instruction is offered by **Active Sports,** 1620 Blanshard St. (tel. 381-SAIL). Beginner three-day lessons (including board and wet suit) start at $120. A unique sailboarding simulator helps first-timers get their balance and learn to set the sail before they ever enter the water.

SAILING Lessons are offered by the **Victoria Sailing Acade-**

my, 481 Head St. (tel. 384-7245), and the **Horizon Yacht Centre,** 1327 Beach Dr., at Oak Bay Marina (tel. 595-2628). Many boat charter operators also have sailboats available for rent by experienced sailors.

If you're contemplating a sail to the Gulf Islands, check with the *Hindeloopen* (tel. 604/656-1768).

SKIING The mountains in central Vancouver Island rise to more than 7,200 feet (2,200m). At this latitude (50°N), that's high enough for a snow cover—and good skiing. The Comox Valley, for instance, gets an astonishing annual snowfall of about 472 inches.

The major resort is **Mount Washington,** P.O. Box 3069, Courtenay, BC V9N 5N3 (tel. 604/338-1386), in the Comox Valley, a five-hour drive north of Victoria. The third-largest area in British Columbia, it has a 1,600-foot (492m) vertical drop and 20 groomed runs for novices, intermediates, and experts, serviced by four chair lifts and a beginners' tow. The area also has 19 miles (31km) of track-set nordic trails, connecting to Strathcona Provincial Park. Full-day rates are $29 for adults, with equipment rentals at $18 daily. Open daily in winter. For a snow report, phone 338-1515.

Nearby **Forbidden Plateau,** 2050 Cliffe Ave., Courtenay, BC V9N 2L3 (tel. 604/334-4744), is the island's oldest ski resort, having opened in 1950. It has a 1,150-foot (354m) vertical and 12 groomed runs, with one chair lift, three T-bars, and a rope tow. Full-day adult rates are $23; complete equipment rentals are $16. Open Friday, Saturday, and Sunday in winter. For a snow report, call 338-1919.

The nearest ski area to Victoria is **Mount Arrowsmith,** P.O. Box 265, Port Alberni, BC V9Y 7M7 (tel. 604/723-9592). It's "only" 120 miles (193km) from the British Columbia capital, a solid 3½-hour drive in winter. Arrowsmith caters primarily to novices, with a 1,000-foot vertical, six runs, two T-bars, and a rope tow.

Near the north end of Vancouver Island, **Mount Cain,** P.O. Box 1225, Port McNeill, BC V0N 2R0 (tel. 604/281-0244 or 956-3744), also offers novice alpine and cross-country skiing.

There are several ski shops in Victoria. For rentals, sales, and service, you might try **Snow Magic,** 570 Johnson St. (tel. 383-5655).

SWIMMING The **Crystal Pool,** 2275 Quadra St. (tel. 361-0720 or 380-7946), is Victoria's largest aquatic facility, with a 50-meter lap pool, a separate children's pool, diving pool, sauna, whirlpool, weight and aerobics rooms, and a cafeteria-lounge. It's open 18 hours a day.

Other good public pools are at the **Juan de Fuca Recreation Centre,** 1767 Island Hwy., Colwood (tel. 478-8384); the **Oak Bay Recreation Centre,** 1975 Bee St. (tel. 595-7946); the **Esquimalt Pool,** 527 Fraser St. (tel. 386-2286); the **Gordon Head Recreation Centre,** 1744 Feltham Rd. (tel. 477-1871); and, of course, the **YM-YWCA,** 880 Courtney St. (tel. 386-7511).

All Fun Recreation Park, 650 Hordon Rd. (tel. 474-4546 or 474-3184), is 8 miles (13km) northwest of Victoria, off Millstream Road. In addition to a three-quarter-mile water slide complex, it has a mini-golf course, bumper boats, go-kart track, games parlor, RV park, gift shop, and ice-cream caboose. The Western Speedway drag-racing track is adjacent.

WHALE-WATCHING Most of this takes place on trips from

Tofino or Ucluelet, about halfway up Vancouver Island's west coast. But there is one firm that takes visitors on trips of 1½–3 hours from Victoria's Inner Harbour into the Gulf Islands or San Juan Islands, with sightings of orcas (killer whales) and porpoises likely during the season (May to September). **Sea Coast Expeditions,** 1655 Ash Rd. (tel. 477-1818), has biologist guides aboard its Zodiac boats during their 20- to 50-mile trips. Rates are $45–$70 for adults, $25–$45 for children 6–16. Three-hour "guaranteed" sighting trips are offered from June to September for $70. Sea lions and marine birds are always around.

CHAPTER 14

STROLLING AROUND VICTORIA

1. THE INNER HARBOUR

2. DOWNTOWN/OLDE TOWN

Weather permitting, Victoria lends itself to walking. Both the Inner Harbour and the Downtown/Olde Town area have a high concentration of fascinating landmarks.

WALKING TOUR 1 — THE INNER HARBOUR

Start: Tourism Victoria Information Centre.

End: Tourism Victoria Information Centre.

Time: Not more than 1½ hours to cover the actual route, but all day if you actually visit each of the attractions.

Best Times: Midsummer, when it's warm and dry and the attractions are all open.

Worst Times: Midwinter, when it's chilly and damp and many of the attractions are closed.

1. **Tourism Victoria Information Centre,** at Wharf and Government Streets on the Inner Harbour, is the ideal starting point. With a highly knowledgeable staff, unfailing helpfulness, and an immense stock of maps, timetables, brochures, and pamphlets, the center can save you valuable time and energy by directing you to the places you want to go; it can also inform you about local sights you might otherwise miss.

   Walk south, along the causeway facing James Bay. On your left is the:

2. **Empress Hotel,** 721 Government St. (see Chapter 11, "Victoria Accommodations"). As you follow the harbor shore west, you look south at Victoria's other major landmark, the:

3. **Parliament Buildings,** 501 Belleville St. Beside the province's legislative center lies:

4. **Heritage Court,** a superb combination of concrete buildings and native plant gardens which you enter by stepping over the petrified prints of a dinosaur. The Netherlands Carillon, a gift from the Dutch people, rises like a slender white column 88 feet (27m) from the mall floor, carrying bells weighing 10,612 pounds (4,813kg).

   Opposite the legislative lawns, at Belleville and Menzies Streets, you'll spot some horse-drawn carriages in front of:

5. **Confederation Garden.** From 10am to 11pm, the carriages offer relaxed tours of this corner of Victoria for up to six people (rates per carriage—*not* per person—are about $1 per minute, up to an hour). The centerpiece of the garden, a monument to

Canadian confederation, is a huge bronze sculpture displaying the coats of arms of the 10 provinces and the federal coat of arms.

Across Belleville Street are two of Victoria's major tourist attractions, the:

6. Royal London Wax Museum and:

7. Undersea Gardens, 490 Belleville St. Behind the wax museum is the terminal of Black Ball Transport's MV *Coho,* a ferry that plies the international route to Port Angeles, Wash.

Opposite the terminal, on the south side of Belleville, is the Captain's Palace hotel and restaurant, with its adjacent:

8. Heritage Village and:

9. Land of the Little People, 321 Belleville St. Continue west on Belleville Street and you will come to:

10. Centennial Park, a lovely and painstakingly maintained stretch of city-owned shoreline, includes Laurel Point and the Laurel Point Inn with its views of the Empress to the east and outer Victoria Harbour to the west.

On the shore opposite the promontory rises:

11. Songhees Point Development. Once an industrial zone, this area is now the home of the new Ocean Pointe Resort. It will soon boast a second luxury hotel, condominium towers, restaurants, pubs, and a walkway through the encircling park.

Follow the main thoroughfare west through a series of staggered junctions and you'll come to:

12. Fisherman's Wharf, at St. Lawrence and Erie Streets. Home of Victoria's largest concentration of fishing boats, this is a great place to catch the flavor of the maritime industry—and buy fresh seafood—when the fleet is in.

Return one block north on St. Lawrence and turn east on Superior Street. Continue through three residential blocks to the corner of Menzies Street and you'll find the:

13. James Bay Inn, on your right, one of Victoria's oldest hotels, dating from 1907. It was the last home of the well-known artist Emily Carr.

Cross Menzies and you're in the government district, with the Parliament Buildings on your left and various provincial office buildings on your right. Turn north (left) on Douglas Street. About halfway down the block, bear left into:

14. Thunderbird Park, notable for its awesome wooden totem poles. Here you'll find two important 1850s heritage buildings:

15. Helmcken House, home of a pioneer doctor, and:

16. St. Ann's Schoolhouse, and beyond them, the:

17. Royal British Columbia Museum, 675 Belleville St. Continue north on Douglas across Belleville Street. On your left is the city bus depot, where connections can be made to Vancouver (via ferry) and to other Vancouver Island destinations. On your right is the:

18. Crystal Garden, 731 Douglas St., once the British Empire's largest saltwater swimming pool, now a lovely greenhouse full of tropical vegetation and birds.

Across the street, north of the bus depot, is the:

19. Victoria Conference Centre, 720 Douglas St. (tel. 361-1000). Opened in 1989, this attractive two-level structure accommodates groups of up to 1,500 people. It was designed with an eye to history as well as to efficiency, since it adjoins the

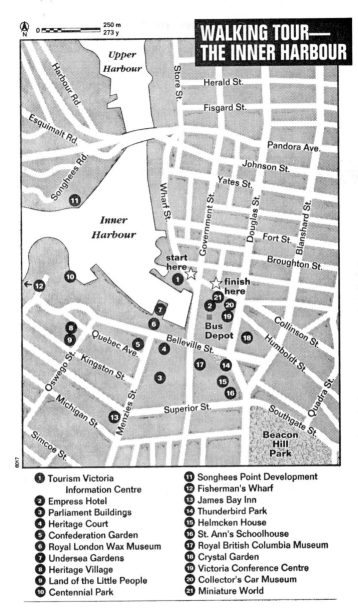

WALKING TOUR— THE INNER HARBOUR

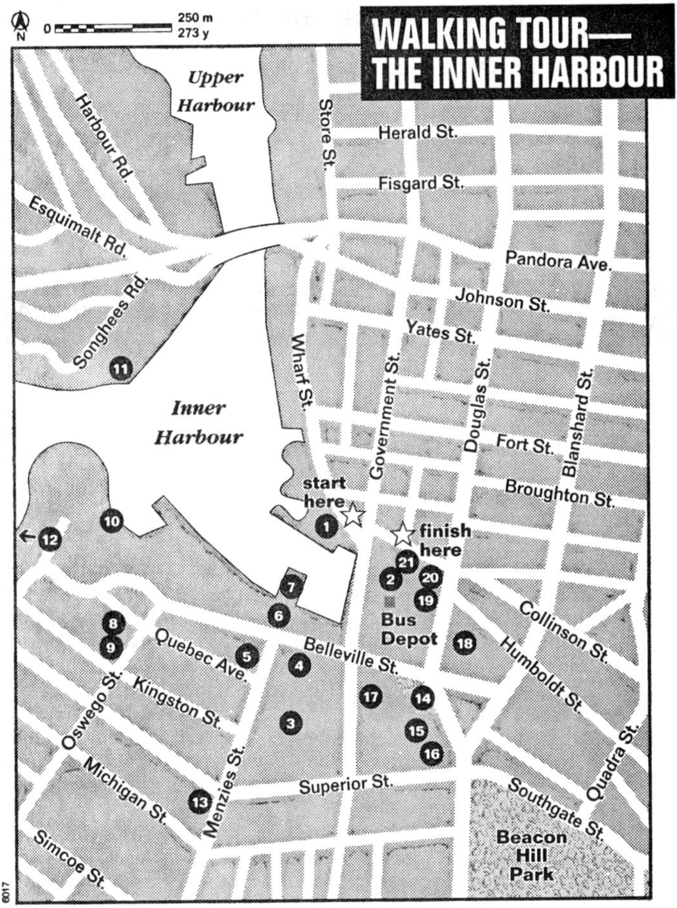
0
250 m
273 y
N
Upper Harbour
Harbour Rd.
Esquimalt Rd.
Songhees Rd.
Store St.
Herald St.
Fisgard St.
Pandora Ave.
Johnson St.
Yates St.
Wharf St.
Government St.
Douglas St.
Blanshard St.
Fort St.
Broughton St.
Inner Harbour
start here
finish here
Bus Depot
Collinson St.
Humboldt St.
Quebec Ave.
Belleville St.
Kingston St.
Oswego St.
Michigan St.
Menzies St.
Superior St.
Southgate St.
Quadra St.
Beacon Hill Park
Simcoe St.
6017

1. Tourism Victoria Information Centre
2. Empress Hotel
3. Parliament Buildings
4. Heritage Court
5. Confederation Garden
6. Royal London Wax Museum
7. Undersea Gardens
8. Heritage Village
9. Land of the Little People
10. Centennial Park
11. Songhees Point Development
12. Fisherman's Wharf
13. James Bay Inn
14. Thunderbird Park
15. Helmcken House
16. St. Ann's Schoolhouse
17. Royal British Columbia Museum
18. Crystal Garden
19. Victoria Conference Centre
20. Collector's Car Museum
21. Miniature World

famous Empress Hotel. The gardens and foyer, both open to the public, display fine art by provincial artists, including a totem pole commissioned by master carver Tony Hunt. (Look for Qwawina, the raven, on top; Sisiutl, the double-headed serpent, in the middle; and Nanis, the grizzly bear, holding a halibut, at the bottom.) Nineteen stores, including arts, fashion, jewelry, and other gift outlets, make up a shopping plaza around the perimeter of the conference center.

At the northeast corner of Douglas and Humboldt Streets is the:

20. **Collector's Car Museum.** Turn left on Humboldt; halfway down this block, in a side door of the Empress Hotel, is:

21. **Miniature World.**

The Info Centre—this walk's starting point—is another half block ahead.

WALKING TOUR 2 —— DOWNTOWN/ OLDE TOWN

Start: Tourism Victoria Information Centre.
End: Tourism Victoria Information Centre.
Time: About 1 hour to Chinatown and another hour to return via Antique Row (if you plan to browse and shop, it's best to plan for a half day).
Best Times: Midsummer.
Worst Times: Midwinter.

1. **Tourism Victoria Information Centre,** at Wharf and Government Streets, is also the beginning point for this walk. Head north on Government Street, a quaint, somewhat narrow thoroughfare lined with shops. The oldest brick building in British Columbia is the:

2. **Windsor Hotel** building (1858), 901 Government St., at the northeast corner of Courtney Street; today, its bricks have been timbered over and it houses gift shops. Canadian Customs is located at the intersection's southwest corner; the two-story Harbour Square Mall shopping plaza is at the northwest corner.

The corner of Broughton and Government Streets, one block north, marks the southeast corner of the former:

3. **Fort Victoria,** constructed by the Hudson's Bay Company in 1843 as the western headquarters of the company's fur-trading empire. Located within the area now bounded by Government and Wharf Streets, Broughton Street, and Bastion Square, it featured 22-foot cedar pickets and two octagonal bastions. It was torn down in 1858 when the Fraser River gold rush led to a real-estate boom.

Just past View Street, a little byway cuts off on the right, running one block to Broad Street. This is:

4. **Trounce Alley,** where bearded miners and roisterous mariners once clustered to spend their gold on female entertainment. A lot of paint, soap, and affection has gone into making this small lane a kind of welcome mat. Lit by gas lamps, hung with heraldic crests, ablaze with flower baskets and potted shrubs, Trounce Alley now offers jewelry, fashions, edibles, and souvenirs.

From Broad Street, circle back west down View Street into:

5. **Bastion Square.** In the late 19th century, this area was bustling with waterfront hotels, saloons, and warehouses. Today it's an enchantingly restored pedestrian mall, with the raucousness tamed down and the renovated old buildings crammed with restaurants, offices, and art galleries.

On the site now occupied by the:

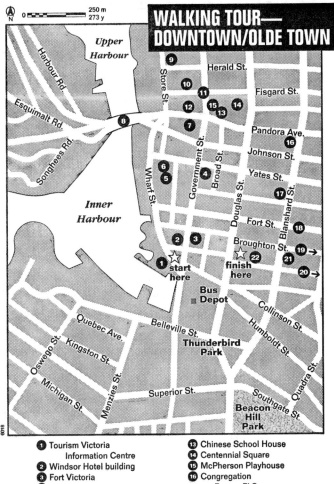

**WALKING TOUR—
DOWNTOWN/OLDE TOWN**

0 ——— 250 m
273 y

Upper Harbour

Herald St.

Fisgard St.

Store St.

Pandora Ave.

Johnson St.

Government St.

Broad St.

Yates St.

Inner Harbour

Wharf St.

Douglas St.

Fort St.

Blanshard St.

Broughton St.

start here

finish here

Harbour Rd.

Esquimalt Rd.

Songhees Rd.

Bus Depot

Quebec Ave.

Belleville St.

Collinson St.

Oswego St.

Kingston St.

Michigan St.

Menzies St.

Superior St.

Thunderbird Park

Humboldt St.

Quadra St.

Southgate St.

Beacon Hill Park

1 Tourism Victoria
   Information Centre
2 Windsor Hotel building
3 Fort Victoria
4 Trounce Alley
5 Bastion Square
6 Maritime Museum
7 Market Square
8 Johnson Street Bridge
9 Harbour Public Market
10 Chinatown
11 Gate of Harmonius Interest
12 Fan Tan Alley

13 Chinese School House
14 Centennial Square
15 McPherson Playhouse
16 Congregation
   Emanu-El Synagogue
17 St. Andrew's Roman
   Catholic Cathedral
18 Antique Row
19 Pioneer Square
20 Christ Church Cathedral
21 Royal Theatre
22 Victoria's Central Library

6. Maritime Museum, 28 Bastion Sq., was the police barracks, where convicted murderers were publicly hanged and buried. Their bones may still lie beneath the paving of the square.

You can get a good feel for the city's historic-preservation efforts by strolling through some of Olde Town's alleyways. From Bastion Square, turn north up Commercial Alley. Cross Yates Street, and a few steps farther west, turn north again up Waddington Alley. On the other side of Johnson Street is:

7. Market Square, a shopping center made up of beautifully restored historic buildings. Its 40-odd stores include seven restaurants, numerous arts-and-crafts shops, bookstores, boutiques, and gift shops. They occupy two levels surrounding an open-air terrace, which is popular for lunching any time of year, but especially on summer weekends when bands and individual musicians often perform for an appreciative audience.

On its western side, Market Square faces the:

8. **Johnson Street Bridge,** the main link between downtown Victoria and the Esquimalt peninsula. The VIA Rail/Esquimalt & Nanaimo Railroad terminal is just across Store Street.

Go north two blocks on Store; across Herald Street, on your left, is the:

9. **Harbour Public Market,** the city's major market for fresh produce. Return down Store Street one block and turn east on Fisgard Street.

You're now in:

10. **Chinatown,** known to many facetious Victoria residents as "China block." In fact, it occupies about 1½ blocks of Fisgard Street. Nevertheless, this is Canada's oldest Chinatown, established in 1858 when the first Chinese arrived as gold-seekers and railroad workers; at one time it covered six city blocks and had a permanent population of around 3,000. Today, most of the buildings are restaurants and gift shops, but three features are of special interest.

Spanning Fisgard on the west side of Government Street is the:

11. **Gate of Harmonious Interest.** Built in 1981, its lavish detail, including dragon-head moldings, symbolized the completion of a major revitalization of the Chinatown area.

Extending one block south from Fisgard, about 50 yards west of the gate, is:

12. **Fan Tan Alley,** the narrowest street in Canada. Not more than four feet wide in places, in the late 19th century this was the main entrance to a maze of streets that comprised "Little Canton." Opium smoking, gambling, and prostitution were rampant behind its doors.

At the east end of Chinatown, halfway down the block between Government and Douglas Streets is the:

13. **Chinese School House** (built in 1907). With its tiled pagoda-style roof, recessed balconies, and "lucky" colors of red and gold, it's the best surviving example of early Chinatown architecture.

Just east is:

14. **Centennial Square,** a 1962 urban-development project which occupies the block south of Fisgard. Surrounding its modernistic fountain and Floral Knot Garden, a replica of one in England's Hampton Court, are the restored 1878 City Hall, the Victoria Police Department, a parking lot, shopping arcade, senior citizens' recreation center, and the:

15. **McPherson Playhouse,** 3 Centennial Sq. (tel. 386-6121). Victoria's main performing arts center occupies the former Pantages Theatre, a vaudeville establishment restored to its 1912 baroque Edwardian style.

From City Hall, at the southeast corner of Centennial Square, proceed east one block on Pandora Avenue. The building at the southeast corner of Blanshard Street is:

16. **Congregation Emanu-El Synagogue,** built in 1863 and now a national historic site. It's the oldest surviving Jewish temple both in Canada and on the west coast of North America.

    If you were to continue farther east on Pandora, you'd encounter a downtown "church row"—Baptist, Methodist, Gospel, and Seventh-Day Adventist places of worship within the next two blocks. Instead, turn south on Blanshard, down "cinema row" and past the impressive:

17. **St. Andrew's Roman Catholic Cathedral,** at the corner of View Street.

    Turn east (left) one block farther, on Fort Street, onto:

18. **Antique Row.** Extending for three blocks to Cook Street, the shops concentrated here carry everything from 19th-century furniture, crystal, and paintings to rare stamps, coins, and books. Just a few blocks beyond Cook, Antique Row approaches the Art Gallery of Greater Victoria (1040 Moss St.) and Craigdarroch Castle (1050 Joan Crescent).

    Turn right off Antique Row at Quadra Street. One short block south is:

19. **Pioneer Square,** one of the oldest cemeteries in British Columbia. Hudson's Bay Company fur traders, ship captains, and crew members from British Royal Navy vessels lie beneath the sandstone markers. Guided tours of this graveyard as well as of Ross Bay Cemetery, between Dallas and Fairfield Roads, are offered on Sunday most of the year by the Old Cemeteries Committee (tel. 384-0045).

    Overlooking the park at Quadra and Courtney Streets is:

20. **Christ Church Cathedral,** 912 Vancouver St., seat of the Anglican bishop of British Columbia.

    Now head back to the starting point by walking west on Courtney. Look north toward Broughton as you cross Blanshard to see the:

21. **Royal Theatre,** 805 Broughton St. (tel. 361-0820), on the right side of the street. It's the home of the Victoria Symphony and host to many touring and local groups.

    In the next block on Courtney is:

22. **Victoria's Central Library.** When Courtney intersects Government Street, turn left, and you're back at the Info Centre again.

VICTORIA SHOPPING

Visitors to Victoria generally find their greatest shopping joys in traditional English goods, both antique and modern, and in British Columbian arts and crafts.

1. THE SHOPPING SCENE

THE DEPARTMENT STORES   As in Vancouver, the corner-stones of shopping are the two big department stores, **The Bay** (Hudson's Bay Company), 1701 Douglas St., between Fisgard and Herald Streets (tel. 385-1311) and Eaton's. The Bay is long established as Victoria's leading department store—of course, it was the Hudson's Bay Company that founded the city! Eaton's has a major outlet in a suburban shopping mall, but its showcase is the new **Victoria Eaton Centre** (tel. 389-2228), which covers most of two city blocks between Government and Douglas, Fort and View Streets. Eaton's (tel. 382-7141) and 103 shops fill this shopping center. The unique architecture of this four-story complex incorporated several late 19th-century buildings and includes two small park areas with fountains and reflecting pools, as well as a rooftop garden patio.

SHOPPING STREETS   As for shopping streets, **Government Street** from Humboldt to Yates, a five-block stretch, is the prime area to search for British goods and Canadian crafts. **Fort Street** from Blanshard to Cook is known as "Antique Row" for the number of collectibles shops and auction houses in those three blocks. **Lower Johnson Street,** in the two long blocks from Wharf to Douglas Streets, has earned a reputation for the trendy and avant-garde. And **Oak Bay Village,** especially Oak Bay Avenue from Foul Bay Road to Monterey Street (six blocks), so resembles a British shopping district—with its hanging flower baskets and Tudor-style storefronts—that it's referred to as "behind the Tweed Curtain."

SHOPPING CENTERS & MALLS   Downtown, in addition to the Victoria Eaton Centre, there are two important shopping centers. **Harbour Square,** on two levels between Government and Wharf, Courtney and Broughton Streets, houses 25 shops selling women's and men's fashions, jewelry, and a variety of imports, plus a small food court. **Market Square,** at the harbor end of Johnson Street and Pandora Avenue, is a charming historic restoration containing 40 shops (see Chapter 14, "Strolling Around Victoria").

Within a short drive or bus ride of downtown are three large shopping malls: the **Mayfair Shopping Centre,** 3147 Douglas St., between Tolmie and Finlayson (tel. 383-0541); the **Hillside Shopping Centre,** 1644 Hillside Ave., at Shelbourne Street (tel. 595-7154); and the **Tillicum Mall,** 3170 Tillicum Rd., at Burnside Road West (tel. 381-7123).

SHOPPING HOURS Hours vary from store to store, but Thursday (for some) and Friday (for all) are late shopping nights in downtown Victoria. Expect stores to be open Monday through Wednesday and on Saturday from 9:30am to 5:30pm, on Thursday and Friday from 9:30am to 9pm, and (in tourist areas) on Sunday from noon to 5pm.

2. SHOPPING A TO Z

ANTIQUES On Antique Row (Fort Street), start at the 1100 block (Cook Street) and work back toward downtown. The most authentic collectibles are at the east end of the row, and they're often missed by people who start their search at the Douglas Street end. Antiques dealers here will happily recommend other shops if they don't have what you're looking for. Worth a look are **Kilshaw's Auctioneers,** 1115 Fort St. (tel. 384-6441), for estate sales, and **Jeffries & Co.,** 1026 Fort St. (tel. 383-8315), for silver.

ART There are fine galleries all over the city, including the **Fran Willis Gallery North,** 1619 Store St. (tel. 381-3422); the **Herald Street Artworld,** 655B Herald St. (tel. 384-3766); the **Marshall Gallery,** 1636 Cedar Hill Cross Rd. (tel. 477-1242); the **Handloom Gallery,** 641 Fort St. (tel. 384-1011), for Canadian crafts work; and the shop at the **Art Gallery of Greater Victoria,** 1040 Moss St. (tel. 384-4101).

BOOKS **Munro's Book Store,** 1108 Government St. (tel. 382-2464), is not only a Victoria landmark, but the city's most important book dealer, with more than 30,000 titles. **Poor Richard's Books,** 968 Balmoral Rd. (tel. 384-4411), offers current and rare editions in an old brick heritage house. **Crown Publications,** 546 Yates St. (tel. 386-4636), offers the largest selection of B.C. titles.

Specialty stores include **Everywomans Books,** 641 Johnson St. (tel. 388-9411); **Playfaire Alternative Toys and Books,** 11-1594 Fairfield Rd. (tel. 595-7444), for children; and **Earth Quest Books,** 1286 Broad St. (tel. 361-4533), for travel books.

For book bargains and remainders, try the **Book Warehouse,** 1301 Government St. (tel. 386-5711).

CHINA & CRYSTAL This is a major item in Victoria—Waterford crystal, Royal Worcester bone china, and so forth. Check **Victoria Limited Editions,** 919 Fort St. (tel. 386-5155); **Sidney Reynolds,** 801 Government St. (tel. 383-3931); **Robert James,** 1005 Broad St. (tel. 386-4588); and **Eaton's** at Victoria Eaton Centre (tel. 382-7141).

CRAFTS Government Street has the largest number of shops specializing in traditional Northwest Coast Native Canadian and Inuit arts and crafts. Native to Vancouver Island are long-wearing Cowichan sweaters, hand-spun from undyed raw wool. Look also for wood-carved masks, boxes, and bowls; jewelry of silver, gold, jade, and black argillite; soapstone and ivory sculptures; and weaving, leatherwork, and basketry.

Among the outstanding shops are **Canadian Impressions,** 605 Courtney St. (tel. 383-2641), and **Quest,** 1023 Government St. (tel. 382-1934).

FASHIONS   This category includes British and European imports, as well as Canadian designers. Government Street and its side streets are the best places to look for both men's and women's fashions. Try **W & J Wilson Ltd.,** 1221 Government St. (tel. 383-7177); **Anthony James,** 1225 Government St. (tel. 381-2152); and **Hughes Ltd.,** 564 Yates St. (tel. 381-4405). Outstanding for men's fashions is **George Straith Ltd.,** 921 Government St. (tel. 384-6912). Women should check out **Sunday's Snowflakes,** 1000 Douglas St. (tel. 381-4461), and **Gibson's Ladies Wear,** 708 View St. (tel. 384-5913). If you're in the market for Scottish tartans, **Prescott and Andrews,** 909 Government St. (tel. 384-2515), may have what you need.

FOOD   What do you look for in a British town? Why, tea and chocolates, of course! **Murchie's,** 1110 Government St. (tel. 383-3112), has custom blends of all major British teas plus its own chocolates made on the premises. Chocoholics may also love **Rogers Chocolates,** 913 Government St. (tel. 384-7021); **Bernard Callebaut Chocolaterie,** 623 Broughton St. (tel. 380-1515); and **Coco's Chocolates,** 722 Broughton St. (tel. 384-2262).

JEWELRY   The most interesting pieces are those crafted by Native Canadian artisans in silver, gold, British Columbia jade, or black argillite (a semiprecious stone mined only in the Queen Charlotte Islands). For this type of jewelry, see "Crafts," above.

For more traditional work, visit **Nugget Jewellers,** 2nd floor, 824 Johnson St. (tel. 385-8444).

PUBLIC MARKET   **Market Square,** 560 Johnson St. (tel. 386-2441), is near Chinatown. Produce, fish, and meat stalls, take-out food booths, and craft and clothing boutiques have created a bustling marketplace.

SOUVENIRS   There are plenty of shops with the requisite junk. My favorites for quality and variety are side by side, a few steps east of Government Street: **Drover's Cottage,** 623 Fort St. (tel. 385-1312), and **Scaramouche Gallery,** 635 Fort St. (tel. 386-2215).

CHAPTER 16

VICTORIA NIGHTS

1. **THE PERFORMING ARTS**
- **MAJOR CONCERT & PERFORMANCE HALLS**
2. **THE CLUB & MUSIC SCENE**
3. **THE BAR SCENE**
4. **MORE ENTERTAINMENT**

Though a relatively small city, Victoria has a surprisingly active nightlife. There's a strong emphasis on "high" culture, including theater, symphony, and opera. But jazz music is also very big, and the city has its share of pubs, discos, and rock clubs.

The **Community Arts Council of Greater Victoria,** 620 View St., Suite 511 (tel. 381-ARTS or 381-2787) keeps an up-to-date list of current and future events scheduled in the city. So does **Tourism Victoria,** 812 Wharf St. (tel. 382-2127). Tickets for most events can be obtained from the box office of the **McPherson Playhouse,** 3 Centennial Sq., Pandora Avenue and Government Street (tel. 386-6121), or at Tourism Victoria. Current listings can be found in the daily *Times-Colonist;* in *Monday Magazine,* a weekly tabloid published on Thursday; and in the bimonthly *Arts Victoria.*

Throughout the summer, there's free entertainment around the shore of James Bay, in Market Square, in Beacon Hill Park, and wherever else people congregate. And numerous festivals bring outstanding artists of all pursuits to parks and performing arts centers at little or no charge. They include jazz festivals in April and June, the classical-oriented Victoria International Festival in July and August, and the avant-garde Fringe Festival in September and October (tel. 361-0820).

---

1. THE PERFORMING ARTS

MAJOR CONCERT & PERFORMANCE HALLS

In addition to the two halls listed below, another important performance hall is the **University Centre Auditorium** at the University

---

MAJOR CONCERT & PERFORMANCE HALLS

Belfry Theatre, 1291 Gladstone St., at Fernwood (tel. 385-6815).

McPherson Playhouse, 3 Centennial Sq., at Pandora Avenue and Government Street (tel. 386-6121).

Royal Theatre, 805 Broughton St., at Blanshard Street (tel. 361-0820).

University Centre Auditorium, at the University of Victoria, Finnerty Road (tel. 721-8299).

of Victoria, Finnerty Road (tel. 721-8299). One of the most acoustically sound in Canada, this auditorium seats 1,233 for concerts, plays, dance performances, and lectures.

MCPHERSON PLAYHOUSE, 3 Centennial Sq., Pandora Ave. and Government St. Tel. 386-6121.

This 800-seat baroque Edwardian theater, restored in 1962, was built in 1914 as the Pantages Theatre for vaudevillians. Today it's the home of the Victoria Symphony Orchestra, the Pacific Opera Victoria, and numerous other musical and theatrical groups. Free noon-hour concerts are often presented in the summer at Centennial Square, adjacent to the playhouse. The box office is open Monday through Saturday from 9:30am to 5:30pm, and on performance days also from 6 to 8:30pm. Bus: 23 or 24.

Admission: Ticket prices vary depending on the performance.

ROYAL THEATRE, 805 Broughton St., at Blanshard St. Tel. 361-0820, or 386-6121 for the box office.

Built in the first decade of the 20th century and renovated in the late 1970s, the Royal is operated by the McPherson. It complements the larger venue's programs as a locale for concerts, dance recitals, and touring stage plays. The box office (at the McPherson Playhouse; see above) is open Monday through Saturday from 9:30am to 1:30pm and 2:15 to 5:30pm, as well as 6 to 8:30pm on all performance days. Bus: 1 to Courtney Street.

Admission: Ticket prices vary depending on the performance.

THEATER

The theater is very active in Victoria, with several companies mounting regular productions throughout the year. The most prominent is:

THE BELFRY THEATRE, 1291 Gladstone St., at Fernwood. Tel. 385-6815.

This acclaimed group—it represented Canada in the Olympic Arts Festival in Calgary in 1988—performs a five-play season from October to April in its own small and intimate, recently renovated playhouse. Programs span the gamut of serious theater; contemporary Canadian playwrights are preferred, but the Belfry has also produced works by Eugene O'Neill, Harold Pinter, and Stephen Sondheim. Artistic director Glynis Leyshon directs ShowFest at Niagara-on-the-Lake, Ontario, in the summer. The Belfry's box office is open Monday through Friday from 9am to 5pm, with extended hours on performance days.

Admission: Tickets cost around $16 for adults; senior and student discounts available.

OTHER THEATER COMPANIES

The **Intrepid Theatre Company,** 620 View St., Suite 602 (tel. 383-2663), produces the annual **Victoria Fringe Festival,** held for 10 days in late September. It offers more than 260 performances in comedy, drama, music, dance, mime, and puppetry. This is where counterculture joins the mainstream. Themes range from absurd and/or existential to leading-edge avant-garde. No production charges over $7 for tickets, but no tickets are sold until an hour before show time once the festival has begun.

The **Victoria Theatre Guild,** 805 Langham Court, Rockland (tel. 384-2142), presents six plays a year at the Langham Court Theatre. Prices are $12 for adults, $10 for seniors and students.

The **Capital Comedy Theatre,** 965 Sunnywood Court (tel. 658-4341), stages its productions on an irregular basis at the McPherson Playhouse.

The University of Victoria's **Phoenix Theatres** (tel. 721-8000), serve up a year-round potpourri of productions at two campus theaters, plus two repertory plays June through August at the campus Faculty Club.

The **Kaleidoscope Theatre,** 715 Yates St. (tel. 383-8124), has drawn raves internationally for its work with young audiences (3–18 years). Kaleidoscope has both a resident company and a touring company, and runs a professional theater school for kids 4–84.

The **Theatre Inconnu,** based in Market Square (tel. 380-1284), is an avant-garde troupe that performs in the shopping plaza and elsewhere around town on an irregular basis.

OPERA

The nationally acclaimed **Pacific Opera Victoria,** 1316B Government St. (tel. 385-0222, 386-6121 for the box office), mounts three productions annually—in September, February, and April—at the McPherson Playhouse. The company has presented Mozart's *The Magic Flute,* Rossini's *La Cenerentola,* Tchaikovsky's *Eugene Onegin,* and Gilbert and Sullivan's *The Pirates of Penzance.* Pre-performance lectures are given nightly by opera scholars on the McPherson mezzanine. Tickets can be obtained at the box office at the McPherson Playhouse (see above), and cost $15–$52.

The **Victoria Operatic Society,** 798 Fairview Rd. (tel. 381-1021), established in 1945, presents a year-round schedule of light Broadway musicals, such as *South Pacific, Kiss Me Kate,* and *A Chorus Line,* at the McPherson Playhouse. Typical prices are about $15.

ORCHESTRAL & CHORAL MUSIC

The year's big event is the **Victoria International Festival,** held from the second week of July through the third week of August. Symphony concerts, classical recitals, ballet performances, baroque concerts, and other events featuring dozens of world-renowned musicians are presented at the McPherson Playhouse, Royal Theatre, University Centre Auditorium and Recital Hall, Christ Church Cathedral, and the St. Michael's University School. Prices of events vary, but a 31-concert subscription can be obtained for $160–$220 ($142–$198 for seniors and students). Get tickets from the McPherson Playhouse box office (tel. 386-6121); for further information, contact the festival coordinators at 3737 Oak St., Suite 103, Vancouver, BC V6H 2M4.

The **Victoria Symphony Orchestra,** 846 Broughton St. (tel. 385-9771), with more than 50 dates scheduled through the year, including summer concerts, has been performing since 1940. Most series are given at the Royal or the University Centre Auditorium, including "Masterworks" (its main classical series), "Seagram Pops," and "Concerts for Kids." Two other shorter series are offered at the

University Centre Auditorium: "Bach to Mozart" and "20th Century Spectrum." Tickets cost $10–$22.50 for adults, with a $1 discount for seniors and students.

The 72-member **Greater Victoria Youth Orchestra** (tel. 477-3870), featuring performers aged 12–24, was founded in 1986. Already its alumni are performing with provincial symphony orchestras in eastern Canada and studying at conservatories from Vienna to Yale. The group plays November and March concerts at the University Centre Auditorium, and makes occasional other appearances.

The **Island Chamber Players,** 851 Pendele Place (tel. 385-6973), performs a September-to-April season of seven concerts at North Park Gallery, 1619 Store St. Tickets are $12 for adults, $10 for students and seniors.

Other notable groups are the **Victoria Choral Society,** whose year culminates in a Christmas-week performance of Handel's *Messiah* with the VSO at the Royal Theatre; the **Victoria Savoyard Society,** which stages about three Gilbert and Sullivan operettas each year; the **Victoria Conservatory of Music,** 839 Academy Close (tel. 386-5311), a professional music school one block east of the Royal B.C. Museum, which presents student recitals; and the **University School of Music,** which offers free concerts by faculty and students on Fridays, plus a full schedule of evening performances.

DANCE

Numerous amateur companies and dance studios present recitals and full-scale performances throughout the year. In addition, companies from across North America frequently perform—usually at the Royal Theatre.

2. THE CLUB & MUSIC SCENE

NIGHTCLUBS & CABARETS

HARPO'S, 15 Bastion Sq. Tel. 385-5333.
Victoria's best intimate showcase for high-profile artists, short of a concert hall, overlooks the waterfront above Wharf Street. A wide variety of artists, from jazz (Joanne Brackeen Trio) to blues (Koko Taylor) to progressive rock (the Oyster Band) to African (Native Spirit) perform behind a fine dance floor. Drinks run $3 and up. The club is open Monday through Saturday from 8:30pm to 2am. Bus: 5.
   Admission: $3–$15, depending on the act.

ROCK MUSIC

Relatively few downtown clubs serve up live rock music on a regular basis.
   The Forge, in the Strathcona Hotel, 919 Douglas St. (tel. 383-7137), is probably the biggest and best. Rock bands provide the beat for a crowd that ranges from new wavers to blue-collar workers. It's open nightly, with a $3–$5 cover charge.
   The Rail, at the Colony Motor Inn, 2852 Douglas St. (tel. 385-2441), is a pub-style spot for hard rockers.

JAZZ, BLUES & FOLK

It's easier to find good live jazz in Victoria than hot rock. To begin with, there are two major jazz festivals here each year: the **TerrifVic Dixieland Jazz Festival** (tel. 381-5277), over 5 days in late April; and the **International Jazz Fest,** at several venues (tel. 386-2441), spreading over 10 days in late June. The Dixieland event brings more than 20 bands from as far away as the British Isles, Latin America, and (of course) New Orleans to perform at venues all over the city, and there's free shuttle service between sites in a double-decker bus. Five-day badges for all performances are $70. The Jazz Fest leans more toward swing, bebop, fusion, avant-garde, riffs, and licks; in 1992, it drew over 200 musicians in 55 performances. Noon-hour and evening performances are focused on Market Square's central courtyard. **Sunfest** is a three-day world-beat jazz festival held on the third weekend of August at Market Square.

Hermann's Dixieland Inn, 753 View St., near Blanshard Street (tel. 388-9166), is like a 1950s time warp. A low-lit jazz club with photos and posters all over its walls, and old trumpets and trombones practically against the ceiling, it specializes in Dixieland jazz, with occasional fusion or blues. Meals are not really gourmet, but feature very generous portions of home cooking. Hermann's is open on Monday from 5pm to midnight, Tuesday through Friday from 11:30am to 12:30am, and on Saturday from 4pm to 12:30am. Full meals cost $9.95–$11.95, drinks are $3, and there's usually no cover charge.

Pagliacci's, 1011 Broad St. (tel. 386-1662), has an eclectic variety of music most evenings, from Latin jazz to big band, jazz fusion to Balkan folk songs. Also try the popular **Soho Village Bistro,** 1311 Gladstone St. (tel. 384-3344).

The **Victoria Jazz Society** (tel. 388-4423) is a clearinghouse of information on jazz activity throughout the greater Victoria area. It often sponsors performances by visiting artists at Harpo's, Hermann's Dixieland Inn, and the Royal Theatre. And when he's in town, Victoria's own world-famous jazz flutist, Paul Horn, can often be convinced to concertize.

A fine selection of jazz recordings is available from **Sweet Thunder Records,** 575 Johnson St. (tel. 381-4042).

For lovers of acoustic music, the **Victoria Folk Music Society** (tel. 386-9530) hosts regular performances, and folk singers perform Wednesday through Saturday nights at **Pluto's Mesquite Diner,** 1150 Cook St. (tel. 385-4747; see Chapter 12, "Victoria Dining").

COUNTRY

The selection here is limited. But the **Esquimalt Inn,** 856 Esquimalt Rd. (tel. 382-7161), fills a need for country music lovers. There's live music here Tuesday through Sunday, and jam sessions starting at 3pm on Saturday and Sunday. Take bus no. 23.

DISCOS

The names change, the places change, but there are always discos with canned dance music. Most are open Monday through Saturday until 2am, on Sunday until midnight. Some of the hot spots at this writing are:

Club California, 1318 Broad St. (tel. 382-1331). An upstairs club with a large dance floor and big-screen rock videos, it's open nightly, with frequent theme nights.

Julie's Cabaret, 603 Pandora Ave., at Government Street (tel. 386-3631). This Top 40 disco shares quarters with Monty's Pub in Victoria Plaza. Open nightly; no cover.

Merlin's, 1208 Wharf St. (tel. 381-2331). A waterfront club that attracts a 20s crowd, it has regular theme nights, including Wednesday and Thursday ladies' nights with male dancers. There's a $3 cover after 9:30pm on weekends.

Pier 42, 1605 Store St., at Pandora Avenue (tel. 381-7437), is in the basement of Swans Pub (and under the same management) and offers Top 40 hits. Open Wednesday through Sunday nights, from 8pm; no cover.

Scandals, 770 Yates St., near Blanshard (tel. 389-0666), has progressive dance music nightly. Doors open at 8pm.

Sweetwaters Niteclub, Market Square, off Store Street (tel. 383-7844), is an elegant singles club that features classic tracks and anything else worth dancing to. There's no cover, but expect a line seven nights a week.

3. THE BAR SCENE

It's only natural that a town as British as Victoria should have outstanding pubs. Be sure to visit at least one brew pub, which manufactures its own beers and ales.

SPINNAKER'S BREW PUB, 308 Catherine St., near Esquimalt Rd. Tel. 386-BREW (386-2739).

This full-mash brew house overlooks Victoria Harbour on the west side of the Songhees Point Development. A great place for a light meal or an evening ale, it draws a mixed clientele of local old-timers and young professionals. Brewmaster Jake Thomas buys his malted barley from Great Britain and cultures his own yeast in the laboratory. He has 30 different recipes, among which the favorites are Spinnaker ale, Mitchell's Extra Strong Bitter, and Empress stout. Phone ahead if you'd like to tour the brewery. Live music is often presented evenings. Meals start at $5.50; beers are $4 and up. The pub is open daily from 11am to 11pm. Bus: 23 to Esquimalt Road.

SWANS PUB, 506 Pandora Ave., at Store St. Tel. 361-3310.

Housed in a converted 1913 feed warehouse, this hotel-café-brewery complex (see Chapter 11, "Victoria Accommodations") is extremely popular with the city's young professional crowd. The pub serves half a dozen British-style draft ales brewed on the premises at Buckerfield's Brewery, and the adjoining Swans Café serves lunch and dinner daily. Main courses run $9–$18; beer starts at $2.40. The pub is open daily from 11am to 2am. Bus: 23 or 24.

4. MORE ENTERTAINMENT

GAMBLING CASINOS See Chapter 9, "Vancouver Nights," for general information about gambling in British Columbia.

Victoria has a sprinkling of legal casinos scattered around the city. Don't expect Las Vegas or Atlantic City: None of them offers a floor show or other diversions, and the decor is modest and devoid of glamour. The main games are blackjack, roulette, and sic-bo.

Among the casinos are **Casino Victoria,** 716 Courtney St., near Douglas Street (tel. 380-3998), and the **Great Canadian Casino,** in the Red Lion Inn, 3366 Douglas St., near Ardersier Street (tel. 384-2614). Both are open from 6pm to 2am every night.

METRIC MEASURES

LENGTH

1 millimeter (mm)	=	.04 inches (*or* less than 1/16 in.)
1 centimeter (cm)	=	.39 inches (*or* just under ½ in.)
1 meter (m)	=	39 inches (*or* about 1.1 yd.)
1 kilometer (km)	=	.62 miles (*or* about ⅔ of a mile)

To convert kilometers to miles, multiply the number of kilometers by .62. Also use to convert kilometers per hour (kmph) to miles per hour (m.p.h.).

To convert miles to kilometers, multiply the number of miles by 1.61. Also use to convert from m.p.h. to kmph.

CAPACITY

1 liter (l)	=	33.92 fluid ounces	=	2.1 pints
	=	1.06 quarts	=	.26 U.S. gallons
1 Imperial gallon			=	1.2 U.S. gallons

To convert liters to U.S. gallons, multiply the number of liters by .26.

To convert U.S. gallons to liters, multiply the number of gallons by 3.79.

To convert Imperial gallons to U.S. gallons, multiply the number of Imperial gallons by 1.2.

To convert U.S. gallons to Imperial gallons, multiply the number of U.S. gallons by .83.

WEIGHT

1 gram (g)	=	.035 ounces (*or* about a paperclip's weight)
1 kilogram (kg)	=	35.2 ounces
	=	2.2 pounds
1 metric ton	=	2,205 pounds (1.1 short ton)

To convert kilograms to pounds, multiply the number of kilograms by 2.2.

To convert pounds to kilograms, multiply the number of pounds by .45.

TEMPERATURE

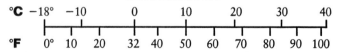

°C	−18°	−10		0		10		20		30		40
°F	0°	10	20	32	40	50	60	70	80	90	100	

To convert degrees Celsius to degrees Fahrenheit, multiply

°C by 9, divide by 5, and add 32 (example: 20°C × 9/5 + 32 = 68°F).

To convert degrees Fahrenheit to degrees Celsius, subtract 32 from °F, multiply by 5, then divide by 9 (example: 85°F − 32 × 5/9 = 29.4°C).

INDEX

GENERAL INFORMATION

SIGHTS & ATTRACTIONS

VANCOUVER

Note: An Asterisk (*) indicates an author's favorite.

VICTORIA

ACCOMMODATIONS

VANCOUVER

Key to abbreviations: * = Author's favorite; $ = Super-value choice; B = Budget; M = Moderately priced; E = Expensive; VE = Very expensive.

VICTORIA

RESTAURANTS

VANCOUVER

Key to abbreviations: * = Author's favorite; $ = Super-value choice; B = Budget; M = Moderately priced; E = Expensive; VE = Very expensive.

VICTORIA

Please Send Me the Books Checked Below:

FROMMER'S COMPREHENSIVE GUIDES
(Guides listing facilities from budget to deluxe,
with emphasis on the medium-priced)

	Retail Price	Code		Retail Price	Code
☐ Acapulco/Ixtapa/Taxco 1993–94	$15.00	C120	☐ Morocco 1992–93	$18.00	C021
☐ Alaska 1994–95	$17.00	C131	☐ Nepal 1994–95	$18.00	C126
☐ Arizona 1993–94	$18.00	C101	☐ New England 1994 (Avail. 1/94)	$16.00	C137
☐ Australia 1992–93	$18.00	C002	☐ New Mexico 1993–94	$15.00	C117
☐ Austria 1993–94	$19.00	C119	☐ New York State 1994–95	$19.00	C133
☐ Bahamas 1994–95	$17.00	C121	☐ Northwest 1994–95 (Avail. 2/94)	$17.00	C140
☐ Belgium/Holland/ Luxembourg 1993–94	$18.00	C106	☐ Portugal 1994–95 (Avail. 2/94)	$17.00	C141
☐ Bermuda 1994–95	$15.00	C122	☐ Puerto Rico 1993–94	$15.00	C103
☐ Brazil 1993–94	$20.00	C111	☐ Puerto Vallarta/ Manzanillo/Guadalajara 1994–95 (Avail. 1/94)	$14.00	C028
☐ California 1994	$15.00	C134	☐ Scandinavia 1993–94	$19.00	C135
☐ Canada 1994–95 (Avail. 4/94)	$19.00	C145	☐ Scotland 1994–95 (Avail. 4/94)	$17.00	C146
☐ Caribbean 1994	$18.00	C123	☐ South Pacific 1994–95 (Avail. 1/94)	$20.00	C138
☐ Carolinas/Georgia 1994–95	$17.00	C128	☐ Spain 1993–94	$19.00	C115
☐ Colorado 1994–95 (Avail. 3/94)	$16.00	C143	☐ Switzerland/ Liechtenstein 1994–95 (Avail. 1/94)	$19.00	C139
☐ Cruises 1993–94	$19.00	C107	☐ Thailand 1992–93	$20.00	C033
☐ Delaware/Maryland 1994–95 (Avail. 1/94)	$15.00	C136	☐ U.S.A. 1993–94	$19.00	C116
☐ England 1994	$18.00	C129	☐ Virgin Islands 1994–95	$13.00	C127
☐ Florida 1994	$18.00	C124	☐ Virginia 1994–95 (Avail. 2/94)	$14.00	C142
☐ France 1994–95	$20.00	C132	☐ Yucatán 1993–94	$18.00	C110
☐ Germany 1994	$19.00	C125			
☐ Italy 1994	$19.00	C130			
☐ Jamaica/Barbados 1993–94	$15.00	C105			
☐ Japan 1994–95 (Avail. 3/94)	$19.00	C144			

FROMMER'S $-A-DAY GUIDES
(Guides to low-cost tourist accommodations and facilities)

	Retail Price	Code		Retail Price	Code
☐ Australia on $45 1993–94	$18.00	D102	☐ Israel on $45 1993–94	$18.00	D101
☐ Costa Rica/Guatemala/ Belize on $35 1993–94	$17.00	D108	☐ Mexico on $45 1994	$19.00	D116
☐ Eastern Europe on $30 1993–94	$18.00	D110	☐ New York on $70 1994–95	$16.00	D120
☐ England on $60 1994	$18.00	D112	☐ New Zealand on $45 1993–94	$18.00	D103
☐ Europe on $50 1994	$19.00	D115	☐ Scotland/Wales on $50 1992–93	$18.00	D019
☐ Greece on $45 1993–94	$19.00	D100	☐ South America on $40 1993–94	$19.00	D109
☐ Hawaii on $75 1994	$19.00	D113	☐ Turkey on $40 1992–93	$22.00	D023
☐ India on $40 1992–93	$20.00	D010	☐ Washington, D.C. on $40 1994–95 (Avail. 2/94)	$17.00	D119
☐ Ireland on $45 1994–95 (Avail. 1/94)	$17.00	D117			

FROMMER'S CITY $-A-DAY GUIDES
(Pocket-size guides to low-cost tourist accommodations and facilities)

	Retail Price	Code		Retail Price	Code
☐ Berlin on $40 1994–95	$12.00	D111	☐ Madrid on $50 1994–95 (Avail. 1/94)	$13.00	D118
☐ Copenhagen on $50 1992–93	$12.00	D003	☐ Paris on $50 1994–95	$12.00	D117
☐ London on $45 1994–95	$12.00	D114	☐ Stockholm on $50 1992–93	$13.00	D022

FROMMER'S WALKING TOURS
(With routes and detailed maps, these companion guides point out the places and pleasures that make a city unique)

	Retail Price	Code		Retail Price	Code
☐ Berlin	$12.00	W100	☐ Paris	$12.00	W103
☐ London	$12.00	W101	☐ San Francisco	$12.00	W104
☐ New York	$12.00	W102	☐ Washington, D.C.	$12.00	W105

FROMMER'S TOURING GUIDES
(Color-illustrated guides that include walking tours, cultural and historic sights, and practical information)

	Retail Price	Code		Retail Price	Code
☐ Amsterdam	$11.00	T001	☐ New York	$11.00	T008
☐ Barcelona	$14.00	T015	☐ Rome	$11.00	T010
☐ Brazil	$11.00	T003	☐ Scotland	$10.00	T011
☐ Florence	$ 9.00	T005	☐ Sicily	$15.00	T017
☐ Hong Kong/Singapore/ Macau	$11.00	T006	☐ Tokyo	$15.00	T016
			☐ Turkey	$11.00	T013
☐ Kenya	$14.00	T018	☐ Venice	$ 9.00	T014
☐ London	$13.00	T007			

FROMMER'S FAMILY GUIDES

	Retail Price	Code		Retail Price	Code
☐ California with Kids	$18.00	F100	☐ San Francisco with Kids (Avail. 4/94)	$17.00	F104
☐ Los Angeles with Kids (Avail. 4/94)	$17.00	F103	☐ Washington, D.C. with Kids (Avail. 2/94)	$17.00	F102
☐ New York City with Kids (Avail. 2/94)	$18.00	F101			

FROMMER'S CITY GUIDES
(Pocket-size guides to sightseeing and tourist accommodations and facilities in all price ranges)

	Retail Price	Code		Retail Price	Code
☐ Amsterdam 1993–94	$13.00	S110	☐ Montréal/Québec City 1993–94	$13.00	S125
☐ Athens 1993–94	$13.00	S114	☐ Nashville/Memphis 1994–95 (Avail. 4/94)	$13.00	S141
☐ Atlanta 1993–94	$13.00	S112	☐ New Orleans 1993–94	$13.00	S103
☐ Atlantic City/Cape May 1993–94	$13.00	S130	☐ New York 1994 (Avail. 1/94)	$13.00	S138
☐ Bangkok 1992–93	$13.00	S005	☐ Orlando 1994	$13.00	S135
☐ Barcelona/Majorca/ Minorca/Ibiza 1993–94	$13.00	S115	☐ Paris 1993–94	$13.00	S109
☐ Berlin 1993–94	$13.00	S116	☐ Philadelphia 1993–94	$13.00	S113
☐ Boston 1993–94	$13.00	S117	☐ San Diego 1993–94	$13.00	S107
☐ Budapest 1994–95 (Avail. 2/94)	$13.00	S139	☐ San Francisco 1994	$13.00	S133
☐ Chicago 1993–94	$13.00	S122	☐ Santa Fe/Taos/ Albuquerque 1993–94	$13.00	S108
☐ Denver/Boulder/ Colorado Springs 1993–94	$13.00	S131	☐ Seattle/Portland 1994–95	$13.00	S137
☐ Dublin 1993–94	$13.00	S128	☐ St. Louis/Kansas City 1993–94	$13.00	S127
☐ Hong Kong 1994–95 (Avail. 4/94)	$13.00	S140	☐ Sydney 1993–94	$13.00	S129
☐ Honolulu/Oahu 1994	$13.00	S134	☐ Tampa/St. Petersburg 1993–94	$13.00	S105
☐ Las Vegas 1993–94	$13.00	S121	☐ Tokyo 1992–93	$13.00	S039
☐ London 1994	$13.00	S132	☐ Toronto 1993–94	$13.00	S126
☐ Los Angeles 1993–94	$13.00	S123	☐ Vancouver/Victoria 1994–95 (Avail. 1/94)	$13.00	S142
☐ Madrid/Costa del Sol 1993–94	$13.00	S124	☐ Washington, D.C. 1994 (Avail. 1/94)	$13.00	S136
☐ Miami 1993–94	$13.00	S118			
☐ Minneapolis/St. Paul 1993–94	$13.00	S119			

SPECIAL EDITIONS

	Retail Price	Code		Retail Price	Code
☐ Bed & Breakfast Southwest	$16.00	P100	☐ Caribbean Hideaways	$16.00	P103
☐ Bed & Breakfast Great American Cities (Avail. 1/94)	$16.00	P104	☐ National Park Guide 1994 (Avail. 3/94)	$16.00	P105
			☐ Where to Stay U.S.A.	$15.00	P102

Please note: if the availability of a book is several months away, we may have back issues of guides to that particular destination. Call customer service at (815) 734-1104.